The Johannine Question

19.39

MARTIN HENGEL

The Johannine Question

SCM PRESS
London

TRINITY PRESS INTERNATIONAL
Philadelphia

Translated by John Bowden from the German

© Martin Hengel 1989

Translation © John Bowden 1989

First published 1989

SCM Press Ltd
26-30 Tottenham Road
London N1 4BZ

Trinity Press International
3725 Chestnut Street
Philadelphia, Pa. 19104

British Library Cataloguing in Publication Data

Hengel, Martin
The Johannine question.
1. Bible . N. T. John – Critical studies
I. Title
226'.506

ISBN 0–334–00795–X

#20634345

Library of Congress Cataloging-in-Publication Data

Hengel, Martin.
The Johannine question/Martin Hengel.
p. cm.
Includes bibliographical references.
ISBN 0–334–00795–X
1. Bible. N.T. John—Authorship. 2. Bible. N.T. Epistles of
John—Authorship.   3. Bible. N.T. John—Criticism, interpretation,
etc.—History—Early church, ca. 30–600.   4. Bible. N.T. Epistles
of John—Criticism, interpretation, etc.—History—Early church, ca.
30–600.   5. Bible. N.T. John—Criticism, interpretation, etc.
6. Bible. N.T. Epistles of John—Criticism, interpretation, etc.
I. Title.
BS2601.H36   1990
226.5'06—dc20   89–28972
                                                                              CIP

Phototypeset by Input Typesetting Ltd, London
and printed in Great Britain by
Richard Clay Ltd, Bungay, Suffolk.

Contents

Preface

This book has a long and somewhat complicated history. It is based on the five Stone Lectures which I gave at Princeton Theological Seminary in autumn 1987. The first two of these lectures in turn go back to a lecture which I gave as a stimulus to discussion two years earlier in various English universities, in Glasgow, at Trinity College, Dublin, and later in West Germany and Switzerland.

The English text translated by John Bowden has been expanded at a number of points but still retains the character of the original lectures; behind it lies a substantially more extensive German manuscript which has yet to be published. Because of the particular difficulties of the topic it seemed to me appropriate to have the Stone Lectures published in the language in which they were delivered, supplemented by notes (which are often extensive), to some degree as a 'preliminary sketch', and to postpone publication of the longer manuscript.

The basic thesis presented in the lectures clearly goes against many views which are popular today. Among other things, I believe that the broad witness (both direct and indirect) of Christian writers of the second century to the Johannine corpus or the Fourth Gospel deserves more attention than it is usually given, especially since the basis of nineteenth-century scholarship shifted considerably as a result of the strikingly good attestation of the Gospel in particular during the second century. Furthermore, it seems to me to unmistakeable that the Gospel and the letters are not the expression of a community with many voices, but above all the voice of a towering theologian, the founder and head of the Johannine school. We need to be interested in his theological thought, which is quite equal to that of Paul, and not in an alleged plurality of apparently contradictory opinions and sketches. I do not think that collectives without a head can really be creative. But the Johannine corpus is a creative theological achievement of a unique order. There was a time when people wanted to attribute the *Iliad* and the *Nibelungenlied*, too, to a multiplicity of authors and redactors. Nowadays, however, we have moved away from this. Here we should learn from the aberrations of other disciplines, which have fortunately remedied them long since.

Nor is the work of this great theologian the primarily hidden product of an insignificant sect, half-Christian and half-Gnostic. Rather, from a relatively early date, starting in Asia Minor in the second century, the Johannine corpus had an amazing theological influence on the church. At this point, the Fourth Gospel had just as good a standing as the Synoptic Gospels, though it is substantially different from them.

The views that I shall be outlining do not contain very much that is really new; but I shall be glad if I can recall some things which have almost been forgotten. Only a little of what I have written here has never been presented at some point in the 150-170 years of critical Johannine research. I am aware of being particularly indebted to some remarks made by Adolf von Harnack in his *Geschichte der altchristlichen Literatur*, II.1, *Die Chronologie der Litteratur bis Irenäus*, Leipzig 1897, 656-80, though I part company with him over many points of detail. I could also say of the thesis offered in this book what Adolf von Harnack said of his own attempt at a solution:

> I do not want to claim that this result, which is intrinsically surprising and therefore suspicious, is completely certain, nor that it solves all the riddles surrounding the Johannine writings themselves and their earliest history. I have continually attempted to force the problem with a variety of possible attempts at a solution, but these lead to even greater difficulties, indeed entangle themselves in contradictions. The attempt made here is the one that so far has commended itself to me the most (677f.).

I believe that some new discoveries and insights which were still unavailable to Harnack in 1897 support an attempt at a solution which moves in the direction of his own. Lesser mortals that we are, today we have every reason to look back on our great forefathers, to whom we owe so infinitely much (even if nowadays we are often unaware of the fact), and learn from them again.

In the narrow sphere of New Testament study, where we move between hypotheses (often to a greater degree than we are aware of or would like), and in so doing sometimes no longer note that a widely acknowledged 'fact' is only a favourite hypothesis of the moment, we cannot allow ourselves any radical scepticism about what is said by the sources of the earliest period unless we begin to maintain a radical silence because we can no longer make out anything in the darkness of earliest Christian history. However, contemporary research is a far cry from that. The more critical it makes itself out to be, the more 'creative' it becomes: what is said by the texts which have come down to us is all too often replaced by more or less free conjecture in the face of text and 'context'.

This book, too, presents a hypothesis, and I am all too aware of the fact. In offering this hypothesis, I am concerned to take seriously the often very disparate phenomena and problems of the attestation of the Johannine corpus in the early church, and indeed to take seriously the Johannine corpus itself, incorporating it into an overall historical picture without at the same time forgetting how relatively little we know and how difficult it can sometimes be to distinguish between the manifold possibilities and what is really probable. However, precisely because we know so little, we cannot afford simply to neglect the clear information that we do have or even to pass over it in complete silence – as often happens today. So like others before me, I still think that an attempt at a reconstruction of the circumstances in which the Gospel came into being must at least be sought in the direction that I have indicated.

As this book is a 'sketch' of limited extent and not an exhaustive monograph, my use of the literature of Johannine research, which has now become virtually too large to cope with, has been limited to particular points; here I have been drawn above all to earlier works in English which are often ignored in Germany. Despite this, the notes have still grown too large.

That the book could be written at all is something that I owe to a year's study leave at the Wissenschaftskolleg in Berlin, during which I was able to give the five Stone Lectures their literary form. I am grateful to John Bowden for his patience – this book should have been ready a year ago – and his admirable translation. It was also his suggestion that the book should appear in this shorter form, related to the lectures.

I have also to thank Inge Böhm of the secretariat of the Wissenschaftskolleg for typing the text in its various stages and my Tübingen secretary Marietta Hämmerle for typing the notes. My assistant Anna-Maria Schwemer and Roland Deines were a great help in reading the typescript and Ulrich Heckel and Jörg Frey in reading the proofs.

I dedicate the book in gratitude to the theological faculties of the universities of Cambridge and Durham. A great scholar, Bishop Joseph Barber Lightfoot, worked in both of them, in the former as a professor, in the latter as a great church leader; our discipline owes much to him for his study of the second century and thus also of the Johannine corpus, and this year is his centenary.

Tübingen   *September 1989*

Abbreviations

AB	Anchor Bible
AGJU	Arbeiten zur Geschichte des antiken Judentums und des Urchristentums
AGWG.PH	Abhandlungen der Gesellschaft der Wissenschaften zu Göttingen, philologisch-historische Klasse
AHAW.PH	Abhandlungen der Heidelberger Akademie der Wissenschaften, philosophisch-historische Klasse
ATANT	Abhandlungen zur Theologie des Alten und Neuen Testaments
AzTH	Arbeiten zur Theologie
BASOR	Bulletin of the American Schools of Oriental Research
BCE	Before the Common Era
BETL	Bibliotheca ephemeridum theologicarum Lovaniensium
BFCT	Beiträge zur Förderung christlicher Theologie
BHTh	Beiträge zur historischen Theologie
Bib	Biblica
Billerbeck	(H. L. Strack and) Paul Billerbeck, Kommentar zum Neuen Testament aus Talmud und Midrasch
BU	Biblische Untersuchungen
BWANT	Beiträge zur Wissenschaft vom alten und neuen Testament
BZNW	Beihefte zur Zeitschrift für die neutestamentliche Wissenschaft
CB.NT	Coniectanea Biblica. New Testament Series
CBQ.MS	Catholic Biblical Quarterly. Monograph Series
CC	Corpus Christianorum
CE	Common Era
CIJ	Corpus Inscriptionum Judaicarum
CorpAp	Corpus Apologetorum

CPJ	Corpus papyrorum Judaicorum
CSEL	Corpus scriptorum ecclesiasticorum Latinorum
EPRO	Études preliminaires aux religions orientales dans l'empire romain
EtB	*Ètudes Bibliques*
EvQ	*Evangelical Quarterly*
EvTh	*Evangelische Theologie*
ExpT	*Expository Times*
FGrHist	*Fragmente der griechischen Historiker*
FGNK	Forschungen zur Geschichte des neutestamentlichen Kanons und der altchristlichen Litteratur
FRLANT	Forschungen zur Religion des Alten und Neuen Testaments
FS	*Festschrift*
GCS	Die Griechischen christlichen Schriftsteller der ersten drei Jahrhunderte
HC	Hand-Commentar zum Neuen Testament
HibJ	*Hibbert Journal*
HNT	Handbuch zum Neuen Testament
HThK	Herders Theologischer Kommentar zum Neuen Testament
ICC	International Critical Commentary
IEJ	*Israel Exploration Journal*
JBL	*Journal of Biblical Literature*
JBTh	*Journal of Biblical Theology*
JEH	*Journal of Ecclesiastical History*
JPTh	*Jahrbuch für protestantische Theologie*
JSS	*Journal of Semitic Studies*
JTS	*Journal of Theological Studies*
KlT	Kleine Texte
KNT	Kommentar zum Neuen Testament
KuD	*Kerygma und Dogma*
LTK	*Lexikon für Theologie und Kirche*
LXX	Septuagint
MNTC	Moffatt New Testament Commentaries
MSS	Manuscripts
MSSNT	Society for New Testament Studies. Monograph Series
MT	Massoretic Text
NF (NS)	Neue Folge (New Series)
NGWG.PH	Nachrichten der Gesellschaft der Wissenschaften in Göttingen. Philologisch-historische Klasse

NHC	Nag Hammadi Codices
NKZ	*Neue Kirchliche Zeitschrift*
NT	*Novum Testamentum*
NTA	Neutestamentliche Abhandlungen
NTA[5]	*Neutestamentliche Apokryphen*, fifth edition, ed. E. Hennecke and W. Schneemelcher
NTD	Das Neue Testament Deutsch
NTS	*New Testament Studies*
NT.S	*Novum Testamentum* Supplements
OrChr	*Oriens Christianus*
ÖTK	Ökumenische Taschenbuchkommentar zum Neuen Testament
PG	J. P. Migne, *Patrologia Graeca*
PL	J. P. Migne, *Patrologia Latina*
POx	Papyrus Oxyrhyncus
PTS	Patristische Texte und Studien
PW	Paulys Real-Encyclopädie der classischen Alterthumswissenschaft
PWSuppl	Supplementary volumes
Qad.	*Qadmoniot*
R	Reihe (Series)
RAC	*Reallexikon für Antike und Christentum*
RB	*Revue biblique*
RGG	*Die Religion in Geschichte und Gegenwart*
RHPR	*Revue d'histoire et philosophie religieuses*
RSPT	*Revue des sciences philosophiques et théologiques*
SANT	Studien zum Alten und Neuen Testament
SBB	Stuttgarter biblische Beiträge
SBLDiss Ser	Society of Biblical Literature Dissertation Series
SC	Sources chrétiennes
SchL	Schweich Lectures
SHAW.PH	Sitzungsberichte der Heidelberger Akademie der Wissenschaften, philosophisch-historische Klasse
SHR	Studies in the History of Religion
SPAW.PH	Sitzungsberichte der Preussischen Akademie der Wissenschaften, philosophisch-historische Klasse
SQS	Sammlung ausgewählter kirchen- und dogmengeschichtlicher Quellenschriften
TDNT	*Theological Dictionary of the New Testament*, ET of *TWNT*
ThJb (T)	*Theologische Jahrbücher*
ThQ	*Theologische Quartalschrift*
ThR	*Theologische Revue*

ThZ	*Theologische Zeitschrift*
TRE	*Theologische Realenzyklopädie*
TS	*Theological Studies*
TU	Texte und Untersuchungen
TWNT	*Theologisches Wörterbuch zum Neuen Testament*, ed. G. Kittel
TyB	*Tyndale Bulletin*
UNT	Untersuchungen zum Neuen Testament
VigChr	*Vigiliae Christianae*
VL	Vetus Latina
WdF	Wege der Forschung
WMANT	Wissenschaftliche Monographien zum Alten und Neuen Testament
WUNT	Wissenschaftliche Untersuchungen zum Neuen Testament
ZDPV	*Zeitschrift des deutschen Palästinavereins*
ZKG	*Zeitschrift für Kirchengeschichte*
ZNW	*Zeitschrift für die neutestamentliche Wissenschaft*
ZTK	*Zeitschrift für Theologie und Kirche*
ZWTh	*Zeitschrift für wissenschaftliche Theologie*

I

The First Step towards an Approach:
The Gospel in the Second Century

'Once upon a time', as we must say now, David Fiiedrich Strauss, the founder of radical gospel criticism in the nineteenth century, compared the Fourth Gospel to 'Christ's seamless robe'.[1] Nowadays, even a conservative theologian would no longer dare to say anything like that; 'Christ's seamless robe' has long become a patchwork 'coat of many colours'. So sometimes scholars hardly dare to speak of a real author of the Gospel, but concern themselves rather with a multiplicity of redactors and sources. Its linguistic and stylistic unity is no longer attributed to an author but to a community. The literary critics, who seek to dissect layer upon layer, redaction upon redaction, have been reinforced by the constructors of a history of the Johannine circle, who combine literary-critical work and the reconstruction of this community. Here Raymond Brown has produced the most impressive hypothesis in his book *The Community of the Beloved Disciple*,[2] which traces the history of this supposed community through seven or eight phases up to the division into the orthodox Christians and the heretical Gnostics.

As I am not nearly so bold, I would like to limit the 'Johannine question' in a rather old-fashioned way[3] to the final form of the writings of the Johannine corpus: the Gospel and the three letters which are attributed to John. The Apocalypse must stand to one side as an ever-perplexing problem. In other words, my concern is to investigate the Johannine writings in the historical context of their origin, beginning with the letters and going on to the Gospel in its present form, including chapter 21. My theme is therefore limited to the problem when, where, by whom and in what circumstances this Gospel and these letters were written and circulated in the mainstream church. Therefore the starting point of our enquiry must be the history of the influence of the Johannine corpus in the second century. Moving backwards from there, I shall first attempt to come

1

closer to the point at which the Johannine writings found their way into the church.

It is a long time since an English author, Maurice Jones, could begin the chapter on the Johannine literature in his book *The New Testament in the Twentieth Century* (London 1914) with the words:

> The question of the authorship of St John's Gospel is perhaps the most fascinating problem of New Testament criticism, and is incomparably the most important of them all. This is realized to the full by those who advocate the Johannine authorship as well as by those who take the opposite view (359).

Twenty-five years earlier, in 1889, Emil Schürer already began a lecture to pastors with the remark:

> No other question of New Testament criticism is of such significance as that of the origin of our Fourth Gospel... So no other question agitates people as much as the Johannine question ('Ueber den gegenwärtigen Stand der johanneischen Frage', now in *Johannes und sein Evangelium*, ed.K.H.Rengstorf, WdF 82, 1973, 1).

Now, as the twentieth century is coming to its end, this question, to which Jülicher devoted a whole chapter in the seven editions of his *Introduction to the New Testament* between 1894 and 1931 (pp.390-423 in the seventh), seems to many scholars to be quite unimportant. However, because I do not believe that the quest for authorship is irrelevant to the understanding of a particular text, I will attempt (with due caution) yet another new approach – even if the result will be neither new nor sensational.

1. Irenaeus: The 'stumbling block' and its Asian traditions

Towards the end of the second century there was agreement over all the problems which we now dispute, finding no end or consensus. Here the main evidence – and for modern 'critical research' the main culprit[4] – is Irenaeus, who gives the first clear information about all four Gospels, the letters of John and the Apocalypse shortly after 180 CE. His well-known survey of the evangelists ends with John: 'Lastly John, the Lord's disciple, who also reclined on his breast, himself produced the Gospel when he was staying in Ephesus in Asia.'[5] Present-day criticism mostly wants to banish this to the realm of legend. However, that would make things far too easy. Let us take, for example, the *sequence* of the four Gospels.

(*a*) According to Irenaeus, the Gospel of Mark came into being after the deaths of Peter and Paul.[6] The Fourth Gospel is much later still, and the last in time. Was Irenaeus wrong here? He takes over the information about Mark from Papias, whose work he knew, or – more probably – from the Roman community archives, and I am convinced that the information about John also comes from the same reliable source and was not invented by him.[7] He reports that this John lived until the time of Trajan, who became emperor at the end of January 98 and died in August 117.[8] He knows that the Beloved Disciple, who reclined 'on the Lord's breast' at the Last Supper, wrote the Gospel from its last chapter, where, after a reference to his death, the disciple is indicated as the author (21.20-24). The time is past when Protestant hypercriticism could put the Fourth Gospel in the middle of the second century. P^{52} makes it improbable that it was written after 110. In other words, the *terminus ad quem* is really the time of Trajan.

On the other hand, the precise information given by Irenaeus that the Fourth Gospel is also the *last* of the four canonical Gospels, along with the reference to the death of the evangelist John in the time of Trajan, and its last verses, where the end of the beloved disciple is put long after the martyrdom of Peter, should warn us against dating the Gospel too early. As the other references, such as the expulsion of Christians from the synagogue, the Logos christology, and the rejection of Docetism, suggest a later origin, we may hardly presuppose a 'final redaction' before 98, i.e. before Trajan.[9]

(*b*) But loud protest continues against the reference to 'John *the Lord's disciple'* and his location at *Ephesus*. In the Fourth Gospel the identity of the mysterious beloved disciple is certainly veiled, and the editor(s) uncover(s) the author's incognito only by hints. Did they want to hide his identity because the author did not come from the acknowledged group of Twelve, and because about 100 his relationship to Jesus as 'beloved disciple' was anything but acknowledged everywhere? This crucial question will accompany us till the end of the investigation.

Now for Irenaeus that was no longer in question. In a stereotyped way he describes John about twenty times as 'the Lord's disciple' 'who reclined on the Lord's breast', who composed the Gospel and the First and Second Letters and saw the visions of the Apocalypse. He himself had oral information about John in his youth in Asia Minor via the 'elders', especially Polycarp.[10] For him, this John is identical with one of the Twelve, the apostle and son of Zebedee, and in his eyes this John is in some ways the most important disciple of Jesus. Here we can agree with the judgment of J.Hoh: 'It is evident that Irenaeus knows about the Fourth Evangelist from far more, and more special, traditions than those about the other three. This fact entitles us to conclude that Irenaeus must have special sources about John.' The one who mentions 'John the disciple of the Lord' about twenty-five times as the author of the Gospel and about ten times as the seer of the Apocalypse surely no longer has any doubts about the authorship of these two works, but takes it to have already been settled for some time. However, it is striking that with one exception – which may be a quotation from the Gnostic Ptolemaeus – he never refers to him directly as 'apostle'. Here he is to some degree removed from the synoptic tradition: for him *'the* apostle' is neither John nor Peter, but Paul.[11]

(c) This fixed terminology already indicates that the tradition of 'John the Lord's disciple' as author of the Johannine corpus must be essentially earlier than Irenaeus' work *Against the Heresies*, which was written soon after 180. That it was taken as a matter of course must be emphasized because in 'critical' monographs, introductions and commentaries we can still read time and again that the 'first sure attestation' of the Gospel of John is Irenaeus.[12] That is certainly not the case. We have a good many earlier witnesses.

So we need to look briefly at clear traces of the Fourth Gospel which are earlier than Irenaeus and – to a large degree – come from Asia Minor. Thus Irenaeus refers – against Valentinian opinions – to an earlier tradition from *'the elders of Asia Minor'* in respect of Jesus' age (almost fifty, according to John 8.57) and to the assertion that his ministry lasted not for one but for several years.[13]

About ten years earlier, around 170, Tatian in Rome, the pupil of Justin Martyr, had already used the framework of the Fourth Gospel and thus John's chronology, in opposition to that of the Synoptics, as the basis of his Diatessaron.[14] A little earlier still, in the writing of Apollinaris of Hierapolis in Asia Minor on the Passover, we find an attack on ignorant Christians who claimed that Jesus ate the Passover on 14 Nisan and suffered on the Great Day of unleavened bread, and who 'say that this is how Matthew describes it. But the Gospels (note the plural, *euangelia!*) seem to contradict them.'[15] In other words, the author begins from the Johannine chronology of Jesus' passion quite naturally and claims that this is the view of all the Gospels. Round about the same time, between 160 and 170, Melito of Sardes, too, makes abundant use of the Fourth Gospel in his Paschal homily.[16] Irenaeus himself attributes to the 'elders' and 'disciples of the apostles' (5.36.1ff.) an exegesis which harmonizes the parable of the Sower (Matt.13.3) with John 14.2 'in my Father's house are many mansions'. Here J.B.Lightfoot and others with some probability conjectured Papias as a written source. In Lyons itself, where Irenaeus, who originally came from Smyrna in Asia Minor, became bishop after the furious persecution in 177 CE, we find hints of the Fourth Gospel in the letter and martyr-report of the Christians there to the communities in Asia and Phrygia. So we have clear evidence that the Gospel was read in the services of the churches in Gaul and Asia.[17]

This special significance of the Johannine Corpus (including the Apocalypse) for theology in Asia Minor becomes especially visible in the paschal dispute and the Montanist movement: the typology of the passover lamb and the chronology of the passion in the Fourth Gospel support the Quartodeciman custom of the paschal feast as practised in Asia Minor;[18] the new prophetic movement starting from Montanus and his prophetesses could hardly have come into being without the link between the Gospel and the Apocalypse; at the same time its success in Asia Minor shows how deeply rooted this mixture of Johannine spirituality and chiliasm was there. In the Montanist prophecy the Paraclete promised in the Farewell Discourses spoke to believers, and according to Maximilla the heavenly Jerusalem of Apocalypse 21 was to descend in Pepuza.[19] However, J.J.Gunther is surely misleading in stating that 'the creation of a Johannine Asian myth started with Montanism'. This new prophetic movement, beginning about 157 (?), already presupposed it. Even in the Martyrdom of Polycarp we find some allusions to the Johannine passion narrative which prove that its usage in Smyrna was a matter of course between 160 (150?) and 170 CE.[20]

2. The last attacks on the Johannine corpus and its broad attestation at the end of the second century throughout the church

It is understandable that this enthusiastic over-estimation of the Johannine writings in Montanist (and other, e.g. Valentinian, see below, 8f.) circles should also provoke opposition. However, we know of open criticism of the Fourth Gospel only in the period between Irenaeus and Hippolytus (between 180 and 220). Irenaeus (3.11.9, cf. *Epideixis* 99) complains that among those who dispute that there are four Gospels are Christians who (probably in their defence against Montanist prophecy) repudiate the Gospel of John because of the promise of the Paraclete. This opposition appears in literature with the Roman presbyter Gaius, who in his dialogue with the

Montanist Proclus asserted that 'the writings (of John) do not correspond with the other apostles'. Both the Gospel and the Apocalypse therefore did not derive from the apostle John, but are forgeries by his opponent Cerinthus. The order of the history of Jesus in the Gospel was in his opinion in such radical contradiction to the three other Gospels, which agree among themselves, that it was manifestly a deceitful fake. Here we can accept Zahn's judgment: Gaius 'in declaring that the Johannine writings were unworthy to be in the church, acknowledged that they were in fact recognized in the church, and in attributing their authorship to Cerinthus, a contemporary of John, acknowledged that they were written during John's lifetime'.[21] Gaius does not argue that the Gospel is quite a new forgery in a way comparable to Tertullian's famous judgment on the Acts of Paul and Thecla (*De bapt*.17.5); his view is that it was written by the most dangerous heretic and enemy of John in Ephesus!

The interplay of these opponents of the Johannine corpus could no longer influence its recognition, which had long been a matter of fact. Almost at the same time we can see the high estimation in which the Fourth Gospel was held in all the centres of the church: with Tertullian in Carthage and even with the North African martyrs of Scili about 180; by the Muratorian Canon and Hippolytus in Rome;[22] in Alexandria by Celsus, the opponent of the Christians, before 177 (or perhaps even earlier, about 160),[23] who read all four Gospels carefully; and a little later by Clement, by the *Physiologus* and possibly even by the syncretistic Poimandres.[24] We also find it about the same time in Theophilus of Antioch,[25] who quotes John 1.1 and mentions the author John as an inspired person; and probably further east in the Syrian Odes of Solomon.[26] About 170/180 it was as well known from West to East as the Synoptics. Its attribution to the apostle John in Ephesus and inclusion in the collection of four Gospels is certainly not a *Diktat* on the part of Irenaeus, but extends far into the second century. How far, we have still to see.

Further support comes from the fact that in third- and second-century Egypt the Fourth Gospel was most prized of all the Gospels. Of the roughly twenty papyrus fragments of Gospels from before the time of Constantine John comes first with eleven texts. Two (or three) of these, the well known P[52] and the recently published P[90], come from the second century, and probably also P[66], in which the inscription *Euangelion kata Iōannēn* has been preserved. The same inscription is found in P[72], which is a little later.[27] At all events, the originals of both manuscripts belong in the second century. In my view, in the case of the Fourth Gospel the title goes back to the circulation of the text as we now have it at the beginning of the same century. The same is also true of the Apocalypse, where the author's name itself is rooted in the text;[28] for the letters this is an obvious conjecture. But if at the same time there existed an *'euangelion kata Iōannēn'* which had meanwhile been edited and multiplied, the question arises, 'Which John?', or 'How many Johns?' This is a special dilemma in the 'Johannine question'.

At the height of the paschal dispute about 190, Bishop Polycrates of Ephesus, who 'led the bishops in Asia... in insisting that it was necessary to keep the custom which had been handed down to them from of old', wrote to Victor of Rome: 'For in Asia, too, great stars have found their resting places..., Philip, from the twelve apostles, who fell asleep in Hierapolis... and also *John, who reclined on the Lord's breast*, bore the (priestly) front shield, was priest, witness to the faith and teacher; he entered into rest in Ephesus.'[29]

Polycrates, born about 125 and (I suppose) about the same age as Irenaeus,[30] refers to the two pillars of the tradition of Asia Minor as Philip and John. Here the 'apostle' Philip comes first; Polycrates (or better, his tradition) confuses him with the evangelist from the Hellenist group of the Seven who is already mentioned – together with his daughters – by Papias.[31] Only in second place does he mention 'John, who reclined on the Lord's breast', the beloved disciple, who according to John 21.24 must be the author of the Gospel. It is striking that he does not mention him first, since in all the lists of apostles in the New Testament John the son of Zebedee is listed before Philip;[32] moreover, he is not given the title apostle. Here Polycrates is evidently following an earlier fixed terminology which we similarly also find in Irenaeus. At all events we have the impression that behind this brief and sometimes cryptic information there is a more intensive John tradition or legend. The tombs of Philip in Hierapolis and John in Ephesus were the counterparts to the famous *tropaia* of the two princes of the apostles in Rome with which the Roman presbyter Gaius confronts the leading Montanist Proclus.[33] Nevertheless John is not called apostle! In my view the last designation, 'teacher', also points indirectly to the writings of the 'beloved disciple'. Presumably Polycrates means to say that for the Christians in Asia John is – now through his writings – the most significant teacher of the past.

3. The Gnostic exegesis of John

At least in the case of one well-known author, John as disciple of the Lord, apostle and author of the Fourth Gospel can be traced back a generation before Irenaeus. In *Adversus haereses* 1.8.5 Irenaeus reports the interpretation of the prologue of John by Ptolemy, the disciple of Valentinus: '*John, the Lord's disciple*, who sought to narrate the origin of all things, according to whom the Father brought forth everything.' In the course of the quotation Ptolemy names John twice more as author of the prologue.[34] Thus the evangelist becomes the key witness to the protological speculations of the famous pupil of Valentinus.

In the Letter to Flora, Ptolemy defends the church's doctrine of creation against a radical Marcionitism and again quotes the prologue: 'Moreover the *apostle* says that the creation of the world is his own (the Logos) – for all things are said to have been made through him and without him was not anything made';[35] i.e. 'the Lord's disciple' and 'the apostle' were already interchangeable as far as Ptolemy was concerned. If, as Harnack and others supposed, he was identical with the Christian teacher Ptolemy in Rome, about whose execution Justin protested in his Second Apology, he would have to be put before c.155.[36] Through Ptolemy we could possibly in this way bring back the attribution to the 'apostle John' to about 150 CE. The period of Ptolemaeus' teaching may have begun c.145, but this dating remains hypothetical. When Irenaeus wrote his *magnum opus* shortly after 180 the pupil of Valentinus was in any case already dead. In his 1943 Cambridge dissertation, J.N.Sanders[37] conjectured that the Alexandrian Gnostics invented this special attribution. However, this distinctive hypothesis is not very probable. Even in Egypt the Fourth Gospel seems to have been, like the other Gospels (as C.H.Roberts has shown), a sacred book of the mainstream church.[38]

Possibly the identification of John the apostle and son of Zebedee with John the disciple of the Lord and author of the Johannine corpus was performed by gnosticizing Christians (like Ptolemy and Valentinus) and mainstream Christians (like Justin, who was converted in Asia Minor c.130-135, see below, 12ff.) at about the same time in Asia Minor, Alexandria and Rome, 'where a self-contained group of Christians from Asia Minor can be proved',[39] and yet there were still a few reservations about John's work up to the end of the second century.

In this way we come to the view, widespread today, that the Fourth Gospel is a semi-'gnostic' Gospel which was first rescued for the mainstream church by the efforts of Irenaeus. But we can see hardly anything of a Gnostic interpretation of the Fourth Gospel in the earliest Gnostics:[40] Menander, Satornilus, Cerdon, Basilides (?) and Carpocrates, and Irenaeus' Simonians and Ophites. Marcion probably knew the prologue, but rejected it.[41] It is quoted first by the disciples of Basilides, and certainly not more but less often than the Synoptic texts. The same thing is true of the rather late Sermon of the Naassenes which presupposes a canon of four Gospels, and of the Book of Baruch by the Gnostic Justin. The Fourth Gospel played no major role in Gnosticism before the school of Valentinus,[42] i.e. 140/150. Whether this great Christian Gnostic theologian, who like Justin lived in Rome between about 135/140 and 150/155 as a free teacher, used the Fourth Gospel remains uncertain, because so few fragments have been preserved. However, it is quite probable,[43] since his pupils were especially fond of it because it was the most 'speculative' Gospel, though they distorted it with their exegesis.

In addition to Ptolemy, I should also mention Heracleon, who was his slightly later contemporary in Rome. Like Ptolemy, he calls John 'the disciple' (as opposed to the Baptist) and reckons him among the apostles. He also wrote the first allegorical commentary on the Gospel of John. The Alexandrian pupil of Valentinus, Theodotus, also often made use of it, calling John and Paul *'apostolos'*.[44]

The important point here is that Valentinus and his school sought to be quite deliberately Christian Gnostics in the sphere of the church and that for a long time the Roman community took no steps against them. The boundaries between orthodoxy and heresy were relatively vague right to the end of the second century, and in Rome church discipline seemed more important than 'true doctrine'.[45]

Among the Nag Hammadi documents, too, it is primarily the Valentinians who use the Fourth Gospel, as in the Gospel of Truth, the Gospel of Philip,[46] the Epistle to Rheginos and other later writings influenced by this school.[47] Elsewhere the Synoptics are cited considerably more often. So we cannot say that the Fourth Gospel was particularly the Gospel of the Gnostics. This is true only for the Christian school of Valentinus. Because the definition of the terms 'Gnosis' and 'Gnostics' is still unsettled and there is a wide range of variations, we should be more cautious about using the perplexing label 'Gnosis' or 'Gnostic' too hastily. It often does not help to clarify a problem but rather darkens it. And in any case we should define more clearly what sort of 'Gnosis' we mean.

In the large collection of Gnostic texts by Werner Foerster, the number of scriptural references to John and Matthew is almost identical (104 to 102). In addition there are 32 parallels to Luke and 6 to Mark.[48] This relationship roughly matches the frequency in the papyri of the Gospels in Egypt before the time of Constantine: 11 John; 9 Matthew; 4 Luke; 1 Mark. Is this mere coincidence?[49] The Gnostics could use Matthew just as well as John, for they could cope with almost any text.

4. Early Johannine apocrypha and apocryphal Gospels

Use is probably also made of the Fourth Gospel in the only apocryphal writing from Nag Hammadi attributed to John, the Apocryphon of John. The framework of the book contains a revelation of the Risen Christ to John the son of Zebedee which he reports at the end to his fellow disciples.[50] Yet Peter is represented much better in the library with four apocrypha;[51] moreover he is mentioned five times more frequently than John. Even Matthew, Thomas, Paul, Jude and James the brother of the Lord are mentioned more often.[52] John is certainly no 'beloved disciple' of 'the Gnostics'.

Here we come up against a new complex of which often too little notice is taken: the New Testament Apocrypha. Mention must be made here first of the Acts of John,[53] the earliest paradigm of this genre. They were probably written soon after 150. The first part has not been preserved. The text as we possess it begins with the arrival of John in Miletus (ch.18). In addition to Ephesus and Smyrna he also visits 'other cities in Asia'.[54] This round trip was probably orientated on the sequence of the seven letters in Revelation 2 and 3. The author puts forward a crude 'monarchian' christology, which identifies the Logos and the Father; the title Son nearly disappears. Neither holy scriptures nor the traditional kerygma of incarnation, death and resurrection of Jesus have a role here. The christology corresponds to a 'naive docetism'. The 'earthly' Jesus already has a mysterious 'pluriformity' which elsewhere we find only with the risen Lord. His body was at one point material and then again non-material; he only seemed to eat and – here (but not in the Gospel itself) my colleague Ernst Käsemann would be right – 'like a God walking over the earth' he left no footprints as he went.[55] The author hoped that his work would have a positive influence on the semi-educated pagan middle classes by removing all offence that the Christian message might cause. Surely he thought himself to be a very modern 'progressive' theologian: we find these people in all centuries of church history. He sometimes used the Gospel, from whose christological dialectic he is far removed, very eclectically, and in addition also synoptic material.

However, the influence of the Fourth Gospel can also be seen on a number of apocryphal Gospels, which must probably be dated as early as the end of the first half of the second century: first of all in the Gospel of Peter,[56], possibly in the Gospel of Thomas,[57] but also in the Gospel fragment contained in the Egerton Papyrus, which represents a free cento of Johannine and synoptic texts.[58] The 'Secret Gospel of Mark' in the letter fragment of Clement is a similar secondary 'mélange' which, if it is authentic – though I doubt this strongly – may go back to the Carpocratians.[59] The earliest text of this kind is the secondary conclusion to Mark, 16.9-20, which is attested as early as the second century not only by Irenaeus but also by the *Epistula Apostolorum* and others.[60] Mark 16.9 reproduces in the briefest form the appearance of Jesus to Mary Magdalene. Subsequent verses give a harmonizing summary of the reports of John 20, Luke 24 and Matt.28 and expand them with apocryphal material which has connections with Papias.[61] The text may have been written between 110 and 130. It is the first attempt at a partial 'gospel harmony', but is still much freer in form than that of Tatian fifty or sixty years later.

In this connection we must also consider the problem, which is easily overlooked, that at a very early stage the Fourth Gospel influenced the text of Matthew and Luke in the passion narrative; this may also in part go back to the first half of the second century. To mention only the most important examples: John 19.2, the *himation porphyroun* in Matt.27.28, Western text; 19.24, the quotation from Ps.22.19 in the Johannine form in Matt.27.35; 19.20, the *titulus* in three languages in Luke 23.38 and the thrust into Jesus' side in Matt.27.49.

These examples and texts would bring us quite close to the time of the origin of the Fourth Gospel. However, so far I have spoken only about its existence and influence; I have said nothing about the evangelist. To combat Gnosticism his name is emphasized in a text which has chosen the more Gnostic form of the revelation discourse of the risen Christ, the *Epistula Apostolorum*.[62] In it the Risen One speaks to the twelve disciples. The content of his revelations is largely identical with material from the four Gospels and Acts; it also has a clear anti-Gnostic tendency. The place of origin is presumably Egypt (or Asia Minor); the time of origin can be established more closely. When the disciples ask when the promised parousia will take place, according to the Coptic text the Risen Christ gives a figure of 120 years.[63] The starting point is the passover of Jesus' crucifixion, 30 CE, which would then make the parousia expected about 150; in that case the work might be supposed to have been composed between 140 and 150.[64] This would also suit its free form, which still does not indicate any awareness of structured church ministry. Simon and Cerinthus, the opponents of Peter and John, are mentioned as the future heretics, but not Marcion, the most dangerous heretic of the second century.[65] It is striking here that, of the Gospels, John is the most important – it passes down the true knowledge of Christ, though Johannine and synoptic material are well mixed. In accordance with this, John, and not Peter, heads the list of the eleven disciples and Nathanael is included among them.[66] The Acts of John, written about ten or twenty years later, is, like the *Epistula Apostolorum*, evidence of the high reputation of John and of the Fourth Gospel in Egypt (or Asia Minor) between 140 and 160, and shows as well that at that time the authorship was already attributed to John, the beloved disciple and apostle.

5. Justin

We have thus reached that area in which knowledge of the Fourth Gospel is often denied in scholarship. However, in this early period no Gospel author is mentioned – if we leave aside the unusual and enigmatic Papias notices. We find John directly named as a Gospel author in Ptolemy and, rather later, Matthew in Apollinaris of Hierapolis.[67] Even Justin mentions no evangelist directly by name and uses the word *euangelion* only three times, and once, as a complete novelty, the plural *euangelia*.[68] Elsewhere he has the designation 'Reminiscences of the apostles' (*apomnēmoneumata tōn apostolōn*); this expressed the unity-in-multiplicity more clearly than the 'impossible' plural *euangelia* and was more understandable to pagan readers, for whom *euangelion* was no literary title at all.[69] Only in one of Justin's three 'Gospel' passages does he introduce a quotation: the saying about authority (Matt.11.27 = Luke 10.22), with the scriptural formula 'In the Gospel it is written'.[70] Immediately before that he says that after his crucifixion Christ will rise from the dead 'which he has received from his Father'. The closest parallel is John 10.18: the Son has authority 'to take back his life again. I have received this from my Father.'[71] Is this a chance point of contact? The question arises in most of the approximately forty texts which are listed in Goodspeed's edition as echoes of the Fourth Gospel.[72] In some, however, the dependence is quite clear. Here are only two examples of many. In *Dialogue* 88.7 it is said that 'men supposed that he (John the Baptist) was the Messiah'. But he himself called out to them, 'I am not the Messiah (*ouk eimi ho Christos*) but the voice of one who cries.' This must be explained from a combination of John 1.15, the crying of the Baptist, his reply to those sent to him in 1.20, 'I am not the Messiah' (*ego ouk eimi ho Christos*), and his definition of himself in 1.23, 'I am the voice of one who cries.' In *Apology* 61.4, we have the most discussed allusion to the Gospel of John in the context of Christian baptism. Baptism happens because Christ said 'Unless you are born again you will not enter into the kingdom of heaven.' This recalls Jesus' answer to Nicodemus in John 3.3, 'Unless someone is born again', and 3.5, 'He cannot enter the kingdom of God.' The fact that here the Johannine text is in the background emerges clearly from the sequel: 'Now it is clear to all that it is impossible for those who have once been born to return to the bodies of their mothers.' This corresponds closely to the foolish interjection from Nicodemus in John 3.4b. Justin alludes to the conversation with Nicodemus without, however, quoting it precisely.[73]

As Justin's Logos christology is inconceivable without the prologue of John, I need not discuss the point further.[74] His pupil Tatian not only uses the Fourth Gospel as the 'backbone' for his *Diatessaron* but also quotes it as holy scripture.[75] Justin's anti-docetic view of the incarnation of the Logos also has close connections with John. The frequently used participle *sarkopoiētheis*[76] refers back to John 1.14, and his realistic interpretation of the Last Supper in *Apology* 64.2 is connected with the same passage and the eucharistic tradition of John 6.51-58. Nevertheless it is beyond question that in his Gospel quotations Justin prefers 'the synoptic tradition'; but here too he often quotes the Gospel texts quite inexactly from memory, i.e. from his teaching practice. The reason for this was first that the Fourth Gospel provided little for practical paraenesis and ethics, which were essential for the life of the church and for apologetics. Possibly also in his time, as the latest of four, it was still not generally acknowledged in the Roman community.[77] For Roman Christians it seemed to be a bit too speculative and 'spiritual'. If we take all the numerous allusions to the Fourth Gospel and Johannine thought together we can hardly escape the conclusion that Justin, coming from Asia Minor to Rome, knew the Gospel quite well but did not use it as much as Matthew and Luke for the reasons mentioned.

When it comes to the authors of the Gospels, Justin once mentions Peter indirectly as author of the Gospel of Mark;[78] elsewhere he says only once that 'the reminiscences *were composed by Jesus' apostles and their successors*'.[79] We might take the latter to apply to Mark and Luke and the former to Matthew and John. Of the disciples he mentions Peter only twice[80] and once speaks of 'John, one of the apostles of

Christ'; however, this is not as the author of the Gospel but as the seer of the Apocalypse, who prophesied the thousand-year kingdom.[81] But we may assume that he also saw the same John as author of the Gospel.

6. The Apostolic Fathers, Ignatius and Polycarp

Justin had become a Christian a few years before the Bar Kochba revolt, which broke out around 132. Before him we have the so-called Apostolic Fathers and the endless dispute over the fragments of Papias. I shall not spend much time on the Apostolic Fathers. These writings do not contain any really trustworthy evidence of having used the Fourth Gospel, though of course that does not mean that it was totally unknown to them. The *argumentum e silentio*, which is so often misused, is no proof that an author did not know a particular text. It only shows that he did not use it explicitly. Unequivocal quotations of any of the Gospels in the Apostolic Fathers are very rare.

It is obvious that John was not known to Clement of Rome because both were writing around the same time. Possibly the author of Hermas and Barnabas and somewhat less probably the unknown preacher standing behind II Clement knew the Gospel of John, but because of the uncertainty this does not take us much further.[82] Given the lively exchange between the main Christian communities through travelling brethren and letters it is quite probable that a Christian teacher and author between 110 and 150 knew the Gospel of John. At this time the community libraries were already quite well equipped. We may deduce this from I Clement and Barnabas and their broad use of Old Testament and Jewish literature.[83] The crucial question is whether or how they acknowledged the new Gospel, and even in Justin's work this point still remains somewhat problematical. Here, however, the most interesting problem is that of the relationship between Ignatius and the Gospel of John.

The letters of Ignatius were written on the bishop's journey to his martyrdom in Rome, at the latest in the early autumn of 113.[84] He wrote them in Asia Minor barely ten years after the 'publication' of the Gospel. If he knew it, which is probable,[85] he read it with different eyes from Justin or Ptolemy thirty or forty years later. For Ignatius, its author was not yet an apostolic authority. In his letter to the Romans he accords Peter and Paul this status;[86] while he describes the Ephesians as *symmystai Paulou*, he does not say a word about John.[87] For he has in mind not the teacher from Asia Minor from the most recent past but the apostle who founded the community and later became a martyr in Rome nearly two generations earlier. Probably this is not because the former is unhistorical but because he regarded him more as an 'older' colleague who was not, as far as he was concerned, an apostle. What connects Ignatius with the Gospel and the letters of John is not a direct 'literary dependence' in the strict sense but a kindred theological milieu – in christology, eucharistic doctrine and abrupt repudiation of the 'docetic' heresy. At the same time his excessive stress on the hierarchy is a point of difference. Here Ignatius looks anxiously at the future of the church, requiring strict obedience of the bishop and the presbyters, while the Johannine writings still live completely under the charismatic authority of the Lord and his spirit, 'who will guide into all truth'. Possibly Ignatius does not mention the 'Elder John' because he had been an antihierarchical, charismatic teacher, without any interest whatsoever in ecclesiastical offices like bishops, presbyters and deacons.

The situation is similar in the (second) letter of Polycarp to the Philippians, which was written not too long after the martyrdom of Ignatius.[88] Although Irenaeus stresses – in my view rightly – that Polycarp knew John of Ephesus,[89] we may not overlook the fact that he also says in general terms that Polycarp was 'taught by the apostles' and was appointed bishop in Smyrna by them.[90] In other words, even for Irenaeus, Polycarp is no 'exclusive' disciple of John but first quite generally an authority from the very early period which reaches right back to the time of the eyewitnesses and apostles. Polycarp had been a Christian for eighty-six years at the time of his martyrdom. Because the date of this event is uncertain, and can be argued for between 156/7 and 166/7, he may have been baptized as a child between 70 and 80 CE and could have seen some aged eyewitnesses and disciples of Jesus in addition to John of Ephesus.[91] When he became a Christian, Pauline influence was still predominant in Asia Minor. The climax of the Johannine tradition is between ten and twenty years later. This is also shown by the letter. The episcopal diplomat reminds the community in Philippi founded by Paul of the authority of its founder, the 'blessed and famous Paul', and of his letters, but also of the 'apostles and prophets who preached the gospel'.[92] In his paraenetic writing he mainly quotes Paul, Jesus tradition and the letter of Peter (which is probably pseudepigraphical) from the time of Domitian, about twenty years later; compared with this, 'Johannine tradition',[93] i.e. that of an older contemporary who died only about a decade or two earlier, is represented relatively sparsely. Nevertheless it is unmistakable at the point where he addresses a 'dogmatic problem': 'For anyone who does not confess that Jesus Christ has come in the flesh is an Antichrist.'[94] That sounds not so much like a scriptural quotation as like a well-tried battle-cry which comes from the Johannine school, though we may of course assume that Polycarp knew the letters (and the Gospel). The next clause, 'and anyone who does not acknowledge the testimony of the cross is of the devil', is also a Johannine formulation;[95] the battle against Docetism already fought by John and Ignatius went on. Above all in the polemic Polycarp seems to have remained – among others – a disciple of John. No wonder that of all that he is said to have told of the legendary teacher in Ephesus, Irenaeus has only handed down the story of the clash with Cerinthus at the public baths of Ephesus.

Down to the time of Irenaeus, in theological terms, the province of Asia Minor was the most influential and fruitful in the early church. Before Pantaenus, from Alexandria we hear only of some Gnostics, and Syria, too, is veiled in silence between Ignatius and Theophilus. I believe that Asia Minor owed this theological influence above all to the Johannine school and – even more – to its corpus of scriptures.

7. Papias of Hierapolis

Before we turn to this, we must look at the few remaining relics of the first *magnum opus* of the mainstream church from the pen of Papias of Hierapolis.[96] We owe most of them to Eusebius, who 'annihilated' the five books by his malicious criticism but himself rescued a few fragments. Had they been preserved, we might conceivably have had a key to the Johannine question.

Papias' work may have been written in the time of Hadrian (117-138), say between 125 and 135;[97] it presupposes a lengthy period of collecting material, which would have extended back over decades. In his prologue Papias describes his method: by interrogating visitors who had connections with the 'elders', he wanted to collect what seemed to him to be reliable traditions and interpret them.[98] But he also 'expounded' texts from earlier Christian writings. Thus (like the Letter of Polycarp) he quoted the First Letter of John and Peter, and moreover – something that Eusebius keeps quiet about – the Apocalypse of John, for like most of the Christians of Asia Minor in the second century he too was a chiliast, a point which made him suspect in the eyes of the Platonizing Origenist Eusebius and later theologians.[99]

Even more significant than the references to the Johannine writings are his reports of 'Johannine persons' in the prologue to his work, which is formulated in good rhetorical style:

And if anyone chanced to come who had actually been a follower of the elders, I would enquire as to the discourses of the elders, what Andrew or what Peter said, or what Philip, or what Thomas or James, or what John or Matthew or any other of the Lord's disciples; and the things which Aristion and John the elder, the disciples of the Lord, say.[100]

Here Papias distinguishes between two different Johns, John the son of Zebedee, who was one of the Twelve, and the presbyter John, who was also a disciple of the Lord, but is separated from the first group of seven disciples and is not mentioned in the synoptic lists of disciples. The sequence of the seven in the first group is unsynoptic. Andrew, Peter, Philip appear in this sequence as disciples only in John 1. After Philip, Thomas is the fourth most important disciple in this Gospel; we find him in another interesting list of seven disciples in John 21.1. ranking directly after Peter. It will be useful to consider these lists in more detail, and compare them with Papias' and others.

As has long been noted,[101] the affinities between the sequence of disciples in John 1.35-51, the list in John 21.2 and in Papias are striking and certainly no coincidence. In his catalogue, Papias, who like John does not use *apostolos* in his fragments but only *mathētēs*, not only has a very similar order of names, which as in John 1.40 begins with Andrew, but also uses the same names (of persons) as John, the only difference being that he has Matthew instead of Nathanael, who is unknown to the Synoptics. In his Gospel John only once has the extra 'Judas not Iscariot' (15.22; cf. Luke 6.16). Surely Papias is to some degree influenced by the Synoptics by having the names of James and John instead of 'those of Zebedee' (John 21.2) as well as Matthew. The Fourth Gospel has a strange reluctance, which is difficult to fathom, to mention these two famous disciples by their proper names. In John 21.2 it is of course taken for granted that the hearer or reader knows who 'those of Zebedee' are: his two sons James and John. It is also striking that Papias and John attach importance to the same names of disciples, in contrast to the Petrine tradition in Mark. In addition to Andrew and Peter, Philip and Thomas are especially prominent;[102] Philip (like Andrew) is also of special significance for the later tradition of Asia Minor.[103] In John and Papias he is possibly identified with the 'evangelist' and second member of the Seven from the Hellenists in Acts.[104] In Mark, Thomas is still on the back bench

Catalogues of Disciples

Papias (7 + 2)	Andrew	Peter	Philip	Thomas	James	John	Matthew	Aristion	Presbyter John	
									(two not of the Twelve)	
John 1 (1 + 4) (one unknown)	Andrew	Peter	Philip				Nathanael			
John 21 (5 + 2)		Peter		Thomas	Nathanael		Sons of Zebedee	two unknown disciples		
Philip of Side (4 + 2)	Peter	John	Philip	Thomas				Aristion	Presbyter John	
Mark 3 (12)	Peter	James	John	Andrew	Philip			Bartholomew	Matthew	Thomas
Acts 1 (11)	Peter	John	James	Andrew	Philip			Thomas	Bartholomew	Matthew
Epistula Apostolorum (11)	John	Thomas	Peter	Andrew	James	Philip		Bartholomew	Matthew	Nathanael
Apostolic Constitutions (12)	John	Matthew	Peter	Andrew	Philip	James	Nathanael	Thomas	Cephas	Bartholomew

in the catalogue of disciples. Another analogy is provided by the two 'disciples of the Lord' who do not belong to the Twelve at the end of the Papias list and the two unknown disciples in John 21.2 who preserve the incognito of the beloved disciple.

Concerning Nathanael it should be remembered that in John he is the ideal believing Jew – 'truly an Israelite in whom there is no guile' (1.47), who confesses Jesus as the Son of God and King of Israel. The old identification with Bartholomew, 'Son of Talmaj',[105] is of course historically possible, but is not important for the purpose of the evangelist, because in his call the stories about disciples in 1.35-51 reach their climax and probably the name chosen by John has a deeper theological meaning: 'Gift of God', 'The true disciple is given to Jesus by God himself.'[106] John is not interested in purely trivial historical information. Other identifications, like the beloved disciple, or even Paul, are still more improbable.[107] But we should not overlook the fact that the one disciple, *Matthew*, mentioned in the Papias list but passed over by John, has a name with a similar meaning, Mattaty(ahu), 'Gift of the Lord'. How easily names with the same connotation could be combined is shown by a tomb near Jericho where a Natan'el also bears the Greek name Theodotos.[108] That the identity of Matthew was in some way puzzling is demonstrated by the fact that the unknown author of the First Gospel identifies Matthew with the tax collector Levi in Mark.[109] It has long been supposed that there may be a connection between Nathanael and Matthew,[110] but this need not be a simple identification. The Nathanael of Cana could be a real disciple of the broader circle. Neither John nor Papias shows a special interest in the group of the Twelve.[111] By idealizing the unknown 'Nathanael' and ignoring 'Matthew', the author of the Fourth Gospel could show his distance from the Greek Gospel according to 'Matthew', which was edited as a pseudepigraphon under the name of an apostle from about fifteen years earlier and in many respects seemed to be the precise opposite of his own work. In the decisive confessions of the Messiah Jesus in 1.41-49 we hear nothing about the 'Son of David', a title which Matthew likes so much, and Philip calls Joseph the father of Jesus (who comes from Nazareth and not from Bethlehem). Possibly the author also has a certain antipathy to Ebionite Jewish Christianity.[112] Is it pure coincidence that Matthew comes right at the end of the Papias list? Moreover in his report about Matthew's Gospel, which in all probability he received, like that about Mark, from the presbyter John, Papias shows a degree of critical detachment from the *Greek* Gospel of Matthew in saying that 'Matthew composed the "logia" (of the Lord) in the Hebrew language and everybody translated them (into Greek) as best he could.' The Greek Gospel of Matthew was probably the most influential of the Gospels as early as the time of Papias. Papias could no longer ignore it, so he disparaged it.[113] As far as we can see, for the Presbyter and Papias it was not a genuine, original collection of the logia of Jesus but had only a second-hand character as one of several translations. Probably Papias still had some knowledge of an older work containing mostly sayings of the Lord, which was said to have been originally written by Matthew in Aramaic. Irenaeus already connects the Gospel of the Jewish Christians with Matthew (1.26.2; 3.11.7) as do Jerome and Epiphanius, for all the differences from the canonical Matthew. Jewish Christians later regarded Matthew as 'their' evangelist. The author of the Fourth Gospel therefore chooses the unknown 'Nathanael' as the 'true' believing Israelite – and not Matthew. We cannot understand the two reports on the Gospels of Mark and Matthew in Papias as coming from the Presbyter if we do not see that they have a somewhat critical attitude towards these older Gospels. Hypothetical though they are, these reflections on the relationship between Nathanael and Matthew in Papias and John, which are not new, may help us to understand this one small difference in the lists of disciples in John and Papias, which on the whole have a similar tendency. That there is a close connection between the two can hardly be doubted.

The special role of Andrew in the Johannine tradition, comparable to that of Philip, is also demonstrated by the Muratorian Canon, where the initiative to write the Gospel is said to have been given through a revelation to Andrew.[114] The Acts of Andrew, which were probably written at the end of the second century, take their hero to northern Asia Minor, to Macedonia and to Achaia, i.e. to the general neighbourhood of Ephesus.[115]

The shorter list in the account by Philip Sidetes shows a 'synoptic' correction of the unusual 'Johannine-Papianic' order and therefore again puts Peter and John first.[116] The *Epistula Apostolorum* (and similarly the Apostolic Constitutions) puts its hero John at the head,[117] followed by Thomas, who in the second century (possibly as a result of John) became an important revealer disciple, not least in Gnostic circles. More notice should be taken of the importance of the order of names in catalogues of disciples for our understanding of the changes in the estimation of authorities in early Christianity.

In any case, this list of Papias is 'late-Johannine' and based on the first and last chapters of the Fourth Gospel. All that is no coincidence, and I am quite sure that Papias knew it; he has what he felt to be the right 'order' (*taxis*), in contrast to Mark.[118] The argument which is often heard, that Eusebius would have mentioned that Papias knew the Gospel of John, is not convincing. Presumably the Phrygian bishop had said things here which 200 years later the Bishop of Caesarea did not approve of. Eusebius's *Church History* is not always very trustworthy on such points: he also passes over the quotations of the Apocalypse by Papias (see above n.99) and suppresses the criticism of the Fourth Gospel by the Roman presbyter Gaius,[119] reporting only his repudiation of the Apocalypse, which Eusebius thoroughly disliked.[120] He also neglects to mention Papias' report about the killing of the sons of Zebedee by the Jews, which we know only through the church history of Philip Sidetes. This often neglected tradition seems to me to be more trustworthy than it is usually supposed to be, because it contains several scattered hints which taken together are not without importance.[121] In his relatively extensive report on the letters of Ignatius Eusebius mentions six of them, but passes over that to the Philadelphians (HE 3.36); he does not go into Ignatius's knowledge of the Gospel of Matthew in Smyrn.1.1 (= Matt.3.15) any more than he goes into his mention of Paul (Eph.12.2: Rom.4.3); mention is made only of the appearance of the Risen Christ to Peter and the disciples around him (Smyrn.3.2 = HE 3.36.11). A 'critical' use of the argument from silence could conclude from this that Ignatius did not know Paul or repudiated him, and instead had been a resolute follower of Peter and the earliest apostles.

We must therefore reckon with the possibility that Eusebius sometimes concealed information which seemed disagreeable to him or omitted it through carelessness. Why should he not have kept quiet about a – hypothetical – notice of Papias that the presbyter John had written the Fourth Gospel? He was only interested in making him the author of the Apocalypse by introducing the tendentious legend of the two Johannine tombs in Ephesus (3.39.6) which was first advanced by Dionysius of Alexandria. Over and above all these considerations, we do not know precisely how Eusebius read the five volumes of Papias, which he did not esteem very highly. His brief quotations give only a very feeble impression of the work as a whole, and the few surviving fragments quoted by later authors lead us to suppose that it was not read very attentively at all.

Whereas the first group of seven well-known names belongs in the rather distant past, the two disciples of the second group come from the time of the author; hence the present *legousin* in contrast to the aorist *eipen* in the case of the seven. Eusebius adds (3.39.7): 'Papias says that he was himself an actual hearer of Aristion and of John the elder. Therefore he mentions them very often in his writings.' We cannot infer from the particle *goun* that Eusebius is exaggerating in his first statement about John's audience and that Papias did not hear John at all. In later Greek the particle often has no restrictive significance but is merely used instead of *oun*. Several fragments agree precisely on the point that there was a direct connection between Papias and the presbyter John.[122] Probably Papias puts his name at the end of his two-stage list of disciples because he himself is most closely connected with John (see above, 17). For the author Papias the 'presbyter John, disciple of the Lord', is the – quite personal – climax in this list of disciples of Jesus.

This John must have been a significant teacher in the generation before Papias, i.e. in the decades before the turn of the century,[123] and the best explanation why Papias from Phrygia mentions him more often than other witnesses and even heard him in person is that he (and Aristion) had also been teaching in Asia Minor and not elsewhere in Syria, Egypt or Greece. When Papias wrote his work these 'disciples of the Lord' were already dead. A late trace of them may be found in the Apostolic Constitutions, where it is said that in Ephesus Paul ordained Timothy as his successor, but the apostle John – speaking in the first person – installed another John, and that in Smyrna the first bishop was Ariston and the second Strateas. Polycarp as his successor is, oddly enough, passed over, and another Ariston follows.[124] A Syriac Peshitta manuscript connects the Gospel of John with a 'John the Disciple' who taught in Bithynia; another Syriac colophon mentions after Ignatius and Polycarp a John as the third disciple of the Evangelist, who was the successor to the apostle in the see of Ephesus and wrote down revelations (*glyn'*) according to 'what he heard from the mouth of the evangelist John'.[125] All this may be the consequence of the two John figures in Papias and the interpretation of them by Eusebius. Having been himself in personal contact with the 'last disciple' John the elder, the Bishop of Hierapolis is indicating by his own work (in five volumes) – and by his polemic against writing books – that the time of oral Jesus tradition has definitely come to an end and the era of intensive book writing has begun.

That is the end of the first stage of our approach; the next awaits us in the following chapter. We have reached this mysterious John the presbyter at the end of the first century, and have observed a concentration of older Johannine traditions in Asia Minor throughout the second century, from the beginning. Our next question will be: 'Is there a bridge from this elder John to the Johannine corpus itself?'

II

John the Elder as the Author of the Second and Third Letters

1. John the elder in Papias

Our journey through the references to the Johannine writings in the second century brought us close to the time of their origin; now we have the task of building a bridge to the writings themselves. That cannot mean introducing the one 'author' immediately. A wealth of hypothetical sources, authors, redactors and even communities has been produced for the Johannine writings, but the results differ more widely than ever.

R.E.Brown, the most significant commentator on the Johannine corpus at the present time, conjectures four different 'Johannine figures': the beloved disciple as the source of the Jesus tradition; the evangelist; the presbyter as author of all three letters; and the final redactor of the Gospel. Rudolf Bultmann even presupposes seven or more such persons.[1] In that case the unsolved riddle is the question how so many different individuals in late first- and early second-century Asia Minor (or somewhere else) could be fused together as one, so that one or two generations later fathers who came from Asia, like Irenaeus and Polycrates (and their informants), knew of only the one John teaching in Ephesus. Nowadays this question is answered by reference to a Johannine circle, school or community.[2] But when, where and how did this come into being, and for how long did it exist? And why do we not possess an independent reference to this 'Johannine' school with its plurality of authors and teachers, like Plato's Academy or the nineteenth-century Oxford Movement, but only to *one* John (though it is true that according to early tradition he was surrounded by a circle of fellow disciples, pupils and bishops)?[3] If we mistrust Irenaeus, who mentions Polycarp and Papias, no name of a later teacher coming from this school is really known to us. The Leucius mentioned by Epiphanius remains quite legendary and about

24

Gaius and Demetrius in the third letter we know little more than their names. There is no sign of a direct personal connection with later Gnostics and even the Montanist movement; all we have is the mysterious enemy Cerinthus. We shall have to consider him later.

Did the school have one founder and leader or a variety or even a succession of different heads, or did it have the quite modern form of a collective of friends and brethren on an equal footing? What was its relationship to the other churches? Did it form a peripheral enthusiastic or Gnosticizing sect[4] or was it already a special church in a pre-Marcionite style? Nowadays, when 'orthodox' has become almost a term of abuse and 'heretical' is almost equivalent to 'individualistic' and 'creative' – in contrast to the 'narrow-minded' and 'stubborn' institutionalized church – such an interpretation seems to be quite attractive. But if that was the case, how could these writings be accepted by the other communities of the mainstream church and gain such broad and deep influence in it as early as the second century, as we have seen in the first chapter? And finally, how did all these different writers and redactors get the un-Greek name John? I have attempted to approach the problem 'from outside' and want to take this method one stage further before going on to consider the Johannine texts themselves. Here I am helped by the fact that today some 'foundation pillars' again provide a basic consensus which perhaps allows us to do some careful building.

1. This is true first of all of the question of *dating*. I have already made the decisive points in connection with that. After all the errors of radical criticism since F.C.Baur (who dated the Gospel around 170, a date which was later brought down to 140, see below, 87f.), we must concede that Irenaeus is largely right here. The Johannine corpus was hardly edited later than shortly after 100 and surely not very much earlier (see above, 2f.).

2. There are now again more and more supporters for the view that the corpus really was written in Asia Minor. This is true above all for the letters. The two earliest witnesses, from barely more than two decades after the composition of the first letter, Polycarp and Papias, come from Asia Minor, as does our key witness, Irenaeus. Moreover the two most important disciples in the first part of the Gospel (chs.1-12) have close links with Asia Minor in the later tradition (see above, 20). One could argue against the misleading objection which is often heard, namely that our testimonies about Ephesus are rather 'late', that they are earlier than anything we learn about the geographical origin of other Gospels. In addition to Irenaeus, further witnesses are Polycrates, who was born about 125,

and the Acts of John written about 150-160, which provides indirect testimony. Ephesus is therefore still the most probable hypothesis.[5]

3. A further foundation pillar is provided by the name John, which gives the corpus its unity. The title of the Gospel, *euangelion kata Iōannēn*, is certainly ancient; it goes back to the final redaction and editing of the work. In the case of the letters we must assume that all three circulated together under the name of John as their author;[6] a separate edition of the second and third letters, each of which occupy just one leaf of papyrus, is extremely improbable: they would never have established themselves in the church in the form of single sheets. Therefore the comment which is made again and again, that the second and third letters were pseudepigrapha, is extremely improbable. It is a miracle that despite the enigmatic sender *ho presbyteros* and their insignificant contents these two letters were preserved at all. One point in favour of a common publication is the use of the first and second letters in Irenaeus, who regards the two as a complete unit.[7] Even if the second and above all the third letter are hardly noted and cited by the fathers, all three letters have been preserved in the known manuscripts since the great uncials of the fourth century, and we also find them in the Old Latin manuscripts. Probably they were together translated into Latin around 200;[8] all three – or at least two of them – are mentioned in the Muratorian Canon. Presumably the (first) letter of John was already called 'the catholic' letter in Asia Minor at the end of the second century.[9] Particularly in view of the natural way in which Irenaeus uses the second letter as part of the one *epistula* of the disciple John we cannot avoid the question how it came to be attributed to John in particular. However, in no way can we think here *a priori* of the son of Zebedee and the apostle.

The name *Iōannēs*, the Graecized form of Johanan, is rather strange in the Jewish diaspora of the Roman empire, but it is extraordinarily frequent in Jewish Palestine. We shall return to this point (see below, 103f.).

4. The title IΩANNOY and the unique information about the sender, that he is 'the elder', clearly suggests a connection with the *'presbyteros Ioannes'* of the Papias fragments, even if in present-day scholarship this point, which was once widely recognized, is all too easily dismissed. As I have already demonstrated in the previous chapter how Papias is dependent on the Gospel of John in his order and selection of the names of the disciples and knows I John and the Apocalypse, we must take a closer look at his terminology. He uses *ho presbyteros* in a quite independent way that is not orientated on the

widespread Jewish-Christian office of the presbyter,[10] which we find quite often in the Christian literature of the last third of the first century and the second (James, Acts, Pastoral Epistles, I Peter, I and II Clement, Ignatius, Polycarp, Hermas). There is no mention of 'church ministries' in the fragments of the work by the Bishop of Hierapolis, a lack of interest which he shares with the whole of the Johannine corpus. As in the Fourth Gospel he is interested only in the 'disciples of the Lord' and the 'truth' of the tradition which emanates from them. His terminology of *alētheia*, truth, here has connections with the Johannine letters.[11] So he seems to me to be a later, very derivative 'offshoot' of the traditions of the Johannine school.

The *presbyteroi* in the plural in Papias are the old bearers of the original tradition: both the immediate disciples of Jesus and their disciples 'who followed the elders'. In the fragment of his prologue he evidently does not make a clear terminological difference between the 'apostles' – a word which he does not use in the fragments which have survived – and the later 'elders'.[12] He also gives the impression that he still had personal connections with such elders. 'John the Elder', right at the end of his list of disciples, stands out from this terminology in the plural; together with Aristion he is clearly distinguished from the previous list by the use of the present, *legousin*. I have already referred to the fact that Eusebius stresses that Papias himself, 'listened to Aristion and the presbyter John with his own ears. Certainly he often mentions them by name, and reproduces their teachings in his writings' (see above, p.22). At the end of his rather superficial account of the work of the Bishop of Hierapolis, Eusebius mentions the two bearers of the tradition once again: Papias 'gives accounts of the Lord's sayings obtained from Aristion or learnt directly from John the elder'.[13] Immediately after that he has his famous note about Mark with the introduction, 'This, too, the elder used to say';[14] again the reference is to John the elder. The later use of 'the' elder or 'elders' after Papias for teachers and bearers of old tradition, which is limited to a few authors – Irenaeus, Clement of Alexandria and Hippolytus – is formally dependent on Papias, but its meaning has changed somewhat. The later 'presbyters' are no longer identical with disciples of the Lord, none of them is called *ho presbyteros* followed by a personal name, and none of them introduces himself as *ho presbyteros*. The term has more of a collective significance, even when a single individual like Polycarp or Pantaenus is meant.[15]

The use of the singular *ho presbyteros Iōannēs*, and *mathētēs tou kyriou*, 'the elder John, disciple of the Lord' almost as a fixed title, differs in a unique way from this later general significance and also from the plural *hoi presbyteroi* in Papias himself. Papias must have mentioned this particular 'elder' in his work quite often. The Mark and Peter tradition, and what follows about Matthew, shows that he is indebted to him for important information. Thus the title for this one particular person was so fixed that it could be used by itself, *ho presbyteros*, even without the name being added.

2. The 'elder' in II and III John

We find a very similar situation in II and III John, where the strange absolute use of 'the elder', *ho presbyteros*, as a self-designation in the prescript is unparalleled in the New Testament and the apostolic fathers. The only exception is the unique note about Mark in Papias, which has already been quoted. Evidently everyone knew who this elder was without further explanation. Here too we come upon a Jewish origin: 'the elder' (*haz-zāqēn*) was a title of honour for great Jewish teachers before 70 like Hillel, Shammai and Gamaliel I when they had become really old men. Rabban Gamaliel I in particular was later called 'the old one' in distinction from his grandson. Probably John the elder was given this name in advanced age to distinguish him from the son of Zebedee, who by that time was probably already dead (see above, 21 n.121). The identification by A.Schlatter and B.W.Bacon of the 'elder John' in Papias with the otherwise unknown John in the list of fifteen 'bishops of Jerusalem' given by Hegesippus is quite out of place. Why should Papias, as a bishop in Phrygia, have had any interest in such a remote and insignificant figure?[16] On the contrary, this 'elder' John in Papias was an important teacher and mediator of the earliest tradition who was said even to have been a 'disciple of Jesus'. This points to a relatively great age and a long period of activity. Papias puts him at the end of his narrative because he feels dependent on him in a quite special way. That he cites so many traditions from the otherwise unknown Aristion and even more from John the elder is at the same time a sign of a relative proximity and also an abiding personal interest which could well be based on the fact that he really was once their pupil.

In the 'elder' of II and III John we similarly have a teacher with considerable authority, who is not bound to a single community but is in a position of giving instructions to other churches, which depend on him.[17] When in III John he counts Gaius among his 'children' (v.4), as in Judaism this points to a teacher-pupil relationship,[18] and the warning in II John 8, 'See that you do not destroy what we have done',[19] contains a reference to a successful missionary activity extending over a lengthy period and beyond the bounds of his own community. This is matched by the reference to travel plans in both letters and the lively exchange of messengers in the third letter.[20]

All ancient and modern attempts to devalue the authority of the 'elder' in the second and third letters are contradicted by the fact that here as in the first letter a teacher can raise his voice independently of all church-hierarchical institutions in an authoritative and self-confident way, because he knows that he has a direct link with the truth 'which was from the beginning'.[21] The 'we' in all three letters[22] is not – as R.E.Brown conjectures – a reference to dependence on a collective of other 'Johannine tradition bearers' standing behind and beside him[23] but an expression of his primal authority with which he then goes on in the name of his faithful pupils and followers to attack the false teachers and false prophets. Brown rightly identifies the presbyter of the second and third letters with the writer of the first, but distinguishes between the author of the Gospel and that of the letters: 'II and III John are true letters in which the author identifies himself by his customary community title (!), whereas in I John he is deliberately wearing the mantle of the evangelist whose work he thinks he is authentically interpreting.'[24] But is such a complicated construction, which has no basis in the Johannine texts, necessary and convincing? If one has to speak of a Johannine school – and I would say that we do – then here we are listening to the authoritative *head of the school*; he alone would merit the unique designation 'the elder'. That he is no longer a man in the prime of life, but also physically an old man, is supported by the fact that he has pupils (III John 4) and addresses his 'school' (or community) to whom he is talking in the first letter as his 'little children'. We also have the same address in the mouth of the Johannine Jesus as the fundamental authority.[25]

Quite another picture is given by Judith Lieu in her recent most thorough investigations of the third and second letters. She depicts the author of the third letter as a last, tired and hardened representative of the Johannine tradition who is far removed from the lively origin of the school and is ending in a blind alley.[26] But can such far-reaching conclusions be drawn from one or two papyrus leaves (postcards, in modern terms)? The preservation of the two letters thus becomes totally inexplicable. So for Judith Lieu their 'acceptance by the wider church within its canon of scripture' becomes an example of 'those enigmatic ironies' which 'stretch the imagination of both historian and theologian.'[27] For my part I see in their content and reception by the church much more genuine Johannine consistency than the irony of historical chance, since in the two brief letters we meet in a more 'private' way the authoritative person behind the Johannine corpus, who in the Gospel and the first letter remains invisible. We find a comparably authoritative 'we' for a leader of a religious group in the unpublished letter from the Teacher of Righteousness to the High Priest in Jerusalem, in which the Teacher gives the reason for the separation of his followers, 'We have written to you (here)', 'for we have noted', but also 'we have separated ourselves from the majority of the people...'[28]

This sovereign authority of the 'elder' was not acquired in a short time; it presupposes a lengthy activity. But if Ephesus, the great metropolis in Asia Minor, is most probable as a place for the letters, then it is hard to see why this unique elder of the second and third letters of John should not be identical with the unique John the elder mentioned by Papias the Bishop of Hierapolis in Asia Minor, who was writing about a generation after these letters had been sent.

3. The Johannine tradition in Asia Minor

This identification would also make the origin of the amazingly varied Johannine traditions there understandable. We hear more about this John of Ephesus in the early church during the second century than about any other figure living in the important period between 70 and 100. We should not be worried that here only a little history may be mixed up with a good deal of legend. No collection of legends has grown up in the relatively short period of about three generations without any historical basis. Moreover, we should remember that great theological stimulus in the church came from known teachers like Peter, Paul and James, who equally were transfigured by countless legends. This Johannine tradition begins with the seer of Patmos and goes further via John the elder in Papias, through the narratives of Polycarp,[29] the *Epistula Apostolorum*, the fantastic Acts of John and the remarks of the Valentinian teachers about John the apostle and disciple, and reaches its climax in Irenaeus and Polycrates of Ephesus. However, the anti-Montanist Apollonius,[30] the Muratorian Canon with its report of the strange genesis of the Gospel and its enigmatic notice about the letters, and Clement of Alexandria with his moving story of the young man who became a robber and the note in his *Hypotyposes* about the spiritual Gospel,[31] or the ascetic story about John and the partridge,[32] also show this variety of different and independent traditions. Tertullian knows of John's martyrdom in burning oil and claims that his hero was a virgin; this may go back to the encratite teachings in the second century.[33] At the end of the chain is the legend which Lessing described as the Testament of John, from Jerome's Commentary on Galatians. Having reached extreme old age the evangelist John in Ephesus said nothing more than a constant 'little children, love one another'.[34] Even if this legend is not 'historical' in the strict sense, it is admirably devised as an 'ideal scene'.

The starting point of these rich traditions and legends[35] is not a fiction but a real historical personality, a teacher and charismatic authority who worked in the Flavian period and early in the period of Trajan in Ephesus and founded a school there. He was that John the elder who played so great a role in the work of Papias as a 'disciple of the Lord' and a bearer of tradition and who as 'the elder', i.e. 'the old one', stands behind the letters of John (and as a prophet behind the Apocalypse of John). That need not necessarily mean that he really composed the Apocalypse as a whole and during the same period; apocalypses in particular were usually written as pseudepigrapha. We can therefore leave aside the historical question of the Apocalypse for the moment. This figure is the only historically tangible teacher known by name between 70 and 100 and between Rome and Antioch; his younger contemporaries Clement and Ignatius fall far behind him in theological significance.

It is further clear that this John is hardly to be identified with the son of Zebedee from the circle of the Twelve. This identification was made only when Papias' account of the death of the two sons of Zebedee was forgotten or suppressed a generation or two later (see above, 21). The nearest analogy is the transformation of Philip the evangelist into an apostle, which is very early and may go back to Papias or even the Gospel of John. For the Christians of Asia Minor it was highly significant later that they too could refer to two great 'apostles' (or 'disciples of the Lord') as having taught exclusively in their province.

The Neoplatonic philosophers Origen and Ammonius are another example of such a deceptive identification of persons living rather more than 100 years later. Eusebius identifies the pagan philosopher Origen with the great Christian teacher, and even Porphyry confuses the Neoplatonic thinker with the great theologian. The identity of names led to an identification of quite different persons.[36] In Asia Minor there was a special interest in the 'promotion' of the 'elder John' and 'disciple of the Lord' to an 'apostle and member of the

Twelve'. Like Rome and Antioch, their great competitors, they now possessed two apostles as founders.

4. The internal evidence of the letters of John and the Gospel

So far we have been approaching from the outside the origin of the Johannine writings, the time, the place and the author; now we must make a new attempt to get the letters themselves to tell us about their author and his school.

In contrast to the Gospel, where the pupils only make an enigmatic reference to the author in the penultimate verse,[37] in the letters the head of the school himself speaks, and above all in the last two letters the 'elder' introduces himself and his problems quite personally. First of all, however, we must defend both letters against their critics.

In contrast to the 'ideal' account of Jesus in the Gospel and the theological admonition of the first letter, the second and third letters discuss quite specific crises in the community. That here they do not develop the same 'theological depth' as the Gospel (and I John) is first of all because of their external form. If one is limited to a single papyrus leaf, one cannot develop an argument with such theological freedom as in a letter almost ten times as long or in a Gospel seventy times as long. One has to limit oneself to formulae, slogans, behind which very much more may stand than our critical academic understanding can grasp. The author not only lacked the room to develop what he understands by 'truth', his main theological term; he also has to apply this concept to practical problems and living people. Could we express ourselves on a postcard in a better way? The third letter with 219 and the second with 245 words are by far the shortest letters in the New Testament:[38] one cannot expect any sharp theology here.

And there is another perspective. In the Gospel, Jesus himself speaks and acts almost exclusively from beginning to end; everything relates to him alone. There is basically only one theme: Jesus himself, the Son and Redeemer sent by the Father into the world, who calls to faith and gives eternal life. It is he alone who speaks and acts in a superior way. Here we should pay more attention to the extreme difference in the literary genre. There is a deep gap between a Gospel with Jesus' 'authentic' teaching, an admonitory letter to all communities, and a very short private letter to one community or even one person. We cannot always expect exclusively the same language in such extremely different writings. I would hope that even a modern theologian displays some stylistic differences between a 'life of Jesus', a sermon and a short and confidential letter to a good friend. Therefore the manifold and in some respects close links between the two short letters and the Gospel, and even more the first letter, are really astonishing.

This is matched by the particular language of the Gospel. Wellhausen rightly compared it with the solemnity of the Priestly codex. With its numerous striking characteristics, the 'hieratic' monotony[39] of its limited vocabulary – 1011 words out of a total of 15416 – it developed only in a lengthy period of school activity and was shaped by the theological and linguistic individuality of the head of the school.[40] Mark has only around 11242 words but a vocabulary of about 1345; in the letter to the Hebrews the ratio is as much as 4951:1038. We find this school language in an even more monotonous way in the first letter,[41] but in another direction. Here it is no longer the Son who is speaking as revealer of himself, but the witness as teacher and admonisher in a situation which threatens the existence of the Johannine school, its 'sympathizers' and even – in his view – the whole church. Here therefore we have a presentation of what is more in the background in the Gospel: a paraenesis which is sometimes quite specific. So Hans Conzelmann has termed the letters 'Johannine Pastoral Letters'.[42] This comparison seems to me to be wrong, since there are about fifty or more years between the authentic letters of Paul and the pseudo-Pauline Pastoral Epistles, and a fixed continuous school connection can no longer be demonstrated there; by contrast, a lengthy period of time cannot be detected between the Gospel of John and the letters: indeed the final editing of the Gospel probably took place after the composition of the letters. The letters nowhere 'quote' the written Gospel; they do not presuppose the written work but the 'impressive' teaching of the head of the school, his theological language, and the existence of his school.

In addition, this comparison overlooks the utter difference in genre, already mentioned, between a 'gospel', i.e. an ideal, normative narrative of the activity, teaching and suffering of Jesus lying in the past, and a current admonition to members of the community about pressing problems of the present. Because of this fundamental difference, which is bound up with the critical situation of the school, the letters cannot simply repeat the christology and pneumatology of the Gospel. Nevertheless the immediate school connection between Gospel and letters is indisputable. In a comparison one might think, rather, of the striking differences between Pauline soteriology and paraenesis, which are sometimes quite considerable, even amounting to apparent contradictions. One could say that the Gospel expresses above all the indicative of salvation, whereas the letters concentrate more on the imperative and life in the community. In the farewell discourses in John 13-17, where the departing Jesus is looking into the threatening future and the imperatives therefore pile up in the Gospel too, we are closest to what the letters say.

These unmistakeable features common to all three letters are best explained from the context of a situation in which the second letter provides the link. In all probability they come from about the same period and from the same hand.

5. III John and the conflict with Diotrephes

The third letter – the most private of all the New Testament letters – gives us the most interesting information about the position of the elder as head of the school and the difficulties associated with that. So we shall begin there and go back from it via the second letter to the first.[43]

Here two points in particular should interest us: (*a*) the position of this writer over against those to whom he is writing, and (*b*) his problems, in particular the false teachers with whom he has to argue.

Formally we may call the third letter a private letter of commendation, but in a somewhat unusual way, since it commends to the recipient travelling brethren whom he already knows personally because he has received them and treated them well before. It is a new threatening situation which makes this letter necessary, a letter which not only commends but, even more, admonishes and announces. In comparison with all the other Johannine writings, the relative linguistic independence of III John is striking. This is connected with its markedly personal character. In no other early Christian writing do we find so many echoes of secular letter themes as we do here, though in a markedly idiosyncratic way. Here 'the elder' is being quite private.[44] Nowhere does the head and founder of the Johannine school face us so personally. The Demetrius mentioned in v.12, who may have delivered this shortest letter in the New Testament to Gaius, probably also explained its enigmatic, brief contents and the critical situation in detail; the letter is simply meant to establish personal contact between the elder and its recipients over and above an oral report and to commend the person of the messenger. Therefore the writer can content himself with allusions.

I shall go on to attempt to give the author – within the framework of the Johannine corpus – a meaningful historical context and at the same time to explain why this quite private and not very edifying letter should have been preserved at all. The further one removes III John from the rest of the Johannine corpus, the more difficult this basic question is to answer. A first important point is that of the three names – the only names we really know from the 'Johannine school' (if we leave aside the more problematical names of Papias, Polycarp, Cerinthus and even Leucius) – in the letter: Gaius, Diotrephes and Demetrius. All three are un-Jewish; one is Latin and two are pagan theophoric names, pointing towards a Gentile-Christian milieu: certainly far from Palestine but still influenced by 'Jewish' behaviour probably going back to the elder himself.

The elder is writing to Gaius, of whom otherwise we know nothing. The elder counts him among 'his children' (v.4),[45] i.e. his pupils. The confidential and personal tone of the letter, the greetings from friends and the request to greet friends at the end also suggest this (v.15). The plural 'friends' is used by Jesus for the disciples in the farewell discourses. It is typically Johannine language.[46] Possibly Gaius is the leader of a house community, and he is certainly a man with social status and influence. He has welcomed Christian travellers, probably because they had close connections with the elder and had been sent out by him. They reported afterwards on this hospitality and the 'faith' of Gaius in the elder's community.

The elder uses the term *alētheia* = truth six times in this context. This favourite Johannine term also occurs five times in II John, partly in similar formulae, nine times in I John and twenty-five times in the Gospel. Its use as a formula in III John and II John need not be the sign of a later decline in theology, as is so often claimed, since in such short letters there was no possibility other than to express the content of faith in bare formulae. Nor is the charge of a deficient christology a just one. It is the quite personal, private form of the letter which prevents the author from using the title Christ, just as in a private letter a Jew avoids the tetragrammaton by periphrasis. Therefore the author prefers to speak of 'the truth', which for him is solely the truth of Christ. *en alētheia*, which is used three times, comes very close to Paul's use of *en kyriō* or *en christō*. The reader who belongs to the school knows what the elder means by it. The name Christ here is paraphrased once – basically in good Jewish fashion – in the description of Christian 'itinerant missionaries' with *to onoma*, 'the name': 'for they have set out for the sake of the name'. That means that the travellers are messengers of Christ. The Johannine Christ, too, sends his disciples out into the world.[47] The conflict is sparked off by these itinerant messengers and the treatment they received. Since – and this too recalls Jewish behaviour – they accept nothing from the

Gentiles,[48] they have to rely on the support of private Christian individuals and communities. This leads to conflict. The elder had earlier written a letter to 'the community' (*tē ekklēsia*),[49] but 'Diotrephes who wants to put himself first among its members (*ho philoprōteuōn autōn*) does not acknowledge us' (v.9). Diotrephes rejected the itinerant brethren – who had presumably at the same time tried to deliver the letter from the elder –, attempted to stop other Christians who wanted to receive them, and expelled those who opposed him from the community (v.10). He was surely not yet the monarchical bishop of a whole city community, but probably the president of a house community, who could exercise his rights as a householder in his capacity as owner of a place where Christians met. An established monarchical episcopacy is not yet in evidence here, but it was probably in the making.[50] Especially in the larger cities like Ephesus, Smyrna, Pergamon, etc., individual house churches probably stand side by side in relative independence: i.e. the letter must have been written some time before those of Ignatius.

This point alone makes it improbable that the letter is a rather late product of the disintegrating Johannine school. The elder now writes the third letter to Gaius, in which he praises his hospitality and asks him to continue to receive and support the travelling brethren (vv.5f.). On no account is he to be led astray by the bad example of Diotrephes and to follow him (v.11). His practical behaviour towards the brethren shows whether he 'comes from God' (*ek tou theou estin*), i.e. in Johannine terms whether he is born of God as a child of God. Anyone who (like Diotrephes) rejects the brethren and breaks off communion with the elder and his community 'has not seen God' (cf. I John 3.6). The elder describes this clear either-or in the language of Johannine dualism as 'doing good' or 'evil';[51] faith and action are inseparably connected in the specific situation of conflict. For him, the human individual is a unity; faith and personal behaviour cannot be torn apart. So for the elder, how one behaves towards a Christian brother at one's own front door is the deciding factor over faith and unbelief, life or death, light and darkness.

We find a certain parallel to the authority of the writer and to the dualistic character of his admonition in the letter from the Teacher of Righteousness to the High Priest which I have already quoted: 'And we have also written to you (a selection) of works of the Torah which we hold to be important, for the good of yourself and your people... Take heed of all these (regulations) and pray God that he may guide your decision rightly and keep far from you the counsel of Belial, so

that you may rejoice at the end of time by acknowledging our words...
may this be counted to you for righteousness.'[52]

As I have already said, those critics for whom II and III John are at
a lower theological level and are characterized by a hardening in the
tradition do them an injustice. In these few lines there is really no
room for fine theological reasoning. Rather, we can see in them how
the head of the Johannine school reacts to real threats. In III John the
individual sovereignty of the elder is particularly clearly in evidence.
In a very personal, even pastoral way, Gaius is asked to prove the
authenticity of his faith in hospitality[53] towards the itinerant brethren
as 'fellow workers in the truth'. Dogmatic truth and existence in faith
are as inseparable in the Johannine school as they are in Pauline
proclamation.

The wicked conduct of Diotrephes is described only briefly, far too
briefly for us, and the writer does not engage in any further polemic.
However, the elder does announce his visit, on which he will then
confront the person concerned quite openly with his calumniations.
The *ean elthō*, 'if I come', announces a firm purpose. It does not mean
'If I possibly should come.' This intention and v.14, 'I hope to see
you soon', which is more than an empty epistolary convention, go
together. It shows that the writer feels fully up to the situation. He
is indicating his real plans for the imminent future. Later, second-
century, legend as it appears in the Acts of John and then in Clement
of Alexandria in the story of the conversion of the robber by John, in
which he is said to have appointed bishops and ordered communities,
is also familiar with a John who travels and visits the churches in
Asia.[54] This is also true of the picture of John as an authority
surrounded by friends and pupils.[55]

In my view, the aversion to letter-writing expressed by the formula
'Though I have much to write to you, I would rather not use pen and
ink' (III John 13; cf. II John 12) shows that he was certainly a master
of the spoken word and of oral teaching, but was not a well-trained
rhetorical writer. This also emerges from the simplicity of his style in
all his works. In view of the expectation of the imminent end, writing
in early Christianity was a makeshift measure and on the whole an
exception. We do not have a personal writing from any of the Twelve,
and the same goes for all early Christian teachers mentioned in Acts
and in the letters of Paul other than Paul himself, Mark, Luke and
James. Only the Christian Gnostics who had had higher education
broke through a barrier here and began a richer literary production.
In the first century the earliest Christian writings – with the one
exception of Luke – extend to only one volume each. Basilides first

wrote an interpretation of the Gospel in twenty-four volumes; Papias is the first 'orthodox' author to have written a 'Pentateuch', and Hegesippus, Apollinarius of Hierapolis (Eusebius HE 4.2.7,1) and Irenaeus follow him. There may be a good reason for the way in which, in the hyperbole in the last verse of John (21.25), a high degree of criticism is also directed at books as opposed to the vivid teaching in the Johannine school. But even for the author Papias, who wrote a work in five volumes, 'the living and abiding word' was preferable to anything in writing.[56] At the same time, however, that means that what is handed down to us in writing in the Johannine corpus is only a shadow of that oral 'testimony' which the teacher gave in a school that probably existed for about thirty years or even longer.

The letter which according to v.9 the elder sent to Diotrephes and which provoked his hostility may have been identical with II John. Possibly Diotrephes had not agreed with the rigorous action of the elder towards his opponents and therefore made the elder's command in II John 10f. rebound on its author.

The fact that the elder writes to Diotrephes and his community and sends messengers to him suggests that Diotrephes too had once been closer to him and perhaps even belonged to a former group of his pupils. This would also explain why the elder, backed by no church institution, with an authority based only on his bare repu-tation as a witness to Jesus and a teacher which had been proven over many years, has the firm intention of delivering a public rebuke to Diotrephes on his planned visit.

With all this the person and function of the elder also comes more clearly to the fore. For a long time he has been the recognized head of a school with a fixed location – presumably Ephesus;[57] it is also possible that the closer circle of pupils there might at the same time represent the 'community' mentioned in v.6, the community to which the brothers 'give testimony' about Gaius on their return.[58] It sends out messengers and receives itinerant brethren. These itinerant Christian preachers, who did not just go around one particular province but sometimes also travelled from one great city to another, were important guarantees of the unity of the church, but at the same time, as II John shows, they could be a source of dangers.[59] In the case of a famous teacher and bearer of tradition like the 'elder' there was thus the possibility that individual visitors would come from further away, even if his activity would be concentrated above all on the densely populated province of Asia. I Peter and the Johannine corpus including the Apocalypse of John with its seven letters, and slightly later the letters of Ignatius, the letter of Pliny to Trajan, those of Polycarp and the Pastoral Epistles are quite contemporary evidence that Christianity underwent a particular successful expansion in Asia Minor between 90 and 110 CE. Up to the time of Constantine this province had the highest proportion of Christians. The wide expansion of Christianity may possibly go back to the activity of this charismatic teacher (and his rivals).

6. II John and the threatened community

(a) The author and the community

The slightly longer second letter has some formal characteristics in common with the third, but in its content as an official letter of the elder to a community it is closer to the first. It lacks the very personal flavour of the letter to Gaius. Private features are almost completely absent from it. Here we can see the same bitter conflict as in the first letter and offensively harsh counter-measures which are to be explained from the basically dualistic position of the elder. The letter of the elder 'to the elect lady and her children' is addressed to an individual community, but this does not exclude the possibility that the elder sent a similar-sounding letter to several threatened churches.[60] In using the quite unusual address 'elect lady' he means to bring out the great worth of the community which he is addressing,[61] a status which applies equally to the 'sister', i.e. the community from which he is writing. If 'lady' and 'sister' denote the communities as a whole, 'the children' denotes individual members of the community. The accumulation of the uses of the term 'truth' which is unique in the New Testament (*alētheia* appears five times in the first four verses) indicates that for him this truth is now at risk. This situation, which in the eyes of the presbyter is acutely threatening, binds all three letters together.

In view of the prescript with its unusual content and clumsy form, we can ask again whether the elder was a fluent correspondent. Probably it was the danger of the conflict that had broken out which forced him reluctantly to take pen in hand. The very first sentence in the body of the letter reveals a complicated situation: 'I rejoiced greatly to find some of your children walking in the truth, just as we received a commandment from the Father.' This sentence means that the elder is making a distinction between the members of the community: he has found some of them who – we must add, in the controversy which has already broken out – match up to his idea of true life from faith. The parallel formula which is used twice in the third letter to Gaius, 'walking in the truth' (v.3f.),[62] shows that there too the conflict is welling up in the background, even if it is not explained in detail.

Now that means that others in the community to which he is writing are not obviously 'walking in the truth'. Since we can hardly suppose that the elder has visited the community, we may assume that some of its members had sought out the elder and informed him of dangers that threatened. The *heurēka*, 'I found', indicates a personal encounter; it is stronger than a mere 'hearing' (*akouein*) and expresses a powerful self-awareness: the elder decides what 'walking in the truth' means on the basis of his authority. He refers it first to the commandment to love received from the Father, which, he impresses on the community, is not a new commandment: 'rather, we have [it] from the beginning' (i.e. the disciples received it from Jesus himself).[63] The whole complex of the argument is very closely connected with the more extensive polemic against the false teachers in the first letter.[64] The elder cannot develop on a single sheet of papyrus the relationship between new and old commandment – old in so far as Jesus gave it at the beginning,[65] but new because in it the overcoming of darkness and the shining of the light becomes manifest in a constantly new way – as it is developed in I John 2 against the false teachers, to be followed by the invitation to the work of love which runs right through the first letter. Nevertheless, he brings his thought to an end in a brief cyclical conclusion by identifying walking in the truth with walking in love. He wants his letter to be understood in terms of these two basic concepts, truth and love.

(b) The false teachers of II John and I John

Only after establishing this basis can he go on to the occasion for the letter. It is concerned with the deadly activity of false teachers: 'For many deceivers have gone out into the world, men who will not acknowledge the coming of Jesus Christ in the flesh; such a one is the deceiver and the antichrist' (v.7).

The repudiation of such false teachers, who are the greatest threat to the Johannine school and the surrounding communities, is the real occasion for the writing of all three letters. In them the elder appears as one fighting for the truth of his message and for that reason giving pastoral admonitions. This is also the most important difference between the letters and the Gospel. In the Gospel we see less of this threatening controversy within the church, and only indirectly (see below, 52); nevertheless, we do see it there (52, 105). The quite acute polemical situation of the three letters, which point to a severe crisis within the school itself, for which there is no room in the Gospel in this direct form, explains why the theological argumentation sometimes sounds different. Here too I John tells us substantially more, but unfortunately 'more' does not mean greater clarity in every respect. One of the riddles of Jewish and early Christian polemic is that it hardly ever really names its opponents, but tends to use derogatory paraphrases. This is true of Essene polemic, which conceals its opponents in ciphers, but it is also true of the rabbis, who can hide quite different groups behind collective terms like *minīm* or *ṣadduqîm*.[66] Even Paul nearly always conceals the names of his most immediate adversaries and sometimes hides them behind taunt-names,[67] and the same is true of Ignatius, who writes to the Smyrnaeans (7.3): 'It is right to refrain from such men and not even to speak about them (the Docetists) in private or in public.'[68]

We get the impression that to mention an opponent by name or to describe him precisely was dangerous, as though it brought the one using the description under the opponent's spell himself; therefore the opponent is just to be rigorously rejected and at the same time veiled. Christian 'heretics' coming from one's own movement here seem to be more dangerous than open Jewish or pagan enemies.

I John 2.18 stresses that the 'last hour', the last time before the end, has now come, and so just as the community is looking for the imminent arrival of the Antichrist[69] – as the protagonist of the last time of terror – so now already 'antichrists' are appearing as his preliminary foreshadowings.[70] This appearance of false teachers as an eschatological signal and warning against them is a relatively widespread theme in earliest Christianity.[71]

2.19 reports that the false teachers 'went out from among us although they were not of us'. Probably by *ex hēmōn*, 'from us', the author means 'from the narrower circle of the Johannine school'.[72] These former pupils appeared with the claim that they were continuing the revelation through the Paraclete, but the community being addressed does not need such new seductive doctrine because it is itself taught by the Spirit (2.20,27). That the false teachers referred to the Spirit follows from 4.1ff., where there is a summons to test the spirits and the false teachers are called 'pseudo-prophets'. Although a whole series of modes of conduct like the claim to sinlessness, hatred and social irresponsibility are attacked in the first letter, the real cause of offence over which Christ and antichrist separate relates to *christology*. II John expresses this most clearly in the sentence that

I have quoted: the deceivers do not confess 'the coming of Jesus Christ in the flesh'. Anyone who rejects this confession 'is the deceiver and antichrist'. This confession stands right at the centre of the struggle.

Equally urgent is the eschatological admonition (v.8): 'Look to yourselves, that you may not lose what we have achieved, but may win a full reward.' In the 'we' of *ha eirgasametha*, literally 'what we have achieved', we have another expression of the awareness of the leader that he is the founder and head of a school which has also produced new communities in Asia Minor as a result of its missionary expansion.[73] Like the 'we' in the third letter the 'we have worked' demonstrates the 'self-conscious... claim by the author'.[74]

The fatal danger of the false teachers consists in their denial of the true understanding of the person of Christ so that they exclude from salvation themselves and those who allow themselves to be led astray by them. They appeal to the Johannine Paraclete 'who will lead into all truth' and derive from him the right to 'go ahead' beyond the teaching put forward by the elder (v.9. *pas ho proagōn*). This teaching by the Paraclete, understood as 'progress', comes into conflict with Jesus' commandment to abide in his word and to keep it, *menein* and *tērein*. Anyone who does not abide in the 'teaching of Christ' put forward by the elder separates himself from God himself, in christological terms, from 'the Father and the Son' (v.9). When the elder speaks of God in the letters, behind his words there is already a concept of God with a binitarian (or even trinitarian) content, which includes the Son who is elevated to the Father. Here the elder presupposes among those being addressed a clear knowledge of true christology in the decisive points of dispute; that is, he has presented this in his 'school' as a nucleus of his activity and now needs only to make a brief allusion to it. First of all it should just be said that here the *sarx Christi*, more exactly the 'coming in the flesh' (v.7), the corporeal, human mode of Christ's existence, plays the decisive role. But the unusual present participle *erchomenon en sarki* needs yet more explanation. We shall return to this point in the next chapter (below, 63). Thus for the 'elder', in the face of 'deceivers' and 'antichrist' the saving truth of belief in Christ is at risk.

That explains his rigorous and to our modern understanding offensive instruction: 'If anyone comes to you and does not deliver this doctrine,[75] do not receive him into the house or give him any greeting; for he who greets him shares his wicked work' (v.10). 'Receive into the house' means that the false teachers are not to be given the hospitality which would otherwise be offered to itinerant missionaries, nor even a personal welcome, which for Christians was not a mere formality but the establishment of a direct inter-personal relationship. For the greeting with the salutation of peace[76] itself creates community and that itself can have fatal consequences in connection with deceivers. The 'wicked works' are not to be misunderstood in a 'moralistic' way,[77] but in connection with the dualistic thought and language of the Johannine corpus. It is a matter of faith and disbelief, of salvation or damnation, truth or lie, life or death. 'Receiving into the house' suggests above all the offer of hospitality in the house community and probably at the same time communion in the eucharist of this community. And the prohibition against a greeting is not so much against a greeting in the street as against greeting the stranger as a guest (and brother) in the house which offers its hospitality. Welcome and greeting are related, as in the case of the greeting to be offered by the disciples in the mission charge in Q.[78] This parallel from the teaching of Jesus shows that the Jewish-Christian greeting of peace was an effective force which could even be withdrawn. It is not to be offered to the false teacher, for one cannot offer the peace to those who are without peace *par excellence*, the 'heralds of the antichrist'.

If we point a moralistic finger at this rigorous procedure on the part of the elder, so contrary to the uncommitted human friendliness in our churches, we do him an injustice. Surely at this point a contradiction to the unconditional commandment of the Lord, 'Love your enemies' (Matt.5.44), emerges, and here we have good reason for a theological critique of the content of the passage as well. But we should not judge from the standpoint of 'enlightened moral superiority'. In the Sermon on the Mount, after Matt.5.44 we also read 7.1-5. First of all we should see the position of the elder in its historical context.[79] Moreover what he says has a wealth of parallels in early Christianity. The Didache enjoins a welcome to all who come 'in the name of the Lord' – and not only them – to be followed by an examination of their ethical behaviour (12.1). Teachers who put forward the instructions of the Didache are to be accepted. But if someone puts forward any other teaching, he is not to be listened to (11.1). We can conclude from this that travellers who were immediately recognized as false teachers simply were not accepted (cf.16.3). The Gospel of Matthew warns against false prophets who though coming in sheepskins are inwardly 'ravening wolves' (7.15). The metaphor of the ravenous beast for the false prophet later became popular;[80] we already meet it in Ignatius: 'For some are accustomed to bear around the name (of Christ, cf. III John 7), but to do what is unworthy of God. You must avoid them as though they were wild beasts. For they are rabid dogs with a treacherous bite.'[81] You do not let savage wild beasts into your house.

We have even earlier parallels in Paul, who repeatedly forbids the Corinthians to have anything to do with members of the community who live in grave sin; here they are excluded from any kind of table fellowship (I Cor.5.9,11). In one instance he can even ask the community to 'deliver the delinquent over to Satan' (5.4f.).[82] His actions against false teachers were even more rigorous. They suffer the anathema,[83] i.e. separation from salvation.

The instructions of the 'elder', presented apodeictically and with self-awareness in a specific situation of danger, do not basically go beyond analogous Pauline instructions. The orders given by both figures express a similar awareness of authority which differs from what comes later in its terse, evocative harshness. The salvation which is at risk necessitates this. According to v.8 those being addressed are not to lose what the elder's preaching of Christ has achieved. In a comparable situation Paul expresses the fear that he may have worked in vain.[84]

One could also refer to the Gospel of John. Certainly the later division of the community because of heretical christology is not a direct theme in the preaching of the Johannine Jesus. But how rigorous the evangelist can be is evident not only from his account of Judas, which is intensified to the degree that he becomes a diabolical figure (6.70; 13.2) and comes to a climax in the dramatic expulsion of the traitor (13.21-30), the 'son of corruption',[85] from the circle of disciples by Jesus himself. The designation of the Jews as 'sons of the devil' (8.44), with the use of a formula which recurs in the polemic of the first letter against the false teachers,[86] shows the harshness of which the evangelist is capable. He was able to react if need be with 'hot hate' (see W.Bauer, above n.79). This is matched by the way in which for him the commandment to love is made concrete only in connection with the disciples. The disciples are to love one another (John 13.34; 15.12ff., 17). I John continues this line, when it forbids intercession for the mortal sinner (I John 5.16). The departing Christ already prays, not for the world but only for the community of disciples (John 17.8). It is God's love alone which saves the world, i.e. humankind (3.16; cf. I John 4.10,19).

The offensive instruction in II John 10f. is meant to preserve the community from diabolical temptation and destruction. Its basic tenor can already be found in the Gospel itself. No break should be supposed here. The roots for this conduct, strange though it may seem to us, are basically Jewish and dualistic. We find the closest Jewish analogies in the exclusion of the *minim* from the community of the synagogue on which the Johannine school looks back, but also already in the separation of the Essenes from the *massa perditionis* of the rest of the populace, which took place about 200 years earlier, and a little later in the formation of the Pharisees, who sparked off a furious rebellion against Alexander Jannaeus; it can also be seen in the abrupt demarcation over against the 'heretical' Samaritans with which the evangelist is familiar.[87] Knowledge of the truth not only binds people together; it can also produce painful separation. We should make a fundamental distinction between the historical question and the problem of ethical justification or even imitation of the presbyter's attitude today. As in John 8.44 or Phil.3.2, we need to reflect on the possibility of criticizing the actual content of the text, on the basis of Jesus' own teaching (Matt.5.43-48; Luke 6.27-36). But before we condemn the greatest teachers of the primitive church, Paul and John, we should try to understand them as men of their time and in special critical situations against which they had to react.

Here in particular the Pauline corpus and the Johannine corpus are closely connected. Both know radical grace, but also the inexorable 'no' against any falsification of the message of salvation which could even lead to expulsion and separation. Anyone who seeks to apply the measure of moralizing criticism here must begin as early as Paul and cannot save it up until II John.

The 'elder', who in contrast to Paul or Ignatius is not a great letter writer, expresses himself very briefly. Soon he wants to pay a personal visit to the threatened community. That he produces as the reason for the announcement of his visit, and the personal conversation that will go with it, the formula 'that your joy may be complete', a formula which also appears in I John (1.4), in Jesus' farewell discourses (16.24) and in the high-priestly prayer (17.13), is no trivial matter, for in such a threatened situation the visit of the elder represents the personal presence of that which 'was from the beginning'. For he himself is the guarantor of the word of Jesus that has been entrusted to him. In I John written testimony is to produce such joy: 'And we write this to you that your joy may be complete'; in II John this joy is to be brought about by the visit that is announced. Thus we are already in the middle of the dispute over I John and its historical context. That will be our theme in the next chapter.

III

I John and the Split in the School

It already became clear from the previous chapter that there is no justification for tearing the Johannine letters apart. Both the title and the history of the tradition tell against that, and their inner connection does so even more. They mutually interpret one another, and indicate a crisis in the school and in the communities focussed on the 'elder'. His life work, the truth of his proclamation of Christ, is threatened. The close interconnection in language and theological content thus becomes evident, despite all the differences in external form, addressees and situation. John the 'elder' speaks from all three letters in an authoritative way, as the head of a quite extended school.

1. The form of I John and those to whom it is addressed

Whereas II and III John are linked by the note about their sender, 'the presbyter', and by their similar form, each occupying a single papyrus sheet, the form of the first 'letter' remains a riddle. It is not in fact a letter, as it has no prescript and greeting. When it was circulated in the communities, with the second and third letters attached as an appendix, the simple title IΩANNOY was evidently enough to gain it broad recognition.[1] But it cannot be a transcript of an oral sermon, since the introductory 'we write' is first followed six times by 'I write to you' in the present; then the author goes over to the aorist 'I have written to you' and keeps this for the rest of the letter.[2] The verb 'write' occurs thirteen times in the first person. Anyone who has to stress this fact in such a way is presumably not very used to writing; the emphatic use of the first person is at the same time a sign of the self-confidence and authority of the writer, which is underlined by the apodeictic style: the letter does not so much argue as decree. It contains mostly assertions and commandments, or better assertions which substantiate the commandments.

46

Nor, however, is the letter a religious tractate, comparable to the Letter to Diognetus or the *Hermetica*. The form of address is much too confessional and imperative for that; moreover, the letter gives the impression of being relatively unarranged: the train of thought and the intrinsic connection often remain unclear. The very simple style is almost more monotonous than that of the Gospel; but despite all the minor differences, the affinity to the Gospel is great: that applies above all to the antithetical apodeictic way in which the elder speaks, akin to the revelation discourses in the Gospel.

> The style of the Epistles, together with that of the Gospel, is one of extreme simplicity all through, with some monotony of construction. Like the fourth evangelist, he is a cultured man, but his Greek is elementary and repetitive, *as if it were the style of an old man.*[3]

I can agree without qualification with this verdict by Nigel Turner: here we have the voice of none other than John the elder. This is also clear from the unique way in which he often addresses those to whom he is writing as *teknia* and *paidia*, 'little children'.[4] Something else that would best be explained by the fact that this is an old man's work is that after the writer has begun on his conclusion in 5.13 he does not draw quickly to an end but, while sometimes repeating earlier matter, also touches on other questions, finally to conclude in v.20 with a confession of the divinity of Christ, to which, however, he immediately adds the almost touching plea and warning: 'Little children, keep yourselves from idols'.[5] For him 'heresy' is identical with apostasy. I myself am now nearly sixty-three years old, but I do not dare to address my students, who are about forty years younger, in this way. No literary-critical operations can resolve this strange ending of the letter; it has to be explained in terms of the unique personality and the special situation of the aged teacher.

Thus the author, less familiar with the customs of literary rhetoric than Paul, Luke or the writer to the Hebrews, has composed an admonition in written form aimed at a wider circle of hearers. R.E.Brown may be right when he conjectures that this work could be addressed to the scattered house communities of pupils in a large city like Ephesus.[6] The author is known to all and need not introduce himself in person. Accustomed to teach by word of mouth, because of an acute crisis for once he had to attempt to address his scattered pupils and their house communities in the vicinity as quickly as possible.

If the first 'letter' was an admonitory circular to different house communities, the lack of an epistolary introduction and conclusion would be more understandable. Possibly the individual letters had variable prescripts and greetings, which were cut off from the archive copy of the community which was later copied along with the second and third letters; or, as seems to me more probable, it was accompanied by several short personal notes from the elder to the different principals of the house communities. The letter was written to be read, like a sermon, in the services of the communities. The fact that no sender is named is surely no argument against authorship by the presbyter. When the letters were published the inscription (and subscript) IΩANNOY A seemed to be sufficient. The sender, John (the elder), was well known to all the important communities between Antioch, Alexandria and Rome. A letter without a prescript – which was probably removed when it was put in the archive of the community which received it – has been preserved in Hebrews, and in I Clement we know the name of the author – as in I John – only through the inscription, which is already attested by Dionysius of Corinth in the middle of the second century (Eusebius, HE 4.23.11). The same is true of the pseudepigraphical letter of Barnabas. The letter to Diognetus does not mention the author at all either in the prescript or in the inscription, and it has no salutation at the end. The 'framework', prescript, postscript and title of the early Christian letters (and literature in general) are dependent on the vicissitudes befalling the *editio princeps*, especially its deposit in the community archive and its later copying.

Furthermore it seems obvious that I John, like II and III John which are addressed to more distant communities, was born out of an acute emergency and therefore has a very polemical paraenetic character. I shall now go on to try to work out this particular situation in order to discover more closely both the profile of the opponents and that of the 'elder' and his pupils. Here we must constantly note what connections there are with the Gospel, since nowadays it is almost a commonplace that the letter presupposes the written Gospel, which is said to come from another author; moreover there is a widespread view that it was the christology and doctrine of the Spirit put forward in the Gospel itself which led to the split in the Johannine community. There the stronger group of secessionists had a docetic christology and an enthusiastic understanding of the Spirit, whereas an 'orthodox' minority, whose spokesman is said to be the unknown author of the letter, resisted this development without much success. The latter were finally taken up into the early catholic mainstream church, to which they brought a revised version of the Gospel and the letters.

This thesis, which is popular today in several variants, is opposed by the fact that at no point does the author quote the Gospel or refer to it as a written work. If we only possessed the letters, we would not even suppose that such a work as the Gospel existed. We have no indication that the Gospel was already in circulation when the letters were written. Of course it is obvious that there are numerous close connections between the letter and the Gospel, but these are better explained by a common basis of teaching terminology and theology in the school or – in my view best – by common authorship.[7] I would venture to say that only on this presupposition does the first letter and its special polemical situation become understandable in a satisfactory way.

Against the assumption of a preliminary form of the Fourth Gospel fixed in writing and widely circulated, to which even the false teachers of the letter could refer, is the fact that no trace is to be found of the existence of such a preliminary form in the text of the Gospel which is already attested in a variety of ways towards the end of the second century. When we consider what influence Marcion's text – edited at a relatively late date (about 144 CE) – had on the textual tradition of the Pauline letters and the Gospel of Luke,[8] we should expect to find at least traces of this earlier version of the Gospel, if it had been circulated in a substantial number of manuscripts in the school and the surrounding communities. An authoritative and widespread written Gospel cannot be presupposed in the letters. Nor can one say that the prologue of the Gospel is already cited in I John 1.1-3. It would be enough here if the author knew the hymn from which the prologue was formed, and we cannot rule out the possibility that he himself composed this confessional hymn to Christ. Here the introduction of the letter is substantially more modest: at the beginning it deliberately does not refer back to the primal beginning in Gen.1.1 – that is a matter only for the divine word of revelation himself – but to the Logos made flesh of 1.14. It therefore inserts between the hearing, seeing and touching the *etheasametha* which also appears in John 1.14: the dispute with the false teachers is indeed over the reality of this being made flesh, i.e. the seeing, observing and touching of the incarnate word of life. The elder legitimates his authority with this introduction, an authority which he takes as for granted as Paul does his apostolic authority. No epigone of the second or third generation talks like this. The author claims that he is still a physical eyewitness who has seen with his own eyes and heard with his own ears. How we are to imagine this we must consider in connection with the beloved disciple. If we want to see

authorities of the second and third generations we should compare
Luke, Hebrews (cf.2.3) or I Clement. The proclamation of the author
which bears witness to what he has seen and heard is the basis of the
koinōnia, community, between those whom he addresses and himself.
This widespread 'community' created by his message at the same
time connects his audience with the Father and the Son Jesus Christ
(who has been exalted to him).

We can only attempt a hypothesis about those to whom the letter
is addressed. Along with I Peter, I John forms the backbone of the
Catholic letters; indeed it is called catholic in a special way. This
designation probably goes right back to the end of the second
century.[9] There is good reason for it. It is true that I John, too,
was written in a quite particular critical situation and is therefore
addressed to a limited group of recipients. However, it is composed
in such a way that it could speak to any Christian of its time and
certainly contains no special 'sectarian' teaching. But that means that
the Johannine school was open to the 'mainstream church' which
was slowly taking shape at the end of the first and the beginning of
the second century, and that we may not talk in terms of strictly
demarcated special Johannine communites. Nowhere in the Gospel
and the letters do we find any real direct polemic against other
Christian communities. The elder comes forward with the claim to
be a teacher of all real Christians, and only in this way can we
understand how one who at the beginning of his activity met
communities already in existence in Asia Minor, which had been
founded by the Pauline mission, also took up and worked over
numerous elements which are already to be found in Pauline theology. This is true of the pre-existence christology with its 'sending'
formula, the understanding of the death of Jesus as an expiatory
death, predestination and election by grace, stress on faith and the
love of God and concentration on the love commandment. What
John and Paul have in common here is much greater than what
separates them: the differences in terminology produced by the
distinctive language of the school created by the elder are greater
than those of content. The close inner relationship between Pauline
and Johannine theological thought is the most fascinating question
in New Testament theology (see below, 120).

We must suppose that John the elder had an influence on the
communities in Asia Minor between about 60/70 and 100 entirely
by virtue of his authority as an old bearer of a special, indeed
idiosyncratic, Jesus tradition and as a charismatic teacher, and that he
attracted pupils who after some time returned to their communities.

There may have been a relatively narrow circle of immediate pupils, around which several wider groups 'gathered'. Since there was not yet an established monarchical episcopate, and the local communities were usually directed more by a college of 'prophets' and elders, being subdivided loosely into house communities, various teaching traditions could be at work alongside and with one another.[10] The theological picture of the church between 70 and 100 – assuming a basic bond with the Kyrios, crucified, risen and exalted to God – is remarkably varied and full of movement.

The Apocalypse was also published in this milieu as a Johannine 'outsider', in my view later than the Gospel and the letters, though this does not presuppose that it (or at least part of it) was not written much earlier. The old hypothesis that the central parts of it were composed in the time after Nero is still worth considering. But that is not our immediate concern here.

All this would fit my hypothesis that not only Polycarp but also Papias had been quite late and theologically quite remote 'pupils' of the 'elder'.

2. The false teachers in I John

This clarification of the 'church framework' is the presupposition for a correct understanding of the decisive text with which the author describes the appearance of the false teachers. We already know it: 'Children, it is the last hour; and as you have heard that the antichrist is coming, so now many antichrists have come; therefore we know that it is the last hour. They went out from us, but they were not of us: for if they had been of us, they would have continued with us' (2.18f.).[11]

We saw in the previous chapter that the eschatological appearance of false teachers was a widespread theme in early Christianity. It is particularly intensified in I and II John by the introduction of the term 'antichrist'. We already find hints of the figure of the eschatological 'enemy of God' who derives from the apocalyptic tradition in Mark 13.14, more clearly in II Thess.2 and dramatically in Rev.13. In I John 2.18 he is defined by the designation 'antichrist' as the eschatological adversary of Christ. It is assumed that those to whom the letter is addressed are familiar with the designation; perhaps the elder himself created it. But as the crisis demonstrates, the 'antichrist' is in reality already present: the false teachers as 'many antichrists' who are already appearing are the heralds of the eschatological deceiver; through them 'the last hour' becomes perceptible, for with them the deceiver himself is 'already present in the world'; however, in contrast to him they come from the midst of the Christian community itself. They introduce that apostasy from the faith which the antichrist will complete with his coming.

The Gospel does not mention the false teachers directly, not because there were not yet any at the time when it was written; at least its final redaction is in fact to be put later than the letters. Rather, they do not fit into the Gospel's conception of Jesus's presentation of himself, in which everything is concentrated on his person. Anything that does not fit into the ministry of Jesus in the past is left on one side, even if it is significant for the school in the present. But even there we find clear signs of the crisis in the community. On the one hand according to the Gospel the apostasy is concentrated primarily on one person, Judas, the *diabolos* and 'son of perdition'.[12] On the other hand a falling away of numerous disciples is on one occasion depicted as a consequence of the offence caused by the abruptly anti-docetic eucharistic teaching (6.60, 66); here Jesus explains the division among the disciples which is brought about and also the apostasy of Judas in predestinarian terms.[13] The unique 'they went out from us but did not belong to us' in I John 2.19 matches John 6.60 and is also to be understood in predestinarian terms: they belonged to the community only by outward, human appearance (but not in accordance with God's saving will); for this will to be manifested, they must fall away. The antichrist-seducer is probably implied in the *allotrios* and the 'thief' (John 10.5,10), and John 10.8 may be a reference to Jewish messianic pretenders and prophets. Finally, mention should be made of the petition for the unity of the disciples (John 17.22f.), which is menaced by the activity of the 'heretics'.

I pointed out in the previous chapter that according to most modern exegetes 'they went out from us' (2.19; cf.13.14) is best understood as a falling away of members of the Johannine school. Yet it would be wrong to draw too far-reaching consequences from this, as for example does R.E.Brown, and conjecture that only a minority of the school remained 'orthodox' whereas the majority fell away to heresy, and that their roots and motives are to be sought almost exclusively in certain theological tendencies of the Fourth Gospel itself.[14] For that would mean that in the Johannine letters we can see a split that only affected the clearly demarcated Johannine special church which did not exist in this isolated form. In the first place, we simply cannot prove that a written primal Gospel had already been circulated there – in my view there is too much against it; and secondly, the Johannine school cannot be marked off from the churches of the province of Asia as a special community; rather, it was closely interwoven into these churches. Conversely, the school was certainly not closed to influences from other church groups and communities inside and outside the province of Asia. The degree to which any pupil was moulded by the head of the school could differ simply depending on the length of time he spent there listening to him, his intellectual abilities and his personal theological interests, and it could of course be connected with the influence of other thought from outside. On the basis of his oral teaching in conversations in the school we must suppose that John himself will have undergone a constant process of spiritual development. The sharp dialectic in his thinking,[15], which is unique in early Christianity, shows that he was no solitary and static dogmatician. Dialectic comes from *dialegesthai*, and behind the whole Johannine corpus – including the Apocalypse, as an 'archaic outsider' – despite the predominantly apodeictic style which is a typical characteristic of the elder, there is a lively school discussion which is at least partially responsible for this tense dialectic in the Gospel and the letters, with their antitheses and apparent contradictions.

The 'school' did not preach separation from other 'non-heretical' Christian groups; for their teacher the 'children of God' are a 'world-wide ecumene', won by the mission of *all* disciples. Moreover the unity for which the departing Jesus prays (17.20f.; cf.20.21; 11.52) is that of the whole church, not of a single sect. I think that all Christians and even interested pagans who wanted to become catechumens were admitted to hear the teaching of the 'elder'.[16] This openness in principle distinguished the Johannine school both from the sect of the Qumran Essenes and from Marcion's special church of a later date. In contrast to such secluded, exclusive groups, there is no distinctive special group order which could mark off the Johannine circle from the communities of the mainstream church. It therefore seems to have been a quite open Christian school. The seclusion from the 'world' is directed against unbelieving Jews, pagan idolaters and 'heretics', who in the eyes of the elder are destroying the foundation of Christian faith. The differences in teaching between the school and the earlier communities shaped by Paul were by no means as grave as for example that between the mainstream church of the second century and the great Gnostic schools of Basilides, Carpocrates and Valentinus.

The closest analogy to the crisis in the school seems to me to be Paul's struggle over the community in Corinth which he founded:

there radical followers of Paul himself had in their enthusiasm exaggerated Paul's most basic teaching, influenced by the Alexandrian wisdom teaching of Apollos and by a typical Greek mystery-like magical misunderstanding of the sacraments. In a similar way idiosyncratic pupils may have drawn one-sided consequences from the elder's doctrine of the Spirit and his christology, at the same time being particularly open to fashionable intellectual trends of their time. Towards the end of the first century CE Christianity progressed to the loftier circles of people familiar with popular philosophy and higher education. The literary standards of Luke, the author of Hebrews, I Clement, Papias, and also Pliny's description are evidence of this, testifying that the Christian mission had reached all classes of men and women.[17] This process intensified in the second century and led finally to the apologetic literature and the great Gnostic systems. In these circles above all the compatibility of the divinity of the Son of God with his real humanity became the problem. In the last quarter of the first century the Samaritan Menander had taught in Antioch that the disciples whom he had baptized 'could no longer die, but would remain alive as immortals without growing old'; the 'gnostics' in II Tim.2.18 claim that resurrection has already happened.[18] Irenaeus mentions Satornilus as Menander's 'follower'. He taught that the redeemer had 'neither body nor form' and only 'apparently appeared as man' and that he saves only those who already bear the spark of life in them.[19] The tradition of Asia Minor connects the controversial figure of the Jewish Christian Cerinthus (who probably came from Egypt) directly with John of Ephesus;[20] the Apocalypse mentions the libertinistic Nicolaitans;[21] Ignatius and Polycarp fight one or two decades later against Docetists who deny the reality of the humanity of Jesus and his death; and the Pastoral Epistles, which are also quite late, demonstrate that 'pseudonymous gnōsis' (I Tim.6.20) was active in Asia Minor in the first or second decade of the second century CE.

Several possible influences may have come together here, the tendency of which one can denote with the term 'gnosticizing' (or even 'Gnostic'; this is merely a question of definition), and it is conceivable that the leader had incorporated into his teaching by his own dialectic and power of integration conceptions and concepts which his 'progressive pupils' then turned against him by destroying this typical Johannine dialectic. Nor do we have any reason to suppose that the 'separatists' of I John 2.19 had a strictly fixed doctrinal system and were a firmly organized group. The picture of the opponents in the letter is too fluid and blurred for such conjectures.

In addition to this the whole matter cannot in any way be limited to an internal dispute in the school. As the Gospel of Matthew, I Clement and somewhat later the Pastoral Epistles, Jude, the letters of Ignatius and II Peter show, it seems to have flared up at a variety of places. The Johannine school and its head, too, could not avoid this fire. Already in a relatively early text, which in my view must be dated around 80 CE, the speech of Luke's Paul to the presbyters of Ephesus, we find a warning about the 'fierce wolves': 'from among your own selves (*ex hymōn autōn*) will arise men speaking perverse things, to draw away the disciples after them'.[22]

That the crisis which was the occasion for the letters of John was not just a struggle within the school but was also caused by other groups which came from outside is suggested by the second direct reference to the false teachers in I John 4.1: 'Beloved, do not believe every spirit, but test the spirits to see whether they are of God; *for many false prophets have gone out into the world.*' Here there is a general reference to Christian false prophets. We might assume that pupils with self-awareness, influenced by 'false prophets' coming from outside, allowed themselves to be prompted to develop the teaching of the elder in a particular direction, to 'understand it more consistently than he understood it himself'. In doing so they supposed that they were up with the theological (and philosophical) development of the time, and therefore found a similar echo in the school and the communities of Asia Minor. The elder is not surprised about that: 'They are of the world, therefore what they say is of the world, *and the world listens to them.*'[23]

R.E.Brown expresses the view, which is shared by many exegetes, that the role of the Spirit retreats in the first letter in comparison to the farewell discourses with their sayings about the Paraclete. This seems to me to be questionable. At least given the extent of the first letter, in it the elder speaks more frequently of the Spirit than happens in the corresponding relation in the Gospel.[24] However, the accents are partly different. The Spirit no longer appears in relatively independent form as the 'Paraclete'; in the letter, rather, this is Christ himself: here the author goes back to an earlier kind of forensic christological terminology (Rom.8.34; Heb.7.25). This is one of the points where the language of the first letter is 'more original' than that of the Gospel. In the letter Jesus Christ, 'the righteous one', himself intervenes as spokesman for Christians when they sin; as a counterpart one could think of the function of Satan as *katēgoros*. Both terms are, moreover, loanwords which are used relatively frequently by the rabbis.[25] The addition *allos* when the Paraclete is first mentioned shows that the Gospel, too, was very well aware of this older christological function of the Paraclete in the school.[26]

This varying terminology must not be seen as an indication of two completely different doctrines of the Spirit and therefore of separate authors. Rather, a careful distinction should be made here between two aspects: the Jesus report, in which he himself speaks; and the admonitory letter, in which the elder speaks. In the Gospel the departing Son of God announces his new post-Easter presence in the community of disciples in the form of the eloquent Paraclete who must therefore have personal features; in the letter the head of the school is speaking to his community, which has received the Spirit as the gift of an 'anointing' and which on the basis of this anointing is in a position to bear witness to Christ in the right way. In the letter, too, the gift and the activity of the Spirit have a christological foundation, for the Johannine circle has 'the anointing of the Holy One', i.e. of the exalted one, who is in unity with the Father, and therefore alone has the correct knowledge (*kai oidate pantes*).[27] The elder is not writing to them because they are ignorant of the truth, but in the confidence that they already know it,[28] more precisely, because they have heard it from the beginning (*ap'archēs*).[29] The elder now recalls what the Spirit taught from the beginning in view of the danger posed by those who are leading the community astray. He can only call on those whom he addresses to remain in what the Spirit itself taught and teaches in testimony to Christ.[30] The christologically based teaching of the Spirit from the beginning and the admonitory reminder of the 'elder' which similarly relates to christology correspond with each other.

Whereas the groups of dissident disciples probably appealed more to a 'progressive'[31] function of the Spirit in terms of John 16.13, 'he will lead you into all truth', for the elder the work of the Spirit in recalling and bearing witness (14.26 and 15.26) stands more in the foreground; here already in the Gospel the formula *ap'archēs*, from the beginning, is essential in connection with the testimony of the Spirit and discipleship. This *ap'archēs* is strikingly frequent in I and II John, but is also used twice in the Gospel (8.44; 15.26). It is a sign that in this dispute within the school between the master and a group of his pupils, influenced by the 'spirit of the age', the *archē*, the very beginning, i.e. the person and work of Christ, was a matter of controversy.

3. The dispute over christology

The texts about the false teachers in 2.18ff. and 4.1 are each followed by what seems to us to be a more precise description of the christological heresies on which all the other warnings are dependent.

2.22: 'Who is the liar but he who denies that Jesus is the Christ? This is the antichrist, he who denies the Father and the Son. [23]No one who denies the Son has the Father. He who confesses the Son has the Father also.'

However, in a way typical of ancient Jewish and Christian polemic this 'heresy' is formulated in such general terms[32] that at first sight virtually nothing can be inferred from them. 'The one who denies that Jesus is the Messiah (or the Son of God) is not a Christian at all.'[33] But in that case, how can he be 'the antichrist'? This new word in 2.19 hardly means all unbelievers, Jews and pagans. Surely it refers to dissident disciples.

The second text already tells us more: 'By this you know the Spirit of God: every spirit which confesses that Jesus Christ *has come in the flesh* is of God, and every spirit which dissolves (i.e. destroys – here I read *lyei* with the earliest witnesses)[34] Jesus is not of God. This is the (spirit) of antichrist, of which you heard that it was coming' (4.2f.).

The reading '*ho lyei ton Iēsoun*' is clearly the *lectio difficilior*. The *ho mē homologei* has presumably found its way in from II John 7 (this correction was made very early; possibly already in connection with the multiplication of the first copies). This use of *lyein*, 'dissolve', 'destroy', has a parallel in I John 3.8: 'to destroy the works of the devil'.[35] Soon afterwards a further three texts follow:

4.15: 'Whoever *confesses that Jesus is the Son of God*, God abides in him, and he in God.'
5.1: 'Everyone who *believes that Jesus is the Christ* is a child of God.'
5.5: 'Who is it that overcomes the world but he who *believes that Jesus is the Son of God*?'

At first sight all these christological statements which all relate more or less to the opinions of the false teachers and deceivers seem somewhat obscure. The elder is not concerned to describe their aims 'objectively'; on the contrary, he deliberately puts them in general terms; indeed, one almost has the impression that in the present crisis any matter-of-fact discussion with the 'apostate' deceivers has become impossible. This explains the ban on their reception in II

John and the questionability of interceding for the mortal sinner. Confronted with the heralds of the antichrist, one can only confess and reject; even to listen to their arguments and as a result necessarily considering them could be dangerous. Apostates who are in league with the devil do not deserve a hearing or any consideration (see above, 44ff.).

The three last mentioned texts, 4.15; 5.1,5, the confession of Jesus as Son of God and the belief that Jesus is the Christ or Son of God are further connected with three other formulations. First 3.23: 'And this is his commandment, that we should *believe in the name* (i.e. the concrete person) *of his Son* and love one another...'; and also 5.13, a remark which sounds like a conclusion to the letter: 'I write this to you who *believe in the name of the Son of God*, that you may know that you have eternal life.'

These statements of the first letter about 'heretical' disbelief (and confession of the true faith in Christ), put in very general terms, are first of all strongly reminiscent of the first conclusion to the Gospel (John 20.31): 'But these are written that you may *believe that Jesus is the Christ, the Son of God,* and that believing you may have life in his name', and the confession about the beloved disciple as an eyewitness under the cross (19.35): 'his testimony is true and he knows that he tells the truth – that you also may believe'. One might regard the statement in 20.31 as a fundamental principle of Johannine (and indeed early Christian) proclamation generally. In addition John 19.35 has strong anti-docetic connotations. The 'elder' is concerned with precisely this 'foundation'. For him the deceivers are jeopardizing the basic confession, the identity of the man Jesus with the Messiah and Son of God, and therefore threatening the gift of salvation, eternal life. So he himself reacts in a way which we modern, post-Enlightenment Christians find strange and intolerant, but which is very similar to Paul's protest in Galatians.

His opponents would of course have contradicted him. They are neither Jews nor Gentiles, but presumably considered themselves as better, 'more progressive', Christians, who thought that they were expressing the true divine nature of the Son of God for the educated hearers of their time, those whose judgment was after all what mattered most, in a better way than the elder with his 'obsolete' uneducated ideas. But what was there in their 'unhealthy' christology which seemed to be such a threat to the elder?

It is striking that whereas elsewhere in the letter the author six times uses 'Jesus Christ' as a proper name,[36] here five times in all he introduces the single word Jesus in connection with confessional formulations:

2.22: who denies that Jesus is the Christ
4.3: any Spirit that dissolves Jesus
4.15: who does not confess that Jesus is the Christ...
5.1: Every one who believes that Jesus is the Christ
5.5: ...except he who believes that Jesus is the Son of God.

These statements are certainly no longer concerned with the dominant question of the Gospel, namely whether and in what way Jesus is the 'anointed', the Messiah. There Jesus never uses the title *Christos* himself; it is always applied to him by others,[37] in complete contrast to Jesus' constant reference to his status as Son. For precisely that reason, in the Gospel the title Christ, which as the fulfilment of the prophetic promise is applied to Jesus by Jews (and the woman of Samaria), needs to be 'expounded' by the designation Son, which alone expresses the true relationship of Jesus to the Father.

In the letter, too, the titles Christ and Son of God are virtually interchangeable in confessional formulations: the belief that Jesus is the Christ at the same time means that he is the Son of God and vice versa, though with twenty-two occurrences 'Son' is substantially more frequent than 'Christ' and 'Jesus'. In the letter as in the Gospel, 'Son' is the decisive title. The christology of the two works is thus extremely closely connected, in spite of the difference in literary genre and situation (a 'report' about the 'earthly Jesus' and an admonition about the right confession of the exalted one); indeed it is basically identical. Towards the end of I John we are told that 'He who has the Son has life; he who has not the Son has not life' (5.12), in what is deliberately a generalized statement which is nevertheless directed against the false teachers.

That their 'unbelief' is quite different from that of the Jews in the Gospel follows above all from the decisive verse 4.3: they 'destroy Jesus', i.e. the man Jesus in his significance for salvation, by denying that he is identical with Christ or the Son of God.

This view is also illuminated by that christology which Irenaeus attributed to Cerinthus, who since Polycarp, the *Epistula Apostolorum* and Irenaeus has been regarded as the opponent of John of Ephesus. Cerinthus, who according to Irenaeus was active in Asia, separated the man Jesus from the heavenly Christ. This separation was necessary because the created visible world and the supreme 'first God' were radically distinct. The world was not made by him *'sed a virtute quadam valde separata et distante ab ea principalitate quae est super universa et ignorante eum qui est super omnia Deum'*. Therefore created mortal beings cannot really take up and become united with the totally transcendent supreme God. Human beings and God must remain separated. Jesus, the son of Joseph and Mary, was a human being like any other human being and different only by virtue of his ethical superiority and intelligence. At his baptism the heavenly Christ, 'the power which is above all' (*ek tēs hyper ta hola authentias*), descended on him in the form of a dove, whereupon he proclaimed the unknown Father and performed miracles. At the end Christ flew away from Jesus again, and Jesus suffered and was resurrected, but Christ himself remained impassible as a spiritual being.[38] Now that means that for Cerinthus Jesus was not the Christ or the Son of God but that Cerinthus made a fundamental distinction between the mere man and the heavenly-spiritual being.[39] In other words, the 'incarnation' of the pre-existent Son of God in the man Jesus is simply apparent.[40]

Irenaeus' account and the polemic of I John meet in one decisive point, the christology. But we cannot of course claim a clear-cut identity between the teaching of the secessionists and that of Cerinthus. The elder does not report on the 'heresies' of his former pupils in an exact way. For him it is sufficent to warn those whom he is addressing in a declaratory, categorical way. Actually to report the teaching of his opponents must have seemed to him to amount to blasphemy. Where he does go into the views of these 'antichrists', he does so in simple confessional statements and allusions, which may be enigmatic for us but which were enough for those to whom he was writing, who were only too well informed.

I think it most probable that Cerinthus was a Judaeo-Christian teacher coming from outside with some popular philosophical learning of the kind widespread in the Greek-speaking synagogue.

He taught in a popular Platonic manner which spoke to the spirit of the time, seeing a fundamental difference between the demiurge of the visible world and the supreme transcendent God. The heavenly, spiritual Christ could not really unite himself with a corporeal human being; he could only enter the human Jesus like an inspiring spirit and leave him before his suffering because as a transcendent divine being he could not suffer at all.

It is, however, somewhat improbable that, as K.Wengst and R.E.Brown have supposed,[41] Cerinthus himself already made use of the Gospel of John in a way which was refuted in the first letter (and the second), for there we only find a stereotyped polemical christology and ethics focussed on the commandment to love. We do not find protology, including the creation of the world – a fundamental question for Cerinthus[42] – in the letter but only at the beginning of the prologue of the Gospel and in a very brief flash at the end of Jesus' last prayer referring back to the *en archē* and *pros ton theon* in 1.1. This looks like a deliberate inclusive structure. The categorical and universalistic statement in John 1.3 excludes all negative dualistic speculation about the creation. But the prologue and the prayer of consecration seem to be among the last keystones in the building of the Gospel, and in my opinion they were added after the acute crises which led to the letters. The crisis did not begin with the question of creation but with christology.[43]

So I do not think that Cerinthus used the Gospel of John, which was finished later and had a clearly anti-docetic tendency, for his argumentation but the older Gospel of Mark which, like John, has no biographical prehistory and knows nothing about the virgin birth, but tells of the coming of the Spirit like a dove and the adoption of Jesus as Son of God during his baptism much more definitely than does John, for whom the story becomes tolerable only by the introduction of John as a witness. Possibly it was because he came from outside that Cerinthus gained influence with his christological teaching on a considerable number of disciples of the elder who with their new opinions separated from the school. This could explain the strange anecdote about John and Cerinthus in the baths at Ephesus. Even the slightest contact with this seductive teacher seemed to be dangerous. Irenaeus gives us information about the different preferences of heretics for the four Gospels: the Jewish Christian Ebionites prefer Matthew, Marcion a 'circumcised' Gospel of Luke, 'but those who separate Jesus from the Christ and contend that Christ remained free from suffering but Jesus suffered, prefer the Gospel according to Mark... The pupils of Valentinus, however, inordinately prefer the Gospel according to John.'[44] We find this separation between the mortal man Jesus and the immortal divine Christ in Cerinthus and in the secessionists in the first and second letters of John; the Gospel also teaches the man Jesus as the Christ and the Son of God from the prologue to the penultimate chapter (20.31).

The repudiation of this christology, which in the eyes of the elder was disastrous, can also be found in the enigmatic verses:

> Who is it that overcomes the world but he who believes that Jesus is the Son of God? This is he who came by water and blood, Jesus Christ, not with the water only but with the water and the blood. And the Spirit is the witness, because the Spirit is the truth.[45]

The man Jesus is as such the Son of God and may not be separated

from him. He 'came' for the salvation of the believers, who have
overcome the world in him,[46] 'through water', i.e. the baptism of
John with which his activity began after the Spirit was sent upon
him, and 'through blood', i.e. his death, with which he completed
his work (cf.4.34).[47] One cannot just speak of the descent of the
heavenly Christ (or the Spirit) in baptism and suppress the physical
reality of the death of the Son of God. This unity of Spirit, water and
blood is attested by the 'Spirit of truth' whom the crucified and risen
one has sent. The Spirit, the baptism and the death of Jesus together
simply comprehend the activity of Jesus Christ which brings salvation; at the same time his 'work' presents itself in the imparting the
Spirit, baptism and the Lord's supper to the disciples and the
community. The Paraclete, 'the Spirit of truth' (4.16, see John 4.17;
15.16; 16.13), does not always give new 'progressive' revelation, but
by testifying to this one truth which is 'from the beginning' he is – as
Christ present in the word – himself 'the truth': 'sanctify them in the
truth, your *logos* is the truth' (17.17; cf.14.6).

Finally, I John 4.7 and II John 7, which similarly belong together,
point in the same direction:

> 'Every spirit which confesses that Jesus Christ *has come in the flesh*
> is of God.'
> '..who do not confess Jesus Christ *coming in the flesh*...'[48]

This formula *en sarki*, in the flesh, describes the coming of the Son
of God as mortal man. Ignatius, who around fifteen years later is
fighting a similar but not identical christological heresy in his letters,
makes a comparable statement in the hymnic passage:

> There is one physician
> who is both flesh and spirit,
> God appearing *in flesh*,
> true life in death,
> both of Mary and of God,
> first passible and then impassible,
> Jesus Christ our Lord.[49]

We find a further parallel in the hymn I Tim.3.16, 'Who was
manifested in the flesh', and above all John 1.14. 'The word became
flesh' has a clear anti-docetic intent, even if in contrast to the
christological confessions of I John it is not put in polemical terms
but has more the assertive character of a confession. A directly
polemical statement would go against the kergymatic form of the
hymn in the prologue. We should not in any way tone down the

importance of the statement that here the divine Logos became 'flesh', i.e. mortal man. Already in the Old Testament and Qumran literature *sarx-bāśār* can be used as an expression of the utterly ungodly weakness of humankind imprisoned in sin and living towards death (Gen.6.3; Isa.40.6). The statement *ho logos sarx egeneto kai eskēnōsen en hēmin* does not contain any kind of qualification to weaken it, but retains the term *sarx* in all its harshness. The following *kai etheasametha tēn doxan autou* is a typical anti-docetic paradox, and not a mitigation of the offence given by the first sentence.[50] This *theasthai* of the evangelist is real only in the realm of faith. It reaches its climax in the deepest humiliation before the cross of the crucified one (19.35). The testimony of the beloved disciple before the cross verifies the *etheasametha* in the prologue.

Whereas in John 1.14 the aorist *egeneto* has in view the unique past event of the incarnation of the eternal Logos (cf. the imperfect *ēn*: 1.1f.,4, 9f.), the perfect *en sarki elēlythota* in I John 4.2 is also concerned with an event in the past but underlines its abiding significance. The Son of God has assumed a human body for ever. He keeps it even as the risen and transfigured one – that is why the Johannine Christ shows his wounds so ostentatiously[51] – and as the one who is to come. I John 3.2, 'and we shall see him as he is', refers to this, as above all does II John 7, the interpretation of which is particularly disputed because of the present, *erchomenon en sarki*, which is possibly to be translated as a future. Unless this is just a sloppy form of expression, the *en sarki erchesthai* may point to the future parousia, which of course includes the incarnation of the Son of God in the man Jesus and his coming to the disciples as the one who is physically risen (see above, n.48). The Son of God, longingly expected soon, bears the recognizable features of the man Jesus. The unique description of the parousia in I John 3.2b which I have just mentioned, *kai opsometha auton kathōs estin*, 'and we shall see him as he is', shows that it is precisely this *kathōs estin*, 'as he is', which seemed to be controversial.[52]

The reference to the 'flesh' (and blood) in John 1.14; 6.51-56; 19.34; I John 1.7; 5.6,8; II John 7, shows (in the Gospel and the letters) the sharpest antithesis to the denial of the true humanity of Christ, a denial repeated a little later among the 'docetic' opponents of Ignatius, who uses similar provocative formulae against them, and by various Gnostic teachers of the second century.[53]

4. Ethics, eschatology and atonement

The 'christological' crisis was at the same time an ethical one.[54] Since I do not have the opportunity here to develop the 'ethics' of the elder and his opponents in detail, I will concentrate on a number of somewhat neglected aspects of its christological foundations, which seem more or less marginal in modern exegesis.

Christ is described four times in the letter as 'the righteous one' (*ho dikaios*), an attribute which in the letter is only one attached to the believer and in the Gospel once to God himself and once to the judgment of Christ.[55] Possibly the opponents did not think the adjective *dikaios* good enough to be applied to God and the heavenly Christ and regarded righteousness only as a lower property of a purely human kind.[56] So in the letter Christ especially is given this predicate 'the righteous one' as the heavenly 'intercessor with the Father' (*paraklēton echomen pros ton patera*, I John 2.1), who 'forgives' the believers who confess their sins and 'cleanses' them (1.7,9). He exercises this function because through his death he effects atonement 'not for our sins only, but for those of the whole world'.[57] Through the atoning death of Jesus God's universal love is made manifest to all men and women (John 3.16). In the Gospel this is matched by the fundamental testimony of John the Baptist (1.29,36) and the whole description of the death of Jesus as the climax of his work (19.28-30). One could put it like this – not in Johannine terminology, but in 'alien' Pauline language: the crucified and risen one, the one true righteous one, pronounces believers righteous and gives them a share in his righteousness. This notion is hinted at in the Gospel by the second of the three 'convincing' functions of the Paraclete in 16.8-11: he convinces the world 'of righteousness, because I go to the Father, and you will see me no more'.[58] The return to the Father 'justifies' (cf. I Tim.3.16) the Jesus who was executed as a blasphemer of God and a transgressor of the law (John 5.18; 10.31, 33; 19.7, etc.) and at the same time all believers are given a share in the liberation from the power of sin and evil which is brought about as a result of his return to the Father: in Pauline terms, they are 'justified' by his death. In his own terminology John, too, knows of the 'justification of the sinner'.

Christ becomes the model, or better the original, of the 'righteous man' for his believers only in 3.7:

'Little children, let no one deceive you. He who does right is righteous, as he is righteous.'

This saying probably refers to the opponents who in their enthusiasm – perhaps based on a false understanding of Paul – believed that they were already in possession of a 'righteousness' which no longer committed them to obedient action (cf. I Cor.6.11). Here the reference to Christ as 'the righteous one' implies his sinlessness;[59] in contrast to him believers, as long as they live, are constantly exposed to the experience of sin and exist from forgiveness.[60]

The starting point of the concrete paraenesis in ch.3 is the expectation of parousia and judgment which emerges relatively strongly in the letter, but is also not completely absent from the Gospel and – given the variety of terminology in which it is expressed – cannot be simply dismissed as a quotation by a redactor with a deficient understanding.[61] As a result of the severe crisis in the school itself, the prospect of the coming Son of God and judge takes on a quite new topicality. For in the crisis the school needs to be warned:

> '...abide in him, so that when he appears[62] we may have confidence and not shrink from him in shame at his coming. If you know that he is righteous, you may be sure that every one who does right is born of him' (I John 2.28f.; cf.3.7,10).

His perfect righteousness is communicated to believers through 'being born of God', and conversely believers are recognized as children of God by their action.[63] For being a child of God is not a consequence of one's own righteous action but a gift of the love of God which brings assurance[64] and the work of the Spirit: 'Anyone who is born of God does no sin, for his seed abides in him.' *sperma* here can refer only to the Spirit that makes present the word of Christ, which brings about the 'abiding' of Christ in the believer and the abiding of the believer in Christ.[65] At this point John does not seem to be too far removed from the Pauline doctrine of the Spirit: in him the imperative is also ultimately grounded in the work of Christ, in the fruit of his death and in the birth from God which is brought about by the Spirit. Most of these themes can also be demonstrated from the Gospel, especially in the farewell discourses, where significantly we also find the majority of the sayings which refer to the eschatological future.

Alongside the 'ethical' terminology of righteousness and the 'physical' terminology of being born from God, there is also the 'cultic' and 'sacramental' terminology which plays a greater part in the Johannine corpus than is often assumed. It is most closely connected with the understanding of the death of God on the cross as an atoning sacrifice. For the secessionists with their 'modern' way of thinking this could no longer have any saving significance; for the Elder, it was precisely here that the reality of redemption was at risk:

'...and the blood of Jesus the Son of God cleanses us from all sins.'[66]
'and he himself is the expiation for our sins...' (2.1)
'and sent his Son
to be the expiation for our sins' (4.10).

For all their distinctive stamp – which is uniquely of a piece for the New Testament – Johannine language and theology remain astoundingly variable; however, it would be foolish to want to attribute these varied nuances to different sources or redactors. Behind them lies the teacher's command of theological language and power of integration.

The climax of the description of the parousia, 'We know that when he appears...' (3.2), is immediately followed by its 'ethical' consequence: 'And every one who thus hopes in him purifies (*hagnizei*) himself as he is pure (or holy, *hagnos*)' (3.3). In John 11.55 the verb is used for the ritual purification of the pilgrims coming to Jerusalem for the Passover. In I John 3.3 it probably means freedom from the *epithymia tēs sarkos* in the widest sense (I John 2.16; cf. John 8.44). In the high-priestly prayer the Christ who goes to the cross uses a similar cultic verb in a pronounced soteriological context: 'Sanctify (*hagiason*) them in the truth: your word is the truth... And for their sake I sanctify myself (*hyper autōn egō hagiazō emauton*) that they themselves also may be sanctified (*hēgiasmenoi*) in the truth' (John 17.19). Both verbs, *hagnizein* and *hagiazein*, were predominantly used in the Septuagint as the translation of the root *qdš*.[67] This terminology presupposes the idea of the sinlessness of Christ, which is important for the letter but which appears as the first great scene of the Gospel in the twofold confession of John the Baptist: 'Behold, the lamb of God, who takes away the sin of the world', for the sacrificial lamb is without spot and fault. The 'sanctity' of Christ appears again in the strange confession by Peter (together with the other remaining disciples), *sy ei ho hagios tou theou*, which describes implicitly the way of the Son who gives his 'flesh for the life of the world' and who will be betrayed by one of the disciples who make this confession (6.69f., cf. 51, 71). The witness of John the Baptist contains a double reference: to the paschal lamb and to the servant of the Lord in Isa.53 who is compared with a lamb (53.7) and who bears (away) the sins of the many (= 53.4,12).[68] From John 1.29 to 17.19 there is a whole series of statements in the Gospel which refer clearly to the vicarious atoning death of Jesus: the preposition *hyper*

appears seven times in connection with Jesus' offering of his life.[69]
In the letter we find *hyper* only once, but alongside it the preposition
peri with the same significance.[70] So in the letter, as in the Gospel, we
come across the use of Isa.52.13-53.12: a typical feature here is the
paradoxical interpretation of 'lift up and glorify' in terms of the
crucifixion or the death of Jesus, which is derived from Isa.52.12.[71]
These statements scattered throughout the Gospel (and the first
letter) contain a soteriological interpretation of the death of Jesus
which is fundamental to the author. They are surely neither later
redactional additions nor unimportant remains of an older source,
but have their well-planned place in the Gospel and prepare for its
climax in 19.30, Jesus' death on the evening of the sixth day at the
time of the passover offering, as the foundation of a new creation.
These relatively numerous references in the Gospel and the letter to
the saving significance of the death of Jesus must have been offensive
to the 'docetic' and perfectionist views of the 'deceivers'. These latter
could refer only to certain parts of Johannine christology, if at all,
in so doing resembling present-day exegetes, who would allow
theological validity only to a heavily corrected and purified 'Gospel
of John'.

In the letter this basic interpretation of the death of Jesus as a
representative atoning saving event is presented in the light of the
acute threat. This union of Johannine *theologia crucis* and ethics of
love reaches its climax in I John 4.7-9:

> Beloved, let us love one another; for love is of God,
> and he who loves is born of God and knows God.
> He who does not love God does not know God;
> for God is love.
>
> Herein is love,
> not that we loved God
> but that he loved us
> and sent his Son
> as expiation for our sins.

This connection between the love of God and the offering up or
sending of the Son can be rediscovered not only in the Gospel (3.16);
earlier forms of it go back to Paul.[72] Here too we can again see
profound connections between the Johannine school and Pauline
thought in christology and soteriology.

5. Is a 'naive docetism' of the Gospel criticized in the letters?

The assertion that in contrast to the letters, whose 'anti-docetic' tendency in the fight against the deceivers can hardly be denied, the Gospel shows naively 'docetic' tendencies, is therefore in my view totally untenable.[73] Following F.C.Baur, Käsemann (and others) attributed such a christology of 'naive docetism' to the evangelist. Thus Käsemann thinks that in John 'incarnation does not have to mean kenosis, total entering into our humanity'.[74] He overlooks the fact that the formulation of John 1.14a is harsher and more evocative than Phil.2.7 or Rom.8.3, but that on the other hand the 'humanity' of the Messiah and Son of God in Paul, John and indeed throughout earliest Christianity is not simply identical with *our sinful* humanity. We may have fallen utterly victim to sin and therefore have merited eternal death (Rom.6.23), but the one who 'knew no sin' accepted death in voluntary obedience (John 10.18f.). Nowhere in earliest Christianity is the 'revealer' depicted only 'in earthly terms *as we are*',[75] otherwise he could not free human beings subject to the slavery of sin and death (John 7.34-36). At this point there is no difference between Johannine and Pauline christology. Nor is the fact that 'judged by the modern concept of reality our Gospel is more fantastic than any other writing of the New Testament'[76] a convincing criterion. The so-called 'modern concept of reality' fails over against *all* the Gospels, and the letters of Paul, Hebrews and Revelation are hardly less 'fantastic' than the Fourth Gospel. The evangelist does not seem to be an ecstatic like Paul; he does not hear 'unspeakable words' in paradise and in the third heaven[77] and he does not present his audience with the virgin birth, the story of the transfiguration, the healing of ten lepers at once or the fantastic exorcism of a legion of demons into a herd of two thousand swine who were drowned in Lake Genessaret. Nor do we hear anything about miracles in connection with the death of Jesus on the cross: there is no darkness at noon, no torn curtain in the Temple and no resurrection of the dead in Jerusalem (Matt.27.52f.). Some of the seven Johannine miracles of Jesus are certainly narrated effectively – in accordance with the progress of the tradition – but on the whole they do not contain any more miraculous features than the synoptic narratives, though their theological significance is developed much more dramatically. Schleiermacher, Neander and other contemporaries before D.F.Strauss's *Life of Jesus* which appeared in 1835 preferred the Gospel of John *inter alia* because it seemed to be less miraculous than the Synoptics.

The difference lies in its deeper theological reflection on the miracles of Jesus. Moreover, raisings from the dead were reported relatively frequently in earliest Christianity. They were attributed to Peter and John, and even Philip's daughters could give amazing accounts: according to Quadratus and Papias some of those raised by Jesus from the dead were alive as late as the time of Hadrian.[78] Many miracles in the canonical and apocryphal Acts of the Apostles far surpass those of the Fourth Gospel in their fantastic colouring – and their readers believed that they had been done by men of flesh and blood. Evidently 'miracles' were familiar in earliest Christianity – to a greater degree than the Jewish Hellenistic environment could take, since it accused Christians, for example, of magic and necromancy. The world of imagination in early Christianity was a truly fantastic one.[79]

The problem lies rather in the 'penetrating monomania' of the Johannine Jesus, his proclamation of himself as the Son sent by the Father as Saviour of humankind,[80], his 'harsh word' about the eucharist (6.60), which seems to be so different from the ethical preaching of the synoptic Jesus, relevant as it is to any period, and his simple but lucid parables and moral teaching. But even here there are more than a few connections. To mention just two examples out of far too many to cite: what fundamental difference is there between Luke 10.18, 'I saw Satan fall like lightning from heaven', and John 12.31, 'Now is the prince of his world cast out'; or between Luke 10.19, 'Behold I have given you authority to tread on scorpions and snakes and no power of the enemy will harm you', and John 16.33, 'In the world you have tribulation, but be of good cheer, I have overcome the world'? Both may sound fantastic to modern ears, but here Luke has reported more original, enthusiastic and elemental material, while John's language has more theological reflection in it, is more 'spiritual' and arises out of much more reflection; that is why it is quite wrong to impute '*naive* docetism' to him. If any New Testament writer is not naive but complex or even sophisticated, ironical and even paradoxical, and sometimes deliberately ambiguous, but at the same time one-sided and clear to the point of monomania, then he is. That is why we exegetes find it so difficult to cope with his dialectic, which is sometimes intensified almost to an intolerable degree.

Almost as though he might have suspected that people would some day accuse him of docetism, he has incorporated some powerful opposition to this misunderstanding into his work. However, it can easily be overlooked by a reader, particularly a prejudiced one with a single-track reading of only parts of the Gospel. Jesus' mother and brothers are spoken of quite openly; leaving aside the preliminary stories, they play a greater role in John than in the Synoptics. Thus the family of Jesus accompanies him to Capernaum, and his mother even stands under the cross.[81] The distance between Jesus and his family, which is certainly historical, is stressed more strongly in the synoptic Gospels.[82] Twice there is mention of his physical father Joseph, about whom Mark says nothing at all, and we are told that Jesus comes from Galilean Nazareth, of ill repute, and not from famous Bethlehem, the city of David.[83] In John 4.6 the evangelist reports that Jesus sits down by the side of Jacob's well exhausted and thirsty from walking in the noontide heat. Where else is the physical exhaustion of Jesus mentioned in the Synoptic Gospels?[84] The evangelist several times reports that Jesus withdraws from the misunderstanding of the crowd (and the murder attempts of his opponents); indeed he hides himself and no longer dares to appear in public.[85] Euripides' *Bacchae* and the Homeric hymn to Dionysus show how a real god in disguise deals with his opponents; Celsus drew express attention to this failure on the part of Jesus.[86] Jesus has to accept the falling away of the majority of his disciples without resisting (6.60ff.), indeed tolerate a representative of the devil in the most intimate circle of his disciples to the very end. In contrast to the *theios anēr* ideal with its philosophical attitude of *ataraxia*, he is subject to very human emotions. As already in Mark he becomes angry, but over and above that he is also disturbed, i.e. he gets very excited, and indeed bursts into tears.[87] This profound emotion (*tarassesthai*) is repeated again in the announcement of his death and during the last supper when he predicts his betrayal. Jesus himself is 'troubled in spirit', but a few lines later he strictly forbids his disciples to be troubled in a similar way.[88] Certainly the passion narrative lacks the theological theme of the Christ assailed by the distance and silence of God, extending from Gethsemane to his final cry,[89] which for Mark is a decisive theological theme and which had to be transformed because it does not fit into the Johannine christology of the ultimate unity between Father and Son that leads to the consequence formulated in 10.17,18.

> That is why the Father loves me,
> because I lay down my life
> in order to take it up again.
> No one has taken it from me;
> rather, I lay it down of my own accord.
> I have the power to lay it down,

and I have the power to take it up again.
This command I received from my Father (translation by R.E.Brown).

The Johannine Jesus cannot therefore entreat his Father, as Jesus does in the Gospel of Mark, to 'let this cup pass from me'; in John 12.27 he therefore directly contradicts the account in Mark:

Now my soul is troubled,
Yet, what should I say – 'Father save me from this hour?'
No, this is just the reason why I come to this hour.
'Father, glorify your name' (translation by R.E.Brown).

But despite the complete affirmation of the Father's will for salvation, which tolerates no personal self-will, 'Jesus' soul is troubled'. The repetition of a similar formula in 13.21 demonstrates that this very human motive of shock and fright, albeit somewhat negative in the eyes of ancient educated readers, was important for the author. Here we may compare the absolute sovereignty of Apollonius of Tyana when he voluntarily appeared before Domitian's tribunal in Rome.[90] Thus over against the Synoptic tradition John stresses that Jesus 'carried his own cross' (19.17). John even reports – in contrast to the Synoptics – a penultimate saying of Jesus which fulfils scripture but at the same time expresses a basic human need, *dipsō* = 'I thirst'; he adds that some people gave Jesus sour wine to drink on a sponge and that Jesus actually took it.[91] This theologically calculated 'realism' surely has a markedly anti-docetic significance. The last cry, *tetelestai*, 'it is accomplished', represents the climax of Jesus' career, the sending of the Son, and thus at the same time is the climax of the Gospel, the completion of the new work of God,[92] or, as we may say in respect of John 1.1-3, Gen.1.1 and 2.1-3, the new creation. His last act, the bending of his head (*klinas tēn kephalēn*) and 'giving up the spirit' represent the real death of the Son of God who has utterly become flesh: for ancient readers and hearers no 'God walking over the earth'[93] dies like this – disgraced and naked,[94] and hanging on the cross; in the understanding of contemporary educated people a divine figure would have to be incapable of suffering and immortal.[95] The evangelist's confession that the Son of God is truly man becomes particularly vivid in the scene with Pilate, where the prefect has Jesus brought out before the leaders of the people and their supporters, bloody from his scourging, crowned with a garland of thorns and clothed in a purple cloak, having earlier been mocked and beaten by the soldiers, and presents him, mistreated in this way, with the words 'See what a man', *Ecce homo*, i.e. *vere homo* (19.1-6). At the latest by this scene it must have become clear to the reader that John has his own *theologia crucis* which, while it takes a different form from that of Paul, is no less deep in its paradoxes than that of the apostle.[96] No author in the New Testament ventures to speak of the suffering and death of God in the man Jesus in this way, provocative as it would have sounded to the ears of people of antiquity. Both texts, 19.28-30 and 19.1-6, are composed with extreme subtlety, and throughout the passion narrative, indeed throughout the Gospel, there is no hint of naiveté, far less naive docetism. I would prefer to say with Karl Barth: 'It is in this that He is *real man*, and may be known in his reality.'[97]

6. The elder, I John and the Gospel

The 'deceivers' of I and II John could take up the christology developed in the teaching of the elder only by dissolving the skilful radical dialectical unity between the earthly Jesus and the heavenly Son sent into the world and appealing one-sidedly and speculatively to the latter. This dialectical and at the same time realistic christology to which the elder appeals polemically in the first and second letters is presupposed in its fullness in the Gospel. The stimulus to the departure of the 'secessionists' from the christology of the school came from outside: the widespread philosophical and religious dogma of the immutability and impassibility of God. Possibly a teacher like Cerinthus had a special influence here. A divine being could certainly for a time take human form and even enter into a man, but could never become truly man, participate in human weakness, suffer and die.

The passionate protest of the elder who here saw a threat to the foundation pillar, the heart, of his testimony to Christ, the incarnation of the Son of God in the man Jesus of Nazareth and at the same time its consummation in his dying on the cross for the salvation of the world, is all too understandable. If he was to remain true to his task he had to confront those who received the first and second letters with a harsh and uncompromising either/or, as did the Christ of the Gospel his Jewish hearers. The Gospel and the letters are thus extremely closely connected in terms of content; indeed they are bound together. What is new and unexpected in the first letter is a result of the acute and perilous crisis in the school, threatening to destroy it, and the totally new situation which it had produced for the elder at an advanced age. On the other hand, we also have a fair number of references to the crisis in the school in the Gospel, which was completed some years after the letters and edited after the death of the elder and which looks back to the ministry of Jesus in Judaea two generations earlier.

The opponents may have orientated themselves on the free and ever-new activity of the Paraclete, but here too the elder can refer to the fact that those who are addressed have known the truth attested by the Spirit for a long time, indeed from the beginning.[98] The 'other paraclete' (14.16) in the farewell discourses indeed does not bear witness to any constantly new 'progressive' truths, but as the 'Spirit of truth' (14.17;15.26;16.12) teaches and calls to mind all that *Jesus* has proclaimed to the disciples (14.25f.), and bears witness about this (15.26). Though the Spirit leads into all truth, he does not make the way free for unbridled 'progressive' speculation, but remains bound to what he receives from the exalted Son in communion with the Father, 'for he does not speak of himself, but what he shall hear, that will he speak, and he will proclaim to you *what is to come*'.[99] Here too is the starting point for the futurist eschatology in the Johannine circle, which therefore rightly emerges more strongly in I John than in the Gospel and is developed above all in the Apocalypse in a way which gives the impression that we are entering a completely different world, though one which nevertheless remains related to the Johannine corpus.

So in our search for the historical context of the Johannine school, for the author(s) of the Johannine corpus, we are pointed by the letters towards the Gospel. We have seen to how great a degree the letters form a unity in the elder's struggle for the truth of his message. In the next chapter I shall ask whether and how the Gospel is a unity and gives at least some evidence of the personal contours of its author.

IV

The Author, his Pupils and the Unity
of the Gospel

Everything that I have said so far about the influence of the Johannine corpus in the second century, John the 'elder' and the three letters associated with him suggests that the Gospel of John is also closely connected with this John the 'elder' who was in the province of Asia towards the end of the first century as a teacher and head of a school. I shall begin by recalling an already familiar argument.

1. The title 'Gospel according to John'

First of all, the title *euangelion kata Iōannēn* is support for this connection. We should not forget that it, too, belongs to the text of the Gospel. It was not given at a later date, but was attached to the work by the pupils of the head of the school when they edited it after the death of their master and circulated it in the communities. The title was necessary for the actual use of the Gospel in the liturgy. Its early origin follows from the lack of any variant titles, despite the widespread attestation to the Gospel as early as the second century. The basis for the title of the Gospel in our manuscripts goes back well into this century, and we already find the attribution to John indirectly in the *Epistula Apostolorum*, and directly with Ptolemy and Heracleon in the middle of that century.[1] These facts make a later transference very improbable. Not only the letters and the Apocalypse, but also the Gospel, were connected with John of Ephesus from the beginning. However, this is not John the apostle the son of Zebedee, but an enigmatic figure who, although he does not come from the circle of the Twelve, was given the honorific title 'the disciple of the Lord' in Papias and in the tradition of Asia Minor. The consistency of this designation 'the disciple of the Lord' is to be understood primarily from this connection with the Gospel. Only the Gospel of John makes exclusive use of the term 'disciple' and never *apostolos* for the men called by Jesus, and it does not set great store by the Twelve. It is also the only one to mention a special 'beloved disciple' as its author. Neither the Apocalypse nor the letters can explain the origin of such an old and fixed epithet as *mathētēs tou kyriou*. Only the *euangelion kata Iōannēn* written by the beloved disciple gives a constant and firm basis for the formula 'John, the disciple of the Lord'.

However, this attribution in the title of the Gospel, *euangelion kata Iōannēn*, was added only after the author's death, by his pupils. In the text of the Gospel itself we find only the 'disciple whom Jesus loved', whom the final editor (or editors) identifies with the author right at the end.[2]

The form of the title, *euangelion kata Iōannēn*, imitated the titles of the earlier Gospels according to Mark, Luke and Matthew which were already quite widespread around 100 CE.[3] The Fourth Gospel presupposes them. The earliest was the *euangelion kata Markon*, which was probably written in Rome around 69 CE and which according to a reliable tradition that we are given by John the Elder was regarded as the work of a disciple of Peter.[4] The *euangelion kata Loukan* may have been published about five or ten years later by Theophilus, to whom Luke had dedicated his work;[5] the first Gospel to bear the name of an apostle, *kata Matthaion*, was composed around 85-90 in southern Syria, Phoenicia or Hellenistic Palestine by an unknown Jewish-Christian teacher who, as the Papias note suggests, transferred the apostle's name, Matthew, from his main source, the logia of Jesus, to his own work to give this apostolic authority also.[6]

Given the lively exchange between the leading communities by messengers and travellers as early as in the period between 70 and 110, we must assume that the four earliest Gospels were circulated among the most important communities relatively quickly. The great work of Irenaeus did not take more than ten years to come from Gaul to the Egyptian Chora and to Africa.[7] This fact tells strongly against the widespread assumption that the elder and his school did not know the other three Gospels (not to mention other similar writings). Another question is how far he is dependent on them or is engaged in a critical discussion with them. The latter is above all the case with the Gospel of Mark. He also seems to use Luke. On the other hand he rather ignored Matthew, which he very probably also knew: it was really at the opposite pole.[8]

If the pupils of John the Elder wanted to establish the work associated with the name of their master in the church over against the already widespread earlier versions of 'the Gospel', they had to connect this work, which was so different, particularly closely with the person and authority of Jesus himself. Therefore they also accepted and used the Pauline-Petrine[9] term *euangelion*, which had previously been avoided in the school because since Mark it had already taken on a widespread stereotyped significance, as the designation of a new genre for the Jesus story in the mainstream church.

2. Peter and the beloved disciple

The starting point for our hypothesis is the identification of the author in 21.24 and the preceding confrontation between Peter and the beloved disciple. The author (or authors) of the final chapter is very well aware of the martyrdom of the prince of the apostles. ' "When you are old, you will stretch out your hands, and another will gird you and carry you where you do not wish to go." This he said to show by what death he was to glorify God' (21.18f.). That means that he (or they) knew that Peter was crucified in Rome – as is also attested by the Acts of Peter and Tertullian.[10]

Peter and the beloved disciple are again contrasted in the four following verses (21.20-23). Peter turns and sees 'the disciple whom Jesus loved following'. This apparently clumsy addition not only has the function of a link between scenes; the strange participle *akolouthounta* is meant to indicate that this disciple who is following behind Peter will also follow Peter in his death and that both together are following Jesus. Now Peter also wants to hear about the fate of the beloved disciple, and Jesus gives him an answer corresponding to the enigmatic character of this follower, which once again stresses the difference between Peter and him: 'If it is my will that he remain until I come, what is that to you? Follow me!' In contrast to the present eschatology, which is dominant (though surely not exclusive) in the Gospel, the additional chapter, like I John already, speaks openly of the parousia of Jesus. So we would do well not to dissolve in a one-sided way the dialectic which is also present in Johannine eschatology.[11] Nowhere in earliest Christianity is there a completely 'present eschatology' without any future element: that is a quite modern theological invention.

The next verse now expresses a manifest dilemma among the group of followers of the 'beloved disciple': on the basis of this saying of Jesus the rumour is said to have circulated among the 'brethren' 'that that disciple would not die' (we should add 'before the Lord comes'). Whereas the earlier parallel tradition Mark 9.1 still says that 'some of those standing here' 'will not taste of death until they see the kingdom of God coming in power',[12] a generation later this privilege – at least in the circle of followers but probably also outside it – was to be attributed to only one outsider, the mysterious beloved disciple. They had been of the view that the one 'whom the Lord loved' had been marked out by Jesus himself as being the only one among the disciples who would still be alive to see the coming of the Lord.

My colleague the Arabist Herr von Ess here drew my attention to a remarkable parallel from the early Islamic tradition: in the earliest period of Islam the 'friends of the prophet', i.e. men and women who had still known the prophet Muhammad personally, were highly regarded in individual provinces as 'bearers of the tradition'. 'In Basra this was Anas b.Malik; he was perhaps the last of them all. When he was very old, the children would run after him and shout, "That is the friend of the prophet who will not die until he has seen the Antichrist." The Antichrist is a sign of the end-time, so it was evidently expected that Anas would live to experience the end of the world' (written communication of 16 January 1987). A modern example is the leading 'apostle' of the Neoapostolic Community, J.G.Bischoff, who died on 6 July 1960 at the age of more than eighty-nine; 'from 1951 he declared it to be a revelation of God that Christ would bring the community home as bride during his own lifetime. The Neoapostolic community quite firmly believed this. Open doubt about it would have been apostasy… Bischoff's death shook them quite considerably.'[13]

The death of the disciple proved this hope to be an error and the widespread rumour was explained as a misunderstanding of that saying of the risen Christ on the part of the 'brethren'. The whole section has an apologetic character as far as the editor (or editors) is concerned.[14] After the event it was possible to explain the false expectation, which had certainly also provoked criticism of the school and its teacher, and in this way lessen the pain of disappointed hope. The recent interpretation of John 21.20 by J.Kügler, who regards even John 21.20-25 as pure literary fiction, including the 'rumour' in 21.23 and the 'redactional' reference to the author in 21.24, is utterly unconvincing and discredits the method of the author, who wants to 'free the way' to denying any historical reality in the Fourth Gospel. In this context (21.18–23) the 'beloved disciple' is no more 'pure fiction' than his counterpart Peter.[15]

The identification of this disciple, who at the end of the Gospel is introduced as the author of the work, with any particular well-known figure among the disciples of Jesus in the Gospel itself, is persistently avoided. He appears for the first time only in the nocturnal farewell discourse less than a day before the death of Jesus; and even in the additional chapter 21, where his incognito could have been lifted, a clear characterization is deliberately made impossible by the reference to the anonymous 'other two of his disciples' (21.2). The reason for this mysterious procedure is difficult to explain. If the disciples of the school knew his name as a matter of course why did they keep it (half-)secret from the other communities to which copies of the Gospel were sent? Had the editors wanted definitely to designate him the son of Zebedee known as the second disciple after Peter, this would easily have been possible. There must be deeper reasons why they leave the question open in an ambiguous way. I need not go further into the other attempts at identification from the Gospel itself: Lazarus, Nathanael, Thomas, or even outsiders like John Mark, Paul or a brother of Jesus.[16]

On the other hand the idea that the 'disciple whom Jesus loved' is an 'ideal figure' must be taken seriously. He really embodies the ideal of the disciple who stands closest to Jesus, who therefore can ask him direct questions, who is the only one to stand under the cross where the dying Jesus entrusts his own mother to him, who is witness to the spear thrust, the first to reach the empty tomb, look in, 'see and believe', and the first to recognize Jesus by Lake Gennesaret.[17] In this way he is quite specially close to Jesus, particularly at critical moments, and is always there before Peter. Of course an 'ideal figure' need not be totally ahistorical and mere fiction. Peter has an 'ideal' character throughout the Gospels and Acts, and the same is true of Timothy, who is addressed as an 'ideal pupil' in the Pastorals. In the Gospel of John in particular, all the disciples have 'ideal' traits.

Two texts in which proximity to Jesus and the pre-eminence of Peter are similarly evident, but which mention only an unknown disciple, who is not explicitly named 'the beloved disciple', are more difficult. This is that 'other disciple' (*allos mathētēs*, 18.15) who together with Peter follows Jesus when he is arrested and makes it possible for Peter to enter the palace of Annas, because 'he was acquainted (or even on friendly terms) with the high priest' (*ēn gnōstos tō archierei*). Already in the exegesis of the Greek Fathers it is almost taken for granted that this 'other disciple' is identical to the beloved disciple (or John), and at a very early stage the article is added to the indeterminate *allos mathētēs* to clarify it (cf.20.2-8). Whether this is the beloved disciple or not is still a matter of dispute, but the overwhelming majority of exegetes, beginning with the church fathers, rightly tend to make the identification.[18] It seems to me that the evangelist himself already wanted to give the impression – he is in fact sometimes fond of ambivalent statements – that this is the beloved disciple, but omitted the epithet because in this context the predicates 'on friendly terms with the high priest' and 'whom Jesus loved' did not go well together. The disciple follows Jesus with Peter; i.e. he was present in Gethsemane and at the farewell meal.

The figure of the unknown disciple of John the Baptist, to whom his master first draws attention to Jesus along with Andrew, and follows Jesus, henceforth to disappear for ever (John 1.35-41), is similar but even more difficult. Here too the double motive of the first connection with Jesus and the disciple's pre-eminence over against Peter are particularly significant.[19] The unknown figure and Andrew spend the rest of the day (and perhaps the following night) with Jesus, and Peter is only called after them; so in contrast to the Gospel of Mark he is not named the first (and last) disciple.[20] It is also striking that the sons of Zebedee, who were of course known in the community, are omitted from the Fourth Gospel there (in contrast to Mark and Matthew); from Peter it moves on straightaway to Philip. Of course the unknown figure cannot be identified as the beloved disciple right at the beginning of the story of Jesus as in ch.13, at the end of Jesus' activity. Kügler's objection to the significance of his person 'that a very careful reading would be necessary to notice the supernumerary disciple at all'[21] overlooks the fact that because of his cryptic approach the author of the Fourth Gospel always requires very close attention. The mysterious anonymous figure right at the beginning cannot be completely insignificant and arouses the curiosity of the reader, but at the same time is deliberately left in the twilight – i.e. he could point to the anonymous disciple 'whom Jesus loved' of chs.13-21. Some of the exegetes of the early church also understood things this way – but not with such unanimity as in 18.15f.[22]

In accordance with Johannine thought, all these 'reports of disciples' have deeper, 'symbolic' meaning, but this need not mean that for the school the disciple was a shadowy, non-existent entity, for at two points this enigmatic, ideal and anonymous figure becomes – ultimately – a 'historical' personality: first the editors stress explicitly that he is the author of the Gospel, and second, this person in advanced old age, long after the martyrdom of Peter, becomes the cause of a painful error: he dies at an exceptionally old age, although among 'the brethen', i.e. his circle of followers, there was a widespread rumour that he would be the only disciple to experience the parousia of the Lord. Something of this kind is incompatible with an unhistorical ideal figure: here there is an allusion to a historical event which was painful for the school and which had to be explained. There is no question that his death had been a sharp disappointment for 'the brethren'. 'Even John died, of whom it had been hoped in vain that he would live to see the coming of the Lord', says Tertullian in connection with the Gnostic Menander – a contemporary of the Johannine school – who had claimed that death could not touch those who had been baptized by him.[23]

So I have to repeat the question which I already raised in the first chapter, whether the information of Irenaeus that the evangelist John lived until the time of Trajan, which nowadays is usually pushed aside with contempt, does not have historical value. If this is the case, in view of the fact that this head of a school, who was a quite special 'disciple of the Lord', someone out of the ordinary, died at a great age – and he was someone to whom unusual hopes were attached in his extreme age and was said to have been the author of the Gospel of John – in view of this figure surrounded by a veil of legend, does not the self-conscious designation 'the old man', viz. 'the elder (*ho presbyteros*) in II and III John or the honorific name 'the elder John, the disciple of the Lord' in Papias, become very specific? The reason why this John was called *ho presbyteros* and not – in better Greek – *ho presbytēs* or *ho gerōn* or something similar lies in the Jewish background of the school and its founder: in the LXX *haz-zaqen* is far and away the most frequently translated *ho presbyteros*. In his person great age was combined with strong authority.

3. John the elder and his school: a provisional assessment

So we can make a provisional assessment. Behind the 'Johannine community' and the Johannine corpus, letters, Gospel (and Apocalypse) there is one head, an outstanding teacher who founded a school which existed between about 60 or 70 and 100/110 in Asia Minor and developed a considerable activity extending beyond the region and who – as an outsider – claimed to have been a disciple of Jesus, indeed – in the view of the school - a disciple of a quite special kind. This teacher, who bore the common Jewish-Palestinian name John, must have attained an extremely great age and therefore was known as 'the elder' in the school and in the communities connected with it; special hopes for the parousia were also associated with his person.

In his last years there was a crisis in the school. It was sparked off by a group of its members who, influenced by the view taken for granted among educated Greeks that a god was incapable of suffering, separated the man Jesus from the divine Logos, Son of God and Christ and radically devalued his significance for salvation. The three letters of John are fruits of the way in which the old school-head combated this threat. They, together with the Gospel, were probably edited soon after his death by his pupils (or one of them) not too long after 100 CE, and this editing appears to be the last visible action of the 'school' (see below).

The school itself, however, seems quickly to have dissolved; there is no indication that there was a further succesion of heads after the elder. So we cannot attribute any of the Johannine writings like I-III John or different redactions of the Gospel to any of the alleged later heads or leading authorities of the school. Its rapid disintegration also makes it very improbable that the 'elder' founded a separate church of his own.[24]

His 'school' or sphere of activity is to be placed firmly in the context of the Christian communities of Asia Minor in the last decades of the first century. The Apocalypse could be an earlier work, the nucleus of which was written in the time after the shock of the Neronian persecution, the beginning of the Judaean war, the murder of Nero and the civil war;[25] possibly it was reworked later, early in the reign of Trajan, by a pupil who depicted the elder as a recipient of apocalyptic revelation and a prophet. The danger of 'secularization' indicated in I John is also evident in the letters to the seven churches. At all events the Apocalypse, too, is to be included in the Johannine corpus in a broader sense.[26]

The reason why the school found no subsequent heads to carry it on in a way comparable to the famous catechetical school in Alexandria beginning with Pantaenus and Clement is connected with the towering figure of the teacher, who in his circle was regarded as the last of the disciples of Jesus still living. It was his ingenuity as a theological thinker who gave the Fourth Gospel its unique stamp which made it the most important theological work in the New Testament after the great letters of Paul. It cannot be the work of a quarrelling collective. The earlier apostles, Peter or Paul, for example, also had no real 'successors'; the later sequences of episcopal successors were first constructed in the controversy with the heads of Gnostic schools round about the middle of the second century, especially by Hege-sippus.[27] They presuppose the monarchical church leadership emanating first from Jerusalem, later from Antioch and ultimately from Rome. In the letters of Ignatius, the Letter of Polycarp and in Papias there is no further trace of the ongoing existence of a Johannine school, but there are signs in Asia Minor of the continuing influence of Johannine traditions, last but not least due to the writings of the Johannine corpus.[28]

In his list of the 'stars' in his province, Polycrates of Ephesus, who was born around 125 CE and refers to seven older relatives who were bishops, and was himself the leading bishop in Asia Minor during the dispute over Easter,[29] mentions Polycarp of Smyrna immediately after the 'apostle' Philip and the beloved disciple and 'teacher' John. As a patriarch who formed a tradition, Polycarp is certainly to some degree analogous to 'John the Elder', but he had neither his theological stature nor such influence extending beyond the region. There is certainly still something (not more) of the Johannine spirit in the letters of Ignatius, and those holding office in the church who are mentioned there may at least in part have had some closer (or more distant) connection with the 'old man', but there is no longer any trace of a 'Johannine school': the growing strength of the monarchical episcopate may have made it difficult for it to continue to exist in an effective way. In Alexandria, too, there were later tensions between the bishop and the catechetical school, as a result of which Origen had to withdraw to Caesarea.

E.Hirsch sees Polycarp as 'a personality who was certainly formed and determined by him' (i.e. the presbyter John), though the only letter of his which has been preserved does not allow us to infer this. However, it may hold for Polycarp's resolution in his battle against doctrinal heretics which is also stressed by Irenaeus that: 'The church in Asia Minor thus seems to have gained through this John of Ephesus the clear and definite line which made it a bulwark against all forms of Gnosticism throughout the East. Here we can detect that the whole shaping of Asia Minor by Palestinian Christianity, i.e. probably by this John, was a great event for the church which brought it a rich blessing.'[30] I would happily agree with this.

In contrast to Alexandria, Antioch and Rome, despite its wealth and its flourishing cultural life, in the second century in particular,[31] and despite its numerous Christian communities which were very aware of themselves, Asia Minor was never the permanent abode of the head of a Gnostic school. If Marcion was active for any length of time at all in the province of Asia, he could not have stayed there long,[32] and the later Monarchians of Asia Minor like Noetus of Smyrna, Theodotus of Byzantium and Praxeas were anything but 'Gnostics', even if they developed their activities in Rome. But this stubborn influence of 'John the Elder' in Asia Minor, in which one must also include the Montanist protest movement from 160, is in no way identical with the continuation of the school under the leadership of a successor as its head. So we cannot make any ongoing school responsible for major literary-critical 'adventures' within the Johannine corpus. The only clear indication of any activity in editing is the *oidamen* in 21.24 or the *oimai* in 21.25. But it is impossible to construct any convincing or extended hypotheses about redactions or strata.

So it is not possible, either, to trace any line directly from the Johannine school going beyond the Gnostic teachers of the second century. Only the relatively later Valentinus (c.135-155) takes up the Gospel (it was very probably him and not just his pupils); nor can any direct line be traced to the Montanists, who were fairly orthodox in their teaching, two generations later. I would prefer to speak of a 'Johannine school', because its founder was foremost a teacher – as Polycrates is still aware – who influenced the Christian communities which already existed in Asia Minor, but he certainly founded no special, separate 'Johannine circle, community or church'. The elder and his pupils may have established individual 'house churches', but they will much more have tried to gain authority in the older communities founded by Paul and his helpers. Here was possibly also a source of some very human conflicts, but these hardly become visible in the Johannine corpus.

Now that we have defined the 'school' and its head more closely, we must look at the Gospel itself in more detail in relationship to its author. That means that we must investigate its literary unity and the history of its origin.

4. The 'we' in John 21.24 and the 'unity of the Gospel'

Together with the episode that precedes them in 21.20-23, the two verses 21.24 and 21.25 are the key to a definition of the historical location of the Gospel, but at the same time also an indication of the literary and theological 'Aporias in the Fourth Gospel'. Eduard Schwartz, the great classical scholar, who in 1907/8 wrote four famous articles with this title,[33] was of the opinion that the Gospel is a 'book made up of a variety of ingredients'. At least he hit the nail on the head in formulating his title: the Gospel really is full of *aporias*, some of which cannot be resolved. The history of the scholarship of the last 150 years shows that it is easier to pile up such aporias than to bring them to a satisfactory solution. For that reason the Gospel of John more than all the other New Testament writings has bred a plethora of hypotheses. Here the ingenuity of exegetes has had full scope.

The special 'key verses' 21.24 and 25 show that the author who is manifested at the end like a *deus ex machina*, the anonymous beloved disciple, cannot be the author of the whole work from A to Z. At least in v.24 the plural *oidamen* is no longer a statement by one author but is made by his pupils (or by one of these pupils) as a plurality of witnesses who guarantee the truth of the work attributed to the beloved disciple; given vv.20-23, we are to suppose that he has died.

It follows from this that the Gospel was first edited and put into circulation by a group of disciples, though given the concluding *oimai* in v.25, an individual may have written on their behalf. The title of the work is to be attributed to this group. In contrast to the letters, which come directly from the elder, the Gospel took on the ultimate form in which we have it only after his death, as a result of this group of pupils. It is therefore not a complete unity in the strictest sense: other hands have worked on it – at least in the last two verses – and the question in dispute is only how many and in what way. On this point views differ widely.

(a) Aporias in scholarship

Here we must take a look at some points in the history of research. Eduard Schwartz, whose verdict I have just quoted, continues with a sharp attack on conservative theologians: 'The Fourth Gospel is composed and pieced together from a variety of... ingredients, as are the narrative books of early Israelite literature. This is a parallel which should be noted by all those who with illogical arguments and flabby interpretation have sought to maintain its unity, which is lost beyond saving, and who do not want to listen to arguments to the contrary.'[34]

Behind this statement is the exchange over the Fourth Gospel which the great classical scholar carried on in Göttingen with Julius Wellhausen, whose commentary *Das Evangelium Johannis* appeared in 1908.[35] In it he worked out an original basic document with narratives and short discourses. For him this was 'the original creation of *a specific personality, a real author*, though he remains anonymous': to this was added a revision made by several hands. According to Wellhausen, among these 'several hands' the first editor is almost a second author.[36] From him come the chronology with the festival journeys, the christology and the sacramental doctrine. Further secondary editors and interpolators followed.[37] However, his concession by way of qualification at the end of his analysis should not be overlooked: 'Despite its different strata it can be seen historically *as essentially a unit*. We are to assume that the expansions mostly come from the very circle within which the basic document came into existence and found its first readers.'[38] Wellhausen resorts to the same method that he had used successfully in his analysis of the Old Testament historical books. Discrepancies in the discourses and narrative and breaks in the texts, along with contradictions in content, are indications for separating various strata of text. Behind this stood the axiom that the simpler is at the same time the more original and is also superior. The question is whether the Gospel of John was the appropriate object, since this procedure blunts and indeed even dissolves the dialectic between humankind and God, glory and suffering, exaltation and humiliation, believing and seeing, flesh and spirit, word and miracle, present and future, time and eternity, human decision and predestination,[39] etc., which dominates the Gospel; it necessarily reduces in a one-sided way the tension in the theology, which is unique in early Christian literature.[40] Here we come up against the real main problem of the numerous attempts to solve the mystery of the Fourth Gospel by literary-critical means.

Eduard Schwartz also distinguished between an original Gospel and at least two editors, leaving aside smaller 'retouching' by inter-polators.[41] In his view, in the end there was an Asia Minor interpolator who inserted John 1.14, and deleted the address of the first letter, replacing it with a beginning dependent on the prologue and the end of the Gospel. He also wrote chapter 21. 'A particular figure gradually emerges from the mist, an inhabitant of Asia Minor, who attributed no less than five writings to the apostle John of Ephesian legend and did not leave any of them untouched by this procedure.'[42] Whether this artificial construction is really more convincing than the conjec-tures of the conservative exegetes whom Schwartz criticizes so harshly is another question.

Whereas Wellhausen was concerned to work out the basic docu-ment, Schwartz was very restrained in his conjectures about the person of the author and the redactors. With him things are the other way round: the greatest aporia, the question of the original form of the Gospel, can no longer be resolved: 'It is difficult, if not impossible, to pass judgment on the original Gospel as a whole; all too often the distinction between the basis and the levels of revision is problemati-cal.'[43] In other words, one can point to the numerous discrepancies and conjecture reworkings, but it is no longer possible to restore the basic document. Nevertheless, Schwartz gives the impression that the original author was 'an extremely original poet who produced a forceful composition' – perhaps too 'forceful' (and modern) a picture of an early Christian author.[44]

However, it must be stressed that the literary-critical 'dissolution' of the Gospel had already begun more than two generations before Eduard Schwartz and Julius Wellhausen with apologetic 'mediating theologians' who by means of reconstructing a Johannine 'original Gospel' tried to save as much as possible of the historicity of the Johannine account in the face of the radical criticism of Tübingen scholars like David Friedrich Strauss and Ferdinand Christian Baur.[45] In the face of such more apologetic attempts, Strauss defended the Gospel as the 'seamless robe of Christ' (see above, 1) and Overbeck mocked that a 'pre-Johannine' Gospel artificially reconstructed in this fashion was just 'a pure scholarly Gospel-homunculus', a 'source-critical game', since 'the whole reconstruction of the source would be without foundation'.[46] With Schwartz and Wellhausen this front changed. The literary fragmentation of the Gospel became the arena for representatives of a 'radical criticism' in the New Testament. Nevertheless, this continued to be confronted by a whole phalanx of critical New Testament scholars, some of whom had fairly major reservations. To mention only some very well-known names: A.Hilgenfeld,[47] A.von Harnack,[48] W.Wrede,[49] A.Jülicher (see below, n.54), H.J.Holtzmann,[50] Hans Windisch,[51] M.Dibelius,[52] and Walter Bauer.[53] They certainly saw the problems in the text of John very clearly, but they could not agree with the literary-critical hypotheses in the body of the Gospel (chs.1-20) which were already very numerous and – as still today – often mutually contradictory. Jülicher, the teacher of Rudolf Bultmann, arrived at a particularly sharp verdict:

> Now the deletions of the critical censors have not been limited to 7.53-8.11 and ch.21; the hypotheses about divisions are already almost beyond surveying... Or a considerably shorter 'original John' is constructed by the assertion that now the 'Galilean' sections, now the majority of the miracle stories, and now the major discourses have been inserted... But the hypotheses must be all completely rejected because they come to grief on the formal and material similarity of all the elements of John... In particular the miraculous actions cannot be detached from the context of the adjacent discourses (e.g. chs.9,11)... In addition, convincing reasons cannot be adduced for the interpolators and those who destroy the order... The unevennesses and contradictions to which people can refer in favour of these hypothetical interpolations and changes in order are characteristic of John in particular. The critics

too often take as criteria their logic, their attention to detail, their need for a logical sequence, in short a Gospel of the kind that they would write themselves, but John's task of carrying through his ideal of Christ in the story of Jesus, of depicting the Christ of God with the material which he drew from a tradition which was still half in the flesh, could not be achieved without inconsistencies. The form he was given was too stubborn to fit with the new content.[54]

Unfortunately the later 'critical censors', above all Emmanuel Hirsch and Rudolf Bultmann, but also their successors down to the present day, never went into the arguments of the doyens of German historical-critical New Testament scholarship. That is all the more reason why we should again listen to them more than we have done, in a time of widespread methodological confusion in the exegesis of John.

It is also all the more the case as the discovery of new texts now makes it impossible for us to give a late dating to the Johannine corpus. In comparison to us, with our better knowledge of the Johannine tradition in the second century, the older exegesis had far more chronological elbow room for its literary-critical speculations.

For so complicated a history of development as has been conjectured by Wellhausen, Schwartz and their followers sufficient time is needed for the Gospel to grow in its various stages. There were many centuries during which the Old Testament Hexateuch or the Deuteronomistic history work could develop from the various sources. Earlier scholarship therefore put the final redaction of the Gospel very late: F.C. Baur claimed a time shortly before 170; E. Zeller reduced it to around 150. Schwartz supposed 'the last edition of the Gospel not very much before 140', because he found in it 'traces of polemics against Basilides and Valentinus'.[55] Wellhausen saw in 5.43 a retrospect 'on the recognition of Bar Kochba as the Messiah on the part of the Jews'. In that case the Gospel would have been edited after 132.[56] By contrast, he claims that the basic writing is almost two generations earlier, in which case one can of course accommodate many redactors and interpolators, since this is a period of between fifty and sixty years. B.W. Bacon even supposed a last revision of the Gospel adding ch.21 'at Rome c.150 AD'.[57] Emmanuel Hirsch, in his analysis of the Fourth Gospel in 1936,[58] also arrived at a similarly complicated history of origins extending over two generations. He begins with an earlier 'sharply anti-Jewish'[59] Gospel, only fragments of which have been preserved, from a 'splintered Christian group' after 70 CE,[60] which a Gentile Christian merchant from Antioch, who also visited Palestine, reshaped into a Gospel proper round about 100.[61] An anti-Gnostic ecclesiastical redactor, who was at the same time the author of I John, revised the Gospel severely and by adding ch.21 attributed its composition to the beloved disciple, whom he identified with John the Son of Zebedee. The letters also come from this redactor. The revised Gospel and I John 'leave to the reader the discovery that the author can only have been John of Ephesus, the disciple of the Lord, long since buried, and that he is identical with the son of Zebedee'. Through this mystification the writer transplanted to Ephesus the 'strange Gospel that had fallen into his hands' (!) and gave it an author who was famous in Asia Minor and at the same time apostolic.[62]

But the romance goes further. A 'collaborator, expander or continuator' further enlarged the Gospel and the letter and wrote II and III John, thus 'making a new link between John of Ephesus and the Gospel and the first letter'. Like Wellhausen and Schwartz, Hirsch comes to the conclusion that 'the Fourth Gospel appeared in its ecclesiastical revision in Asia Minor not too long before 140'.[63]

More recent radical critical scholarship has not got far beyond the 'knitting pattern' presented here. Granted, Bultmann rejected attempts at reconstructing a 'basic document';[64] in his research its place is taken by several sources, like the signs source which is particularly popular today, along with a passion narrative and the originally Gnostic revelation or speech source; then follows the evangelist himself, who was perhaps a converted Gnostic disciple of a baptist sect, and after him one or more redactors and interpolators extending to the author of the appendix in ch.21. The first redactor is then usually identified with the author of I John, the unity of which is itself again in dispute. II and III John can then – depending on taste – be regarded as very early or as late forgeries.[65]

(b) Arguments for relative unity

The earlier warning voices of leading scholars against these radical operations, including their historical consequences, which sometimes went into the realms of fantasy, were mostly overlooked, at least since Bultmann's impressive commentary.[66] Nevertheless two new important recognitions have set limits to the unbounded whimsicality of literary critics and the constructions associated with it. One year before Hirsch's study, in 1935, C.H.Roberts had published p[52] with parts of the text of John 18, which according to Aland is now 'by general consensus put at around 125'.[67] As a result the final redaction of the Fourth Gospel must be put at least a generation earlier than was usual in so-called critical scholarship. The Gospel of John in its present form (and the letters) was surely published a decade or so before the letters of Ignatius, since there is no longer any trace of the Johannine school in these letters addressed to five communities in Asia Minor (see above, 14f.).

Meanwhile two further Johannine papyri from the second century have become known. Aland again comments: 'This threefold attestation of a New Testament text from the second century is unique, just as the early tradition of the Gospel of John generally is unique'.[68] All three texts already display typical Christian characteristics: codex form, *nomina sacra* and a fixed text. Nowhere is there any evidence of alleged primal forms of the Gospel which have not yet been shaped by the final redaction. That is reason enough for doubting the existence of such primal forms circulated in copies.

A second fact which limits the literary 'deconstruction' of the Fourth Gospel is the unity of language and style which is also unique in the New Testament. It had already been brought out in the two volumes by E.A.Abbott, *Johannine Vocabulary* and *Johannine Grammar* (1905/6). Then E.Schweizer in 1939[69] showed by means of thirty-three stylistic characteristics which he discovered that the earlier hypotheses suggesting divisions into sources could not in any way be supported 'on stylistic grounds'. E.Ruckstuhl refined Schweizer's method further in 1951 and also applied it to Bultmann's commentary which appeared in 1941.[70] He could point out that from a stylistic point of view there is no justification for Bultmann's numerous literary-critical operations. It is striking that ch.21 also shares in the unity of the Gospel, while the pericope about the woman taken in adultery, 7.53-8.11, which found its way in at a secondary stage, shows no signs of Johannine style. Granted, Ruckstuhl's conclusions, which are uncomfortable for all literary critics of the Fourth Gospel,- have been doubted, but they have never really been refuted.[71] Let me recall them briefly. The Fourth Gospel is 'a unitary work throughout', 'it has a clear ground plan of its own' and forms 'an unusually strong stylistic unity' which includes ch.21. Its aporias must not be attributed to the involvement of 'several hands', and this unity makes even the hypothesis of an 'ecclesiastical redactor' improbable. 'Style criticism in John does not demonstrate' any underlying literary sources. Glosses cannot be excluded, but they must be demonstrated by textual or stylistic criticism. We should therefore be suspicious of literary criticism based only on 'theological tendencies' and supposed or real inconsistencies in argument and narration. The strongest argument is the stylistic one.

Ruckstuhl developed his older investigation, which is still valid, in his article 'Johannine Language and Style', in it taking apart piece by piece the opposed theses of R.T.Fortna.[72] The detailed investigations of Schweizer and Ruckstuhl suggest a 'normative' figure as author, and who other would this be than the head of the Johannine circle? It is to him that the Johannine corpus owes its unitary language and its main theological ideas, and the Gospel its basic structure. It is a step back in terms of method for modern authors by contrast to postulate a separate Johannine church which simply cannot be demonstrated, with a 'clearly definable history of its own' and its 'own authoritative canon' and even claim, as J.Becker does, that this is an 'undisputed fact'. Justified though the assumption of a Johannine school is, there are doubts about conjecturing the existence of a sect which existed 'in relative separation and with little contact with Christianity'.[73] As though the Johannine school were not an important part of 'Christianity' during the lifetime of its head! And precisely what do we really know about a 'mainstream church' and separated 'sects' or 'groups' in Christianity around 100 CE?

If anyone feels that nevertheless, on the basis of the existing breaks and contradictions in the Gospel, the conjecture of 'various hands' of quite different personalities is indispensable, these must be brought very near in time, place and spirit to the head of the school.[74] The 'history' of the school is first and foremost the 'history' of its master and head between 60/70 and 100/110 CE. The more redactors and authors who are introduced – even with opposed theological views – the more difficult it is to explain the origin of both the corpus and the Gospel with its stylistic unity, unique in earliest Christianity, and the closed nature of its thought-world.

In 1982 J.Becker was still of the opinion that in essentials a certain consensus had become visible in the reconstructions attempted on a literary-critical basis.[75] In the meantime, however, a certain degree of sobriety is gaining ground in the face of the luxuriance of speculation based on an almost unlimited trust in the possibilities of literary criticism.

Above all H.Thyen, who for many years reported on Johannine research in the *Theologische Rundschau* and in so doing emphatically argued for hypotheses of strata and development, has considerably revised his earlier views. His new view, which begins from the traditional text as a basis with a coherent content for any meaningful exegesis of John and attacks the postulate of fortuitous and contradictory 'strata' in the Gospel, has been expressed in his major articles on the Gospel and the letters in the *Theologische Realenzyklopädie*.[76]

This insight has been supported not only by the argument from style, but also by linguistic studies by R.Kieffer, B.Olsson,[77] and above all R.A.Culpepper,[78] which indicate the narrative coherence of the Fourth Gospel, and by the extraordinarily thorough investigation by G.van Belle[79] of the stylistic unity of the approximately 180 'notes' in the Gospel, which point to one hand and can hardly be attributed to different authors. Kügler's dissertation on the beloved disciple, which has already been quoted several times, and which shows more confidence in the possibilities of literary criticism, nevertheless stresses that the 'redaction' of the Gospel in Bultmann 'takes on the role of destruction of the text' and that we also need to ask 'whether... an all too great gulf between tradition and redaction is probable', since 'to revise a text... means to take it over partially or as a whole.' Kügler therefore stresses 'that the redaction is a *Johannine* one, i.e. that it is reworking its own tradition'.[80] Here, however, a wealth of questions arises: for example whether such a 'redaction' *ipso facto* presupposes 'another hand', i.e. another person, and how one is to see the collective editing of a 'group text' – what are we to understand by that? Is not the author most often his own redactor? And given a style which is amazingly of a piece, how are we to find sure criteria for the need to assume such 'another hand' or, better, 'another head'?

As for dependence on the Synoptics, we are to presuppose knowledge of them and sometimes also their direct influence – but in a very free manner. Quite often knowledge of a synoptic narrative is simply presupposed. The author was too independent a writer to copy in a straightforward way. A leading Christian teacher in the capital of the province of Asia, i.e. the central province of the Eastern part of the empire, could not ignore these older writings. However, he wrote his Gospel with an original theology and often in clear opposition to the Synoptics. Whether he used other alien sources alongside them remains uncertain. The one thing that we can be sure of is his excellent knowledge of the Old Testament texts. Of course we cannot know whether he himself, or pupils closely connected with him, made more or less private notes and collections of material, for instance of miracles, which were used for the Gospel. Here we have to reckon with a vast field of possibilities. However, all material from outside was fused stylistically and theologically into the Johannine text.

The existence of a signs source with a *theios anēr* christology supposedly contrary to the Fourth Gospel cannot be demonstrated

in terms either of style or of the history of religion.[81] For the Fourth
Gospel the 'signs' are not an alien body but a basic ingredient of its
picture of Jesus. They are chosen and described in the Gospel in
order to demonstrate Jesus' sending as Son of God in connection
with Old Testament prophecy, a sending which is consummated in
the atoning death of Jesus. At best one can talk of a 'signs source' in
the sense that the teacher (and his pupils) collected miracles of Jesus.
He interpreted them as 'signs' and chose seven of them for use in the
teaching of the school. That this collection was larger is shown by
20.30: 'Many other signs did Jesus before the disciples...' (cf.21.25).
Probably several signs already selected for oral teaching were interpreted by an attached 'revelation discourse', a custom which may go
back to the oral instruction of the elder. Possibly the miracle story
about the feeding of the five thousand was used as a starting point
for the definition of Jesus as 'the bread of life coming from heaven',
a topic the climax and conclusion of which was a reference to the
eucharist (6.51a-58). This central Christian 'sacrament' was thus
transferred into the midst of the ministry of Jesus, and instead of the
traditional eucharistic words during the last supper, the knowledge
of which on the part of the hearers is presupposed, the teacher can
combine this fundamental revelation discourse with the testimony
of the beloved disciple standing before the cross to the blood and
water which flow out from the spear wound (19.34f., cf. 6.53-56) after
Christ had fulfilled his work (19.28,30). The strong 'antidocetic'
tendency is even more evident here than in other miracles.[82] A
collection of miracle stories (or more) could have been kept in written
form for use within the school. But already this is hypothetical.
However, if there was such a collection (or collections), this was no
alien body nor an independent 'Gospel'. One can hardly expect that
a self-conscious head of the school, who did not accept even the
Petrine Gospel of Mark (as Luke and Matthew did), the oldest Gospel
which was recognized widely, but dissociated himself from it and
criticized it, would accept an obscure alien 'miracle gospel' into his
own work. He was not a man who would mechanically, indeed
almost slavishly, write out substantial parts of an 'alien body'.
Therefore 20.30f. cannot be the end of this supposed 'source' either.

Even more questionable are the more extensive constructions,
starting from a basic document, which develop a 'history' of the
Johannine 'special community' from its Jewish Christian beginnings.
Thus Georg Richter began from a basic Jewish Christian document
which was written as polemic against the community of John the
Baptist and in which Jesus was confessed as eschatological prophet

and Messiah. The evangelist, breaking out of this Jewish-Christian group, is said to have introduced the pre-existent Son of God under the influence of Gnostic and Mandaean ideas; the one sent by the Father returns to him and through the Spirit gives 'the birth from above' which has a predestinarian basis; because of the docetic dangers lurking in the work of the evangelist a 'secondary (anti-docetic) redactor from whose spiritual milieu the Johannine letters also derive' again put strong stress on the humanity of Jesus and the practical proof of faith. His influence can be detected above all in the prologue, in the farewell discourses and in the letters, where he opposes the docetists and compels them to secede. Last of all, his group was forced into the ghetto by the hierarchy which arose in the mainstream church. That is evident in the third letter. Christology above all was the cause of these divisions. For Richter, to talk of *the* Johannine community is misleading since 'there is only... a series of Johannine communities... the splintered existence of which is expressed in the various chronologically successive strata of the Gospel of John or in the Johannine writings generally'.[83]

The historical picture painted by Jürgen Becker has some affinity to Richter's outline. He presupposes a lengthy history for the 'Johannine association of communities' somewhere in Syria. The first starting point for him is the 'cursing of the heretics' in the Eighteen Benedictions of the synagogue around 90. The Gospel is said to have been written by an anonymous author between 90 and 100 and to take up a *sēmeia* source which contained almost all the historical tradition and a passion narrative. The Gospel underwent a far-reaching 'redaction in several phases' by various redactors. I John is also to be attributed to a redactor: II and III John followed later. These writings then became the canon of the somewhat independent association of Johannine communities which is said to have lasted until about 130.[84] That we have no evidence whatsoever of a 'Johannine church' between 110 and 130 does not worry him. If New Testament scholars proclaim a pre-Christian 'gnosticism' before Paul without any real evidence in the sources, why may an 'uncritical criticism' not postulate a 'Johannine church' in the first half of the second century? None of these conjectures about a number of sources and levels of redaction can solve the riddle of the Fourth Gospel; that applies all the more to a 'history of the Johannine communities' which is built on them.[85]

The conjecture that there is one dominant creative and theological authority and teacher behind the Johannine corpus is very much more probable. In favour of it is the unity of style and the impressiveness of the overall theological outline which also makes itself felt in the influence it exercised later on the early church. Neither the differences in the Gospel nor those in the letter necessitate the assumption of a whole series of authors and redactors who more or less contradict one another in theological terms.

We may not forget that the head of this school, who had been a dominant figure for a long time, had been involved in a critical discussion, indeed even a deep conflict, with a group of his own pupils who were influenced by 'new ideas' from outside, which they mixed one-sidedly with some provocative theses from their teacher. At an advanced age he had to react to these challenges with new emphases, also stressing in the letters and later parts of the Gospel a rather more 'conservative' standpoint which he himself may possibly have shared in earlier decades. There are many examples in church history from Paul to the German Church Struggle after 1933 of the way in which a new and unexpected crisis compels a theologian to make more precise or even correct opinions which could be interpreted in a misleading way. Augustine was not the only one who had to write *retractationes* in which he partly corrected himself. As a basically dialectical thinker, the head of the school did not have to change his teaching substantially, since the 'elliptical' structure of his thought had always had two focuses. When the secessionists from his own school overemphasized or even separated one, for example the divinity of Christ, the presence of salvation or immediate revelation by the Spirit, he could reinforce the other: the reality of the humanity of Jesus Christ, the future horizon of eschatology and the preservation of the word of Jesus through the Paraclete. Why should we not discover traces of this spiritual conflict and the development resulting from it in the so-called 'redactional layers' of the Gospel itself? And why should not the head of the school become his own 'redactor' in a critical situation, rewriting or redefining his own (unpublished) manuscript?

(c) Some basic assumptions

Starting from this point we have to ask a series of questions and make some assumptions:

1. The Gospel was not written down quickly in a few weeks or months, but grew quite slowly, as the written deposit of the oral christological teaching of John the elder.[86] This slow growth may, among other things, also be connected with the novelty and difficulty of the task. Indeed the author was writing against the predominant Petrine-Synoptic tradition. But this itself could also explain why he

hesitated over publication right up to his death. As with most works, the prologue was added last: perhaps it was composed earlier as a hymn, but this too will have been after careful reflection. John 17 was also added at a later stage as an *inclusio*, but not by a redactor: both prologue and ch.17 clearly show the genius of the author.

2. We do not know over what period and in how many stages the Gospel grew, what written sources the author used in addition to those he used only sometimes and in a dissociated manner: the Gospels of Mark and Luke and Old Testament texts – the Pentateuch, the Prophets and Psalms.[87] If he used alien sources at all, they were totally fused in style and theology and it is impossible to reconstruct them. A rather 'archaic' (if we can use this word in a tradition history of about sixty years) Jewish Christian stratum in his Gospel may be the legacy of his own Palestinian provenance, which we shall discuss in the last chapter. Nor do we know how often he reworked individual parts of the Gospel, whether he wrote himself, or dictated to one or more scribes and pupils. Possibly he changed his custom of writing when he became older and needed a secretary, so that he wrote the earliest parts himself and the latest were written by a secretary; we can guess quite a lot, but we know nothing exactly. The style in the Gospel does not give any indications here. We may also suppose that discussion with his pupils influenced the text, but we cannot see to what extent and in which periods. I think that he was a rather self-conscious teacher, just as we meet him again in the letters; nevertheless he was a teacher, and teaching was possible only in more or less dialogue form.

3. The different 'strata', breaks, supposed 'contradictions', inconsistencies and explanatory glosses are best explained as a result of this slow growth of the Gospel, parallel to the teaching activity of the master in his 'school' in Asia Minor. There, a Palestinian Jewish Christian, he taught mostly pupils of pagan origin. Can we guess from afar what he himself altered, corrected, expanded and reduced in his own manuscripts, and what was done by him personally and what by helpers? The problem with the radical literary critics is that they overestimate the possibilities of their knowledge far too much. Nowadays they surely risk succumbing to uncritical naivety far more than the more cautious conservative exegetes.

4. How may we expect to understand (and criticize) easily the strange work of an early Christian charismatic teacher, an author who has been occupying himself for years (ten or twenty – who knows?) with the same subject since he made his first notes? And we must not forget that this was an author who was probably no man of

letters nor even a very practised writer, as his style shows[88] – in complete contrast to his nineteenth- and twentieth-century critics who write and judge so quickly? Nor should we forget that authors grow older, and that here we encounter someone who according to tradition was an old man.

5. This greatest theological thinker in the earliest church alongside Paul, who in some decisive points is related to him,[89] founded his school and instructed (or even shaped) his pupils – like nearly all great wise men in antiquity - by his oral teaching. The four (or five?) writings collected in the Johannine corpus are only by-products of this teaching, a teaching which may have lasted more than a generation. His few texts, written late, became something like his testament. We should not forget that what we possess from earliest Christian instruction and pronouncement by written sources is only a shadow of the richness of original teaching. And what can we expect from the literary method of a Jewish-Christian writer of the first Christian century who neither received the usual rhetorical training of the educated Greek upper class nor had lessons in philosophical logic? Must every trace of a theological distinction or even contradiction be attributed straight away to someone else? We may think about the extent to which views have changed among German theologians (even among some experts on John) over the last fifty years! The metamorphoses which people seek to trace in the Johannine corpus seem to me small by comparison. Sometimes we can discover quite astonishing changes even in different volumes of the same commentary on John!

Excursus:
Susan Sontag, Franz Overbeck and 'John the Elder'

I hope I may be excused for quoting some extracts – in a way which is historically quite inadmissible – from an interview with one of the most famous essayists of our time, Susan Sontag. These show better than any literary-critical and linguistic analyses (in which the personal feelings of the dissecting scholar often make a formal appearance) what a difficult phenomenon even a modern text and its author are. The argument 'how much more?' is compelling. How much more difficult may be a largely almost unknown author and his text, which will soon be two thousand years old and comes from another completely different cultural and spiritual environment, an author who in addition wants to bring a unique and strange saving message of Jewish origin for all humankind!

First of all there was the question of the form, which she found so problematical, the limitations and necessary reductions in an interview.

Does not a written Gospel represent an enormous limitation and reduction on oral teaching, in which the possibilities of misunderstanding constantly lurk which the author can no longer put right? Does not the whole history of exegesis bear witness to such misunderstandings?

She was afraid of being quoted with ideas, sentences and paragraphs which she had in fact thought, said or written and which could nevertheless be misleading.
Not just because of the context.
They could be misleading simply because she spoke, thought or wrote about them much more, in a much more sophisticated way *and* also *in a way which was quite the opposite* (my italics): 'I can't get away from the idea of how thought is to be depicted where each and no matter which sentence by itself must seem a reduction.'
She is happy if one of her books finally begins to live a separate life, if she loses control of the book and if the reader detects in it things which coincide with her original intentions and if in the reading it also satisfies needs which had not been envisaged when it was being written down.
'Like anyone who has had a career of any length,' she sighed, 'I'm the prisoner of stereotypes which are derived from my previous work.'

Did John the Elder deliberately hold back the tremendous text as long as he could teach because he did not want to lose control over the work, because he did not want to become the prisoner of the stereotypes which it contained – almost as though he suspected the way in which Gnostics and sceptics, ancient and modern, would deal with it?

When she is writing she does not think in the same way as when she is speaking. She says that it is one of the mysteries of writing that one makes discoveries in the process of writing. *Again and again, newly revised drafts of her articles differ enormously from one another* (my italics). But the later drafts would be impossible without the earlier ones. For her there is no direct way.

It is a tedious process. She worked for a year on the ninety pages of 'AIDS and its Metaphors'. Thomas Mann, I think, defined a writer as someone who found writing difficult.

'Of course I sense in myself *the impulse to contradict myself...* Every one of us does that. That shows that we are alive. If I have done something for a while in this way, I ask myself how I can do it like that.' Inconsistency? Contradictions? From this she filters new, splendid options. Options, visions, ways into the future.[90]

In my view, undoubtedly the elder found it very difficult to write his one book. This is no draft written with an easy hand. And probably the one hand wrote many more drafts (some of them contradictory) than we suspect. There were already waste paper baskets in those days. Why do we want to complicate the history of the writing of the work – which was certainly unspeakably difficult – by the postulate of as many hands as possible, some of them even contradictory? Is not the one hand which keeps taking up the pen time and again enough here – circumspect though it may have been? And does not the old proverb 'Too many cooks spoil the broth' apply here?

If the example of the famous American essayist seems inappropriate, I would like to refer to the work of a great Johannine critic which appeared posthumously and which was reviewed by one who was even greater.

Here is Harnack's concluding verdict on the extensive study on John by Franz Overbeck, edited by Bernoulli:[91]

Overbeck did not edit this work himself, but he wanted it to be edited. However, I am certain that he would not have wanted this form; for the work is not only full of repetitions, but *also displays contradictions* (Overbeck's own judgments were once different, and traces of this are still left) and inconsistencies; above all there are whole paragraphs which should not have been printed as they are because they are simply *incomprehensible*. Overbeck could write very well indeed every now and then, but as a rule he wrote densely and badly; such statements as occur countlessly in this work he should have allowed to be printed only after repeated checking or rejected them completely. In addition there are numerous misprints and at some points, I suspect, misreadings of the manuscript which destroy the sense. The editor should have applied himself more assiduously to his work.[92]

Was John the elder in a better position than one of his sharpest critics? Bernoulli certainly did not deliberately falsify or corrupt the work of his teacher. In a short reply he stressed that he only wanted to put into book form 'the special character of my teacher with all its peculiarities' (n.92). May one not then suppose that the completely unknown redactor(s) had the same intention? If only our literary critics, who are sometimes so brash, would reflect more about the complicated reality of life as it is and would not constantly confuse what is possible (and indeed sometimes impossible) with what can be made probable by historical means. Harnack's criticism of Overbeck culminates in the sentence: 'A virtuoso driller is not yet a virtuous master builder.' That may apply to many of us critics of John, but it does not apply to the evangelist. His splendid building stands unshakeable, despite all the defects which have been sufficiently criticized over the past 150 years, since Strauss and Baur.

6. Apart from our profound ignorance, the tendency to suspect another redactor or glossator for each difficulty or 'contradiction' could even lead to a destruction of the basic dialectical theology of the work which gives the whole its tension, creating instead an artificial construct in accordance with one's own wishes, which is then said to be the true Gospel. The great teacher who stands behind the real Gospel, the author of the most significant theological text in the New Testament alongside Romans and Galatians, was the first to take the profound dialectic between the *vere homo* and the *vere deus* as the starting point for his christological thought in all its dimensions – how could such a work fail to be full of tension to the end? He is the one who later acquired the honorary title *ho theologos*: no collective of an anonymous school or a series of partly derivative redactors could have achieved this.

7. The elder John was not able to complete his Gospel and left his work unfinished in advanced old age (probably in small parts). We have no evidence that there was an earlier completed Gospel from his hand which was already published and put into circulation during his lifetime in the circle of his disciples and in the communities of Asia Minor. The concluding verses show that it was first edited by his pupils. In a reference to his *Metamorphoses* in his *Tristia*, Ovid complains bitterly during his exile that he was unable to edit his great work himself. What he says may in some respects also be valid for the author of the Fourth Gospel.

18712

All you who touch these scrolls bereft of their father...
Let your indulence be all the greater because these were not
published by their master,
but were rescued from what might be called his funeral.
So whatever defect the uncompleted poem may have
I would have corrected, had it been permitted me (I,7,35-40).

May an early Christian author not beg his modern critics for a similar
indulgence because he died before he could publish his work himself?

That problem again leaves two questions: (*a*) In what state did the
pupils find this unfinished work? (*b*) What did they add to it or
change in it?

First of all I suppose that the work was essentially complete. Despite
some discrepancies which led to hypotheses about transpositions the
structure is on the whole amazingly clear and consistent; presumably
the disciples were initiated into the elder's plans for the Gospel and
the work had grown in conversation with them. On the other
hand these discrepancies suggest the possibility that the author had
sometimes written several outlines side by side which his pupils then
incorporated into the work after his death. In this way, for example,
we could explain the much-discussed break between 14.31, where
the farewell discourse really ends, having a smooth continuation in
18.1f., and the abrupt new beginning in 15.1ff. But even that is only
one possibility among many.

The numerous 'disruptive elements' in the Gospel could have
arisen in very different ways. We must not therefore claim the
existence of several redactors. Who of us has not inserted additional
sentences into his or her own manuscript, thus breaking the sentence
sequence without noticing? In an author unused to literary work like
the head of the school it would be remarkable if this did not happen
here and there. The clumsiness which is sometimes visible – and this
is only literary – cannot disguise the fact that he was an ingenious,
powerful and passionate teacher who could arrange his material in
an impressive and dramatic way. The assumption of the direct
intervention of two, three or more conflicting redactors – whether
clever or stupid – remains an extreme resort as a hypothesis.

There are other possibilities. For example, that 'interruptions' were
inserted quite deliberately to serve as signals, to provoke the hearer
in the liturgy of the community (these – and not so much private
readers – were the important ones), to prepare for later more detailed
statements or even quite simply to give additional explanations.[93]
The Gentile-Christian audience needed explanations of this kind. We

must also keep in mind the influence of the oral interplay of question and answer in the school which I have already mentioned, continuing in parallel to the growth of the work. What we have here are not the written desk-productions of individual professors of the kind that are usual today. The radical literary critics use too little imagination about these *innumerable possibilities* for the origin of such 'disruptive' elements and are therefore too imaginative in their own constructions 'thus and not otherwise', as they can no longer distinguish between the very different possibilities and what seems to be most probable.

The wide-ranging consensus over the Synoptic Gospels can exist only because the basic evidence is much stronger. If we possessed only Matthew or Luke, Mark could hardly be reconstructed, though ninety per cent of his Gospel is contained in them. In the case of John, where we know much less, opinions differ very widely. The aporias are too great, the unknowns too numerous. The current fashion in New Testament literary criticism which overlooks the limits of the possibility of stringent proof, and in its lack of concern exceeds even the radical fathers at the beginning of the century, is a sign of the loss of historical reality.

8. Of all the possibilities, the most improbable is that in the Gospel we have an almost chaotic hubbub of voices of ecclesiastical redactors, sometimes in conflict with one another, resounding in chorus with stupid interpolations.

How are we really to imagine the work of so many different hands on the Gospel one after another? If it had already been circulated by the evangelist in the communities, we would inevitably discover text-critical references to these earlier authentic preliminary stages in the admirable attestation of the text of John since the second century, as is the case with the conclusion to Mark (16.9-20) or the end of Romans (16.25-27).

If the work had not yet been edited shortly after the death of the evangelist, the question arises how the various, sometimes contradictory, redactors came into possession of these posthumous papers. Photocopiers had not yet been invented. Were they handed down from one rapidly dying head of the school to his designated successor and supplemented by each according to his taste? But was there really a successive series of heads of schools who were also a chain of redactors within about ten years or less? Or did one redactor secretly filch the completed or half-completed manuscript from another by night to edit, expand and even adulterate it,[94] the last of them bringing it as a dowry on his return to the bosom of the church? If the evangelist died around 100 CE, or soon afterwards, there is not too much time for such an eventful fate, and in historical terms it is even less probable.

5. My own attempt at a solution

Following on what I have said so far, I want to develop my own hypothesis, and hope that it has some plausibility in the present state of our knowledge.

1. As already stated, the work of John 'the elder', the Gospel, was not written down over a short period but grew relatively slowly in parallel to the development of the teaching of the school. So it contains in some way the deposit of the christological teaching experience of the head of the school over quite a long time, possibly several decades.

2. As literary 'sources' of which the author takes account without really being dependent on them in the strict sense we should look primarily to the earlier Synoptic Gospels, above all Mark and Luke: the development of the Fourth Gospel took place in antithesis to the Synoptic tradition. Nowhere does the evangelist refer, as Luke 1.1f. does, to alien tradition, but he does refer to the presence of the Paraclete. His work is legitimated by the testimony of the Spirit of truth. This gives the evangelist his unprecedented freedom towards historical 'facts' and the authority to remodel tradition radically.

3. In addition to this there is 'eye witness' to the human reality and the *doxa* of Christ, hidden and open – however the evangelist may understand the true testimony of the eye-witness. The seven signs in the Gospel are a selection from a more extensive collection of the signs of Jesus in the school. They are regarded as a necessary part of the activity of Jesus and do not derive from an alien source. They also illustrate the anti-docetic tendency of the Gospel: the miracles are the work of the creator of the physical world (1.3) who is going to his death; at the same time they have a deeper 'spiritual' significance.

4. We may not judge the work of the teacher, who in contrast to Paul or Luke had little or no literary training, by the criteria we would apply to an ancient author versed in rhetoric. He is writing neither a clearly arranged theological treatise nor a typical biography. His work is basically *sui generis*. The strangeness of the work applies both to the Gospel and to I John. The connection with the oral teaching and the discussions in the school must always be kept in view. It leads to some of the breaks and offensive passages that are protested about, which in fact often introduce surprising new aspects. The explanatory glosses have also largely, even predominantly, been caused by this.

5. The entire work is dominated by the extremely bold dialectic of the teacher in the field of tension between the *vere deus* and the *vere homo*. His basic theological approach is to give reality to the impossible paradox expressed in Gellert's Christmas hymn, 'Godhead and manhood both unite'. In the man Jesus as the incarnate pre-existent Logos and Son of God the love of the Father for all human beings becomes event in order to save them. The sending of the Son by the Father bound up with the call to faith is the one message of salvation which pervades the whole Gospel. Therefore the author associates and dissociates, makes radical separations and connections: God and world, the divinity and humanity of Jesus, the love of God and the world's hatred, suffering and return to the Father, crucifixion and exaltation, flesh and spirit, salvation in the present and salvation in the future, predestination and decision, sacrifical lamb and victor, sign and word, seeing and believing, Israel as people of God and the Jews, the sending of the Paraclete and the presence of the exalted Jesus, the demand to believe and the call to love, the recollection of the word of Jesus and leading into all truth: one could go on like this for a long time.

6. This is matched by the ambiguity of numerous terms: seeing the glory of the incarnate one, the lamb and servant of God, being born anew and from above, Spirit and wind, comprehending and overcoming (1.5), being exalted and being glorified, living spring water and water of life, and many more.

7. In addition there is the underlying symbolic significance of the miracles and actions of Jesus, the 'multiplicity of approaches' which express the one action of God, the sending of the Son for the salvation of the world, in constantly new metaphors and imagery and, like the walker going round a mountain, describe the one great wonder in constantly new forms. Modern thought may then distinguish various christologies here. We also find the same method in the elaboration of narratives which are extended in midrashic fashion, with the introduction of new aspects and persons, at the same time letting the old narrative structure shine though. How do we know that the teacher and his pupils always saw contradictions where we conjecture them? Perhaps they even wanted them as a provocation!

8. One special feature which probably goes back to the oral teaching is the underlying Johannine irony with its partly comic (2.10; 6.5,26; 9.27ff.; 13.9), partly critical effects of alienation. It is because of the particular situation that it fades away in the polemical, almost imprecatory letters. Closely bound up with it is the theme of misun-

derstanding affecting everyone, both disciples and opponents, which is applied in an almost penetrating way.

9. Despite all the tensions and breaks, no New Testament thinker has such integrating, fusing power as the author of the Fourth Gospel. This power not only shaped his unique language but at the same time brings together in his work the threads of the history of religion from all sides: from Qumran, Jewish apocalyptic and wisdom literature; from rabbinic Midrash and from Jewish *hekhalot* mysticism to Philo, the Hermetica and – later – Gnostic texts. The Jewish element predominates, but the Hellenistic aspect is not absent.

10. Much is only hinted at in the Gospel and remains incomprehensible because the pupils were 'initiated' and we are not. So we must reckon with the possibility that behind the written work there is a kind of more extensive esoteric oral teaching, remotely comparable to Plato's Academy. In and behind its teaching, despite its apparent uniformity, there is a richness of imagination and possibilities which we can hardly reconstruct. Therefore even the Apocalypse had its place at the edge of the Johannine school.

11. The author, his work and his school cannot be classified and put in pigeonholes any more than can Paul. He, too, was a theological original of fascinating spirituality through and through, an original in the best sense of the word. The same is true of the christological thought: in no New Testament writing are more christological titles collected than in the Fourth Gospel, but at the same time they are all developed and connected idiosyncratically, to result in an impressive multiform unity derived from 'different christologies'.

12. Here, then, was a towering creative teacher who ventured with reference to the activity of the Spirit Paraclete to paint a quite different picture of the activity and proclamation of Jesus from that which we can see in the Synoptic tradition, and who introduced the post-Easter pre-existence and exaltation christology quite massively into his description of the Galilean master. We must assume that such a 'theologian', who was the opposite of a mere tradent, did not fix the dialectical positions that he expressed at one stage once and for all as immovable principles. In a specific situation of crisis he ventures to take up new focal points and even in some circumstances to correct himself – dialectically. Therefore for all his stress on a 'high christology' we may accuse him neither of playing down the true humanity of Jesus nor of completely rejecting the future aspect in eschatology. His reference to the Spirit paraclete and the revelation continued by him do not exclude abiding in and maintaining the word given 'in

the beginning', any more than his concentration on christology rules out certain considerations on 'ecclesiology'.

13. That such a teacher possessing the highest authority and with rich experience going back over two generations could react sharply and clearly to a controversy with a group of pupils who were adapting themselves to the 'spirit of the time' is not surprising. In his view these former pupils of his (and their seducers, coming from outside) threatened the existence of his school and all the Christian communities in Asia. The letters are such a reaction of the elder, and the same is also true of some much-debated passages in the Gospel, the prologue and chapters 6 and 10, and passages in the farewell discourses and the passion narrative, texts which today are so readily attributed to some kind of redactors.

We should not doubt that the author, the 'elder' of the second and third letters, himself led and survived the battle which becomes evident in the letters. It is obvious that this would also make some mark on his still unpublished work, the Gospel.

14. However, there is an uncertainty factor here, even if it is relatively small. We do not know just how far the Gospel was already completely fixed – it seems to me that almost all of it was nearly in this state – and whether the elder left behind some notes or sketches, perhaps deriving from his oral lectures, some of which were inserted into the Gospel after his death by his pupils. We might also think of marginal notes in the author's own manuscript, and at the same time we may assume that pupils knew of the existence of the work and of its growth. Possibly he had read parts of it to some of them: but here we know nothing and can conjecture much.

15. As long as the elder was alive, of course his own personal oral teaching activity was more important than written works from his hand. The reason why we do not have so many different writings as we do from Paul is connected with the elder's relative reluctance to write and the fact that as a teacher working in a fixed place who undertook minor journeys here and there in the province, he had no occasion to engage in constant correspondence with his pupils and followers or no interest in doing so: he was a man of the spoken word and not a man of letters. Presumably only the crisis in the school made him a letter writer and compelled him to give the last touches to the Gospel.

16. The Gospel was published after his death and sent to the other communities, possibly together with the letters, the publication of which took place not too long afterwards. This certainly did not happen as a forerunner to the tailored Marcionite canon for a sectarian

'community association'. Gospel and letters are addressed to all Christian communities; there is no open polemic against the Christianity of any other church. Any form of gnosticizing arrogance towards mere 'believing Christians' is alien to it. The aim of the Gospel is faith in Jesus Christ the Son of God, sent by the Father to save humankind, and nothing else: the faith which is expected from every true Christian. If the whole had been designed as a sectarian canon for a separate church, it would certainly no longer have been accepted by the other communities.

17. The external form in which the Gospel and the letters were published in the community can also be indicated with some probability. As all earlier Christian biblical texts were circulated as codexes, i.e. in book form and using *nomina sacra*, in my view we may presuppose that this would already be the case with the first edition. This is one of the fixed Christian writing practices which go back to the first century. Use of the codex set Christians apart from the Jews with their scrolls, just as by the *nomina sacra* they distinguished the holy names God, Christ, Spirit from the Jewish tetragrammaton. We may already presuppose this clear demarcation from Judaism in the Johannine school.[95] It was also an external sign of the unity of the church.

18. This new Christian form of church literature, the beginning *en archē* similar to Genesis 1.1, like the climax in 19.30 alluding to Gen.2.1-3 and the *tauta de gegraptai* in 20.31 (cf.21.24), make it probable that the work was composed as a new sort of 'holy scripture'[96] for the communities and churches, and its publication as *euangelion kata Iōannēn* in succession to the earlier 'Gospels' underlines this: it was to be read in Christian liturgy. In a very similar way the Apocalypse of John was published as *the* 'prophetic book' of the church, which was also to be read in the worship of the communities.[97]

19. The pupils, or a redactor commissioned by them, now put the Gospel (which was not quite, but almost, finished) and the notices and outlines which were possibly attached, into the one form that we have; this may explain those discrepancies which have constantly led to transposition theories, e.g. in chs.5-7. Theoretically it is conceivable that they also added some individual smaller passages and observations which could themselves again derive from the oral teaching of the Elder. A few of the explanatory glosses could also go back to this final redaction, but all this remains quite uncertain. That these interventions were made sparingly and cautiously is evident from the fact that such disruptive breaks and 'contradictions' have been left without being attended to. How easy it would have been to

omit the offensive demand in 14.31b! No one would have then supposed that this was the 'original ending' of the farewell discourse. The same is true of other 'difficulties' in the text of the farewell discourses. For a skilled redactor it would have been no problem to smoothe out the beginning of ch.13 or correct the misunderstanding of all the disciples (including the beloved disciple) in 13.28.[98]

20. The reason why the letter contains more stylistic difficulties and obscurities than the Gospel is connected with the fact that the author, an old man, dictated it quickly and in understandable agitation, whereas the Gospel grew slowly and was corrected in the final redaction. In Paul, II Corinthians, which is the most passionate letter, presents the most syntactical problems.

21. In the actual editing there will have been one editor who wrote, but with a number of colleagues behind him. This could explain the change between the first person plural *oidamen* and the singular *oimai* in 21.24,25.[99] We need not suppose that theological rivalries from later generations were involved in the work itself. There is no evidence of deeper interventions or fundamental changes. It would have been easy for the pupils to delete manifest 'heresies' of the elder, but there were no such 'heresies' whatsoever; the work contains none. The problem of 'heresy' in the Fourth Gospel seems to be quite a modern one, since it became fashionable for theologians proudly to call themselves 'heretics' and to look with some disdain on the 'orthodox' mainstream church.

22. If we ask where the redactors really made additions, we naturally come to ch.21, though here too it is probable that there were earlier basic traditions or even a sketch of the text for vv.1-20; other additions could be in 19.35 (though I can hardly believe that) and then above all in the beloved disciple passages, which may in part have the character of insertions. At this point a relatively small uncertainty factor remains. In itself this or that could have been added or removed. Judgments here are largely estimates, often conditioned by theological prejudices. Here I incline more to restraint. A really far-reaching redaction should truly have strengthened the unity of the whole work again – or must all redactors be stupid in principle, people who can only make things worse? Or must we even suppose that the really decisive theological achievement was that of the last redactor, who in that case would be the true 'evangelist', despite the assertion in 21.24? Surely not!

23. The title *Gospel according to John* also comes from the editors. They resorted to it to give the already known Gospels (the Synoptics) with their predominantly Petrine tradition a rival which expressed

the mystery of the person and work of Jesus Christ and the nature of faith in him better than its predecessors. The name John denoted the well-known elder John, the disciple of the Lord (but it could easily be related to John the son of Zebedee, one of the Twelve).[100]

Of course this remains hypothetical (like all attempts to solve the Johannine question in the last 150 years): the attempt to assign to the Johannine corpus one particular historical location – already well attested in the early church – and one towering theologian and founder of a school as its author. However, I think that after a century of critical attempts at deconstruction such a hypothesis (which is not new at all) has more to be said for it than against it.

V

'John the Elder', his Origin and the Historical Setting of his School

In the previous chapter we investigated the Fourth Gospel itself and the debate about its composition; now, finally, I want to turn to the person of the author, his origins, his cultural and religious background, his relation to the beloved disciple and the foundation of his school. In so doing I shall use the Gospel mainly to the degree that it gives us information about these topics.

1. A Jewish-Palestinian home

(a) The name John

As I have already said, the author's name points back to Jewish Palestine, where John was a favourite name at the time of the Second Temple, especially in priestly circles, following the model of the Hasmonaean priest-princes[1] John Hyrcanus I and II and earlier the 'Oniad' high priests before the Maccabaean rebellion. Onias, Chonya, the short form of Johanan,[2] was the most frequent high-priestly name between the time of Alexander the Great and Antiochus IV Epiphanes. In the New Testament John the Baptist is of priestly origin and in Acts 4.15 alongside Annas, Caiaphas and Alexander there appears a high priest John, perhaps identical with the son of the high priest Theophilus and grandson of Annas, who occurs on an ossuary inscription of his daughter Johanna. David Flusser comments on this that 'Yehohanan was with Eleazar the most common name of priests in Jewish antiquity'.[3] Of course the name was not only used in priestly families, but the testimony of I and II Maccabees and Josephus shows that there was some preference for it in aristocratic circles,[4] and certainly it was not a distinctive name outside Palestine. In the New Testament we find six different Palestinian Johns, at least two of which were of priestly origin – one was probably a Levite.[5]

(b) Language, style and Jewish background

But quite apart from the name, numerous historical details indicate that the author of the Gospel had a Palestinian origin, although the work itself was not written in a Jewish milieu. That the author comes from the Jewish mother country is shown, for example, by the fact that, as Adolf Schlatter[6] and Klaus Beyer have demonstrated, he writes a *koine* Greek which has a marked semitic, even Hebraic, flavour,[7] a feature which is also typical of the Apocalypse.[8] Nevertheless this is no translation Greek, but a quite simple and correct *koine*. An expert in Greek style and literature like A.I.Festugière comes to the interesting conclusion that the composition and style of the work are those 'of a man who is not a Greek and who was not brought up in a Greek way. On the other hand, they do not seem to me to be those of a beginner.'[9] The reasons which have been produced for a non-Jewish Syrian (or Greek) origin since Bretschneider and Baur are more than questionable.[10]

It is also striking that the Gospel contains a series of Jewish-Aramaic terms which are transliterated into Greek, e.g. twice Messiah, which is unique in the New Testament, Cephas, Rabbi or Rabbouni, and Thomas-Didymus, the twin. Special knowledge becomes evident through the precise names of Peter, 'Simon son of John', and of Judas (son of) Simon Iscariot or (as some manuscripts rightly translate only in John) the man from Kariot.[11] It further introduces Aramaic or Greek place-names and adds their respective translations, Siloam, Gabbatha[12] and Golgotha, or uses the Aramaic term only: Bethesda[13] and the *wadi* Kedron.[14] Moreover particularly in Jerusalem (but also in Samaria and even in Galilee) it hands down astonishingly accurate geographical, historical and religious details,[15] and adds interesting information about Jewish customs and festivals.[16] Probably these translations, interpretative remarks and geographical details had been part of the oral teaching of the author, who explained even Aramaic names to his audience. It is typical of him that he is not always consistent in doing this, possibly because he thought that a term was already known. For this reason even E.Hirsch conjectured that the author must have visited Jewish Palestine as an Antiochene merchant and Gentile Christian.[17] As these notes relating to Judaism and his mother-country are very numerous and extend from allegedly secondary glosses[18] through the discourses up to the texts which are attributed to the signs source, superficial experiences from a journey are no better an explanation than the unprovable hypothesis of an originally non-Johannine Jewish-Christian basic document.

John knows halachic regulations, for example that the command to circumcise breaks the sabbath (7.22), that the richer people in Palestine were fond of using stone vessels (as these do not incur impurity from the dead), and that vast amounts of water are necessary for baths of purification (2.6); he knows about the period of forty-six years between the beginning of the building of Herod's temple and the time of Jesus (2.20), and the deep hatred between Jews and Samaritans, as also the village of Sychar as the main place in Samaria, by Jacob's well, opposite the holy Mount Gerizim;[19] he is familiar with the Jewish manna haggada,[20] and he is the only one in the New Testament to mention Tiberias, newly founded by Antipas.[21] He also knows the importance of the last, seventh, day of the festival of Succoth and the water poured out in front of the altar.[22] Moreover he is the first author to use *ta enkainia*, the Greek designation of the feast of Hanukkah, and knows that this festival of the dedication of the temple is celebrated in winter.[23] We also hear from him about the deep contempt of the leaders of the people for the unlearned *'am ha-'àreṣ*[24] and the appeal of the Jews to their descent from Abraham as the basis for their claim to freedom and salvation;[25] the stoning of the blasphemer;[26] the Jewish day of twelve hours (11.9); the pilgrimage of country people to Jerusalem for the feast of Passover and the ritual purification associated with it,[27] the 'day of preparation for the feast of the Passover'; and the high priests' fear of becoming unclean and thus unfit to eat the passover lamb by entering the Roman Praetorium to meet Pilate.[28] He also has knowledge of the prohibition against breaking the bones of the passover lamb and the special significance of the sabbath following the day of Jesus' death, which coincided with the first day of the feast of the Passover.[29]

The numerous linguistic and theological Qumran parallels, especially in the sphere of dualism and the doctrine of election, also point to Palestine.[30] The *poiein tēn alētheian* = *'aśah 'emet*,[31] is striking, as are the designation of spring water as the 'water of life',[32] the light of life,[33] the *erga tou theou* = *ma'ªśē 'el*,[34] the *pneuma tēs alētheias* = *ruªh 'ēmet*[35] and the 'sons of light'.[36] Here too the list could be extended a long way. The Qumran discoveries are a landmark for a new assessment of the situation of the Fourth Gospel in the history of religion. Here we can only note the fact; we cannot go into more detail. In the text 11QMelch which is significant for Essene dualistic soteriology we find Michael (Melchizedek), the prince of light, as an eschatological heavenly redeemer who is himself called '*elohim*, is related to the divine predicates, and as a representative of God carries out his work of redemption including judgment on the powers of darkness, and is glorified for it.[37] In his 1963 study *Der Paraklet*, my friend Otto Betz indicated the connections between the Johannine Paraclete and Michael as the Spirit of truth and spokesman for Israel even before the appearance of this text.[38] A few years later Wayne Meeks then interpreted the theme of the eschatological prophet and king in the Fourth Gospel against the background of Jewish-Samaritan veneration of Moses.[39]

In addition to the Qumran texts, newly edited Samaritan sources like Memar Marqa, the Samaritan Liturgies and Chronicles have had a most important impact on Johannine research.[40] A 1977 Tübingen dissertation by J.Bühner explained the motive of the heavenly messenger of God which is fundamental to Johannine christology from the context of messenger law in Judaism and the ancient Near East.[41] The investigation *Weisheit und Messias* (Wisdom and Messiah) by my pupil G.Schimanowski shows by means of a broad range of Jewish source material how much the concept of the 'pre-existence' not only of wisdom but also of the Messiah/Son of Man is at home in Jewish salvation-historical and eschatological thought.[42] That the Jewish myth of the pre-existence of wisdom, its mediation at creation and the sending of it underlies the description of the Logos in the prologue is an old insight, which has taken on new contours in most recent times as a result of our more profound knowledge of ancient Judaism.[43] But other forms of heavenly angelic intermediary figures with the function of being a divine representative in creation, revelation history and eschatology are also possible.[44] The most important more recent investigations into Johannine christology and its background, which differ widely in their starting points, come to amazingly convergent results in respect of the Jewish background. Here a comparison with Pauline statements shows that the development of Johannine high christology cannot be separated from the rest of earliest Christianity but has close connections with ideas which we meet in 'Jewish-Hellenistic' communities inside and outside Palestine, in Paul and in Hebrews, in Jewish apocalyptic and in Philo. The ingredients, rather, are completely Jewish in origin and to a large extent can be demonstrated specifically in Palestinian Judaism. We should not underestimate the multiplicity and creative power of Jewish-Palestinian religion before 70 CE, and the synthesis between Judaism and 'Hellenistic thought' had also been a phenomenon in the motherland for centuries. However, direct pagan influence cannot be demonstrated anywhere.[45]

(c) 'Gnosis' and 'Hellenism'

The old dispute over 'gnostic influence' in the Fourth Gospel is closely connected with the question of the definition of what one means by Gnosticism. If the term is used in a very wide sense, as it still was at the beginning of our century, to include the dualism of Qumran and other Jewish apocalyptic texts, *hekhalot* mysticism, Hermeticism, Philo and Neoplatonism, we may also call the Fourth Gospel Gnostic. The richness of the traditions developed in the Fourth Gospel demonstrates the richness of the spiritual climate in Palestine during the first century CE.[46] But if Gnosticism is defined more precisely in terms of the anti-cosmic dualistic-ontological systems from the second and third centuries with strong philosophical features, which interpret the creation of the material world as the work of very inferior angels, and reject the salvation history of Israel and the physical death of Christ, then the Johannine corpus is certainly not Gnostic. As I have already demonstrated (above, 53ff.), it is in sharp antithesis to speculations of that kind. The rather later writings from Nag Hammadi have not contributed much that is new to the understanding of the Fourth Gospel. In the case of the Tractate on the Trimorphic Protennoia, which at present is the object of a lively discussion, and behind which a gnosticizing preliminary form of the Johannine prologue has been conjectured, one can start from the basis that this late Gnostic text already knew the Fourth Gospel.[47]

That does not mean that the Gospel is clearly cut off from the world of 'Hellenism'; certainly not. Rather, it belongs in it to the degree that ancient pre-rabbinic Judaism in its creative multiplicity is also part of the 'Hellenistic world', in Palestine *and* in the Diaspora. The work was written in simple unliterary *koine* Greek, steeped in the language of Jewish piety. This Greek was also spoken by the upper classes in Jerusalem. About forty per cent of all epitaphs there are in Greek; there Greek-speaking Jews met from all over the empire, scripture was read in Hebrew and Greek, and prayer and discussion went on in both languages.[48] So with some justification the Johannine corpus has been associated with the 'Hellenists' of the circle round Stephen (Acts 6; 7). But their bridge function was very varied, and was not limited to the Johannine school, which grew up substantially later. Thus the 'Hellenists' are less the expression of a historical genealogy of the school than a representation of a milieu which was close to that from which John the elder came. We must not forget that when Jerusalem was destroyed in the year 70 it had been influenced by 400 years of Hellenistic civilization. It was there, and not in Alexandria, that tens of thousands of pilgrims from the Greek-speaking Diaspora met at the great festivals. And the Jewish aristocracy itself adopted the alien language. To an intensified degree in Herodian times a special Hellenized Jewish upper class with its own culture developed in Jerusalem. Paul, who studied the Pharisaic law in Jerusalem;[49] John Mark, the author of the Second Gospel; and the author of the Gospel of John and the letters derive from it.

2. The controversy and the Jews

So over the last thirty years insight into the Jewish background of the Johannine corpus has grown considerably. This is a background which is much more multiform and therefore broader than Schlatter and Billerbeck supposed. Accordingly, today a large number of scholars see the Johannine community or the evangelist as being engaged in a bitter controversy with the Jews. They are the real enemies of the community.[50] For that reason Klaus Wengst even wanted to put this community and the Gospel in the territory of Trachonitis and Batanaea ruled over by King Agrippa II, at some point before the 90s, because there Judaism after 70 CE, recovering and growing stronger again under the leadership of the Pharisees, would have had the possibility of executing Christians.[51] This hypothesis is especially based on John 16.2: 'they will put you out of the synagogue; indeed the hour is coming when whoever kills you will think he is offering service to God.' The key word *aposynagōgos*, which we find only in John, already also occurs in 9.22 in connection with the arrest of the man born blind: 'For the Jews had already agreed that if any one should confess him to be Christ, he was to be put out of the synagogue', and then at the close of Jesus' public ministry in 12.41: 'Nevertheless many even of the authorities believed in him, but for fear of the Pharisees they did not confess it, lest they should be put out of the synagogue.'

These statements are now related directly to the present experience of the Johannine community and connected with the introduction of the cursing of the 'heretics' into the Eighteen Benedictions by the so-called 'Synod of Jamnia', which is said to have taken place around 90.[52] But this event is historically problematical, and that is even more true of the one-sided interpretation of the three texts quoted only in terms of the author's day. The 'expulsion' of Christians from the synagogue took place, rather, in a lengthy and painful process which began even before Paul with the martyrdom of Stephen. I would suppose that the 'Hellenists' in Acts 6-8 were already driven out of Jerusalem as *aposynagōgoi* by the members of the Greek-speaking synagogues there.[53] The foundation of the Pauline mission communities was often associated with an actual expulsion from the synagogue community; the fivefold flogging by the Jewish authorities mentioned in II Cor.11.24 demonstrates the violence of these controversies. Stephen and James the son of Zebedee were certainly not the only martyrs. Acts 12.1 speaks explicitly about a *kakōsai tinas tōn apo tēs ekklēsias* by Herod (Agrippa I), i.e. that he did severe harm to several Christians around 43 CE. The reference to the suffering of the 'communities of God in Judaea' in I Thessalonians 2.14 shows that these were not isolated but repeated events. The taking over of the leadership of the community between 43 and 48 by James the brother of the Lord, who was a strict observer of the law, may have improved the situation somewhat, but his execution by stoning in 62 along with other leading Jewish Christians (*tinas heterous*) on a verdict of breaking the law (*hōs paranomēsantōn*) given by Annas II, the son of the Annas of the Fourth Gospel, is fully in accord with what John 16.2 says.[54] We may also recall the old tradition that the second son of Zebedee, John, was also 'killed by the Jews' (above, 21 and 158f. n. 121).

It seems to me that the much-discussed flight of the earliest community to Pella took place soon after this event.[55] The *birkat hamminim*, the exact date of which we do not know, is simply the ultimate consequence of a development full of combat and suffering. We should also bear in mind the fact that this curse was not only directed against the Jewish Christians but against all Jewish 'heresies'. The addition of the *nosrim* seems to be later. For pagan Christians it was meaningless. That the Fourth Gospel originated and the Johannine school was active in the territory of Agrippa II is utterly improbable. There is not the slightest hint in the Fourth Gospel that it was written in northern Transjordan, a region which – apart from its capital Caesarea Philippi, only mentioned by Mark (8.27) and Matthew (16.13) – is even more out of the way than Galilee, with a predominantly Aramaic-speaking population. The Gospel is not at all interested in this region but in Jerusalem and Judaea. Wengst's conjecture is also refuted by the fact that according to Josephus, Agrippa II protested energetically against the execution of the Jewish Christians by the high priest Annas II in 62 CE, that Luke describes him in positive terms,[56] and further, that we know nothing of any Jewish rights to inflict capital punishment in his predominantly

Gentile sphere of rule.[57] After 70 the Jews had relatively little influence on the way in which Agrippa governed his territory. Greek was spoken by the Jews only in the few larger centres like Caesarea Philippi. The existence of a Greek-speaking Christian school with a Johannine stamp in this territory is therefore an invention of scholarly fancy. There is nothing to indicate it inside or outside the Gospel.

By contrast, the Jews of Asia Minor remained relatively untroubled by the negative consequences of the Jewish War and were very influential in particular cities. The beginnings of the Diaspora there go back to the Persian period; it had been strengthened by Jewish military settlers from Babylon towards the end of the third century BCE. The Jews in the important cities of the province of Asia had been given special privileges by the Romans, and numerous inscriptions and synagogues bear witness to their power and reputation.[58] To mention just two examples: the huge synagogue of Sardes in the middle of the town with its inscriptions demonstrating that members of the synagogue belonged to the town council illustrates the influence of the Jews there. The same is true of the newly published inscription of the Jewish community in Aphrodisias containing about 150 names, half of them pagan godfearers, many of whom were also members of the town council. Both show us how powerful the Jewish communities in Asia were between the second and the fourth centuries.[59] The letters to the communities in Smyrna and Philadelphia in the Apocalypse demonstrate the tense relationship between the Christians of Asia Minor and the Jews there. The twice-repeated *synagōgē tou satana*[60] directly recalls John 8.44: 'Your father is the devil.' We can understand only too well that there would be vigorous complaints from the Jewish side against the Christians, who were a very active missionary sect: the Jews must have regarded its enthusiastic missionary and eschatological teaching as dangerous competition which might bring them into discredit with the organs of state. The Martyrdom of Polycarp attests the participation of the Jews in a persecution of Christians in Asia Minor; here their conduct is depicted as being usual in such events. The Martyrdom of Pionius from the Decian persecution depicts this feature even more strongly. There can be no doubt that hatred was considerable on both sides and could lead to insults and attacks; at the end of the first century and during the second the Jews were in a politically more favourable situation than the Christians, a situation which changed only in the fourth century.

In contrast to the Jews in Syria, Palestine and Egypt, these Jews had not been restricted by the catastrophe of the first Jewish war in

66-70 CE. So John 16.2 need not refer to an acute bloody persecution by Jewish authorities in the time of the evangelist and his school, but is meant to describe the situation of the post-Easter community generally: in the view of the evangelist it was persecuted by the Jews 'from the beginning', in Judaea and in the province of Asia. As the correspondence between Pliny and Trajan shows, if charges were laid against Christians before the Roman governors, the Christians had to expect the death penalty simply for the name itself (*nomen ipsum*) and because of their obstinacy (*Ep.* 10.96.2). The Christians in Lyons in 177 CE in their letter 'to the brethren in Asia and Phrygia' understood John 16.2 as a prophecy of the Lord which was being fulfilled in their persecution by the pagans as well (Eusebius 5.1.15).

At the same time, however, it has to be maintained that the abrupt controversy between Jesus and the Jews in the Fourth Gospel is in no way simply a reflection of the attacks of Jewish opponents on Johannine Christians in the present alone. We have to be more subtle than that here. That Jesus was involved in critical controversy with the religious and political leaders of his own people and was handed over to Pilate by them was a firm and basic ingredient of the Jesus tradition prior to John, which John develops in an idiosyncratic way. The Synoptic Gospels mention primarily the scribes and the Pharisees as the opponents of Jesus before the passion narrative; in Mark they are distinguished, in accordance with circumstances before 70, whereas Matthew presupposes the consolidation under Pharisaic leadership after 70 and speaks formally of 'scribes and Pharisees' as a unity. From the beginning of the conflict in Jerusalem the representatives of the Sanhedrin appear, represented by the 'high priests and scribes', or more precisely as a threefold group, with the addition of the elders.[61]

Things are quite different in John. Like Matthew, he too presupposes that the Pharisees are the spiritual leaders in Jerusalem; he avoids the designation *grammateis* completely, and does so deliberately. In this way he presupposes that the Pharisees are claiming to be the only ones to interpret scripture in a legitimate way and to be 'teachers of Israel' (3.1,10; cf. 7.48). However, he denies this claim: they are not real *grammateis*, authorized expounders of the *graphē*, which gives a clear testimony to the coming and the suffering of the Son of God. He knows the Pharisaic pretension of spiritual and legal oversight, but he does not acknowledge it. Scripture and thus even their hero, Moses, bears witness against them.[62]

At the same time John is well aware that the political power in Judaea lay with the high priests, and so he introduces them and the

Pharisees at the first climax of the conflict over the question of the Messiah in 7.32. Both groups send out 'servants' together to arrest Jesus. High priests and Pharisees are mentioned together five times, the *archiereis* always appearing first.[63] Fundamentally the formula 'the high priests and Pharisees' corresponds in content to the Synoptic 'the high priests and scribes' in the last struggle in Jerusalem. Whereas the stress on 'scribes (and Pharisees)' in Matthew is presumably connected with the fact that, like Paul, the author had had a Pharisaic, scribal education, in John the formula 'high priests and Pharisees' may refer to a priestly view of the leading forces in Judaism. For the leading priests, as for Christians, scribal learning was not a prerogative of the Pharisees!

In the trial itself the action comes from the 'Jews' and the 'high priests'. As a body, they are the ones mainly responsible for the execution of Jesus (*ho paradous me soi*, 19.11b; cf. the 'delivering over' to the Jews in 19.16). John alone knows of the double role of Annas, the *eminence grise* in Jerusalem, and of his son-in-law the high priest Caiaphas in the trial.[64] The term *synhedrion* occurs only once - as in Josephus – not as a fixed body but as an *ad hoc* assembly which agrees to the death sentence at the 'prophetic' prompting of Caiaphas.[65] So John has a sometimes quite vivid conception of events in Jerusalem which in some individual points may be more precise than the Synoptic tradition, and moreover is even more dramatic and polemical; but given his peculiarity of fusing present and past, tradition and spirit-inspired interpretation together, very often against all historical reality, the original event is distorted almost to the point of becoming unrecognizable. His picture of conditions in Jerusalem is a strange mixture of interesting and probably reliable facts, present polemics and christological interpretation. The theological intention is always prevalent in John.

In contrast to the Synoptic Gospels, in his work *hoi Ioudaioi* occurs extremely often: seventy-one times – almost as often as in the historical account in Acts. This designation is certainly used most of the time (but not always) in a negative way, rather like *kosmos*, but in a few cases it is also used positively. Jesus himself is in fact a Jew[66] and at individual points we almost have a positive salvation-historical concept of Israel, 'for salvation comes from the Jews',[67] and not a few Jews believe in Jesus.[68] However, from 5.10, the healing of the paralysed man on the sabbath day, the term is applied in a predominantly negative way to 'the Jews' as the enemies of Jesus, who from this healing on seek his life; and in the dramatic trial scene before Pilate they also act hand in glove with the high priests. Here, strictly speaking, he is using the designation of the whole for part of the people, their leaders or speakers, so 'the Jews' sometimes become nearly identical with 'the Pharisees'. As has long been seen, the Jews thus appear basically as the historically concrete cipher for the *kosmos*, the human world separated from God and hostile to him (cf. Paul in Rom.5.10,6; Col.1.21), a term which John similarly can also sometimes use in a neutral way, though the negative connotation is much stronger. This detrimental usage of 'the Jews' comes to a climax in chapter 8: the Jews are not the true sons of Abraham, but like Cain are sons of the devil. When they seek to kill Jesus they are only doing the work of their father, who is a murderer from the beginning.[69] It is part of the mystery of evil that the Messiah and Son of God is betrayed by one of his nearest disciples and put to death by his own people. The fate that Jesus meets at the hands of his own people is matched – above all in the farewell discourses – by a reference to the world's hatred towards the disciples.[70] Just as in the Gospel, on the basis of Jesus' battle over his own people, the Jews appear as a paradigm of the human world, so in I John we have the secessionists who are of the world and are therefore its enthusiastic audience.[71] The polemical sharpness is the same in both Gospel and letters.

3. The predominantly Gentile-Christian character of the Johannine school and the recipients of the corpus

This unique and idiosyncratic terminology means that John the Elder, his school and the communities of Asia Minor surrounding it had long since parted company with the synagogue. The 'expulsion' lies quite far in the past and was not dependent on one historical act of excommunication or upon the specific decision of an alleged Jewish 'synod' in Palestinian Jamnia. The controversy with the Jews and their leaders takes place with a glance back to the situation of Jesus in Jerusalem two generations earlier. Therefore the Johannine Jesus, though himself a Jew (and through him the author as a Jewish Christian), talks to his Jewish hearers of 'your' and to the disciples of 'their' law, while the Jews speak of 'our' law.[72] Three times a festival in Jerusalem is called a 'feast of the Jews', and twice the evangelist speaks of 'the passover of the Jews'.[73] This is clear evidence that the Gospel was written for a mainly Gentile-Christian audience, probably somewhat similar to the earlier Pauline communities.

But there is one great difference from the situation of the apostle to the Gentiles: the question of the law and 'orthopraxy', i.e. the question of the fulfilling of the commandments of the Torah of Moses and their significance for salvation, which dominated the early period of Christianity between 30 and 60 in Paul and still even in Acts (one reason why Acts should not be dated too late), and which also plays an essential role in Mark and in the rest of the Synoptic tradition, fades right into the background in John. The reproach in 7.19, 'but none of you does the law', sounds like late reflection, a statement which had long since become a commonplace, introduced by John only with the purpose of exposing the plan to kill Jesus as a violation of the law.[74] The law of Moses, like the prophets, has only one function, to bear witness to the Son of God sent by God.[75] Scripture is exclusively orientated on christological fulfilment. The scriptural quotations are therefore mostly concerned with proving this fulfilment and refer above all to the passion of Jesus, especially in the second part of the Gospel.[76] Now that means that the fight to establish the insight that it is not the law of Moses but only faith in Christ, the Son of God, which saves, is long over, and the 'works of the law' are no longer a topic for discussion. The older controversial question 'Christ *or* the law?', which is typical of Paul, or 'Christ *and* the law?', which Matthew still goes into in his own way, has been decided for John unconditionally in terms of *solus Christus* and *sola fide*. We could therefore regard John as the greatest, the true, successor of Paul. Wellhausen and Jülicher already saw that: 'John stands on Paul's shoulders',[77] though not as a disciple of Paul but as a congenial, independent theological thinker of radical grace.

All this points to the origin of the typical Johannine doctrinal tradition being after 70. Its preliminary stages cannot be traced back in a clear and distinguishable way to the time of the first generation. The 'history of the Johannine school' can be seen only after this first period of early Christianity, between 30 and 60, which so considerably shook both Jews and Christians, and is essentially identical with the 'history' of the head of the school, its teacher, and what he left behind. The reason why the catastrophe of 66-70 nevertheless emerges so little in the Gospel is because in contrast to the Gospel of Luke, which is still quite near to it (c.75 CE), this event already lay two or three decades in the past. Moreover, its consequences (or better, its aftermath) were not felt so strongly in Asia Minor as they were at the time in Rome (Mark) or later in Syria (Matthew). Only hints, like the warning of the high priest Caiaphas against Roman intervention or the announcement that worship on Gerizim and in Jerusalem will have an end,[78] point to it. The former world-shaking events which happened in Judaea are already quite far removed – in time and space. Western Asia Minor is a long way away from Judaea in geographical terms. Possibly the last confession of the chief priest before the execution of Jesus, 'We have no other king than Caesar' (19.15), may also be an indirect 'ironical' allusion to the catastrophic result of the Jewish war.[79]

Now all this means that the Gospel and the letters, which primarily address the school, are not predominantly aimed at Jewish Christians but at Gentile Christians. The immediate controversy with the Jews has long ceased to be the main theme of the school. At the centre of the theology of the head of the school there stands the right spirit-inspired understanding of the person and saving work of Christ for all humankind (3.16; 4.42; 12.47, etc.), his call to faith and knowledge of the sending of the Son and his 'exaltation' to the cross, the message which brings salvation equally to Jews and Gentiles and which is repudiated by both, the Jews standing in the Gospel for all unbelievers, because Christ did not preach to pagans but only to his own people.[80] Nevertheless the work is not mainly a missionary writing. It was hardly suitable as an 'advertising brochure' for unbelievers or a *protreptikos* for catechumens. The markedly ethical Gospel of Matthew was much more useful for this purpose and was therefore also more successful in the church from the start. By contrast John sought to give 'solid food' – to use the language of Hebrews 6.12-14 – to the circle of disciples and Christian communities who were ready to listen to the old teacher and to accept his message. The saving faith in Jesus as the Messiah and Son of God in John 20.31 includes knowing (*ginōskein*), abiding (*menein*) and keeping (*tērein*), and that means being constantly reminded and led by the Spirit.

Here it seems to me that the Gospel, which is sometimes alienating but at the same time cryptic and sometimes indeed uncanny, has from the beginning been open to an esoteric allegorizing interpretation going right to the depths. No wonder that the markedly ecclesiastical Gnostics of the Valentinian school took a fancy to it and Clement of Alexandria, the great 'Gnostic' of the mainstream church, praised it as the spiritual Gospel, the *euangelion pneumatikon*.[81] But in the end the elder had to draw in the reins which esoterically had become too loose, since a number of his pupils had gone beyond him; so in the first letter he reserves for himself the right interpretation of what the Paraclete says.

There is much to indicate that, among other things, the Gospel has the mission to the Gentiles in view. Nowhere is Jewish particularism evident in respect of the preaching of faith and salvation: we have no analogy to Matt.10.5; 5.18f.; or 23.3. The Jesus who confesses to the Samaritan woman that 'salvation comes from the Jews' is in the end confessed by the Samaritans as the 'saviour of the world',[82] and in saying that the speaker bursts the Jewish framework. God as Spirit is worshipped in the right way neither on Gerizim nor in Jerusalem but from now on 'in Spirit and in truth' (4.23f.). Jesus brings this salvation, and thus the right way of worshipping, to the Samaritans in Sychar, i.e. to 'semi-Gentiles', who here stand as representatives of all Gentiles (see n.80).

Whereas in Jerusalem, among the disciples of John the Baptist and later in Galilee Jesus comes up against misunderstanding and unbelief, these forerunners of the Gentiles confess the Messiah's universal power of deliverance (John 2.11-6.65).

Here we may not forget that in the Hellenistic-Roman period there was a Samaritan Diaspora with its own Greek Bible. There is evidence for it above all in Egypt, but Samaritan synagogue inscriptions have also been found on the island of Delos from around 100 BCE and from Thessalonica around 400 CE.[83] There was certainly also a Samaritan synagogue in Ephesus. The Fourth Sibylline Oracle and Epictetus give evidence that even disciples of John the Baptist existed not only in Transjordan but also in centres of the Roman empire like Rome, and Acts attests them in Ephesus.[84] The rabbinic accounts of great journeys by the Tannaite authorities to Rome and other parts of the Empire suggest that after 70 Pharisaic scribes also visited the province of Asia in order to pick up the threads to the Palestinian motherland and to collect money for the impoverished communities there.[85]

The brief references to the future Gentile mission which will burst the bounds of Judaism go still further. There is the question of the 'Jews' about Jesus' prophecy of his return to the Father: 'Where does this man intend to go that we shall not find him? Does he intend to go to the Dispersion among the Greeks and teach the Greeks?'[86] *Hellēn*, Greek, here probably means 'Greek-speaking Gentile' rather than 'Greek-speaking Diaspora Jew'. With typical Johannine prophetic irony that points to the west, i.e. to the remote areas in which the elder John had taught the new universal message of salvation through the sending of the Son of God, Jesus here is speaking of Greeks, not of Syrians. The work was certainly not written in a corner of Syria or Eastern Palestine.

The last great scene of the public activity of Jesus after the entry into Jerusalem is introduced by the question of 'Greeks' who want to see Jesus (12.20-22). That means that now even proselytes or Gentile sympathizers are coming to Jesus. That in so doing they turn to Philip, who according to the tradition of Asia Minor is identical with the Philip of the Hellenists in Acts and who first preached to the Samaritans (Acts 8.5ff.), is of course an artifice of the narrator. Philip addresses Andrew, the second disciple with a Greek name. In later traditions both are connected with Asia Minor: Philip with Hierapolis in Phrygia, Andrew with Pontus and Bithynia.[87] Together they present Jesus with this wish of the 'Greeks'. He replies with the image of the grain of seed which has to die in the earth in order to bear much fruit. That means that he produces this abundant fruit by his death. We could add that the successful mission among the 'Greeks' in the west is a living sign of this 'bearing fruit'. The 'greater works' which the believers will do because Jesus 'goes to the Father' (14.13) refer, among other things, to this mission in the power of the Spirit, which will have greater success.

'The other sheep which are not of this fold' and who similarly are to belong to 'one flock' (10.16), the gathering of the 'scattered children of God into one' (11.52), and the petition of Jesus in the high-priestly prayer for those who come to faith through the word (of the disciples), 'that they may all be one' (17.20f.), equally presuppose the world-wide mission among the Gentiles in John. All in all, the references to later mission to the Gentiles are certainly not less, but more varied, in John than in the Synoptic Gospels. The Johannine school and its head can therefore no longer be placed in a predominantly Jewish context, even if the founder of the school himself was a Jewish Christian from Palestine. He is working in a Gentile-Christian milieu and presupposes the Gentile mission and the solution of the question of the law. Here again a chronological framework between 60/70 and 100 is the most probable, and no convincing objections can be made to the activity of the author John in Asia Minor.

By contrast, as I have already said, a reconstruction of the development of the school before 60/70 seems to me to be quite impossible. It is utterly uncertain whether the elder John already had pupils before he came to Asia Minor and whether he was accompanied by them when he arrived there. We know virtually nothing specific about his personal pre-history. In all probability the school was first founded as such in Asia Minor after the teacher had moved there. Nowhere is there any sign of a transplanting of the school as a group, say from Palestine, Transjordan, Syria or Phoenicia.[88] The stages of development which scholars want to reconstruct in Johannine christology from a Jewish-Christian apocalyptic Son of Man messianology to a high christology orientated on the Father sending the pre-existent Son relate to the formation of christology in the primitive church generally and cannot be shown to be a specifically Johannine way of thinking.

4. The person and development of the head of the school and its relation to the 'beloved disciple'

The question of the origin of the head of the school, John the 'elder', is therefore to be kept separate from the 'history of the school', which cannot be traced back beyond 70/60 CE. Here of course we find ourselves on the thin ice of hypotheses which are difficult to prove. So I intend what I am going on to say as no more than very hypothetical considerations.

The fact that the Gospel contains numerous pointers towards Jerusalem has already been commented on often. From ch.5 (or 7) onwards it is there and in its immediate surroundings that all events take place, with increasing drama: Jesus' appearance in Galilee offers merely a relatively short introduction to this, which is already interrupted by the first journey to Jerusalem (and Judaea) in 2.13-4.3. The Johannine Jesus even baptizes in Judaea (3.22; cf.4.1-3). This special and deliberate stress on the southern province and the capital is one of the reasons which make it extremely improbable that the Gospel was written or even prompted by a Galilean disciple. The balance of the activity is shifted completely to Jerusalem, in contrast to the synoptic tradition. In its topographical (and historical) information about Jerusalem and Judaea the Gospel is far superior to the Synoptics.

That the author comes from the upper class in Jerusalem could follow from the marked 'aristocratic' character of the work, which has nothing of the 'aura of poverty' surrounding Galilean peasants and fishermen. We find the term *ptōchos* only in the anointing scene in 12.5-8 and in 13.29, both times in connection with Judas. John uses it in a more restricted sense than the Synoptic Gospels. No wonder that in the letter the 'elder' has to emphasize responsibility for those in distress over against the enthusiastic and anti-social indifference of his apostate pupils. It is a result of his own tendency, which in the end became dangerous for his own group.[89] The wedding at Cana takes place on a prosperous estate, social problems recede completely into the background and by contrast an air of luxury pervades the whole story. D.F.Strauss already called it a 'luxury miracle'.[90] The relatively few people who have dealings with Jesus – leaving aside those who are healed: the blind beggar and the paralysed man in Bethesda[91] – belong to the upper class: the royal steward (*basilikos*) in

Capernaum,[92] Nicodemus, the Pharisee and 'ruler of the Jews',[93] the two sisters Mary and Martha and their brother Lazarus in Bethany,[94] and Joseph of Arimathea, whom along with Nicodemus the author probably reckons to be one of the secret believers from the circle of the leaders of the people who do not confess their faith 'for fear of the Jews'.[95] Finally, mention should be made here of the mysterious 'other disciple' who gains direct access to the palace of Annas, at that time the most influential man in Jerusalem, because he was well acquainted with him or a friend of his (18.15f.: *ēn gnōstos tō archierei*). He can therefore introduce Peter into the palace. We should have no doubt that the beloved disciple is meant here (see above 73 n. 22).

This brings us back to the figure of the 'beloved disciple', who indeed appears only on Jesus' last day, and then again in the last appearance in Galilee. At least the editors associated him with the author of the Gospel, i.e. in my view with John the 'Elder'. From him, standing as he does closest to Jesus in an ideal way and as the more successful 'rival' of Peter, the idiosyncratically 'wholly other' Fourth Gospel takes on its authority, which is meant to make it superior to the Synoptic-Petrine Gospels and their Jesus tradition. It seeks to see the 'history' of Jesus better, in the right *taxis*, order (according to Papias), and at the same time in a much deeper christological understanding (see above, 21 and 157 n. 118; 69ff.).

The difficult and indeed almost insoluble question is whether there are historical points of contact which make a connection between the beloved disciple and John the elder conceivable – over and above the identification of the beloved disciple and the elder made by the authors in the last verses (21.20-25). First of all I should point out briefly that with the young man in Gethsemane (14.51f.) the earlier rival Gospel according to Mark similarly contains an enigmatic 'signature' in the passion narrative which could point to the author, though no such claim to authority is associated with it as there is in the case of the beloved disciple. Possibly this 'predecessor' in Mark who is so enigmatic to us today, but whom the author of the Fourth Gospel could evaluate much better at the end of the first century, was a model for the introduction of the much more effective 'beloved disciple'. We could also go on to ask – as was often done earlier – whether the report of Polycrates of Ephesus in his letter to Victor of Rome about John 'who was a priest and wore the high-priestly plate on his forehead' is connected with John 18.16, 'he was known (or related) to the high priest', indeed whether Polycrates, who was born about 125 CE and bound to earlier Asian Christianity by many ties of family relationships, and of course knew very much more than he writes in the letter, wanted in this way to indicate that the disciple 'who reclined on the Lord's breast' was, like John the Baptist, of priestly descent.[96]

Even if we doubt John of Ephesus's direct authorship of the Apocalypse in the time of Domitian, the report of his stay on Patmos is to be taken seriously in historical terms. It is surely no legendary fiction. How otherwise would one arrive at this very small unknown island in the Aegean, about forty miles west of Miletus? Insignificant provincials were not banished to islands; even among Roman citizens that was reserved for members of the upper class. For serious crimes – and banishment was a possibility only in such cases – ordinary people were either executed or deported to the mines as state slaves.[97] Two high priests, Ishmael and Helkias, were kept in Rome as hostages in 61/62, and Ishmael was subsequently banished to Cyrene, where he was later beheaded.[98] For John to be banished to Patmos indicates that he had high social status. However, the dating and duration of the banishment are uncertain. Irenaeus mentions the last years of Domitian; this time was probably significant for the Johannine school and for the composition of the Johannine corpus generally, but might not the event have taken place earlier, at a time when Roman provincial justice was not yet as strict against Christians as it was in the time of Ignatius and Pliny the Younger, when adherents of the new superstition (and especially their leaders) were sentenced to death? Might the enforced stay of John the elder on Patmos have encouraged the rise of docetist secessionists in the school, or did it already happen in late Neronian or early Flavian times? One can only guess. I personally tend towards the latter possibility.

The Apocalypse, which as a literary work seems to be more peripheral to the school, contains further indications. First, its style is more strongly marked by Hebraisms than the Gospel; even the numerous allusions to the Old Testament depend more on the Hebrew text than on the Septuagint; and large parts of it point directly to Palestinian apocalyptic tradition.[99] Secondly, the John who speaks there is depicted as a prophet and in no way as an apostle. The twelve apostles are authorities of the past. Their author does not make the claim that the John who receives the revelation of Jesus Christ as a Christian prophet himself belonged to the circle of the Twelve.[100] Nevertheless he appears as an inspired and indisputable authority, who wrote with the claim of creating a sacrosanct 'holy scripture'.[101] A late dating of the exile on Patmos has the further difficulty that a real persecution under Domitian has become very doubtful. I am therefore inclined to presuppose an earlier date between about 68 and 70 when eschatological expectation was very fervent – as Mark 13 shows. Is it so improbable to suppose that the Apocalypse – archaic as it is – was written in this earlier period by John 'the elder' but reworked and edited by his pupils after his death? Or was it a pseudepigraphic work by a pupil? In the former case we have to look for a further theological development of the author in the direction of an eschatology more strongly orientated on the present and a linguistic development towards a better knowledge of Greek *koine*. Why should this not be possible over twenty or thirty years? In the author's last years, during his confrontation with the secessionists, we would understandably find once again a return to earlier positions. The 'progressive' who became more 'conservative' in the crisis: is this not quite a realistic hypothesis? At all events, the Apocalypse belongs to the Johannine corpus, and the John in Rev.1.8; 20.8 denotes the same person as the 'John' in the title of the Gospel and in the letters.

In the Gospel things are no less complicated and ambivalent. The title apostle does not appear at all, the Twelve appear only once in the consolidation of the disciples in Galilee after the eucharistic discourse which causes offence and in the closer definition of Thomas as 'one of the Twelve'; otherwise the Gospel speaks only of 'disciples', seventy-eight times in all, more often than the other Gospels.[102] The terminology 'John the disciple of the Lord', typical of Asia Minor, here seems to receive its substantiation. There is no mention of the beloved disciple in the context of the two passages which refer to the Twelve. It remains unclear whether the evangelist presupposes only the Twelve in the farewell discourses. In 13.1 only *hoi idioi*, his own, appears, which is familiar from the prologue (1.11), where it means God's 'own' people in the Old Testament. When in 15.27 Jesus says that the disciples bear witness 'because you were with me from the beginning', this *ap'archēs* does not mean 'since the baptism of John', as it does in Acts 1.21, but as in I John 1.1ff. refers to the origin of their testimony in the person and word of the Son of God. The author names only nine disciples in the Gospel: Andrew, Peter, Philip, Nathanael (who is not attested by the Synoptics, but is perhaps comparable with Matthew[103] in Johannine garb), then, very late, Thomas, who has a favourable position only in Acts 1.13 in a pair with Philip,[104] once, in the farewell discourse, Judas 'not Iscariot';[105] also Judas the betrayer, and only in the appendix 21.2 'the sons of Zebedee'. The references of 11.16; 14.5,22 and 21.2 show how naturally the Gospel presupposes the Synoptic narrative tradition and at the same time sets itself above it in a sovereign way. In addition there are the anonymous beloved disciple and again in 21.2 the 'two other disciples'. This vagueness is deliberate (see above, 77ff.).

The unknown author of the First Gospel already changes the publican Levi into Matthew and adds 'the publican' to Matthew in the catalogue of disciples. There may be oral tradition behind this. On the basis of the title *euangelion kata Matthaion* the reader can identify the author in the Gospel and thus recognize it as the first apostolic one. Its author becomes the tax collector, who was called by Jesus in Capernaum.[106]

The editors of the Fourth Gospel, who did their work about ten to fifteen years later and for whom it was therefore even harder to establish their Gospel as an 'apostolic' one, are not so open-minded. On the basis of the 'picture puzzle' in 21.2 the author, who is said to have been very close to Jesus, the only witness at the cross, the first at the tomb, the ideal disciple *par excellence*, who is also said to have long survived Peter – maybe by about a generation – could be one of the sons of Zebedee, and indeed because of the title of the Gospel could be John the apostle of the Synoptic Gospels – but need not be, for there are also some features which tell against this; he could just as well be one of the two anonymous disciples, indeed that might be more likely. As we have a guessing game at the beginning of the Gospel with the unknown disciple of John the Baptist and colleague of Andrew, so at the end we have another in 21.1,7,20ff. with the beloved disciple and his identification. The editors – like the author – want the riddle to remain unsolved, the issue to be left open.

So they take the reader some way towards the sons of Zebedee but refuse, indeed prevent, a truly unequivocal identification. This feature, too, is one of the deliberate contradictions in the Gospels. The redactors could truly have made things easier for themselves and their readers. The Gospel of Peter, which came into being about twenty or thirty years later, and which already makes powerful use of the Fourth Gospel, makes Peter speak clearly and unambiguously in the first person. Here all problems are solved. The same is true of the Protevangelium of James, where the pseudepigraphical 'author' introduces himself: 'But I, James, who have written down this story . . .' (25.1), and of the Childhood Gospel of Thomas, which begins: 'I, Thomas, the Israelite, announce and make known to all' (1.1). Both Gospels may have been written in the middle of the second century. Even with the mystification over its author, the Fourth Gospel is completely outside this framework.

In my view this is because the editors did not want simply to identify one specific individual – a certain John – as the true disciple. He was meant to be and remain 'ambivalent'.

Franz Overbeck had already pointed to the paradigmatic significance of John the Baptist for the Fourth Gospel.[107] In the Gospel according to John, in contrast to the Synoptic Gospels, John the Baptist is the 'primal disciple', the first true witness to Jesus. His testimony already contains the whole message of salvation in a nutshell. Because he comes before Jesus, on the one hand he belongs among the Old Testament witnesses to Jesus like Abraham, Moses or Isaiah. However, on the other hand by giving testimony to the present Jesus he is in some way already a disciple of Jesus.

It is therefore only consistent for the Gospel that the first two disciples of Jesus should come from the circle of John the Baptist, indeed should be led to Jesus by the testimony of John the Baptist before Jesus' call. Those familiar with the synoptic tradition – the author simply presupposes knowledge of it – could draw conclusions from the way in which just as one of the two disciples of John who are mentioned, Andrew, passed the message about Jesus on to his brother Simon Peter, so the same thing happened with the anonymous second member of the pair, and that this other unknown person was John, who led his brother James to Jesus. For the four appear in the sequence Simon, Andrew/ James and John in the call stories in Mark and Matthew.[108] However, that remains only one possibility: the hearer (or reader) could also leave the question open, for the sons of Zebedee are not mentioned until the additional chapter, in 21.2, so that only someone familiar with Mark and Matthew misses them. Because we can presuppose that the school and the audience knew these Gospels, I believe that that the editor(s) (and of course the author) meant them to be missed.

In 21.2, as I have already said, the audience again has a choice: either one can start with the title of the Gospel and identifies the beloved disciple, who now according to 21.24 is also the author, with John the son of Zebedee, or one can identify him with one of the two other disciples, who in that case similarly bore the typical Jewish name John, which was very popular in Jewish Palestine (see above, 109f.). In the latter case there would have been two different Johns, one of them belonging to the wider circle of disciples, just as – above all if one includes the brothers of Jesus – there were not just two but at least three Judases, Simons or Jameses[109] in the lists of disciples in the Gospels.

Did the final redactor(s), who composed at least the last verses of the beloved disciple passages in ch.21, starting from John the Baptist the primal disciple, quite deliberately project two different Johns on to this shimmering ideal form and combine them: John the son of Zebedee, who therefore may not appear elsewhere in the Gospel, and John the presbyter, head of the Johannine school, who came from the Jerusalem aristocracy?

This would mean that this figure has a double aspect; not, however, like a Janus head looking in two directions but like a photograph which has been exposed twice, containing the pictures of two different persons merged together on the same film. First it shows the face of the second man after Peter in the earliest community and then that of the founder and head of the Johannine school, John the elder, of whom the tradition said that he too had been one of Jesus' disciples. First, then, that of an 'old disciple' of great repute who later became a martyr, and then that of quite a young hearer of Jesus, who later settled in Asia Minor as a result of the turmoil of the Jewish war, as did Philip, who was probably close to him. Did this younger John appeal to the older John as his teacher and thus prepare for the 'immortalizing' of the two persons in the one beloved disciple?

This hypothesis may sound fantastic. But the Fourth Gospel as a whole is a 'fantastic' book, deliberately full of more mysteries and more provocative contradictions than are found in other works of earliest Christian literature.

In reality it is quite simply a matter of understanding in a meaningful way the manifold attestation of the second century to the Johannine corpus and to the statements of the Johannine writings.

There are too many historical reasons against supposing that the Gospel was composed by John the son of Zebedee, which was the predominant view from the middle of the second century on.[110] They have already been given: this Gospel cannot come from a Galilean fisherman, and is also hard to reconcile with the significance that John had for a long time in the Jerusalem community as one of the three pillars (Gal.2.9). Its abrupt dissociation from the Synoptic tradition would similarly be inexplicable. Granted, I would not unconditionally accept the argument that a disciple standing close to Jesus and an eyewitness could not have written a Gospel which deals so violently with historical reality and reshaped it radically in favour of the proclamation of the pre-existent and exalted Son of God in the figure of Jesus. The great mistake of the nineteenth-century critics and apologists of the Gospel was that they transferred their own, modern, understanding of history and historicity to a first-century Palestinian author, who did not think in our categories of 'historical' and 'unhistorical' but in a 'haggadic' way and within the categories of higher religious truth – and precisely for that reason preferred to write a kind of 'theological poetry' rather than 'brute facts'.

In his old age, Plato made hardly less violent changes to the teaching of the 'historical Socrates' in his late dialogues in favour of quite a new understanding of philosophical truth. Can we forbid John what was allowed to Plato (no one denies that he was a real disciple of Socrates)? We should on no account project our very modern understanding of historical reality on to ancient authors here. If Paul, who became a Christian a few years after the ministry of Jesus, had earlier received his education as a pupil of learned Pharisees in Jerusalem, and after his conversion, between about 33 and 50 CE, was surely several times in personal contact with eyewitnesses, including Peter and the physical brother of Jesus,[111] could develop his quite specific high christology, are we to deny it to a disciple of Jesus who had grown old, some fifty, sixty or even seventy years later? Anyone who still adheres to the authorship of the Gospel by the son of Zebedee cannot in so doing rescue the historical trustworthiness of the Fourth Gospel, which was the most controversial problem in earlier generations of Johannine research: in most parts the Gospel really is important and ingenious, 'inspired' christological 'poetry' and not real 'history'.

But what one would have to concede to the son of Zebedee can even less be denied 'John the elder, the disciple of the Lord'. However, we can only make conjectures about his earlier fortunes before his activity in Asia Minor.[112] His work and name make it probable that he comes from Jewish Palestine, possibly from the priestly aristocracy in Jerusalem; the extreme age at which he died around 100 and the designation 'disciple of the Lord' in Papias, together with his own claim to be an eyewitness, suggest that in some way as a young man he came into close contact with Jesus in the Holy City and was deeply influenced by him. Indeed his Gospel describes how the proclamation of Jesus even had an effect on the Jerusalem aristocracy. On the other hand he knows that the real faith and understanding of Christ is a gift of the Spirit Paraclete after Easter, a point which is already prepared for by the Marcan theory of the disciples' permanent failure to understand.[113] How far the specific 'beloved disciple' passages go back wholly to him and how far they are partially shaped by the redactional work of the editor(s) is hard to decide. If we begin from ch.21, the latter seems a possibility which cannot entirely be excluded.

Given the unique way in which the figures of John son of Zebedee and the teacher of the school and author of the Gospel are deliberately superimposed in a veiled way, it would be conceivable that with the 'beloved disciple' 'John the elder' wanted to point more to the son of Zebedee, who for him was an ideal, even *the* ideal disciple, in contrast to Peter, whereas in the end the pupils impressed on this enigmatic figure the face of *their* teacher by identifying him with the author in order to bring the Gospel as near to Jesus as possible. Therefore I cannot believe that this ideal figure is pure fiction. In the teaching of the Evangelist and in the discussions of the school the beloved disciple had not only an ideal but also some kind of 'historical' significance which was – ultimately – related to two figures: the 'apostle' John from the Twelve and the author himself. At least in the scenes in the high priest's palace and by the cross we might consider whether here features have not entered in of a disciple who did not belong to the group of Twelve but to the priestly aristocracy in Jerusalem. Nor are 'his own', *hoi idioi*, in 13.1 limited to the group of the Twelve. Indeed, we must ask how his pupils came to claim this of the head of the school and the author of the work.

Here one thing seems to me to be quite probable. The Fourth Gospel is not a completely free 'Jesus poem', however much the theological concern of the author has altered, indeed we might even say violated, his personal recollections and church tradition, and with them historical reality, so that it is visible only as a shadow which we can therefore barely verify any longer. Here we must distinguish between those traits which are historically plausible and others which remain chiefly suppositions. An inability to prove the historicity of something does not mean that it is pure unhistorical fiction. Certainly the evangelist is not narrating historical, banal recollections of the past but the rigorously interpretative spirit-paraclete leading into truth, which has the last word throughout the work.[114]

Nevertheless, we find features in the Fourth Gospel which some-times sound more realistic than in the Marcan-Petrine outline. In my view these include the lengthy activity by Jesus of at least two years covering three Passovers; the original connection with John the Baptist, who is also the intermediary with his first disciples, which perhaps even led to Jesus beginning his own activity as one of the Baptist group; the numerous journeys to Jerusalem – according to Mark, too, Jesus already has close personal connections with Bethany;[115] individual happenings in Jerusalem; the significance of Annas as the *éminence grise* who pulls the strings,[116] and finally the even greater importance of the messianic question in the final arguments. The totally unmessianic Jesus whom people attempted to read out of the Synoptic Gospels was a typically modern, but nevertheless fundamental, mistake of German scholarship. Perhaps the controversy with the authorities in Jerusalem was drawn out longer and took a more dramatic course than the few scenes in Mark indicate.

Not only Schleiermacher in the first decades of the nineteenth century[117] but even Bultmann in the 1920s reckoned with the possibility that 'Johannine Christianity' represents an earlier type than Synoptic Christianity. By this he meant 'that the appearance and proclamation of Jesus were perhaps more closely connected with the Gnostic-Baptist movement in terms of which the Gospel of John is to be understood than the Synoptic tradition suggests'.[118] Cullmann, who started from similar considerations, has attempted to outline a development of the Johannine circle which begins from the Hellenists of Acts.[119] But is not the 'Johannine circle' in the – decisive – early period between 30 and 60 CE reduced to the former fortunes of 'John the elder, the disciple of the Lord', later the head of the school in Ephesus, which are unknown to us?

I shall close with some very hypothetical comments – how could they be otherwise? – on this figure to whom we ultimately owe the Johannine corpus. Hardly anything in them is new; most of the suppositions can be found in the older literature, especially in English.

If he died about 100 he may have been born in Jerusalem around 15 CE as a member of the priestly aristocracy. In the second century we know several Christian authorities who died at an advanced age: Polycarp, Pothinus of Lyons and the legendary nephew of Jesus, Symeon of Jerusalem. Another paradigm from a single school is provided by some members of the Tübingen school, which was so hostile over accepting the authenticity and an earlier date for the Gospel and the letters, and even the existence of John the elder. Eduard Zeller (22 January 1814 – 19 March 1908) died at the age of ninety-four; Adolf Hilgenfeld (2 June 1823 – 12 January 1907) at the age of eighty-three; and Gustav Volkmar (12 January 1809 – 9 January 1893) nearly at the age of eighty-four. Why should we not believe in the existence of this 'old man John', who was an eye-witness and died in the time of Trajan?[120]

The revival movement of John the Baptist appealed to him as a very young lad and he was attracted by the activity of Jesus. We should not be put off by what seems to us to be the rather young age of this figure. Josephus in his autobiography acknowledges that at fourteen he had already reached a very high level of learning and that by sixteen he 'determined to gain personal experience of the several sects into which our nation is divided'. 'Not content, however, with the experience so gained,' he became the 'devoted disciple of the Jewish ascetic named Bannus and stayed with him for three years'. After all these experiences he decided to become a Pharisee. Surely the young John in Jerusalem was no less a seeker of truth than Josephus had been.[121]

Already in personal contact with Jesus, he witnessed Jesus' fate in Jerusalem at close quarters and still at quite a young age belonged to the wider group of adherents (or disciples) and then to the earliest community. Presumably he had closer connections with John the son of Zebedee, and also with Philip – who was probably somewhat older – from the group of Seven, who had perhaps moved over from the Twelve into the Hellenist community. Possibly he had also, like Philip, left Jerusalem because of Jewish pressure. The sharpness of the controversy with the Jews may, among other things, go back to early traumatic experiences of this kind. The link with Philip could have aroused his interest in the mission to the Samaritans and to the Gentiles.

The tense situation during the fifties and early sixties before the outbreak of the Jewish war, with the trial of James and other Jewish Christians in Jerusalem in 62 CE instigated by Annas II, son of the Annas in John 18, the terrorism of the Sicarii and riots in Hellenistic Caesarea,[122] compelled him, like Philip, to emigrate to Asia Minor in the early sixties, where at about the age of fifty he founded his school, which flourished for about thirty-five years. Then among his pupils in Asia Minor he was regarded in later years as the 'old man' and as 'the beloved disciple of Jesus' or 'the disciple of the Lord'. During the earlier period of his stay in Asia for a time he was exiled to Patmos.

His authority grew because he survived most or all other disciples. In his quite original theological work, which is a fruit of his old age, and in which typical 'Jewish Palestinian' reminiscences are combined with more 'Hellenistic', 'enthusiastic' and indeed even Pauline approaches into a great synthesis, the christological doctrinal development of primitive Christianity reaches its climax.

The fact that, thirty or forty years after his death, church tradition identified him with the son of Zebedee and two hundred years later gave him the unique honorific title *ho theologos*,[123]was a recognition of his unique theological achievement. Behind that his individual personality retreated to such a degree that down to the present day research has almost completely lost sight of it. But with the unique theological individuality of his work we should try to rediscover at least the shadow of this great teacher to whom the church owes a good part of its foundation.

Notes

I. The First Step towards an Approach: The Gospel in the Second Century

1. Preface to the conversations of Ulrich von Hutten, *Gesammelte Schriften* VII, ³1877, 556; original edition Leipzig 1860, XLIV: 'Might not this very Gospel itself be said to be that seamless robe of which it tells us, about which one may draw lots but which one may not divide?' Reprinted in W.F.Howard, *The Fourth Gospel in Recent Criticism and Interpretation*, London 1931, 258. For the dispute over the unity of the Gospel see below, 83ff.

2. R.E.Brown, *The Community of the Beloved Disciple*, New York, Ramsey and Toronto 1979; for other comparable attempts at a solution see Georg Richter, *Studien zum Johannesevangelium*, Regensburg 1977; J.Becker, *Das Evangelium des Johannes*, ÖTK 4.1, 1979, 25-61; J.Louis Martyn, *The Gospel of John in Christian History*, New York, Ramsey and Toronto 1979; id., *History and Theology in the Fourth Gospel*, Nashville ²1979; a different view is taken by K.Wengst, *Bedrängte Gemeinde und verherrlichter Christus. Der historische Ort des Johannesevangeliums als Schlüssel zu seiner Interpretation*, BThSt 5, Neukirchen ²1983. For criticism of these attempts see J.S.King, 'Is Johannine Archaeology really Necessary?', *EvQ* 56, 1984, 203-11; A.Dauer, 'Schichten im Johannesevangelium als Anzeichen von Entwicklungen in der (den) johanneischen Gemeinde(n) nach G.Richter', in *Die Kraft der Hoffnung. Festschrift für Alterzbischof DDr Joseph Schneider zum 80.Geburtstag*, Bamberg 1986, 62-83; U.Schnelle, *Antidoketische Christologie im Johannesevangelium*, FRLANT 144, 1987, 11ff., 49ff., 168ff., etc.; J.Kügler, *Der Jünger, den Jesus liebte*, SBB 16, 1988, 73ff.

3. Becker, *Evangelium* (n.2), 40-8: the question of authorship is 'nowadays... rightly seen as a peripheral question... and at all events of little significance for the understanding of John' (48). Similarly W.Marxsen, *Einleitung in das Neue Testament*, Gütersloh ²1978, 264. Cf. also R.Schnackenburg, *Das Johannesevangelium. Ergänzende Auslegung und Exkurse*, HTK IV, 4, 1984, 33: 'As the question of the authorship of the four writings, the language and theology of which belong closely together and yet which display unmistakable differences from one another, seems almost insoluble, one might shed more light on the literary development by reflection on the communities which are addressed.' – As if that were simpler! How 'old-fashioned' the subject of my investigation is can easily be seen from the Preface of R.T.Fortna, *The Fourth Gospel and its Predecessor*, Philadelphia 1988, XI: ' I intended at first to entitle

this work *The Evangelist John and His Predecessor*... Why then avoid speaking of the former in the title? Because... the provisional title was sexist, most obviously in the possessive pronoun "his" but also in using the traditional name "John." The feminist movement in biblical studies has convinced me that these conventions, supposedly innocent in intent and justified by the canon, must be given up. Just as we have no idea of the Evangelist's identity and name, so also of his or her gender. And like all of the Gospels, that according to "John" is in fact anonymous, its apostolic attribution added roughly a century after it was written and on spurious grounds. We cannot know even the degree of likelihood that the writer was a male. So the custom of calling "him" by the traditional name "John" ought to be abandoned.' Nevertheless, I think it is time to speak out against this or similar 'progress' towards an ahistorical nirvana.

4. See for example the judgment of E.Schwartz, *Gesammelte Schriften* 5, Berlin 1963, 175f.: 'Irenaeus was the first to set in motion, and perhaps even invented, the fable of the elderly John in Ephesus, the teacher of Polycarp in Smyrna, with refined untruthfulness, in order to place on his own head the halo of an indirect disciple of the apostle...' Ernst Haenchen, *The Gospel of John*, ed. R.W.Funk and U.Busse, Hermeneia, Philadelphia 1980, 9-13, gives a somewhat milder account, but one which is nevertheless condescending. For the 'fateful' role of Irenaeus see e.g. also B.W.Bacon, 'The Elder of Ephesus and the Elder John', *HibJ* 26, 1927/8, 112-34: 'For the confusion of the elder John with the Apostle John, Irenaeus is responsible...' (125). '...misunderstanding... his probably defective copy of Papias' (126). This American scholar's view may be taken as representative of many. In some modern introductions the testimony of Irenaeus is now completely disregarded. Thus in H.M.Schenke/K.M.Fischer, *Einleitung in die Schriften des Neuen Testaments II: Die Evangelien und die anderen neutestamentlichen Schriften*, Gütersloh 1979, 168-97. Instead, as the author is conjured up a 'prominent Christian Gnostic who, after living and working within Christian-Gnostic groups, and coming into contact with a Christianity that was bound more strongly to tradition, was involved in a process of rethinking with the aim of finding a connection with this Christianity and a place in it for himself and his group' (193): the testimonies of the fathers are suppressed and their place is taken by a modern 'critical' romance about the evangelist.

5. *Adv.haer.* 3.1.1 = Eusebius, HE 5.8.4: ἔπειτα Ἰωάννης, ὁ μαθητὴς τοῦ κυρίου, ὁ καὶ ἐπὶ τὸ στῆθος αὐτοῦ ἀναπέσων, καὶ αὐτὸς ἐξέδωκεν τὸ εὐαγγέλιον, ἐν Ἐφέσῳ τῆς Ἀσίας διατρίβων, cf. 2.22.5 = HE 3.23.3f.; 3.3.4 = HE 4.14.3-8; *Ep.ad Flor.*, HE 5.20.4-8, on John and his Gospel in Ephesus. As my former assistant Klaus Thornton shows in a dissertation, Irenaeus' information about the Gospels (3.1.1) probably comes from a list of writings in the community library in Rome, which Irenaeus knew from his visits to Rome. It bears a striking similarity to the information about authors in ancient library catalogues.

For the following all too brief account of the influence and attestation of the Fourth Gospel in the second century see W.von Loewenich, *Das Johannes-*

Verständnis im zweiten Jahrhundert, BZNW 13, 1932; J.N.Sanders, *The Fourth Gospel in the Early Church. Its Origin and Influence on Christian Theology up to Irenaeus*, Cambridge 1943; F.M.Braun, *Jean le Théologien et son Évangile dans l'église ancienne*, I, Paris 1959; R.Schnackenburg, *The Gospel of John*, I, Tunbridge Wells 1968, 77-91, 193,202; R.E.Brown, *The Gospel according to John*, AB 1966, LXXXVIII-XCII; C.K.Barrett, *The Gospel according to St John*, London [2]1978,62-6, 100-13; H.von Campenhausen, *The Formation of the Christian Bible*, London and Philadelphia 1972, Index, 336, s.v. The older nineteenth-century literature is indispensable: T.Zahn, *Geschichte des Neutestamentlichen Kanons* I.1-II.2, Erlangen 1880-1892; J.B.Lightfoot, *Essays on the Work entitled Supernatural Religion*, London and New York 1893; id., 'External Evidence for the Authenticity and Genuineness of St John's Gospel', in *Biblical Essays*, London and New York [2]1904, 45-122. Also impressive are the short study by an 'American outsider' to the European discussion of the time, Ezra Abbot, *The Authorship of the Fourth Gospel. External Evidences*, Boston 1880, and the thoroughgoing investigation by J.Drummond, *An Inquiry into the Character and Authorship of the Fourth Gospel*, London 1903, 72-351; V.H.Stanton, *The Gospels as Historical Documents, Part I, The Early Use of the Gospels*, Cambridge 1903, 18ff., 51-91, 162ff., etc. The co-founder of the Tübingen school, E.Zeller, 'Die äusseren Zeugnisse über das Dasein und den Ursprung des Vierten Evangeliums', *ThJb(T)* 4, 1845, 579-659; 6, 1847, 89-174, is extremely critical, with numerous untenable dates; see also the earlier Introductions to the New Testament: W.M.L.de Wette, *Lehrbuch der historisch-kritischen Einleitung in die kanonischen Schriften des Neuen Testaments*, [6]1980, 223-9; A.Hilgenfeld, *Historisch-kritische Einleitung in das Neue Testament*, 1875, 392ff., 682ff., 695ff; H.-J.Holtzmann, *Lehrbuch der historisch-kritischen Einleitung in das Neue Testament*, [2]1886, 477-88; B.Weiss, *Lehrbuch der Einleitung in das Neue Testament*, [2]1889, 609-21; A.Jülicher/E.Fascher, *Einleitung in das Neue Testament*, [7]1931, 390-423. As a rule the treatment in the modern introductions to the New Testament is inadequate. The Harvard dissertation by M.R.Hillmer, *The Gospel of John in the Second Century*, 1966, is one-sided and some of its judgments are unreliable; the learned but quite speculative article by J.J.Gunther, 'Early Identifications of Authorship of the Johannine Writings', *JEH* 31, 1980, 407-27, also discusses the sources with a preconceived view which leads to a polemical caricature of church developments in the second century; cf. also id., 'The Alexandrian Gospel and the Letters of John', *CBQ* 41, 1979, 581-603. There is an excellent account of the question of authorship in W.Bousset, 'Der Verfasser des Johannesevangeliums', *ThR* 8, 1905, 225-44, 277-95.

6. Against the slightly later information of Clement of Alexandria, who has the Gospel written still during Peter's lifetime, and the later church tradition, see M.Hengel, *Studies in the Gospel of Mark*, London and Philadelphia 1985, 1-30.

7. See n.5 above. For Papias' note see Hengel, *Studies in Mark* (n.6), 47ff.; Papias has his account from the presbyter John, see below, 17ff.

8. *Adv.haer.* 2.22.5 and 3.3.4 = Eusebius, HE 3.23.3f. For the legends on the death of John or his translation and his age (between 80 and 120

years) see R.A.Lipsius, *Die apokryphen Apostelgeschichten und Apostellegenden, Ergänzungsband,* 1890 (reprinted in Vol.I, 1976), 207, index s.v. 'Lebensausgang'.

9. The great acuteness which Bishop John A.T.Robinson, who died all too early, employs in his last work *The Priority of John,* London 1985, to overturn the almost unanimous testimony of the early church tradition is not enough to make his theory really convincing. However, his most learned book is an interesting example of the way in which many of the modern 'critical' arguments can be turned round. Even the Introduction by Schenke/Fischer (n.4), 197, tends towards a modified early date 'in the decade between 75 and 85 CE'. However, we have no reason to doubt the clear information of Irenaeus, which rests on earlier tradition. The sequence of the Gospels predominantly attested since the second century (in addition to Irenaeus cf. p⁴⁵ and p⁷²) with John at the end of the four Gospels supports this. I myself would date the Gospels as follows: Mark 69/70; Luke 75-80; Matthew 85-90; John c.100, or perhaps even very slightly later. The decisive factor here is the date of its editing and multiplication, i.e. distribution in the communities. There is no way in which we can put the Fourth Gospel very much earlier. Another factor against that is the transference of the title θεός to Christ and its relative historical distance from Palestinian Judaism before 70, which was more pluralistic than it is depicted as being in the Fourth Gospel, along with the final break with the synagogue (and conservative Jewish Christianity).

10. *Adv.haer.* 3.1.1 (above n.5) (= Eusebius, HE 4.14); 3.3.4 (= Eusebius, HE 3.23.4): Ἰωάννης ὁ τοῦ κυρίου μαθητὴς ἐν τῇ Ἐφέσῳ, cf. ibid., end. John remained in Ephesus until the time of Trajan: 'he is a truthful witness to the apostolic tradition'. For the composition of the Fourth Gospel see 3.8.3; 3.11.1-4,7,9; 3.15.2,5,8; 3.16.5 (author of the Gospel and letter); 3.16.8 (on I and II John as a unity); 3.22.2; 4.2.3;4.6.1;4.10.1; 5.18.2: *Johannes Domini discipulus, in Evangelio dicens…;* 5.33.3: *Quemadmodum Presbyteri meminerunt, qui Johannem discipulum Domini viderunt.* See already in 1.8.5 (with a quotation from the exposition of the prologue by Ptolemy, the disciple of Valentinus); 1.9.1-3; 1.16.3 (II John 11); 2.2.5; 2.22.3; *Epideixis* 43.94. For the Apocalypse see 4.30.4: *Johannes discipulus Domini vidit in Apocalypsi,* similarly 5.26.1; 1.26.3; 4.17.6; 4.20.11; 4.21.3; 5.28.2; 5.34.2; 5.35.2. The information which Irenaeus will have received from the 'Elder' is collected together in E.Preuschen, *Antilegomena,* Giessen ²1905, 101-7. For Irenaeus and the Johannine Corpus see J.Hoh, *Die Lehre des Hl.Irenäus über das Neue Testament,* NTA VII.4,5, 1919, 5ff., 32ff., 54ff., 150ff.

11. Hoh, *Irenäus* (n.10), 32f. However, Hoh is too concerned to make a close connection between the 'disciple John' and the apostles. In so doing he overlooks the special features of the terminology in Irenaeus. In 1.9.2 in the report on the exegesis of John by Ptolemy there is mention first of the evangelist and then, a few lines later, of the apostle. This will be based on Ptolemy's terminology, see above, 8; 3.3.4 end: the designation of John as witness to the tradition of the apostles would not necessarily in itself (strictly speaking) term him apostle, cf. also 2.22.5: *non solum Johannem, sed et alios*

apostolos viderunt; further 2.24.4 and 3.12.3,5. Peter and John in Acts 4.22; *Ep. ad Vict.*, Eusebius, HE 5.24.16: Polycarp, who had been together 'with John the disciple of our Lord and the other apostles'. Irenaeus would hardly have written such a sentence in a tense situation in which he was arguing for the Easter usage of the Christians of Asia Minor, i.e. the opposite side to the bishop of Rome, had this statement been his own invention. Cf. the similar formulae '...with the others who had seen the Lord' in a letter to an opponent, in *Ep ad Flor.*, Eusebius, HE 5.20.6 and Polycarp, ad Phil.9.1. For Irenaeus and John see also von Loewenich, *Johannes-Verständnis* (n.5), 115-41; Braun, *Jean le Théologien* (n.5), 331-4.

12. Thus the most recent work on John, a 1986 Münster Habilitationsschrift by J.W.Taeger, *Johannesapokalypse und johanneischer Kreis*, BZNW 51, 1989, 3. Without himself examining the sources and the most important secondary literature the author has evidently allowed himself to be led astray by the deficient and in part inaccurate account by Haenchen, *Gospel of John* (n.11), 6-19.

13. *Adv.haer.* 2.22.5, cf.1-6. This interpretation of John from Asia Minor is in itself in clear opposition to the Synoptic tradition as it is formulated in Luke 3.23, which Irenaeus similarly cites. The Valentinians (and also Basilides) are here on the side of Luke and the Synoptics. It remains uncertain whether this interpretation goes back to Papias, as is often conjectured. The argument that in that case one would have to expect a reference in Eusebius, who knew both works and in HE 3.23.3 cites the decisive passage about the unanimous testimony of all the ' "elders" who were in Asia with John the disciple of the Lord', is not conclusive, because Eusebius overlooks many things that do not interest him. Possibly this is a later (special) exegesis of John 8.57 with an anti-Gnostic character. Cf. also *Adv.haer.* 5.36.1f., where similarly an exegesis of John is attributed to the '*Presbyteri Apostolorum discipuli*'. Here there is more reason for dependence on Papias because of the parallelism of the statements to the Papias quotation in 5.33.3 which is directly connected with the testimony of 'the elders who saw John the disciple of the Lord' (cf. below n.17).

14. This 'unification' of the four Gospels directed against the threat by the Marcionite 'Gospel of unity' presupposes the recognized use of all of them in church worship. Here, as the fragment from Dura Europos shows (see Aland, *Synopsis* [13]1985, 493), Tatian uses the text of the Gospels with scrupulous exactitude. At that time, even before Irenaeus, apocryphal Gospels no longer play any essential role in worship. The letter of Bishop Serapion of Antioch to the Christians in Rhossus (Eusebius HE 6.12.206) shows that the use of the Gospel of Peter there was already an exceptional case. For the Diatessaron see Ephraem, *Commentaire de l'évangile concordant ou Diatessaron*, ed.L.Leloir, SC 121, 1966. A substantial number of pages of the Syriac Diatessaron commentary which have been recently acquired by the Chester Beatty Foundation are about to be published. The work begins with John 1.1 and ends with John 21.19-23 (and Luke 24.49); cf. Leloir, 16: 'Divers indices, et notamment le choix de l'evangéliste Jean pour commencer

et terminer le Diatesseron, permettent en outre de conclure que Tatian concevait le quatrième évangile comme la clef des synoptiques.'

15. Quoted in the *Chronicon paschale*, ed. L.Dindorf, Bonn 1832, I, 13f. = PG 92, 80C-81A; see also A.Harnack, *Geschichte der altchristlichen Literatur, Erster Teil, Die Überlieferung und der Bestand*, 1893, 243-6 (244f.); *Méliton de Sardes, Sur la Pâque (et fragments)*, ed. O.Perler, SC 123, 1966, 244-7. The fragments show the degree to which Apollinaris prized the Fourth Gospel. For the question of Easter and Apollinaris see H.Merkel, *Die Widersprüche zwischen den Evangelien*, WUNT 13, 1971, 37-41.

16. In addition to the edition by Perler cited above, see S.G.Hall, *Melito of Sardis, On Pascha and Fragments*, Oxford 1979. Among other things, a work 'On the Devil and the Apocalypse of John' is also attributed to him, see Eusebius, HE 4.26.2. Possibly these are two titles, as Rufinus and Jerome distinguish two works: see 171f. n. 69 below. While the refined and highly poetic Asiatic rhetoric of Melito's work on the passion prevents direct quotations from the Gospels, he does work in the Fourth Gospel with the Synoptics in a harmonizing way. 25,501: John 1.32-37; 44f.,411f.: John 1.17; 46,50,771: John 1.29, 34 cf.36; 62: John 20.28; 195-8: John 11.50-52; 257f.: John 3.12; 288ff.; John 2.19ff.; 8.23; 311f,781ff.: John 1.1-3.14; 360f.: John 8.44; I John 3.15; 397: John 19.28-30,36; 473ff.: John 8.34-36; 3.19; I John 2.9; John 5.24; I John 3.14; 511,550f., 656: John 11.17-44; 563: John 6.63. As in Apollinaris, the much-discussed text 565-80 clearly presupposes the death of Jesus on the evening of 14 Nisan, i.e. at the time of the passover sacrifice, and shortly before the beginning of the passover meal. Jesus dies and is buried while Israel is celebrating the passover feast as a feast of joy. On this see Hall, *Melito*, p.43 n.45; 590f.: John 1.18; 5.37; 9.35-41; 595-7: John 1.4f.; 549, 653f.: John 9.1-7; 565, 692, 694, 704: John 19.20 and 19.14 (the time of the crucifixion and nearness to the city: Melito, who had visited the Holy Land and knew the place [Eusebius, HE 4.26.14], makes this ἐν μέσῳ Ἰερουσαλήμ, i.e. in the midst of Aelia Capitolina! 709 τίτλος: John 19.19f.; cf. also the 'I am' sayings, 769ff., 733, 776: John 11.25; 14.6; 774: John 8.12; 778: John 6.39, 44, 54; 779: John 12.32; 14.3; 780: John 14.8f.; 790f.: John 5.27; 17.2,5, cf.3.17; 12.47; 792f.: Rev.1.8f.; 21.6. For the fragments see fr.6* (Hall, 68-70) lines 25f.: the period of Jesus' activity as three years (according to Anastasius Sinaita). However, the authenticity is disputed by Hall; fr.9* (Hall, 74), 7f., cf. John 19.17; fr.16b* (Hall, 84f.), lines 3, 6, 7: the participles σαρκωθείς, ὑψωθείς, δοξασθείς as basic christological statements (see below 151 n. 76).

17. *Essays on the Work entitled Supernatural Religion*, London and New York 1893, 3ff., 194-8. M.J.Routh, *Reliquiae Sacrae*, Oxford ²1846, I, 10, already includes this tradition among the fragments of Papias. F.Loofs, *Theophilus von Antiochien...*, TU 46.2, 1930, 310ff., 325ff., 376, 383f. in particular wanted to derive the whole 'Asia Minor tradition about the *seniores*' from the work of Papias, see also n.10 above. For the Martyrs of Lyons see Eusebius, HE 5.1.15: John 16.2; 5.1.22: John 19.34 cf.4.10; 7.38; 5.1.48: John 17.12; 5.1.23: I John 4.18; 5.1.10: Rev.14.4; 5.1.58: Rev.22.11.

18. For the letter of Polycrates of Ephesus see Eusebius, HE 5.25.2-7;

J.Quasten, 'Osterfeststreit', *LTK* 7, 1962, 1273-5; B.Lohse, *Das Passafest der Quartodecimaner*, BFCT II, 54, 1953; against this, wrongly, W.Huber, *Passa und Ostern*, BZNW 35, 1969, 21-5; cf. Hall, *Melito* (n.15), 43 n.45 against Huber and Perler. It follows from the Letter of Polycrates, Eusebius, HE 5.24.6, that Melito was a Quartodeciman.

19. Gunther, 'Early Identifications' (n.5), 410. For Montanism see P.de Labriolle, *La crise montaniste*, Paris 1913, 37ff.: Oracles 1-3; 54ff.: Or.8; 69f.: Or.12 + 13; 86ff.: Or.17; 129ff. on the Paraclete sayings of John 14-16: 'Cette description du Paraclet, de son rôle, Montan au gré de ses fidèles, y répondait trait pour trait' (133). H.G.Opitz, 'Montanus', *PW* 16.1, 1933, 206-10; H.Paulsen, 'Die Bedeutung des Montanismus für die Herausbildung des Kanons', *VigChr* 32, 1978, 19-52; W.Schneemelcher in *New Testament Apocrypha* 2, London 1965, 686ff., the prophetic sayings 1-3; 8 (cf. John 21.19); 9; 15 (Eusebius, HE 5.16.17); however, the separation of 'prophetic' and 'apocalyptic' movements by Schneemelcher seems to me to be a mistake. Sayings 11 and 12 presuppose the influence of the Apocalypse and the expectation of the imminent end.

20. Loewenich, *Johannes-Verständnis* (n.5), 23f.; B.Dehandschutter, BETL 52, 1979, 217, 233-58 (239f., 251ff.) is too cautious. For the martyrs of Lyons see n.17 above.

21. Epiphanius, *Pan.*51.4.5-12.6 (quotation 4.5); also the account by Dionysius Bar Salibi, in *Apocalypsim*, CSCO 60 Script.Syri 20, trans.I Sedlacek, Louvain 1962, 1f.; cf. A.Bludau, *Die ersten Gegner der Johannesschriften*, BSt(F) 22, 1928; de Labriolle, *Crise montaniste* (n.19), 190-202; Merkel, *Widersprüche* (n.15), 34ff.; Braun, *Jean le Théologien* (n.5), 147ff.; 34-7: S.G.Hall, 'Aloger', *TRE* 2, 1978, 290-5; for the Zahn quotation see his article 'Aloger', *PW*[3] 1, 1896, 386-8 (387); similarly already Abbot, *Authorship* (n.5), 18: 'The fact that they ascribed the Fourth Gospel to Cerinthus, a heretic of the first century, contemporary with the Apostle John, shows that they could not pretend that this Gospel was a recent one.' Gunther, 'Early Identifications' (n.5), 411f., excessively exaggerates the significance of the 'Alogoi' (the equivocal term first appears in Epiphanius, who invented it), who were perhaps limited to Gaius and his circle.

22. *Acta mart.Scil.*16 (in the dialogue with the Roman governor): *ego imperium huius seculi non cognosco*, cf. John 18.36. The *libri* in v.12 will primarily mean the four Gospels. *Acta Perp. et Fel.* ch.5: I John 1.1,3; ch.12: Rev.4; ch.19: John 16.24; *Muratorian Canon* lines 9-34: the distinctive text stresses the assent of all the apostles to the Fourth Gospel and indicates the problem of its differences from the other Gospels, perhaps because there were still difficulties in Rome around 200. For the letters see 23ff., 68f. Hippolytus, the pupil of Irenaeus, calls John 'apostle and disciple of the Lord' in *De Antichristo* 18 (GCS Achelis 23); for him there is no longer any question that John wrote the Gospel, letter and Revelation.

23. The fact is readily overlooked that Celsus (or his Jewish informant) knew the Gospel of John well and engaged in vigorous polemic against it: see Origen, *c.Cels* 1.70, cf. John 4.6f.; 21.13 (on this see R.Bader, *Der*

ΑΛΗΘΗΣ ΛΟΓΟΣ *des Kelsos*, Stuttgart 1940, 61f.); 2.30f. cf. John 1.1-14 (Bader, 70f.); 2.37f. cf. John 19.28 (Bader, 73); 2.47 cf. John 8.44f.; 12.31; 14.30; 16.11; I John 3.8; 2.49 cf. John 8.11; 14.6; 2.55 cf. John 20.1, 11-18; 2.27 (Bader, 79); 6.17 cf. John 4.24 (Bader, 171). Celsus counts it with Matthew, Mark, Luke and the letters of Paul among the acknowledged Christian writings, see Origen, *c.Celsum* 2.74: ἐκ τῶν ὑμετέρων συγγραμμάτων, from which he draws his arguments. Cf. also 2.27 (Bader, 69): his criticism of the 'three-, four- and manifold' form of the Gospel. For an early date around 160 see H.-U.Rosenbaum, 'Zur Datierung von Celsus' ΑΛΗΘΗΣ ΛΟΓΟΣ', *VigChr* 26, 1972, 102-11 and J.Schwartz, 'Du Testament de Lévi au Discours véritable de Celse', *RHPR* 40, 1960, 126-45 (137).

24. For Clement of Alexandria see his famous verdict from *Hypotyposes* Book VI = Eusebius, HE 6.14.7 on the Gospel of John as πνευματικὸν εὐαγγέλιον. In the famous legend *Quis dives?* 42 he speaks in a matter-of-fact way (in contrast to Irenaeus and Polycrates) of the 'apostle John' (42.1) or simply of the 'apostle' (42.10). That seems to be Alexandrian tradition (see n.45 below). For the *Physiologus* see K.Alpers, 'Untersuchungen zum griechischen Physiologus und den Kyraniden', in *All Geschöpf ist Zung' und Mund*, ed.H.Reinitzer = *Vestigia Bibliae* 6, 1984, 13-87. The time of composition is between 180 and 200, see pp. 14, 27, 38. John 19.34 is presupposed in the symbol of the pelican, ch.4 (ed. F.Sbardone, Rome 1936, 17ff.); John 10.18 in ch.7 (25ff.); John 3.14 in ch.3 (15); John 1.14 in ch.1 (4) and ch.22 (82); John 1.11 in ch.32 (105); John 1.29 in ch.41 (127); John 1.29 in ch.44 (135). See also D.Offermanns, *Der Physiologus nach den Handschriften G und M*, Beiträge zur Klassischen Philologie 22, 1966, 31.7; 38.1ff.; 84.16; 104.8; 116.18f.; 128.8; 134.17f.; 148.2f. For Poimandres see J.Büchli, *Der Poimandres. Ein paganisiertes Evangelium*, WUNT 2R. 37.

25. *Ad Autolycum* 2.22: '... and all those inspired of the Spirit, of whom John says: "In the beginning was the Word"', cf. 2.10: John 1.3; 1.14; John 20.27. Jerome reports several times that Theophilus wrote a commentary on a harmony of the Gospels (?). For the problems of this account see Harnack, *Geschichte der altchristlichen Literatur* (n.15), I, 2, 498f.: *Ep. ad Aglasiam* 121: '...qui quattuor evangelistarum in unum opus dicta compingens'. If this report is reliable, Theophilus would have also been the second commentator on the Fourth Gospel, after Heracleon.

26. For the parallels see R.A.Culpepper, 'The Odes of Solomon and the Gospel of John', *CBQ* 35, 1973, 298-322: 'It is clear that the Odes and John contain innumerable and impressive parallels' (320). This sentence deserves full assent. But the way it goes on is misleading: 'and that these neither suggest that the Odes depend on John nor the reverse. Both reflect the same milieu, probably somewhere in Western Syria, and both were probably composed in the same community.' The Syriac Odes are at least two generations later than the Fourth Gospel. It is because of their poetic form that they do not 'quote' John directly. The Johannine parallels show a clear further development in them. See also Braun, *Jean le Théologien* (n.5), 238ff., who conjectures that Bardesanes was the author. That is hard to prove. For

the date of the Odes see L.Abramowski, 'Sprache und Abfassungszeit der Oden Salomos',*OrChr* 68, 1984, 80-90. The Syriac *Didaskalia* at the beginning of the third century also presupposes the Fourth Gospel as a matter of course. The same goes for the Pseudo-Clementines, which in the nineteenth century were put far too early by the Tübingen school.

27. C.H.Roberts, *Manuscript, Society and Belief in Early Christian Egypt*, SchL 1977, 1979, 12f., 61; K.Aland, 'Der Text des Johannesevangeliums im 2.Jahrhundert', in *Studien zum Text und zur Ethik des Neuen Testaments. Festschrift zum 80.Geburtstag von Heinrich Greeven*, ed. W.Schrage, BZNW 47, 1986, 1-10, on p^{52}, p^{66} and the new p^{90} (= POx 3253): 'This triple attestation of a New Testament text from the second century is unique, as the early tradition of the Gospel of John generally is unique'. p^{75}, p^{45}, p^{5}, p^{22}, p^{28} and p^{80} belong in the third century (some of them in the early part). That, too, 'is quite exceptional' (1). For the superscriptions of the Gospels see Hengel, *Studies in Mark* (n.6), 64-84, 162-83.

28. Rev.1.1,4,9; 22.8. However, 18.20 and 21.14 probably tell against an origin of the seer in the circle of the twelve apostles, see below, 126, n. 100.

29. Eusebius, HE 5.25.1-7 (2.3), cf. 3.31.3: καὶ γὰρ κατὰ τὴν Ἀσίαν μεγάλα στοιχεῖα κεκοίμηται... Φίλιππον τῶν δώδεκα ἀποστόλων, ὃς κεκοίμηται ἐν Ἱεραπόλει καὶ δύο θυγατέρες αὐτοῦ γεγηρακυῖαι παρθένοι καὶ ἑτέρα αὐτοῦ θυγάτηρ ἐν ἁγίῳ πνεύματι πολιτευσαμένη ἐν Ἐφέσῳ ἀναπαύεται· ἔτι δὲ καὶ Ἰωάννης ὁ ἐπὶ τὸ στῆθος τοῦ κυρίου ἀναπέσων, ὃς ἐγενήθη ἱερεὺς τὸ πέταλον πεφορεκὼς καὶ μάρτυς καὶ διδάσκαλος οὗτος ἐν Ἐφέσῳ κεκοίμηται... The 'witness' may refer to the exile on Patmos; for the 'breast-plate' see Ex.28.36, LXX; John 18.16; Acts 4.6 (see below, 124ff.), and the account of James the brother of the Lord by Epiphanius, *Panarion*, 29.4.3f. He mentions as further witnesses in order 'the bishop and martyr Thraseas of Eumenea who fell asleep in Smyrna', 'the bishop and martyr Sagaris who fell asleep in Laodicea', and 'the blessed Papirius and *Melito* (see n.16 above) the eunuch' who now rests in Sardis. He puts the whole tradition of witness and martyrdom in Asia Minor in the balance, and presupposes that it is also recognized in Rome.

30. Polycrates gives his age as sixty-five (5.24.7) and also refers to his family tradition. Seven of his relations have been bishops. His testimony cannot be estimated highly enough. Transferred to our time it would correspond, say, to reports which I gave from oral tradition dating from the period around 1900. At that time my father was eleven, and I could still tell of details of that period on the basis of my father's accounts (I was born in 1926). When Irenaeus was bishop in Lyons in 177 he may have been around fifty years old: he himself in fact puts strong stress on the *perfecta aetas magistri* in *Adv.haer.* 2.22.4f. (see n.13 above). His literary work is that of a mature older man. The criticism usual today, which is abstract and historically barren, far removed from real life in history, is only possible because it dismisses all too lightly what is clearly stated in the tradition of the early church.

31. The account by Polycrates about the three daughters of Philip which goes into detail gives the impression of reliability precisely because of its

difference from Acts (21.9 speaks of four, as does the Montanist Proclus in the dialogue of Gaius quoted in Eusebius, HE 3.31.4). The Bishop of Ephesus knows the work because he quotes Acts 5.29 at the end. For Papias see Eusebius HE 3.39.9 and for the Montanist tradition HE 3.31.4; 5.16.3.

32. Mark 3.17f.; Matt.10.2f.; Luke 6.14; Acts 1.13. In the lists of the three in Mark and Matthew, John always comes after Peter and James, but Luke sometimes changes them round, putting John in second place: 8.51; 9.28; cf.22.8 and Acts 3.1ff. Papias is quite different, following John 1, see below, 17ff.

33. Eusebius, HE 2.25.7.

34. The Latin version is abbreviated here; the original Greek text is preserved in Epiphanius, *Panarion* 31.27.1:῎Ετι δὲ Ιωάννην τὸν μαθητὴν τοῦ Κυρίου διδάσκουσι (i.e. Ptolemaeus), τὴν πρώτην ὀγδοάδα μεμηνυκέναι, αὐταῖς λέξεσι λέγοντες οὕτως (now the quotation begins): Ἰωάννης, ὁ μαθητὴς τοῦ Κυρίου, βουλόμενος εἰπεῖν τὴν τῶν ὅλων γένεσιν... At the end there is the explicit reference to Ptolemaeus: *Et Ptolemaeus quidem ita*.

35. Epiphanius, *Panarion* 33.3.6: ἔτι τε τὴν τοῦ κόσμου δημιουργίαν αὐτοῦ ἰδίαν λέγει εἶναι τά τε πάντα δι᾽αὐτοῦ γεγονέναι καὶ χωρὶς αὐτοῦ γεγονέναι οὐδὲν ὁ ἀπόστολος.

36. A.von Harnack, *Die Mission und Ausbreitung des Christentums in den ersten drei Jahrhunderten*, Leipzig ⁴1924, 599 (not in the ET) ; id., *Marcion, Das Evangelium vom fremden Gott*, Leipzig ²1924, 29; G.Lüdemann, 'Zur Geschichte des ältesten Christentums in Rom.I. Valentin und Marcion, II. Ptolemäus und Justin', ZNW 70, 1979, 86-114, esp.100-2; P.Lampe, *Die stadtrömischen Christen in den ersten beiden Jahrhunderten*, WUNT 2R, 18, ²1988, 200-3. Justin's protest against the Valentinians is evident only in *Dial*. 35.6, i.e. about 7-10 years later.

37. J.N.Sanders, *The Fourth Gospel in the Early Church. Its Origin and Influence on Christian Theology up to Irenaeus*, Cambridge 1943, 45: 'The first identification of the Beloved Disciple with John the son of Zebedee may have been made by the Alexandrian Gnostics', cf. 35 n.4. Sanders (86f.) conjectures that the work was written in Alexandria, whereas the letters (which he thinks are earlier) came from Asia Minor. One main argument for his theory is the alleged early use of the Gospel among the Gnostics. In reality this preference was restricted to the Valentinians. For the question of Alexandria or Ephesus see also below, 161 n. 5.

38. Roberts, *Manuscript, Society* (n.27), 49ff.; see also Aland, 'Text des Johannesevangeliums' (n.27), see above, 6f.

39. H.Lietzmann, *Kleine Schriften*, TU 67, 1958, I, 107; cf. id., *Geschichte der Alten Kirche*, 2, 1936, 246f.

40. On this see von Loewenich, *Johannes-Verständnis* (n.5), 62ff.; however, the picture is very fragmentary, cf.Sanders, *Fourth Gospel* (n.37), 46ff.; Drummond, *Inquiry* (n.5), 296-334. Drummond conjectures that Basilides already knew the Fourth Gospel; the problem was debated in the nineteenth century after the discovery of Hippolytus' *Philosophoumena* (ed. E.Miller,

Oxford 1851). In fact a large proportion of the fragments attributed to him seem to go back to his disciples.

41. Harnack, *Marcion* (n.36), 249ff., 253: 'It is not impossible that he discussed the foot-washing in the *Antitheses*.' The Marcionites are aware of Johannine themes, see also T.Zahn, *Geschichte des neutestamentlichen Kanons*, I.2, Erlangen 1889, 663f., 675-80, and Irenaeus, *Adv.haer*. 3.11.2; cf. also in detail Drummond, *Inquiry* (n.5), 286-95. His pupil Apelles used John, see Hippolytus, *Ref*. 7.3.8,4: John 20.20,25.

42. von Loewenich, *Johannes-Verständnis* (n.5), 63-9. In Irenaeus, who evidently does not know the works of Valentinus but only those of his disciples (*Adv.haer.*, Prol. §2), only Valentinian Gnostics refer to the Fourth Gospel, and he complains bitterly about this (3.11.7): '*Hi autem qui a Valentino sunt eo* (= *evangelium*) *quod est secundum Iohannem plenissime utentes....*' Only in Hippolytus do quotations from John also appear in non-Valentinian Gnostic texts. This is discussed in detail by Drummond, *Inquiry* (n.5), 265-85.

43. According to A.von Harnack, *Geschichte der altchristlichen Litteratur* II.1, *Die Chronologie bis Irenaeus*. Leipzig 1897, 720, Valentinus came to Rome between about 136 and 140, i.e. roughly at the same time as Marcion. Given the small number of his fragments, the question whether he used the Fourth Gospel must remain uncertain. Because of the predilection of his disciples for it, however, that seems to me to be highly probable. Some fragments could indicate a knowledge of the Gospel of John, e.g. frs.4,6,7 (Völker); cf. also Sanders, *Fourth Gospel* (n.37), 56-66. Hippolytus, *Refut.*35.1 = John 10.8 and 34.1,4 = John 12.31 and 3.29, on the other hand probably do not go back to Valentinus himself but to his disciples. See also Drummond, *Inquiry* (n.5), 269: 'If... Tertullian was correctly informed, we must concede that Valentinus made use of the Fourth Gospel.' According to *Praescr.haer*.38.8ff, Valentinus – in contrast to Marcion – used all the Gospels (*integro instrumento uti videtur*).

44. For Heracleon see W.Völker, *Quellen zur Geschichte der christlichen Gnosis*, SQS NF 5, 1932, 63-86; also E.Pagels, *The Johannine Gospel in Gnostic Exegesis*, Nashville 1973; J.-M.Poffet, *Le méthode exégétique d'Héracléon et Origène*, Paradosis 28, Fribourg 1985. For Theodotus see F.Sagnard, *Clément d'Alexandrie, Extraits de Théodote*, SC 23, 1970, 246f. John appears three times as ὁ ἀπόστολος, 7.3; 35.1; 41.3, and Paul five times; nowhere is he called μαθητής: note the difference in terminology from his contemporary Irenaeus: 'disciple of the Lord' indicates a special tradition from Asia Minor which is of historical value.

45. Lampe, *Stadtrömische Christen* (n.36), 325-9.

46. *Ev.Ver*. (NHC I) 25.36ff. = John 3.19; 26.4-9 = John 1.14; 30.14ff. = John 9.10f.; 30.25-31.7 cf. I John 1.1ff.; John 6.52-58; 20.20,27; 20.22; 4.34; 5.37; I John 4.2; *Ev.Ver*. 42.25-33, cf. John 14.6,10f.; 43.13ff.; cf. I John 3.9. There are further examples in C.K.Barrett, 'The Theological Vocabulary of the Fourth Gospel and the Gospel of Truth', in *Essays on John*, London 1982, 50-64; cf. also W.C. van Unnik, 'The "Gospel of Truth" and the New Testament', in *The Jung Codex*, ed. F.L.Cross, London 1955, 72-129 (115-22). *Ev.Phil*. (NHC

II) 52.7-15, cf. John 11.25; 55.13ff., cf. John 6.32; 57.2ff. cf. John 6.53; 59.7ff. cf. John 19.25; 61.6-10 cf. John 8.44 and I John 3.12; 74.23f. cf. John 14.10f.; 76.30ff. cf. John 4.23 (reading uncertain); 77.16ff. cf. John 8.34; 82.27f. cf. John 8.56; 84.7ff. cf. John 8.32. Matthew is quoted even more often.

47. *Ep.Rheg* NHC I, 45.36f., cf. John 12.32; 49.23ff., cf. John 11.25. On this see also M.L.Peel, *The Epistle to Rheginos*, London and Philadelphia 1969, 26: the author also knows Mark and John, among others. Further Johannine influence is visible in the Tractate of the Trimorphic Protennoia (NHC XIII.1), see Y.Janssens, 'The Trimorphic Protennoia and the Fourth Gospel', in *The New Testament and Gnosis*, Festschrift for R.McL.Wilson, ed. A.H.B.Logan and A.J.M.Wedderburn, Edinburgh 1983, 229-44 (cf. also below 212f. n.47). For the Apocryphon of James see P.Perkins, 'Johannine Traditions in Ap.Jas. (NHC I.2)', *JBL* 101, 1982, 403-14. Further texts which show points of contact with or quotations from the Fourth Gospel are the two Apocalypses of James (NHC V.3,4); the *Testimonium Veritatis* (NHC IX.3), which already presupposes Valentinus and Basilides; the writing of Thomas the Contender (NHC II.7), the twin brother of Jesus, the *Tractatus tripartitus* (NHC I.5), the *Sophia Jesu Christi* or *Eugnostos the Blessed* (NHC III.3 and V.1), etc. As for the most part these texts belong to the third century and probably none of them comes from the first half of the second century, we need not go into them further here. I can also pass over what I believe to be the mistaken conjectures about a dependence of the Fourth Gospel on texts from Nag Hammadi, as they are presented *inter alia* in the *Sophia Jesu Christi* and the *Trimorphic Protennoia*. These and other texts are rather for their part more influenced by the Gospel of John and to some extent contain polemic against its incarnational christology, see e.g. K.Koschorke, *VigChr* 33, 1979, 392 n.18.

48. W.Foerster (ed.), *Die Gnosis*, 2, 1971, 476; cf. also the index of references in B.Layton, *The Gnostic Scriptures*, London and New York 1987, 522-4: Matthew and Luke predominate by far. For the use of the Synoptics in the Nag Hammadi texts see C.Tuckett, *Nag Hammadi and the Gospel Tradition*, Edinburgh 1986. For the Gospel of Matthew see also W.-D.Köhler, *Die Rezeption des Matthäusevangeliums in der Zeit vor Irenäus*, WUNT 2R.24, 1987, 339-427, and E.Massaux, *Influence de l'Évangile de Saint Matthieu sur la littérature avant Saint Irénée*, 1950, who in each instance also goes into the Johannine parallels, see Index, 693ff.

49. Cf. M.Hengel, *Studies in Mark* (n.6), 67; cf. also C.H.Roberts, *Manuscript, Society* (n.27), 61f.

50. It has been preserved in four manuscripts and two recensions, three manuscripts of which come from Nag Hammadi; for the bibliography see E.Hennecke/A.Schneemelcher/R.McL.Wilson, *New Testament Apocrypha* I, London and Philadelphia 1963, 315f. and Layton, *Gnostic Scriptures* (n.48), 26f. The whole is a Sethianic-Valentinian interpretation of Gen.1-6, which ends with a revelation discourse of the perfected Pronoia. John appears only in the narrative framework. The conclusion 'Jesus is the Anointed One' (II.32.6) could be an allusion to John 20.31.

51. 1. The Acts of Peter and the Twelve Apostles (NHC VI.1); 2. The

Apocalypse of Peter (VII.3); 3. The Letter of Peter to Philip (VIII.2); 4. The Acts of Peter (BG 8502.4). Only the second and third works are really Gnostic. Of James we have three (I.2; V.3,4), and of Paul and Thomas each we have two (I.1; II.2; II.7; V.2) apocrypha among the NH texts.

52. See the index of names in J.M.Robinson (ed.), *The Nag Hammadi Library in English*, Leiden ³1988. As far as I can see, John appears indirectly as 'Beloved Disciple' only once, in the non-Gnostic Acts of Peter and the Twelve Apostles (VI.11.2-5; cf. John 13.23-25).

53. See now the excellent new edition by E.Junod and J.-D.Kaestli, *Acta Iohannis*, CC SerApoc 1/2, 1983. For the attribution of the Acts of John to the otherwise unknown author Leucius (Charinos), which is quite common, see the rightly critical account of the situation in E.Junod and J.-D.Kaestli, *L'histoire des Actes Apocryphes du IIIᵉ au IXᵉ siècle*, CRTP, Neufchâtel 1982, 137-45. He appears for the first time in Epiphanius, Pan. 51.6.9, as a supporter of John in the battle against Ebion (!) and Cerinthus. Only in Photius in the ninth century does he become the author of all the apostolic acts (Bibl.114). Nowhere does he appear as the author only of the Acts of John.

54. Chs.55-59: the journey runs from Ephesus to 'Smyrna and the other cities of Asia' (ch.55), and via Laodicea back to Ephesus. There is a gap in between.

55. Ch.93; cf. E.Käsemann, *The Testament of Jesus*, London and Philadelphia 1968, 9, 75f.: here Käsemann refers to F.C.Baur, G.P.Wetter and E.Hirsch. John is the disciple who reclined on Jesus' breast (89.11) or whom he loved (90.7); cf. also 90.16 with John 20.27. The editors regard chapters 94-111, which have a particularly strong docetic-Gnostic colouring, as a Valentinian elaboration towards the end of the second century; cf. for example the reinterpretation of the passion narrative in 101.7-11, which is directed against a literal understanding of the statements about the passion in the Fourth Gospel. By contrast, cf. the fairly moderate 'docetism' of Valentinus; see fr.3 (Völker = Clem.Al., *Strom.*, 3.59.3): Jesus 'ate and drank in a special way and did not excrete the food. So great was the power of continence within him that not even the food was "corrupted" (φθαρῆναι) within him as he had no "corruption" (in him).' Clement of Alexandria also knows the tradition of the special 'spiritual' material nature of the body of Jesus: *Adumbrationes* on I John 1.1; GCS 17.2 = Clement of Alexandria III, ed. O.Stählin, 1970, 210.12ff. For the Jewish background to such conceptions see Tobit 12.19 BA (S and the Vulgate differ), and the Targumim on Gen.18.8 and bḤag 16a; GenR 8, in Billerbeck 1, 891. But cf. John 19.28f., and below, 71.

56. See the collection of instances from John in M.G.Mara, *Évangile de Pierre*, SC 201, 1973, 233-5. They are so numerous and so far-reaching that it is impossible for them all to be derived from a common source (which is completely hypothetical). In many respects the author follows the Fourth Gospel and the Apocalypse in his theology (214); as a place of origin Mara conjectures Asia Minor (217f.) in the first half of the second century. The unclear and vacillating judgment of W.Schneemelcher, in *New Testament*

Apocrypha I, 180f., is completely unsatisfactory. In reality the author makes free use of all four Gospels and adorns them with legendary additions.

57. The references are not completely clear, and the parallels to the Synoptic Gospels are very much stronger, cf. J.-E.Ménard, *L'Évangile selon Thomas*, NHS 5, 1975, 25. For Logion 19 cf. John 15.8; 8.52; 11.25; Logion 38, cf. John 7.34,36; Logion 69a, cf. John 4.23; Logion 77a, cf. John 8.12; 9.5 and 1.3f.; Logion 88, cf. John 1.51; Logion 91 (and 43), cf. John 8.25 (1.19;16.5). See also R.E.Brown, 'The Gospel of Thomas and St John's Gospel', *NTS* 9, 1963/4, 155-77. For the *Protevangelium Jacobi* cf. chs.19f. and John 20.25.

58. H.I.Bell and T.C.Skeat, *Fragments of an Unknown Gospel*, London 1935; J.Jeremias and W.Schneemelcher in *New Testament Apocrypha* I, 94-7 [at this point it should be noted that this English translation is from the 1959 edition of Hennecke-Schneemelcher, *Neutestamentliche Apokryphen*, the fifth edition of which (Tübingen 1987 = *NTA*⁵) has additions or corrections. Where the passage or reference is only in the German, that edition will be cited.] *NTA*⁵ says of the dating of the papyrus: 'more around 200 than around 150' (82).

59. M.Smith, *Clement of Alexandria and a Secret Gospel of Mark*, Cambridge, Mass. 1973; H.Merkel, 'Auf den Spuren des Urmarkus? Ein neuer Fund und seine Beurteilung', *ZTK* 71, 1974, 123-44; id., in *NTA*⁵ I, 89-92. Here Mark is closely connected with Alexandria. The Fourth Gospel is also used in the Strasbourg Coptic papyrus, see W.Schneemelcher in *NTA*⁵ I, 87ff. and probably also in P.Ox 840, ibid., 81f.

60. *Adv.haer*.3.10.6; *EpAp*: C.Schmidt, *Gespräche Jesu mit seinen Jüngern nach der Auferstehung*, TU 43, 1919 (reprinted 1927), 220f., 224, cf. C.D.G.Müller, in *NTA*⁵ I, 205-33 (208 n.8; 210 nn.31, 40; 222 n.129). Cf. also Gospel of Peter 27; Justin, *Apology* 45.5; *Dialogue* 108.2; *Asc.Is*. 3.18-20; 11.22. Perhaps this special appendix to the Gospel of Mark goes back to the presbyter Aristion, thus according to a note of the Edshmiadzin Evangeliar of 989: A.Jülicher and E.Fascher, *Einleitung in das Neue Testament*, Tübingen ⁷1931, 311; T.Zahn, *Einleitung in das Neue Testament* ²II, Leipzig 1900, 230f., 238f. This would explain its special points of contact with information in Papias. The Armenian fathers still seem in part to have known the work of Papias. On this and the Evangeliar see F.Siegert, in J.Kürzinger, *Papias von Hierapolis und die Evangelien des Neuen Testaments*, Eichstätter Materialien 4, 1983, 128-38.

61. Eusebius, HE 3.39.9; cf.also Fragment XI from the church history of Philip Sidetes in F.X.Funk and K.Bihlmeyer, *Die apostolischen Väter*, SQS 2R. 1, 1924, 138f. (= Fragment 16 Kürzinger) and Mark 16.8b.

62. Schmidt, *Gespräche Jesu* (n.60).

63. Müller, *NTA*⁵ (n.60), 205-33. Ch.IX in Schmidt, *Gespräche Jesu* (n.60), 57, 59; numbered by *New Testament Apocrypha* (n.60) I, 201 as ch.17.

64. Thus rightly against the late dating by Schmidt, *Gespräche Jesu* (n.60), 337f., 397f. (180 CE), H.Lietzmann, *ZNW* 20, 1921, 174, see also Müller, *NTA*⁵ (n.60), 207. Cf. L. Gry, 'La date de la Parousie, d'après l'Epistula Apostolorum', *RB* 49, 1940, 86-97; M.Hornschuh, *Studien zur Epistula Apostolorum*, PTS 5, 1965, with c.120 probably arrives at too early a date.

65. Thus ch.1 (Schmidt, *Gespräche Jesu* [n.60] 25, cf. also 169, 171, 195): they

are the heretics of the apostolic period. The letter is not directed 'against Montanists or Marcionites, but against decided representatives of the Gnostic heresy'.

66. Ch.2 (Schmidt, *Gespräche Jesu* [n.60], 26, cf. 229f.). For the special position of the Gospel of John in the *Epistula Apostolorum* see Schmidt, 224ff., 241f.: 'Indeed, in the eyes of the author the Gospel of John is apparently *the* Gospel which communicates true knowledge of Christ' (225). Cf. also von Loewenich, *Johannes-Verständnis* (n.5), 57-9.

67. See above, 4. n.14; below n.76. In my view the designation εὐαγγελιστής for the author of a Gospel appears for the first time in Hippolytus (?) or Origen, see G.W.H.Lampe (ed.), *A Patristic Greek Lexicon*, Oxford 1969, 559. It is referred above all to John cf. Origen, *Comm. in Io*. 1031. 199. For Gregory of Nazianzus he is the personification of the 'evangelist' οἱ δὲ τῇ θεολογίᾳ προσέβησαν (*Or*. 43.69, PG36.589C).

68. Singular in *Dialogue* 10.2; 100.1; plural in *Apology* 66.3: the apostles in the reminiscences composed by them which are called Gospels (οἱ ἀπόστολοι ἐν αὐτοῖς γενομένοις ὑπ᾽ αὐτῶν ἀπομνημονεύμασιν, ἃ καλεῖται εὐαγγέλια).

69. The 'Reminiscences of the Apostles' appear time and again in Dial.100-107 in the exegesis of the passion narrative in connection with Ps.22. Behind this is probable the earlier exposé of an anti-Marcionite account of the passion of Jesus in connection with an exegesis of Ps.22. Elsewhere we find the expression only in the description of the reading of scripture in worship in *Apology* 67.3 and – for the first time – in 66.3, where the term, which is unusual for Christians, is explained with a reference to the Christian designation *euangelia*. The verb *apomnemoneuein* already appears in Papias, Eusebius, HE 3.39.15 in the Mark notice (cf. the simple form in 39.3), and Justin, *Apology* 33.5, cf. R.Heard, *NTS* 1, 1954/55, 122-9. Certainly for Justin the model of Xenophon's biographical reminiscences of Socrates plays a part since he knows them and quotes them (II Apology 11.3). In his day *apomnemoneumata* was a relatively well known book title for all kinds of collections, e.g. anthologies (Favorinus of Arles, Aulus Gellius, etc.). Cf. Origen, *c.Celsum* 6.41, the *apomnemoneumata* of the magician and philosopher Apollonius of Tyana by Moiragenes.

70. *Dialogue* 100.1: ἐν τῷ εὐαγγελίῳ γέγραπται. Here Justin is presumably quoting from memory in a version of his own. In *Dialogue* 100.4 he then speaks again of 'Reminiscences of the Apostles'.

71. *Dialogue* 100.1: ὁ ἀπὸ τοῦ πατρὸς αὐτοῦ λαβὼν ἔχει, cf. John 10.18: ἐξουσίαν ἔχω πάλιν λαβεῖν αὐτὴν (viz. τὴν ψυχήν μου)· ταύτην τὴν ἐντολὴν ἔλαβον παρὰ τοῦ πατρός μου. The statements in *Dialogue* 100.2,4 about the pre-existence of Jesus and his being made flesh (or man) have points of contact in substance with John 1.1f.; 1.14, cf. also II *Apology* 6.3 and 5; *Dialogue* 105.1 with John 1.18, 14; here John 1.1-18 is evidently included in the 'Reminiscences of the Apostles'.

72. For the problem see Zahn, *Kanon* (n.41) I, 522f.; von Loewenich, *Johannes-Verständnis* (n.5), 27-31; Braun, *Jean le Théologien*(n.5), I, 1959, 135-44, with a synopsis on pp.136ff. The problem was already discussed at length

and argued over in the nineteenth century, see E.Zeller, *ThJb(T)* 4, 1845, 599-618; J.Drummond, *The Theological Review* 14, 1877, 155-87, 332-4; id., *Inquiry* (n.5), 84-162; Abbot, *Authorship* (n.5), 20-52; Stanton, *Gospels* (n.5), I, 81-91. I see authentic echoes also in *Apology* 32.10 = John 1.14; *Dialogue* 17.3 = John 1.19; *Dialogue* 63.2 = John 1.13; *Dialogue* 91.4 = John 3.14, 17; *Dialogue* 106.1 = John 13.3; cf. also *Dialogue* 105.1: Christ as μονογενὴς... τῷ πατρὶ τῶν ὅλων (John 1.14,18; 3.16,18) and 105.5: ἀποδιδοὺς τὸ πνεῦμα, which most likely corresponds to John 19.30, παρέδωκεν τὸ πνεῦμα.

73. For this disputed passage see Gunther, 'Early Identifications' (n.5), 409; for details Drummond, *Inquiry* (n.5), 87-103, in the argument with Zeller.

74. Cf. Drummond, *Inquiry* (n.5), 107-45. One can ask whether the *Kerygma Petri*, which was written in the first half of the second century and is also apologetic, presupposes the Fourth Gospel, see *New Testament Apocrypha* II, London and Philadelphia 1965, 94ff.: in fr.1 Christ is called 'Law and Logos'; in fr.2 God 'who has created all things through the word of his power (here, in contrast to Heb.1.3 we have λόγῳ δυνάμεως), which is his Son' (= Clem.Alex., *Strom*.VI 5.39.3); fr.4: 'I have chosen you twelve' (ἐξελεξάμην ὑμᾶς δώδεκα, from Clem.Alex., *Strom.* VI 6.48.2), cf. John 6.70 and 15.16. However, it is impossible to demonstrate 'literary dependence' from these few fragments.

75. Here he concentrates above all on the prologue. 13.1 quotes John 1.5 with an introductory formula, cf. 13.2; 5.1 and 19.4. 4.1 end could refer to John 4.24. For the Diatessaron see above, 4 n.14.

76. *Apology* 32.10; 66.2; *Dialogue* 45.4; 84.2; 100.2.

77. B.H.Streeter, *The Four Gospels*, London ⁹1956, 441, supposes: 'it was Justin Martyr who first effectively commended both the Fourth Gospel and the Logos doctrine to the acceptance of the Roman Church.' However, at the same time this is also done by Valentinus and his disciples, albeit in a way which fundamentally goes against the Fourth Gospel. Justin's *De resurrectione*, which in my view is authentic, also contains references to Johannine theology, cf. already the introductory statements which end up in the remark: λόγος δὲ ἀληθείας ἀπὸ θεοῦ πέμπεται (ed. J.C.T.von Otto, *CorpAp* III, ³1879, 210) or ibid., 212 bottom on resurrection and eternal life and the clear reference to John 20.25, 27 or I John 1.1 in ch.9 (p.244 top).

78. *Dialogue* 106.3 with a reference to Mark 3.16f.

79. *Dialogue* 103.8.

80. *Dialogue* 100.4; 106.3.

81. *Dialogue* 81.4. *Dialogue* 123.9 could refer to I John 3.1.

82. von Loewenich, *Johannes-Verständnis* (n.5), 7-18, who arrives at a very balanced verdict. For II Clem. see above all 9.5; for Barnabas 5.10f.; 6.14; 11.19f. and 12.7. See also Braun, *Jean le Théologien* (n.5), I, 163ff.; 84ff. The common elements of the prayer language in Didache 9 and 10 and in John 17 and elsewhere go back to common Jewish-Christian tradition, see von Loewenich, *Johannes-Verständnis*, 18ff., and Braun, *Jean le Théologien*, 255ff.; Massaux, *Influence* (n.48), 39ff., 87ff., 162ff.

83. For the exchange of writings and the early Christian libraries see M.Hengel, *Studies in the Gospel of Mark*, London and Philadelphia 1985, 74f., 77ff.

84. Trajan left Rome on 27 October 113 to travel to the east and there prepare for the Parthian War. After this time the governor of Syria would hardly have sent Ignatius to Rome. The persecution in Pontus under Pliny the Younger and that in Antioch are very close together in time, see W.H.Gross, *PWSuppl* 10, 1965, 1094.

85. W.R.Inge, in *The New Testament in the Apostolic Fathers*, by a Committee of the Oxford Society of Historical Theology, 1905, 81-3: 'Ignatius' use of the Fourth Gospel is highly probable, but it falls some way short of certainty' (83); Massaux, *Influence* (n.48), 112-17, however, affirms only a common milieu. von Loewenich, *Johannes-Verständnis* (n.5), 25-38, is more precise: 'The spiritual affinity seems to be strengthened by literary knowledge - at least there are no serious difficulties in the way of this. Possibly it is also simply to be derived from a common homeland, which at all events has to be assumed' (38). In accordance with the trend of the time, against Loofs, v.d.Goltz and Harnack, Loewenich conjectures 'Syrian Gnosticism' rather than 'the theology of Asia Minor' as its environment; but here he is simply explaining an x with an even more unknown y. We simply do not know anything about the development of Ignatius. His name (Egnatius) was Roman or old Italian, see J.B.Lightfoot, *The Apostolic Fathers* II.1, 1889 (reprinted 1973), 22ff., not Greek or Syriac. Probably he was a Roman citizen. His letters show that he was quite familiar with circumstances in Asia Minor. It is just as possible that Ignatius came from Asia Minor as that the Fourth Evangelist comes from Syria-Palestine. Finally, though, we should concede that we know very little indeed about the Syrian communities in the first and second centuries. The relationships with the 'tradition of Asia Minor' worked out by E.v.d.Goltz, *Ignatius von Antiochien als Christ und Theologe*, TU 12, 1895, 165ff., are very much clearer than the 'Gnostic' background of the Ignatians worked out in the Bultmann school. For Ignatius, John and Justin cf. also the table, 196ff. See also the survey of research by W.J.Burghardt, *TS* 1, 1940, 1-26 and C.Maurer, *Ignatius von Antiochien und das Johannesevangelium*, ATANT 18, 1949, who comes to the conclusion that 'Ignatius had read the Fourth Gospel' (100) in doing which he 'did literary violence' to both John and the Synoptists (101); further Braun, *Jean le Théologien* (n.5), I, 262-82 (270ff.: Rom.7.2f.; Eph.9.1; Magn.8.2; Philad.7.1; 9.1.; Smyrn.3.2).

86. Rom.4.3: 'I do not command you like Peter and Paul. They are apostles, while I am a condemned man.' Braun, *Jean le Théologien* (n.5), devotes a whole section to the 'silences d'Ignace et Polycarpe' (I, 342-5).

87. Eph.12.2. He continues in a somewhat pleonastic way: 'who in every letter remembers you in Christ Jesus', cf. 11.2: Ignatius wanted to be found in the heritage of the Christians of Ephesus, who also always agreed with the apostles in the power of Jesus Christ. For Ignatius the apostles are an absolute authority, bound up with Christ. They are already at some distance from his time (cf. Magn.13.17f.; Philad.9.1). Nevertheless as bishop and

martyr he claims their authority (Trall.3). This pronounced 'hierarchical' use of *apostolos* is at some remove from its complete absence from the Gospel and the letters of John.

88. The second letter comprises chs.1-12 and perhaps also 14. For the dating cf. ch.9: the recollection of the martyrs, whose death is probably not even decades in the past, see J.A.Fischer, *Die Apostolischen Väter*, Darmstadt [8]1981, 236f. In his second letter Polycarp is not yet fighting against Marcion; Fischer therefore assumes that the date of its composition is 'some months, at the latest one or two years, after I Phil' (237). The first letter (ch.13) was written still during the lifetime, 'in all probability during the last journey of the Bishop of Antioch' (235). However, the date for the second letter may be a bit too early.

89. *Ep.ad Flor*, Eusebius, HE 5.20.1, 4-7; cf. *Adv.haer*. 3.3.4 and Eusebius HE 4.14.3-9; see above, 000.

90. Irenaeus, *Adv.haer*. 3.3. = Eusebius, HE 4.14.3: οὐ μόνον ὑπὸ ἀποστόλων μαθητευθεὶς καὶ συναναστραφεὶς πολλοῖς τοῖς τὸν κύριον ἑωρακόσιν, ἀλλὰ καὶ ὑπὸ ἀποστόλων κατασταθεὶς εἰς τὴν Ἀσίαν ἐν τῇ ἐν Σμύρνῃ ἐκκλησίᾳ ἐπίσκοπος.

Cf. *Ep.ad.Flor.*, HE 5.20.4,6. There is no deeper historical significance in the fact that there is no mention of John in the *Vita Polycarpi*, which was written around 400 (text in J.B.Lightfoot, *The Apostolic Fathers, Part II: Saint Ignatius, Saint Polycarp, Vol.III*[2] 1889, 433, 465, reprinted 1979) but that Polycarp is appointed third bishop of the city after Strateas and Bukolos were nominated bishop by Paul with the collaboration of bishops, presbyters and deacons through the anonymous choice of the laity (chs.22f.), since this is such a late makeshift work. Perhaps there is a glimpse here of the old competition between Smyrna and Ephesus. The counterpart is that in the *Apostolic Constitutions* 7.46f., 8, pp.454f. Funk, Polycarp is passed over as the successor of the bishops Ariston and Strateas, see below, 82. Tertullian's assertion, *De praescr.haer*. 32.2, that Polycarp was appointed bishop in Smyrna by John as Clement was appointed bishop in Rome by Peter, spins out the remark by Irenaeus in a tendentious way. But cf. the indication of the plural without mention of any names in Eusebius, HE 3.36. Regardless of what the position is over the historicity of all these reports, Irenaeus does not stress *any* exclusive dependence of Polycarp on John. John was only one of his teachers, perhaps not even the most important one. But that means that this John of Ephesus did not make any 'apostolic claim to exclusiveness'.

91. *Martyrdom of Polycarp* 9.3 on the date of his death, see H.Musurillo, *The Acts of the Christian Martyrs*, 1972, XIII.

92. 3.2 (cf. 9.1; 11.2f.); 6.3 (cf.9.1: Paul and the rest of the apostles). In Polycarp oral and written tradition are inextricably intermingled, cf. Irenaeus, *Adv.haer.*.3.3.4 = Eusebius, HE 4.14.4 and *Ep.ad Flor*. = HE 5.20.6: 'Polycarp related all that he had learned from those who were eye-witnesses of the word of life, in accordance with scripture.'

93. See the index of references in Funk and Bihlmeyer, *Apostolische Väter* (n.61), 160-2. As in the letters of Ignatius, points of contact with the New

Testament far outnumber those with the Old. However, there are only a few 'parallels' from the Gospel of John, which are by no means clear and very general: Polycarp 10.1 (John 13.34; 15.12,17) in connection with the quotation from I Peter 5.9 and 12.3b (John 15.16). Cf. also Polycarp 5.2 with John 13.15-17; 5.21; 6.40; Polycarp 7.1 with John 8.44, see n.96. On this see the Oxford Committee, *New Testament* (n.85), 84ff., 100f., 103ff.; Drummond, *Inquiry* (n.5), 191, refers only to 5.2; see also H.J.Beardsley, 'The Testimony of Ignatius and Polycarp to the Writings of St John', *JTS* 14, 1913, 207-20.

94. 7.1, cf. I John 4.2f. and II John 7. See on this the Oxford Committee, *New Testament* (n.85), 100: 'The numerous coincidences of language render it probable that Polycarp either used John or was personally acquainted with its author.' Massaux, *Influence* (n.48), 'Un contact littéraire... est indubitable'.

95. I John 3.8; John 8.44; cf. 17.12. The subsequent πρωτότοκος τοῦ Σατανᾶ which Polycarp is said to have hurled at Marcion (Irenaeus, *Adv.haer*.33.3.4 = Eusebius, *HE* 4.14.7) and which probably comes from Polycarp Phil.7.1 thus has a degree of Johannine colouring. In I John 3.12 Cain is the prototype of the 'son of the devil', see N.A.Dahl, 'Der Erstgeborene Satans und der Vater der Teufels Polyk 7.1 und Joh 8.44', in *Apophoreta. Festschrift für Ernst Haenchen*, BZNW 30, 1964, 70-84.

96. See now U.H.J.Körtner, *Papias von Hierapolis*, FRLANT 133, 1983, though he arrives at an early date around 110 CE which does not convince me; he discusses the reports about the Gospels in an unsatisfactory way and puts forward absurd conjectures about the second and third letters of John; see also Kürzinger, *Papias von Hierapolis* (n.60); on this see F.Siegert, 'Unbeachtete Papiaszitate bei Armenischen Schriftstellern', *NTS* 27, 1981, 605-14, and id., in *Papias von Hierapolis* (n.60); E.Schwartz, *Über den Tod der Söhne Zebedaei. Ein Beitrag zur Geschichte der Johannesevangeliums*, AGWG. PH 7,5, 1904, in *Gesammelte Schriften* 5, Berlin 1963, 48-123 (57-79); W.Bousset, *ThR* 8, 1905, 236-44, 280ff.; Merkel, *Widersprüche* (n.19), 44-51; M.Hengel, 'Literary, Theological and Historical Problems in the Gospel of Mark', in *Studies in Mark* (n.6), 31-58. For the English literature, which I found particularly illuminating and which Körtner largely overlooked in his bibliographical survey, see E.H.Hall, *Papias and his Contemporaries*, Boston and New York 1899; Drummond, *Inquiry* (n.5), 194-254; Dom John Chapman, *John the Presbyter and the Fourth Gospel*, Oxford 1911; Stanton, *Gospels* (n.5), I, 1903, 52-7, 166-73, 217f., 223-5; H.Latimer Jackson, *The Problem of the Fourth Gospel*, Cambridge 1918, 15, 26ff., 143ff.; H.J.Lawlor, 'Eusebius on Papias', *Hermathena* 43, 1922, 167-22; C.F.Nolloth, *The Fourth Evangelist*, London 1925, 45-7, 58-71; J.E.Carpenter, *The Johannine Writings*, London 1927, 41-3, 209-17; V.Bartlet, 'Papias' "Exposition": Its Date and Contents', in *Amicitiae Corolla...* *to James Rendel Harris*, ed. H.G.Wood, London 1933, 15-44.

97. The dating of the work depends on whether one accepts the authenticity of the note fr.16 (Kürzinger) = fr.12 (Funk-Bihlmeyer) from an excerpt of the church history of Philip in Side (see C.de Boor, TU 5.2, 1888, 170), that according to Philip some of those of Christ had lived *in the time of Hadrian* and

this is not a confusion with the report from the Apology of Quadratus, Eusebius, HE 4.3.2. As the wording is completely different, I do not regard this as certain. Irenaeus calls Papias a contemporary (an older contemporary) or friend (ἑταῖρος) of Polycarp (5.33.4 = Eusebius, HE 3.39.1); see below n.123.

98. The whole account is contained in HE 3.39.2-17; the prologue 39.2-4 with an interpretation added, 5f.; Eusebius attaches importance to two Johns in Ephesus so as to have a non-apostolic author for the Apocalypse.

99. HE 3.39.17: for the use of the Apocalypse see fragments 11-13 (Kürzinger, *Papias von Hierapolis* [n.60], 110-13) = fr. 9,5,4 in Funk and Bihlmeyer, *Apostolische Väter* (n.61). The fragments come from John of Scythopolis (no.11 or 9), and Andrew of Caesarea (nos.12f. or 5 and 4); cf. also the substantial Armenian fragment discovered by Siegert in Kürzinger, 129ff. For Papias and the 'apocalypticism of Asia Minor' see Körtner, *Papias von Hierapolis* (n.96), 127ff., 185ff.

100. Eusebius, HE 3.39.3,4 = fragment 4 in Kürzinger, *Papias von Hierapolis* (n.60), 98 and fr.2 in Funk and Bihlmeyer, *Apostolische Väter* (n.61), 134: εἰ δέ που καὶ παρηκολουθηκώς τις τοῖς πρεσβυτέροις ἔλθοι, τοὺς τῶν πρεσβυτέρων ἀνέκρινον λόγους· τί ᾽Ανδρέας ἢ τί Πέτρος εἶπεν ἢ τί Φίλιππος ἢ τί Θωμᾶς ἢ ᾽Ιάκωβος ἢ τί ᾽Ιωάννης ἢ Ματθαῖος ἤ τις ἕτερος τῶν τοῦ κυρίου μαθητῶν, ἅ τε ᾽Αριστίων καὶ ὁ πρεσβύτερος ᾽Ιωάννης, τοῦ κυρίου μαθηταί, λέγουσιν. The literature on this much discussed and disputed text is legion. For a selection see n.97 above. Körtner, *Papias von Hierapolis* (n.96), and Kürzinger, *Papias von Hierapolis* (n.60), give something of a survey here. In essentials I presuppose, (a) that the first-mentioned John and John the 'Elder' are two different people for Papias; (b) that the text does not need any emendation, but is understandable as it is and that it is a quotation from the work of Papias. It is not significant that the Syriac translation omits 'the disciple of the Lord' after 'John the elder'. It is certainly not a secondary addition but contains the *lectio difficilior*.

101. There are some examples in Körtner, *Papias von Hierapolis* (n.96), 319 n.11. To these should be added F.Overbeck, *Das Johannesevangelium*, ed. C.A.Bernoulli, Tübingen 1911, 334f.; C.von Weizsäcker, *Das apostolische Zeitalter der christlichen Kirche*, Freiburg im Breisgau 1886, 502. However, Körtner's discussion of the list of apostles in 177-82, cf. 197ff., is not very satisfactory. He overlooks the essential feature, the attention to the list from John 21.2, which he mentions only on the side. The question whether Papias knows the Fourth Gospel is, moreover, quite independent of the questionable attribution of it to the son of Zebedee. As the one unknown disciple of John in John 1.37-40 remains anonymous, he cannot be listed as a disciple with a name. This first anonymous figure and the last two anonymous figures in 21.2 are deliberate mystifications, see below, 79, 127ff.

102. Philip appears twelve times in John, Thomas seven times (but both only once each in the Synoptic Gospels) and Andrew six times (four times in Mark, twice in Matthew).

103. T.Zahn, *Apostel und Apostelschüler in der Provinz Asien*, FGNK VI, Leipzig 1900, 158-75, 220ff. Cf. John 12.20ff. and below, 122f. W.Bousset, *ThR* 8, 1905, 286ff. For Andrew see also below nn.114, 115.

104. Cf.Acts 6.1,5; 8.2ff.,19ff.; 21.8 and also the role of Philip in John 12.20ff. Papias evidently does not make any distinction between the 'disciple' Philip (HE 3.39.4) and the father of the daughters who settled in Hierapolis (3.39.9). Eusebius uses the title 'apostle' in his report as does Polycrates of Ephesus, see above n.28 (but cf.3.31.5). This shows that his quotation is inconsistent on this point.

105. From the time of Isho'dad of Merw (ninth century), see R.Schnackenburg, *Gospel of John* (n.5), 314.

106. John 6.37, 39; 10.29; 17.2-12; 18.9.

107. Further examples in H.J.Holtzmann and W.Bauer, *Evangelium, Briefe und Offenbarung des Johannes*, HC IV, ³1908, 70f.

108. R.Hachlili, 'The Goliath Family in Jericho: Funerary Inscriptions from a First-Century AD Jewish Monumental Tomb', *BASOR* 235, 1979, 31-65. For Mattathias as Theodotus see II Macc.14.19 and B.Bar-Kochva, *Judas Maccabaeus*, Cambridge 1989, 521 n.7.

109. Matt.9.9 = Mark 2.14; cf. the addition 'the publican' in Matt.10.3.

110. A.Hilgenfeld, *Die Evangelien nach ihrer Entstehung und geschichtlichen Bedeutung*, Leipzig 1854, 244 n.2; id., *Das Evangelium und die Briefe Johannis nach ihrem Lehrbegriff*, Halle 1849, 271; H.Spaeth, 'Nathanael', *ZWTh* 11, 1868, 168-231 (171ff.), on 'the symbolic significance of the name'; Overbeck, *Johannesevangelium* (n.101), 334ff.: '...a bloodless shadow, which is introduced in such a mystical way that one is formally compelled to seek an allegory under this name'; J.Grill, *Untersuchungen über die Enstehung des vierten Evangeliums* II, Tübingen 1923, 31 n.87, 354; K.Hanhart, 'The Structure of John I.35-IV.54', in *Studies in John. Presented to Prof. Dr J.N.Sevenster*, NT.S 24, 1970, 22-46 (25f.); R.Stichel, *Nathanael unter den Feigenbaum*, Stuttgart 1985, 24 n.34 (with bibliography).

111. The Twelve appear only in John 6.70f., in connection with Judas, and in 20.24 in a formal way with Thomas. They are never listed by name as they are in the other Gospels. Mark mentions the Twelve in connection with the disciples eleven times, Matthew nine times and Luke seven, cf. also Acts 6.2 and I Cor.15.3.

112. Cf. the judgment on the brothers of Jesus in John 7.5. The contradiction between John and the birth narratives of Matthew and Luke seems obvious to me; see John 1.45f.: 6.42; 7.26f., 42. On the other hand he stresses the significance of the title *basileus* for Jesus almost more strongly than Matthew, albeit in a meaning which is abruptly directed against any *political* messianic hope: 6.15; 1.49; 12.13 (cf. Matt.21.5): the motive of the king is intensified by the *hypantēsis* of the people of Jerusalem who go to meet Jesus, cf. also 18.33-19.13, 19. According to Irenaeus the later Ebionites reject the virgin birth, although they only use the Gospel of Matthew (in abbreviated form?): Irenaeus, *Adv.haer.* 1.26.22; 3.11.7; 3.21.1; 4.23.4; 5.1.3. See below, 119ff.

However, it is questionable whether the Jewish Christians shared in this repudiation around 90. Perhaps John rejected the virgin birth, too.

113. Eusebius, HE 3.19.16. 'Logia' of itself denotes words of divine origin, including inspired words of scripture: Rom.3.2; Heb.5.12, see W.Bauer, W.F.Arndt, F.W.Gingrich and F.W.Danker, *A Greek-English Lexicon of the New Testament*, Chicago ²1979, 476; and Lawlor, 'Eusebius on Papias' (n.96), 189f.

114. Lines 13ff.: *eadem nocte reuelatum andreae ex apostolis ut recogniscentibus cuntis (sic!) iohannis suo nomine cuncta discriberet*. In line 9, in accordance with the tradition of Asia Minor John is described as being *ex decipolis* (*ex discipulis*). Text after E.Preuschen, *Analecta SQS*, 1 R, Vol.8, Part II, 1910, 27f.; translation in *New Testament Apocrypha* I, 43.

115. P.M.Peterson, 'Andrew, Brother of Simon Peter', *NTS* 1, 1958, 4f., 8ff., 24ff.; *New Testament Apocrypha* II, 276ff. See also above, n.101.

116. Fr.16 (Kürzinger, *Papias von Hierapolis* [n.60], 116f.) = 11 (Funk and Bihlmeyer, *Apostolische Väter* [n.61], 138f.). Jerome, *De vir.ill.* 18, however, keeps Papias's (= Eusebius's) order.

117. *Epistula Apostolorum* (n.60), ch.2, p.192, and 218, 223f. The catalogue from the *Apostolic Constitutions* is related, see T.Schermann, *Die allgemeine Kirchenordnung, frühchristliche Liturgien und kirchliche Überlieferung. 1.Teil: Die allgemeine Kirchenordnung des zweiten Jahrhunderts*, Paderborn 1914, 12: John, Matthew (!), Peter, Andrew, Philip, Simon, James, Nathanael, Thomas, Cephas, Bartholomew, Judas son of James and almost identically in the Syriac *Didascalia*, 3.6; cf. A.Vööbus, *The Didascalia Apostolorum in Syriac*, CSCO 402,I, 1979, 30f.: John, Matthew, Peter, Andrew, Philip, Simeon, James, Nathanael, Judas son of James, Thomas, Cephas, Bartholomew: here the two different evangelists stand united at the head. With two minor exceptions they give their admonitions in this order. The apostle John similarly stands at the beginning in the Jewish-Christian Gospel from which Epiphanius quotes and which was attributed to Matthew, see *Panarion* 30.13.3 (translation in *New Testament Apocrypha* 1, 125). Here the *Evangelist Matthew, who speaks in the first person, puts himself at the end*. That in Papias the presbyter John, to whom he owes so many traditions, stands at the end is therefore no coincidence. He is nearest to the author and to some degree forms the bridge to him.

118. The critical qualification by the presbyter John, Eusebius, HE 3.39.15, οὐ μέντοι τάξει, presupposes the knowledge of a *better* literary and chronological ordering of the Gospel material. In my opinion, the indication that Mark was not a hearer and follower of the Lord also points indirectly towards the Gospel of an allegedly real 'disciple', who need not have belonged to the Twelve. The note by Papias or the presbyter begins from a superior standpoint. On this see A.Wright, 'τάξει in Papias', *JTS* 14, 1913, 298-300: 'He upholds St John by declaring St Mark to be wrong' (300).

119. We know of this first from Epiphanius and the commentaries on the Apocalypse by Bar Salibi, see above, 142 n.21, on the Alogoi.

120. Eusebius, HE 3.39.5-7, 12ff.: the attack on Papias and his chiliasm, which is indeed directed against an 'orthodox' mediator of old traditions, is quite unusual when put as sharply as this. See also HE 7.24f., the account on

the criticism of the Apocalypse of John by Dionysius of Alexandria. It is very probable that a predilection for chiliasm was already attributed to Cerinthus by the 'Alogos' Gaius and then by Dionysius, in order to discredit him (cf. HE 3.28.4f.). The later fathers then to some degree retained this charge against Cerinthus. J.A.F.J.Klijn and G.J.Reinink, *Patristic Evidence for Jewish-Christian Sects*, NT.S 36, 1973, 5ff., see below, 183 n.38.

121. This report is said to have appeared in the second book of Papias' work: Fr.16 (Kürzinger, *Papias von Hierapolis* [n.60], 116) = 11 (Funk and Bihlmeyer, *Apostolische Väter* [n.61], 138f.); fr.17 (Kürzinger, 118) = 12 (Funk/Bihlmeyer, 139). That this information is reliable follows from:

(a) An epitome of the Church History of Philip of Side which was composed between 434 and 439, coming from the seventh century (Cod.Baroccianus 142), see C.de Boor, TU 5. 2, 1888, 165-84 (170);

(b) From one of the earliest manuscripts of the Chronicles (Cod.Coislinianus 305) of Gregorius Monachus (Hamartolus), ed. H.Nolte, *ThQ* 44, 1882, 464-8. For a critical view of the two texts see Braun, *Jean le Théologien* (n.5), I, 407-11, whose theory (shared by numerous scholars) is not satisfied by a confusion with John the Baptist. At all events the historical value of this account cannot be shaken by this argument. There is further information in

(c) the earliest Syrian martyrology of the year 411 from Edessa, which in turn goes back to a Greek text of the first half of the fourth century from Nicomedia: H.Achelis, *Die Martyrologien, ihre Geschichte und ihr Wert*, AGWG.PH NF III.3, 1900, 30-71, which commemorates the death of Stephen on 26 December, the martyrdom of 'the apostles John and James' on 27 December and of Paul and Simon Cephas on 28 December; see H.Lietzmann, *Die drei ältesten Martyrologien*, KIT 2, 1911, 7f.;

(d) in the Martyr Calendar of Carthage, in which the 'Commemoration of John the Baptist and the apostle James, whom (*quem*) Herod murdered', is also put on 27 December. Here the reference was probably originally to the brother of James rather than John the Baptist. See id. on H.Achelis, *Martyrologien*, 18-29; Lietzmann, *Martyrologien*. There are further indications

(e) in the prophecy Mark 10.39 = Matt.20.23;

(f) in the fact that the Valentinian Heracleon in Clem.Alex., *Strom.* 4.71.3, mentions only 'Matthew, Philip, Thomas, Levi and many others' among the disciples who did *not* 'make the confession with their voice and departed from life', but not John, of whom later tradition did not know any violent end. However, in itself this argument from silence does not carry much weight;

(g) in the homily *De persecutione* of the early Syrian church father Aphraates (*Patrologia Syriaca* I,1, Paris 1894, cols.987f.), who also mentions the sons of Zebedee as martyrs after Stephen, Simon (Peter) and Paul: 'James and John went in the footsteps of their master Christ. Other apostles too made their confessions in various places and proved themselves to be true martyrs';

(h) in the 'Martyrdom of Andrew', (Lipsius/Bonnet, *Acta Apostol.Apocr.* II, 1, 46f.), Peter is sent to the Jews, James and John to the East (ἀνατολή), Philip to Samaria and Asia Minor and among others Andrew to Bithynia, Greece, and so on.

This information is probably to be distinguished from later accounts which report the execution of John (the Baptist) and James (the son of Zebedee) by the sword, see E.Riggenbach, *NKZ* 32, 1921, 692-6; C.L.Feltoe, 'St John and St James in Western "Non-Roman" Calendars', *JTS* 10, 1909, 589-92. As the tradition of the martyrdom of John the son of Zebedee represents the *lectio difficilior* over against the later church tradition, in my view the report of Papias, which was soon suppressed in favour of the apostolicity of John of Ephesus, of whom there is no tradition of any martyrdom with a fatal outcome, has a certain plausibility. As exile to Patmos was no longer sufficient for the apostle, probably towards the end of the second century the report of his martyrdom in oil came into being (in Rome?), see Tertullian, *De praescr.haer.* 36, which was written in 203 CE, see H.D.Saffery, *RSPT* 69, 1985, 265-72. The martyrdom of the two sons of Zebedee need not have taken place at the same time, cf. Acts 12.1f. and Gal.2.9. John was evidently killed later. There is an excellent brief account of the problem in Jackson, *Problem* (n.96), 142-50, cf. also W.Bousset, *ThR* 8, 1905, 225-31, 295.

122. Most important here is the testimony of Irenaeus, *Adv.haer.* 5.33.4 (cf.Eusebius, HE 3.39.1): *Haec autem et Papias Iohannis auditor, Polycarpi autem contubernalis, vetus homo, per scripturam testimonium perhibet...*'. Although Eusebius HE 3.39.2 contradicts Irenaeus over the fact that in his introduction Papias states that 'he had neither heard nor seen the holy apostles' and clearly distinguishes the apostle John from the presbyter, the later authors who cite Papias very often designate him a disciple or hearer of the evangelist. This is even true of Jerome, see frs.6-9 (Kürzinger, *Papias von Hierapolis* [n.60], 106-9); Apollinarius of Laodicea (or Hierapolis?): fr.5 (ibid., 104) = 3 (Funk and Bihlmeyer, *Apostolische Väter* [n.61]); John of Scythopolis, fr.11 (Kürzinger, 110) = 9 (Funk/Bihlmeyer); Anastasius Sinaita, fr.14 (Kürzinger, 114) = 6 (Funk/Bihlmeyer); id., fr.15 (Kürzinger, 114) = 7 (Funk/Bihlmeyer); Philip of Side, fr.16 (Kürzinger, 116) = 11 (Funk/Bihlmeyer); Georgius Monachus, fr.17 (Kürzinger, 118) = 12 (Funk/Bihlmeyer). The last elaboration of this connection, which must have had some basis in the work of Papias, is the relatively late assertion that John dictated his Gospel to Papias, thus frs.20,21 (Kürzinger, 122-5), cf. 13 (Funk/Bihlmeyer). Presumably Irenaeus read a quotation from John 14.2 (and indeed others) in Papias, etc., see above, 4f. n.17, cf. also n.125.

123. As Irenaeus calls Papias not only a 'hearer' of John but also a 'contemporary' (ἑταῖρος) of Polycarp' and a 'man of the old time' (*Adv.haer.*5.33.4 = Eusebius, HE 3.39.1), he will have been about the same age as Polycarp. In that case he would have been born between about 70 and 80. It seems important to me here that he knew the well-known John as 'the elder'. So he could have been around two generations older.

124. *Apostolic Constitutions* 7.46.7f. (pp.452ff., Funk), cf. above n.88.

125. A.Mingana, 'The Authorship of the Fourth Gospel. A New Document', *BJRL* 14, 1930, 335-9. These confusing reports are probably reflections on

Eusebius, to which the second colophon possibly refers. Nevertheless it would be worth investigating this area more closely (see also n.122).

II. John the Elder as the Author of the Second and Third Letters

1. R.E.Brown, *The Epistles of John*, AB 30, 1982, 30 n.71; cf. id., *The Community of the Beloved Disciple*, New York, Ramsey and Toronto 1979. In that case the seer of Patmos would be a fifth 'Johannine' figure. For Bultmann see his commentaries on the Gospel and letters: in the Gospel there are the authors of the revelation discourses and the signs source, the evangelist and the church redactor (and possibly several others); in the first letter the author of the original work, the real author and again a church redactor, and also the unknown 'elder' of the third letter and the forger of the second.

2. R.A.Culpepper, *The Johannine School*, SBL Diss.Ser. 26, 1975; O.Cullmann, *The Johannine Circle*, London and Philadelphia 1976; a particularly bold view is taken by G.Richter, 'Zum gemeindebildenden Element in den johanneischen Schriften', in id., *Studien zum Johannesevangelium*, ed. J.Hainz, BU 13, 1977, 383-414: 'But Käsemann and Schweizer are also far too uncritical (!) in not recognizing the plurality of the term "Johannine community". There is no such thing as the "Johannine community" of which Käsemann and Schweizer speak... but only... a series of Johannine communities..., whose existence is expressed in the fragmentation – indeed largely in an opposition – in the various strata which follow one another in time in the Gospel of John or in the Johannine writings generally' (413). In his review of the book in *TLZ* 106, 1981, U.Wilckens rightly speaks of a dreadful wrong turning in Johannine scholarship. See also the fundamental criticism of A.Dauer, 'Schichten im Johannesevangelium als Anzeichen von Entwicklungen in der (den) johanneischen Gemeinde(n) nach G.Richter', in *Die Kraft der Hoffnung. Festschrift für Alterzbischof DDr Joseph Schneider zum 80.Geburtstag*, Bamberg 1986, 62-83: 'The theological differences demonstrated by Richter are artificial, sometimes arbitrary and not verifiable' (78). In his original literary study, *Anatomy of the Fourth Gospel*, Philadelphia 1983, Culpepper brings out the astonishing literary unity of the Gospel, despite the school hypotheses (on this see below, 88–94).

3. *Muratorian Canon* 10: *cohortantibus condescipulis et ēp̄s* (= *episcopis*) *suis*; Clement of Alexandria, *Hypotyposes* VI = Eusebius, HE 6.14.7: 'encouraged by his friends (or pupils: γνώριμοι)'; Jerome, *De vir. inl.* 9: *rogatus ab Asiae episcopis*; Prologue to the four Gospels (Aland, *Synopsis*, 546): *coactus est ab omnibus paene tunc Asiae episcopis et multarum ecclesiarum legationibus*; Monarchian prologue (ibid., 538): *convocatis discipulis suis in Epheso*. Cf. already Irenaeus, *Adv.haer.* 2.22.5 (Eusebius, HE 3.23.3): *omnes seniores..., qui in Asia apud Johannem discipulum domini convenerunt*. For the legendary pupil Leucius, see Chapter I, n.53 above.

4. E.Käsemann, *The Testament of Jesus*, London and Philadelphia 1968, 39, sees in it 'a Christian conventicle... being pushed to the church's periphery'. In the fourth German edition (*Jesu letzter Wille nach Johannes 17*, Tübingen

1980, 87) he adds that the christology of the Gospel suggests a 'special church group'. [Since this edition is a much expanded version of the edition translated into English, it will be cited where relevant.] In my view this theory of a conventicle contradicts the amazing influence of so late a Gospel as early as the second century.

5. See above, 7, 10. There is very little to support the derivation from Syria which is so popular today. Above all, in complete contrast to Asia Minor, the Gospel cannot be said to have had any particular effect there. The hypothesis put forward by K.Wengst, *Bedrängte Gemeinde und verherrlichter Christus. Der historische Ort des Johannesevangeliums als Schlüssel zu seiner Interpretation*, BThSt 5, Neukirchen ²1983, that it was written in the reign of Agrippa II in northern Transjordan has no support in the Gospel. Moreover he still has to shift the letters to Asia Minor. For this see below, 114ff. Alexandria would otherwise seem most likely. It has been and still is conjectured that the Gospel originated there, see John J.Gunther, 'The Alexandrian Gospel', *CBQ* 41, 1979, 581-603 (who gives the earlier literature); however, he connects this conjecture with the absurd hypothesis that the beloved disciple was a brother of Jesus, namely the Jude of John 14.8f.: 'The Relation of the Beloved Disciple to the Twelve', *ThZ* 37, 1981, 129-48. H.C.Shape, 'The Fourth Gospel, Ephesus and Alexandria', attempts a compromise: 'that the author belonged to a church which had close connections with Alexandria, that he came from Alexandria to Ephesus acquainted with Philo's works and that... through this connection, his gospel became known in Alexandria at an early date' (8). However, if it came from there one would expect in some way traditions from Egypt about the author and his school. But these are *completely* absent. Neither Gnostic authors like Basilides and his school, nor Valentinus and the Eastern branch of his school, nor Clement of Alexandria, who takes over the report of John of Ephesus from earlier tradition (*Quod dives* 42), give any hint. One cannot explain this silence, as Gunther and others do, by saying that all information was lost as a result of the Jewish rebellion in 115-17. It was precisely the Gnostic groups which seem to have survived the catastrophe. The evidence of the papyri (see above, 6) tells us little, because they have *only* been preserved in Egypt. The Fourth Gospel was certainly no less widespread in Asia Minor in the second century than in Egypt. The alleged letter of Clement of Alexandria with the Secret Gospel of Mark knows only the Alexandrian tradition about Mark, see above, 149, n.59.

6. The problem of the book titles in the New Testament has been completely neglected by scholars. Here at most it is the case with the Vulgate – which contains no evidence – that they are quite secondary and very late. However, the *clear* early tradition of the titles points in the opposite direction. Against the widespread view that most New Testament writings were circulated anonymously must be set the fact that in that case we would have to expect a great variety of titles, given the excellent tradition of the texts, since for practical reasons these anonymous writings read out in worship *had to be given a title* in the different community libraries. The communities certainly wanted to know which text was being read out to them. Nor were people

completely uninterested in the name of the author. And it is precisely this multiplicity, necessary in the case of a secondary addition in a variety of communities, which cannot be demonstrated in the New Testament. Moreover where a writing circulated anonymously, as for example Hebrews, which was probably taken into the Pauline corpus with this title, an author's name was not added subsequently, see Hengel, *Studies in the Gospel of Mark*, London and Philadelphia 1985, 64-84; 162-83. That means that in practice the giving of a title – possibly a pseudepigraphical one – was associated with the final redaction and sending to other communities. Completely anonymous writings were not very popular and were looked on with mistrust. See below, 74.

7. Irenaeus quotes the letters five times: the first, three times; the second, twice (the Gospel about twenty times and the Apocalypse more than ten times): *Adv.haer.* 1.16.3 = II John 11; 3.16.5, quotation of John 20.31; I John 2.18-22 (*in epistola sua*), a little later (3.16.8) a quotation from II John 7f. (*in praedicta epistola*); there follows a quotation from I John 4.1f. (*et rursus in epistola ait*); then I John 5.1 (*rursus in epistola clamat*). In other words Irenaeus regards the first and second letters as a unity. Here we may recall the combination of the first and second letters of Polycarp into one. The reason why the third letter was used so little in the early church is connected with its deficient theological and fundamentally 'private' content. For what purpose would it be cited? It was hardly suitable even for a liturgical reading. Moreover, for an 'apostle' the situation depicted in it seemed very painful. In my view the letters were edited together and at first partly regarded as a unity.

8. For the attestation and 'canonization' of the second and third letters see J.Lieu, *The Second and Third Epistles of John: History and Background. Studies in the NT and its World*, 1986, 5-36. For the Vetus Latina see W.Thiele, *Wortschatzuntersuchungen zu den lateinischen Texten der Johannesbriefe*, AGLB 2, 1958, 42; id., VL, *Epistulae Catholicae* 26, 1, 87*ff. The vocabulary of the Vetus Latina of the short letters of John has an antiquarian stamp because 'the texts were not worked over so often as in I John' (87*). Evidently they were regarded as a theologically insignificant 'appendix' to the first letter.

9. For the mention of the letters in *Muratorian Canon*, 26ff., 68ff., see the suggestions for a solution in Lieu, *Epistles of John* (n.8), 20ff., and especially 23 n.62 from P.Katz, *JTS* NS 8, 1957, 273f., who wants to emend the incomprehensible *et superscrictio* (sic!) *iohannis duas in catholica habentur* into *in dua(e) sin* (transcription of *syn*) *catholica*, and similarly C.F.D.Moule, *The Birth of the New Testament*, London 1962, 206 n.1, who sees the original Greek text as being πρὸς τὴν καθολικήν, from which the πρός was wrongly translated 'in'. The original text would then presuppose three letters (see also 27: *constanter sincula etiã in epistulis suis proferam*). Towards 197 CE the anti-Montanist Apollonius complains that the Montanist Themison has 'composed a Catholic letter in imitation of the apostle' (μιμούμενος τὸν ἀπόστολον καθολικήν, τινα συνταξάμενος ἐπιστολήν, Eusebius, HE 5.18.5). 'The apostle'

is probably John; in other words his letter is evidently described as 'catholic' in Asia Minor in the last decades of the second century.

10. Compare the fundamental investigation by D.J.Chapman, *John the Presbyter and the Fourth Gospel*, Oxford 1911, though he contradicts his own conclusion by finally identifying the 'presbyter John' with the son of Zebedee and apostle. For the sender of the letters see Lieu, *Epistles of John* (n.8), 52-63, though for all her good insights she fails to recognize the uniqueness of this terminology in II and III John and Papias. Most recently Udo Schnelle, *Antidoketische Christologie im Johannesevangelium*, FRLANT 144, 1987, 60, argues for an identification.

11. In the first part of the Papias prologue, before the list of disciples (Eusebius, HE 3.39.4), ἀλήθεια appears twice and τἀληθῆ once. Papias is not pleased at those who present strange commandments (ἐντολάς) from memory (μνημονεύουσιν) but at the (commandments) given by the Lord to faith, which come from the truth itself (καί ἀ̓παθῆς παραγινομένας τῆς ἀληθείας). That the concept of truth is historicized here is conditioned by the special interests of Papias and his time. So (against Körtner, above 16 n.96) one should not put him too early.

12. For discussion see Chapman, *John the Presbyter* (n.10), 9ff., though he wants to distinguish between the presbyters and the disciples. However, he has to concede that the simplest solution here is to identify 'the words of the presbyters' and 'what Andrew said'. Cf. D.G.Deeks, *ExpT* 88, 1976/7, 297: 'The most natural interpretation of the clauses... is that "presbyter" and "disciple of the Lord" are synonymous.' The distinction which is now usually made here is less clear syntactically. C.K.Barrett, *The Gospel According to St John*, London ²1978, 107, differs. Here too the terminology of Papias differs from the later terminology of Irenaeus or Clement. One should not read their understanding of 'presbyter' into Papias, who in his designation 'elder' does not yet clearly distinguish between the disciples of Jesus and their pupils.

13. Eusebius, HE 3.39.14: καὶ ἄλλας δὲ τῇ ἰδίᾳ γραφῇ παραδίδωσιν Ἀριστίωνος τοῦ πρόσθεν δεδηλωμένου τῶν τοῦ κυρίου λόγων διηγήσεις καὶ τοῦ πρεσβυτέρου Ἰωάννου παραδόσεις.

14. καὶ τοῦθ' ὁ πρεσβύτερος ἔλεγεν. Here we have the nearest parallel to the absolute ὁ πρεσβύτερος in the prescript of II and III John.

15. See G.W.H.Lampe, *A Patristic Greek Lexicon*, Oxford 1969, 1129-31; G.Bornkamm, πρέσβυς κτλ., *TDNT* 6, 651-83: 671ff..

16. Billerbeck 2 (n.16), 636ff.: Gamaliel I; Bornkamm, πρέσβυς, 659 n.47 (Hillel and Shammai); E.Schürer, *Geschichte des jüdischen Volkes im Zeitalter Jesu Christi* ⁵II, 1907, 425 nn.30,35. For the 'bishop' John in Jerusalem see A.Schlatter, 'Die Kirche Jerusalems vom Jahre 70 bis 130' (first published in 1898), in id., *Synagoge und Kirche bis zum Barkochba-Aufstand*, 1966, 129ff.; B.W.Bacon in numerous publications, ZNW 12, 1911, 186-7; JTS 23, 1922, 134-60 (136ff.); HibJ 26, 1927/28, 122-33; HTR 23, 1930, 305-7: 'The Mythical "Elder John" of Ephesus', HibJ 29, 1931, 312-26; 'John and the Pseudo-Johns', ZNW 31, 1932, 1-50; *The Gospel of the Hellenists*, New York 1933.

17. On this see A.von Harnack, *Das 'Wir' in den Johanneischen Schriften*,

SPAW.PH 1923, 96-113 = *Kleine Schriften zur Alten Kirche*, Leipzig 1980, 2, 626-43. For the authority of the author of the third letter see 98f.= 628f. It becomes clear from the 'we' in III John 9,10,12 that the author 'also claims solely for his person an authority equivalent to the community of believers itself speaking' (104-634), see also 36f.

18. See Billerbeck 2,559 on John 13.33: 'frequent address of the teacher to his pupils'. Cf. 3,331, 341 and below 168 n.45. There is a little-noted parallel to the 'we' (ἡμεῖς) which underlines the authority of the author, the designation of 'pupils' as παῖδες and of the bearers of tradition as 'old men' (γερόντων ἀνδρῶν) in the *Vitae Prophetarum* in the introduction to the 'legend' of the translation of the bones of Jeremiah at the founding of Alexandria (*Vitae Proph.* 2.5, ed.T.Schermann, *Prophetarum Vitae fabulosae...*, Leipzig 1907, 71.12f.; 61.22f.; 44.16f.). I am grateful to A.M.Schwemer for this reference.

19. Against Harnack, *Das 'Wir'* (n.17), 97 = 627, εἰργάσαμεθα and not εἰργάσασθε is to be read (see n.73 below). Paul can use κοπιᾶν with a similar significance, I Cor.15.10; Gal.4.11; Phil.2.16.

20. These references may not just be put aside as epistolary topoi which do not say anything. In both short letters the author sometimes uses stereotyped language, but that does not indicate that he does not mean what he says: cf. III John 10.14; II John 12: see below, 37f. Things are just the same with our postcards and short notes.

21. II John 5f.; cf. I John 1.1; 2.7,13f.,24; 3.11; John 1.1ff.; 15.27; 16.4. On this see Harnack, *Das 'Wir'* (n.17), 104 = 634: the author 'must be aware of himself in a special sense as seer, hearer and proclaimer of the word of life'. However, against Harnack I would say that in this way he is at the same time making the claim – in some way that we can no longer see clearly – of having been the 'eyewitness of Jesus'. The question is how far his claim was generally recognized (see below, 49f.).

22. Here Harnack has seen the situation correctly, see *Das 'Wir'* (n.17), 98 = 628 on III John 9,10,12. By changing from 'I' to 'We' 'the author... wants to stress his authority strongly. So the plural ἡμεῖς is a plural of authority which has an extraordinarly powerful effect as it stands right next to ἐγώ. That applies 'even more strongly' to the third 'we' in v.12. Cf. in Paul e.g. Rom.1.5;3.9; II Cor.10.3ff.,11 etc.; for this see K.Dick, *Der schriftstellerische Plural bei Paulus*, Halle 1900, in critical discussion with the theory that a Christian collective (for example all the apostles) always underlies the first-person plural in Paul. Significantly it is absent from Ephesians and the Pastorals. Classical Hebrew, too, does not know this 'writer's plural' so it is absent from the LXX and the pseudepigrapha (17f.; cf. 30ff. on I John). However, see n.28 on the Teacher of Righteousness! Still, it is not always insignificant, but is to be explained from the contexts, see also F.Slotty, 'Der sog. Pluralis modestiae', and 'Der soziative und der affektische Plural der ersten Person im Lateinischen', *Indogermanische Forschungen* 24, 1927, 188-90, 264-305: 'unless it denotes a... concrete plurality of persons, the plural stands either for a feeling of community (sociative) or to indicate an "affect"

(affective) or to denote both (sociative-affective)'. In Paul and John the latter is often the case. The 'affect' is often connected with claims of authority over the communities which are addressed.

23. Brown, *Epistles* (n.1), 86ff., 94ff.: 'The "We" of the Johannine School'. The author of I John, who is quite markedly dependent on the Gospel, understands himself 'as a traditionbearer of the Johannine School'. 95f.: 'The Beloved Disciple was the Johannine witness *par excellence*, and so the whole Johannine community can speak of itself as "we" because it shared his witness.' 'Since the author of I John regards himself as writing in order to preserve the testimony of this gospel (1.5), he is part of the "we", as is also the redactor of the Gospel of John.' Here the school becomes the phantom which suppresses the unique significance of the head of the school and the author. Nowhere is a plurality of 'presbyters' evident. The uniqueness of the title becomes clear from the absence of the name. There is only one elder, who speaks on the authority of the 'eyewitness' and whom everyone knows.

24. Brown, *Epistles* (n.1), 91.

25. III John 4 (τὰ ἐμὰ τέκνα); I John 2.1,12,28; 3.7,18; 5.21; John 13.33 (τεκνία); I John 2.18; 3.7; John 21.5. For the subject see the unfortunately completely forgotten work by G.Hoffmann, *Das Johannesevangelium als Alterswerk*, Gütersloh 1933, 182f., etc.

26. Lieu, *Epistles of John* (n.8), 148–65. At the end there is a devastating judgment on these two texts (216): 'Both Epistles may also know the Gospel or at least some material within it, although they are not moulded by its theology. Perhaps... not all understood the Fourth Gospel... even within its own community. We may not be able to exclude the possibility that *historically* with 2 and 3 John Johannine theology followed a "no through road".' Can one theologically and morally annihilate an otherwise unknown author so completely on the basis of two 'postcards'?

27. Lieu, *Epistles of John* (n.8), 165.

28. E.Qimron and J.Strugnell, 'An Unpublished Halakhic Letter from Qumran', *The Israel Museum Journal* 4, Spring 1985, 9–12. Here I am to some extent quoting from the translation of the part of the text reproduced, which has been kindly supplied to me by my colleague H.Stegemann. We may hope that this text, which has long been known, will finally appear. It contains some surprises. Cf. n.52 below.

29. Irenaeus, *Adv.haer.* 3.3.4 = Eusebius, HE 4.14.6; cf. *Adv.haer.* 1.26.1.

30. He writes around 196/97 that John raised a dead man in Ephesus, Eusebius, HE 5.18.14. Also obscure is the report of Epiphanius that Leucius had been a companion of John in the fight against Cerinthus, *Pan.* 51.6.9, see above, 148 n.53.

31. Clement of Alexandria, *Quis dives*, ch.42, and R.A.Lipsius, *Die apokryphen Apostelgeschichten und Apostellegenden* I, Brunswick 1883 (reprinted Amsterdam 1976), 349: 'The origin of this narrative in Asia Minor is probably not to be doubted.' Clement of Alexandria, *Hypotyposes* Book VI, quoted in Eusebius 6.14.7: 'Lastly John, when he saw that the bodily things (τὰ σωματικά) had been made known in the Gospels, composed a spiritual

Gospel, admonished by his friends and inspired by the Spirit.' Clement received this tradition 'from the old presbyters' (τῶν ἀνέκαθεν πρεσβυτέρων, HE 6.14.5).

32. On this see E.Junod and J.-D.Kaestli (eds.), *Acta Iohannis,* CC Ser.Apoc. 1, 1983, 145-58. It is independent of the Acts of John and probably goes back to an early ascetic circle. Moreover a whole series of similar ancient legends of John exist, ibid., 109ff., cf.157: 'Behind these texts we suspect the existence of an ancient tradition, oral or written, which is difficult or impossible to localize.' 'Generally associated with Ephesus and Asia Minor, they stress the role played by the apostle in the edification of the church and the fight against heresy' (158).

33. *De praescr.haer.* 36.3: could this tradition in the West have been a counter to the calling of John in Ephesus? There are other traditions about John in Tertullian, see ibid., 32.2 and *adv.Marc.* 4.5.2. The latter passage could be directed not only against Marcion but also against people like Gaius in Rome. For the virginity of John see *Monogam.* 17.1: *Ioannes aliqui Christi spado* (cf.Matt.19.12). This could perhaps go back *inter alia* to John 19.26f. and Rev.14.4. On this see P.Corssen, *Die Monarchianischen Prologe zu den Evangelien,* TU 15.1, 1896, 87ff., though he overestimates the significance of the prologues to the Gospels. He conjectures an origin in Gnostic circles (95) and constructs an old *historia ecclesiastica* on the evangelists (78ff.). For the text of the prologue see J.Regul, *Die antimarcionitischen Evangelienprologe,* AGLB 6, 1969, 42f. lines 1f.: *qui virgo electus a Deo...*; for the context see 223f.

34. Jerome, *Comm. in ep. ad Galat.* 3.6, PL 26, 462: *Beatus Joannes evangelista cum Ephesi moraretur usque ad ultimam senectutem, et vix inter discipulorum manus ad ecclesiam deferretur, nec posset in plura vocem verba contexere, nihil aliud per singulas solebat proferre collectas, nisi hoc: Filioli diligite alterutrum...*'; G.E.Lessing, *Werke,* ed. H.G.Göpfert, VIII, Munich 1979, 15-20.

35. The best survey is in R.A.Lipsius, *Die apokryphen Apostelgeschichten* (n.31), I, 348ff., see also the indexes in the supplementary volume, 206ff. (included in vol.1 in the reprint): 'After Peter and Paul there is no apostle of whom church tradition preserves a richer treasury of legends than of John, the apocalyptist and beloved disciple of Jesus' (348). John of Ephesus is no more a mere 'fiction' than are Peter and Paul. *Ex nihilo nihil fit.* Theologians who think far too much about their 'historical-critical method' should finally also learn that. It is amazing that so rich a tradition could arise about this 'disciple of the Lord' who was at work a generation later.

36. H.Dörrie, in 'Ammonius, der Lehrer Plotins', *Platonica Minora,* Munich 1976, 324-60 (350-56). If such confusions take place in a milieu of critical scholars, how much more is that likely among the Christians of Asia Minor between 130 and 150! Cf. also the two Hippolyti in Rome.

37. 21.24, on this see below, 76ff.

38. R.Morgenthaler, *Statistik des neutestamentlichen Wortschatzes,* Zurich and Frankfurt 1958, 164, according to Nestle, 21st edition. With 335 words the letter to Philemon is almost 50% longer and with 452 words the letter of Jude is almost 100% longer. Even in I John (2137 words) one may not expect the

same 'fullness' as the Gospel (15416). I Thessalonians is much worse here in comparison with Romans. If the Gospel and I John *must* have different authors, would one not have to follow F. C. Baur in assuming that here?

39. J.Wellhausen, *Das Evangelium Johannis*, Berlin 1908, 146. Reprinted in id, *Evangelienkommentare*, Berlin and New York 1987, 746: 'The Johannine language is marked out positively by its measured gravity; in this way it is as far removed from the popular character of Mark as from the somewhat literary character of Luke and approaches the Priestly Codex in the Pentateuch... One has the same impression of pedantry as in the Priestly Codex... The language is meant to be hieratic.' In my view 'the elder' comes from a similar milieu, see below, 109ff.

40. A modern parallel is the typical 'school language' of Bultmann, which according to oral tradition the master is said to have forced on his pupils by requiring the use of his technical terminology in his seminar. However, the 'sociolect' of the Marburg New Testament seminar was far from achieving the unity that we find in the Fourth Gospel and the letters. Therefore we do not need to assume different authors in John.

41. Unfortunately Morgenthaler (*Statistik*, n.38) lumps together I-III John in his statistics (164). The three letters have 2601 words with a vocabulary of 302 (cf. Galatians, 2229/526; Ephesians 2418/529 and Titus 658/303!). The poverty of vocabulary in I John with its didactic monotony is even more striking than in the Gospel. This fact alone tells in favour of a common authorship. The explanation in terms of the sociolect is far too simple. We have nothing comparable anywhere else in early Christianity! As a specifically private letter III John is somewhat richer (see n.44 below). The tables of word statistics in Lieu, *Epistles of John* (n.8), 217ff. (cf. also Schnelle, *Antidoketische Christologie* [n.10], 62f., are no evidence for different authorship because of the essentially different genres. In the Gospel itself the miracle stories and the passion narrative also of course have a richer vocabulary than the revelation discourses.

42. H.Conzelmann, *Theologie als Schriftauslegung*, BEvTh 65, 1974, 214. Lieu, *Epistles of John* (n.8), wants to relate this hardly flattering predicate above all to II and III John, 94 n.114, 165, 172. F.C.Baur, 'Die johanneischen Briefe', *ThJb* 7, 1848, 295-377, already denies in connection with I-III John that 'these letters contain particular individual and historical features' (315); for him they are 'only the echo of the Gospel resounding in weak tones'. Like his pupil Planck a year earlier (*ThJb* 6, 1847, 468f.), he wants to assign them to 'the Montanist circle of ideas'. A more blatant false historical judgment is hardly possible. Baur not only led off radical 'historical criticism' in Germany, but also perpetrated a not insignificant series of radical historical errors.

43. There is abundant bibliographical information in G.Wagner, *An Exegetical Bibliography of the New Testament, John and 1, 2, 3 John*, Macon, Ga. 1984, and in Lieu, *Epistles of John* (n.8), 230ff. See also below, 176 n. 7.

44. With 219 words the letter is the shortest work in the New Testament; with 245 words the second letter is about 11% longer. However, when it comes to vocabulary the situation is reversed; here the third letter has around

9% more terms, with 104 words; indeed with its four *hapax legomena* in the New Testament it has more than the first and second letters put together. Within the Johannine corpus we find 17 special words in it as opposed to 6 in the second letter. This is exclusively connected with its private character and is no argument in the question of authorship.

45. See I Tim.1.2; Titus 1.4. The formula τὰ ἐμὰ τέκνα is stressed. The fourfold address as ἀγαπητός (1,2,5,11) also points to an intimate teacher-pupil relationship. In I John ἀγαπητοί appears six times as a form of address. See also above n.18.

46. III John 15 twice, cf. John 15.13-15; 11.11 and Luke 12.4.

47. John 20.21; 17.18, 20.

48. Cf.I John 5.21; Rev.2.20. It is striking that in the Fourth Gospel, apart from the 'Greeks' in 12.20 and 7.35, where possibly Greek-speaking Diaspora Jews are meant, and Pilate, who cannot be dispensed with, in contrast to the Synoptic Gospels no Gentiles appear, nor are Gentile areas or places in Palestine mentioned. The *basilikos* in 4.46ff. is not a Gentile, in contrast to the parallels in Matt.8.5-13 and Luke 7.1-10, but a Jew, as an official (of Antipas). For Judaism see Billerbeck 3, 421f.: participation in pagan meals could be understood as idolatry in ignorance. See also the abundant material in 4, 366f., 374ff. The non-Jews are the (ritually) 'unclean': mMaksh 2, 3, cf. mShek 8.1. For a refusal to accept food from the hand of non-Jews see Josephus, *Vita* 14. In the Johannine community the 'purification' – which is no longer understood in a ritual way – takes place through the word of Jesus (John 15.3) or baptism (13.10f.). However, the problem of making unclean by indirect contact with idolatry remains (cf. Rev.2.14,20). Pagan food is *ipso facto* under suspicion of being connected with idolatry: cf. E.Bickerman, *Jews in the Greek Age*, 1988, 248ff., see also Acts 15.20,29. The problem was more complex in early Christianity than it appears to us from a Pauline perspective.

49. The term is lacking in the Gospel and in the first and second letters, but we find it twenty times in the Apocalypse. The third letter uses it three times: vv.6 (plural), 9 and 10. Here the difference is visible between the 'school language' in the Johannine circle with its theological stamp and general Christian language, though of course the elder could also make use of the latter when he wanted to.

50. The same problem emerged in Rome, see P.Lampe, *Die stadtrömischen Christen in den ersten beiden Jahrhunderten*, WUNT 2.R 18, ²1988, and probably also in Antioch: it is precisely for that reason that Ignatius fights so bitterly ten to twenty years later to impose monarchical episcopacy. There was still no monarchical bishop even in the community in Philippi, to which Polycarp is writing.

51. Cf. John 3.20f.; 5.29f.; 7.7; 8.39; 10.32; I John 2.11, 29; 3.4,7f.,10,15.

52. See above, 165 n.28. I am also indebted to the kindness of H.Stegemann for this passage: he deciphered the text photograph in the article by Qimron and Strugnell (n.28) and translated it.

53. The later exegesis of the early church, which had its difficulties with this letter, the apostolicity of which was disputed, interpreted the

ἀγαθοποιεῖν in v.11 as φιλοξενία and made it an ἐπιστολὴ περὶ φιλοξενίας, see J.A.Cramer, *Catenae Graecorum patrum in Novum Testamentum* VIII, Oxford 1840 (reprinted Hildesheim 1967), 149.

54. See above 30 n.31. The formation of this legend will have been influenced not only by the seven letters of the Apocalypse but also by the second and third letters.

55. Clement of Alexandria, *Hypotyposes* VI = Eusebius 6.14.7; *Muratorian Canon*, 9ff.; Monarchian prologue to the Gospels, text in Regul, *Evangelienprologe* (n.33), 43 lines 18f.: *convocatis discipulis suis*. Cf. n.3 above.

56. Eusebius, HE 3.39.4. Cf. also Irenaeus, *Ep. ad Florinus*, in Eusebius, HE 5.20.7f.; so influential and long-lived a teacher and bishop as Polycarp wrote only a number of letters to communities and private individuals, of which two letters to the Philippians have been preserved (as one).

57. Gunther, *CBQ* 41, 1979, 601f. completely distorts the situation in contrasting the elder of II and III John with the seer who writes from Patmos as a brother to the seven communities – among which Ephesus stands at the head – and stating that John of Patmos 'did not teach as a proto-archbishop of Ephesus'. Indeed he did not, any more than the elder of the letters of John 'taught as a proto-archbishop of Alexandria'! Here Gunther is reading the later conceptions of the John legend into the text (see above, n.5). At the time of the Johannine school there was still no clearly acknowledged monarchical episcopate, far less were there any 'archbishops', either in Asia Minor or elsewhere. His thoughts on the community structure in Egypt at the end of the first century are pure speculation. We simply know nothing about them. Polycarp, whom he cites as a supra-regional authority, was active around a generation after John. His 'supra-regional' influence, like that of Ignatius or Dionysius of Corinth, rested on the force of his personality, not on his local ministry.

58. We probably find an identity of school and house community in the *Acta Justini*: Justin was condemned with six companions mentioned by name (and perhaps also others). Recension A adds καὶ τῆς συνοδίας αὐτῶν after the seven names. To the prefect's question about the place of meeting Justin mentions his abode 'above the baths of Myrtinus'. 'I know no other place of meeting than there. And if anyone wanted to come to me, I gave him a share in the words of truth.' Euelpistus from Cappadocia replied to the question as to who taught him: 'I was fond of hearing the words of Justin', see H.Musurillo, *The Acts of the Christian Martyrs*, Oxford 1972, 42ff., chs.3-7, cf. also Acts 19.9 with the addition of Codex D and other Western witnesses. The 'pupils' of Christian Gnostic teachers like Valentinus or Marcion before his break with the church and then later the catechetical school in Alexandria must be imagined to have had a similar form.

59. Cf. Didache 12f. The requirement of hospitality which is constantly made corresponds with this, see A.von Harnack, *The Expansion of Christianity in the First Three Centuries*, London 1904, I, 219-24, 435-44; also D.Gorce, 'Gastfreundschaft', *RAC* 8, 1972, 1061-1123 (1103ff.). For the dangers see also I Tim.3.6 and the complaint of Irenaeus about the drive of the Valentinian

Marcus and his itinerant preachers as far as Gaul, *Adv.haer.* 1.13.1ff., 4.6.7. For early Christian travelling see Hengel, *Studies in Mark* (n.6), 80, 181 n.104. We urgently need a monograph on the correspondence and travel activity in the church of the second century.

60. Among other things the exegesis of the early church conjectured a letter to a Christian woman: J.A.Cramer, *Catenae Graecorum patrum* (n.53), Vol.8, 147. Clement of Alexandria even thinks of a Babylonian woman with the name of Eklekte, cf. I Peter 5.13, but the metaphorical interpretation in terms of the church predominated, which probably facilitated the recognition as a 'Catholic' letter, see Lieu, *Epistles of John* (n.8), 31. According to Clement the whole letter was addressed to virgins (*ad virgines scripta*), *Adumbrationes*, in Clement of Alexandria III, GCS 17.2, ed.O.Stählin, 215, thus also as the *subscriptio* in a Sahidic codex, see Thiele, *Epistulae Catholicae* (n.8), 285; Lieu, *Epistles of John* (n.8). Some few late Greek and Latin textual witnesses and sources speak of a letter to the Parthians. The same form of address also appears in the first letter in different variations or slips of the pen in Old Latin manuscripts and in the Latin fathers after Augustine, see Thiele, 241ff., 385-99 and introduction 81*, 87*. Here one could conjecture a misreading for πρὸς παρθένους and a transference of the title from the second to the first letter. See A.Bludau, 'Die Epistula ad Partos', *Theologie und Glaube* 11, 1919, 223-36; R.E.Brown, *Epistles*, 772-4; Lieu, *Epistles of John* (n.8), 28f.; Theodor Zahn, FGNK II, 1884, 92, 99ff.

61. The interpretation by T.Zahn, *Einleitung in das Neue Testament*, Leipzig ³1907, II, 593, is still plausible: 'The community is not only the bride of Christ (John 3.29; Acts 22.17), but also his spouse (Acts 21.9; Eph.5.22-32, cf. Rom.7.4), and what applies to the whole church can also be said of the individual community (II Cor.11.2) except that it is not "the spouse" but in its part "spouse of the κύριος", and therefore κυρία without the article.' One could also refer to the woman who embodies the people of God in Rev.12 and Tertullian, *ad Mart.* 1.1. In the visions of Hermas an old woman appeared who is frequently addressed as κυρία and who represents the church, see H.Kraft, *Clavis Patrum Apostolicorum*, Darmstadt 1963, 286. In *Visions* 2.4.1 (= 8.1) she is presented by the interpreting angel as the church. For the whole question see Lieu, *Epistles of John* (n.8), 66f. Perhaps one might point out that the royal bride in Song of Songs 6.9,10 is described as ἐκλέκτη, and that in 7.1. the name of the bride, the Shulamite, is assimilated to that of king Solomon (šᵉlomo): the designation κυρία points to κύριος. The formula ἀδελφή μου (νύμφη)' also appears a number of times: 4.9f.,12; 5.1; cf. also 8.8. In Judaism the allegorical interpretation of the Song of Songs had already long been in fashion; see W.Riedel, *Die Auslegung des Hohenliedes in der jüdischen Gemeinde und der griechischen Kirche*, Leipzig 1898. IV Ezra 5.24ff. and R.Akiba already interpret the Song of Songs allegorically, see H.P.Rüger, 'Das Werden des christlichen Alten Testaments', *JBTh* 3, 1988, 175-189: 180. I am grateful to A.M.Schwemer for this observation. Perhaps a first Christian indication is visible here.

62. II John 4: περιπατοῦντας ἐν ἀληθείᾳ; III John 3: ἐν ἀληθείᾳ περιπατεῖς; 4:

ἐν τῇ ἀληθείᾳ περιπατοῦντα. The introduction in II John 4, Ἐχάρην λίαν, and III John 3 is identical, as is also the conclusion II John 12 and III John 13f. In my view this indicates that the letters belong together in time and in terms of situation. The formal περιπατεῖν ἐν ἀληθείᾳ is a Hebraism which has a parallel in the LXX: IV Reg. 20.3 (cf. III Reg.3.6).

63. Cf. the twofold ἵνα ἀγαπᾶτε ἀλλήλους in John 13.34 and 15.12, see also n.21 above.

64. Cf. I John 2.3-11: the heretics do not keep the commandments (2.3f.), therefore the truth and God's love is not in them (2.4f.). The 'commandments' concentrate on the one 'old' commandment, i.e. the one which was given at that time by Jesus and observed by the community (2.7f.), which Jesus himself first made possible (John 13.34: καθὼς ἠγάπησα ὑμᾶς, cf. I John 4.19), see below, 67.

65. In the farewell discourses, John 13.34, it is of course the *new* commandment of Jesus: the evangelist and author of the letter is probably aware of the difference in time between then and now.

66. For Essene and Pharisaic polemic see M.Hengel, 'Rabbinische Legende und frühpharisäische Geschichte. Schimeon ben Schetach und die achtzig Hexen von Askalon', AHAW.PH 2, 1984, Abh. 2.

67. Nowhere in the letters of Paul do we discover the names of the opponents. Cephas, James and Apollos cannot really be called opponents. Taunt-names or periphrases appear in II Cor.11.5,13f.; 12.11; Gal.5.12; Phil.3.2; cf. also Gal.1.7; 3.1,10; 4.17; II Cor.2.17; 4.2; Rom.3.8; 15.31. Nor are the troublemakers in Corinth mentioned by name in I Clement. In Rev.2.20 the pseudo-prophetess Jezebel is similarly a cover name, as is the 'teaching of Balaam' (2.14). The Nicolaitans, presumably an old and well-known group, in 2.6,15 are probably identical with the representatives of the teaching of Balaam (see 54 n.21 below). Only in the pseudepigraphical Pastoral Epistles do the names of (fictitious – or former) opponents accumulate; that is harmless. In a Johannine pseudepigraph one would really expect the name of Cerinthus. See above 11 on the *Epistula Apostolorum*.

68. Cf. Smyrn.7.2: 'It is right to refrain from such men and not even to speak about them in private or in public, but to give heed to the prophets and especially to the gospel.' This attitude also explains the widespread silence of the rabbis about the Jewish Christians. Only with Justin, Melito, Irenaeus and the anti-Gnostic, anti-Marcionite and anti-Montanist authors, i.e. at the same time at a higher literary level, does this attitude change: now the opponent is mentioned by name and also quoted, as was customary in controversies between philosophical schools. But even so educated a Jew as Philo withholds from us the names of the 'false teachers' in his polemic, e.g. against the radical allegorists, *Migr.Abr.* 89ff.

69. It appears in the New Testament only in the Johannine letters: I John 2.18,22; 4.3; II John 7. The term is absent from the Apostolic Fathers with the exception of Polycarp from Asia Minor, Phil.7.1, where the dependence on I or II John and at the same time the Johannine school tradition is quite

tangible (see above 16 n.95). Cf. Brown, *Epistles* (n.1), 333: 'Thus the Johannine School may have coined the term "Antichrist" for a concept designated less vividly elsewhere.' It then presumably again plays a role in Melito in his work on 'The Devil and the Apocalypse' (Eusebius, HE 4.26.2) and after that above all in Irenaeus, who in *Adv.haer*.1.13.1 describes the Valentinian and 'magus' Marcus as the *praecursor...Antichristi*. Cf. also 3.6.5; 3.7.2; 3.16.5 (quotation from I John 2.18f.,21f.); 3.16.8 (II John 7f. and I John 4.1-3); 3.23.7; 5.25.4; 5.30.4, etc. Here Irenaeus brings in theology from Asia Minor and may be dependent in detail on Papias and Melito. The same is even more the case with Hippolytus and his interpretation, and his writings on Christ and the Antichrist, and on the Gospel of John and the Apocalypse against Gaius. The term is not unknown even to Clement of Alexandria, see *Excerpta ex Theodoto* 9.1. For Tertullian see below, 175 n.1.

70. Against Brown, *Epistles* (n.1), 337, the *antichristoi* did not replace the '*Antichristos*' who comes, but they are his forerunners, who indicate the 'last time'. The author did not want to correct the traditional conception of the eschatological enemy of God, but to make it more precise in view of the new critical situation. They had 'heard that the Antichrist is coming' as the teaching of the school.

71. Cf. Mark 13.22 par.; Acts 20.29f.; II Thess.2.3ff.; I Tim.4.1ff.; II Tim.3.1ff.; 4.3ff.; II Peter 2.1. The conception goes back to the Jewish expectation of an apostasy from the faith in the last time: Dan.11.32ff.; 1QpHab 2.5ff.; mSota 9.15; on this see C.Spicq, *Les Épitres Pastorales*, EtB ⁴1969, 1, 495ff.; 2, 772f.

72. That this problem is not just limited to the Johannine school or community follows from Acts 20.30: καὶ ἐξ ὑμῶν αὐτῶν ἀναστήσονται ἄνδρες...The fourfold stress on ἐξ ὑμῶν and the corresponding μεθ᾽ἡμῶν in I John 2.19 shows that this is a group close to the author, see Brown, *Epistles* (n.1), 338. II John 7, ὅτι πολλοὶ πλάνοι ἐξῆλθον εἰς τὸν κόσμον, is formulated in more general terms: perhaps because here the author is writing to a community in another place for which the emphatic ἐξ ὑμῶν could have been open to misunderstanding. At the same time we must reckon with the possibility that the instigation towards being led astray came from outside, see below 55.

73. Here εἰργασάμεθα is to be read with Nestle/Aland²⁶ instead of εἰργάσασθε, thus with the original of Vaticanus, Cod.P, the majority text, the marginal reading of the Harclean and the Sahidic version. This is certainly the *lectio difficilior*, as it interrupts the sequence of the 'you' which twice precedes it and follows it, see Brown, *Epistles* (n.1), 670. With additional perceptive reasons see Lieu, *Epistles of John* (n.8), 88f. against R.Schnackenburg, *Die Johannesbriefe*, HThK XIII.3, ³1965, 314 etc.

74. Lieu, *Epistles of John* (n.8), 89, gives this as one of the reasons for the – unjustified – preference for the second person plural by numerous exegetes. However, she fails to see that here there is 'an unusually self-conscious note'. The special feature is that the elder is quite naturally speaking in the name of the Johannine circle – which he founded.

75. The φέρει has the significance of 'bringing' or 'presenting' teaching, see K.Weiss, φέρω, *TDNT* 9, 1974, 58.

76. The secular-sounding χαίρειν αὐτῷ μὴ λέγετε indicates a Gentile-Christian milieu (see above, 35 and 168 n.51), 48; however, what is meant is the Christian greeting among brethren, cf. III John 15; John 20.19,21,26, see also John 14.17; 16.33. The peace in the Christian greeting promises the other the peace of Christ. H.Windisch and H.Preisker, *Die katholischen Briefe*, HNT ³1951, 139: 'The prohibition of the greeting indicates that the greeting was not a matter of form for Christians or for the people of the ancient East generally, but represented an interpersonal contact.'

77. Cf. III John 10f.; John 3.19ff.; 5.29; 7.7; 8.41; I John 3.8, 12.

78. Matt.10.12f. = Luke 10.5f. Cf. also Isa.48.22; 57.21 and Rom.3.17: one cannot promise the peace of Christ to the herald of the Antichrist; cf. Isa.48.22; 57.21. The concrete procedure depicted here signifes more than a periphrasis of the refusal of 'church community': against H.Conzelmann, χαίρειν κτλ, *TDNT* 9, 367 n.64. Everyday elementary living and 'church community' are here still indissolubly connected. 'Church community' in fact takes place completely in private houses.

79. Whereas Irenaeus, *Adv.haer.* 1.16.3 cites II John 11 with approval, Clement of Alexandria, *Adumbrationes in II Joh.*, GCS III², 215, tones down the text for moral reasons: *Tales non salutare prohibet et in hospitium suscipere; hoc enim inhumanum est, sed conquirere vel condisputare cum talibus ammonet eos qui non valent intellegibiliter divina tractare, ne per eos traducantur a doctrina veritatis, veri similibus inducti rationibus* (according to M; V differs significantly and says: *Tales salutare prohibet… hoc enim* in huius modi *est inhumanum, sed nec conquirere…*). Nor is prayer together in the house allowed, because the prayer is followed by salutation, *quae… gaudii [est] et pacis indicium*. Here is the voice of the educated intellectual who can no longer understand the rigorous consistency in the command of the elder. The moral protest also appears in F.C.Baur, 'Die johanneischen Briefe', *ThJb (T)* 7, 1848, 295-336 (331f.) against the exegesis by F.Lücke, *Commentar über die Briefe des Evangelisten Johannes*, ³1856, 460f., on II John 10f.: 'But one should not so lightly, from the orthodox standpoint, declare such a proclamation of *the most loveless partisan hatred* (my italics) to be Johannine Christianity.' W.M.L.de Wette, 'Kurze Erklärung des Evangeliums und der Briefe Johannis', in *Kurzgefasstes exegetisches Handbuch zum Neuen Testament* I/3, ³1846, 279, is chided for his judgment which in terms of the content is correct: 'This prohibition is completely appropriate for the character of John as this is presented in his behaviour towards Cerinthus (see below, n.74) and appears with similar statements by the apostle Paul (Phil.3.2; Gal.1.8; I Cor.16.22) in the polemical zeal and defence against what seemed damaging to the preservation of the church, its justification.' Now the Gospel also shows that the author of the Johannine corpus could hate. For that very reason we should leave general moral judgments on one side in our historical questions about the author. Even the apostles were no moral saints. The substance of W.Bauer's remarks in *Das Johannesevangelium*, HNT 6³, 1933, 248, are correct:

'John reacts to the antipathy of the world outside with hot hatred... Rather we are confronted with a polemical nature ready at any time to intervene with every means in defence and attack for the beloved brotherhood, its masters and its faith.' That is true of both Gospel *and* letters.

80. Acts 20.29; Did.16.3; Ignatius, Philad.2.2; II Clem.5.2ff. (apocryphal gospel tradition); Justin, *Apology* 16.13; *Dialogue* 35.3 (both times quotations from Matt.7.13). According to Eusebius, HE 5.16.17 the Montanist prophetess Maximilla twice says: 'I am persecuted like a wolf from the sheep; I am not a wolf...' In his work against Marcion and his disciples, Tatian's disciple Rhodon calls Marcion the 'Pontic wolf': Eusebius, HE 5.13.3; cf. also HE 4.24 and Lampe, *Lexicon* (n.15), s.v. λύκος.

81. Eph.7.1 and no less sharply Smyrn.4.1: 'But I guard you in advance against beasts in the form of men, *whom you must not only not receive, but if it is possible not even meet...*', cf. 7.2; Philad.2.2; Trall.9.1. For the prohibition against contact see also Titus 3.10f. and on this Spicq, *Épîtres pastorales* (n.71), II, 687: 'an official rejection of brotherhood'. See also Polycarp and Cerinthus, according to Irenaeus, *Adv.haer.* 3.3.4 = Eusebius, HE 5.20.7; if Polycarp had heard such false teaching he would have 'stopped his ears' and he would have 'run out of the places in which he... heard such teaching...'

82. I Cor.5.4f. Paul's example continues to have an effect: I Tim.1.20; Rev.2.22ff.

83. Gal.1.8f.; I Cor.16.22; cf. II Cor.11.13-15; Rom.16.17; Phil.3.2.

84. I Thess.3.5; Gal.4.11, cf. 2.2; 3.4; Phil.2.16; I Cor.15.2b.

85. John 17.12. In II Thess.2.3 the υἱὸς τῆς ἀπωλείας is the enemy of God in the end time.

86. I John 3.8,10,12; cf.4.3. Polycarp, Phil.7.1: ...ἀντίχριστός ἐστιν... ἐκ τοῦ διαβόλου ἐστίν... πρωτότοκός ἐστι τοῦ σατανᾶ. Here we have a polemical line of tradition which can be demonstrated from the Gospel of John through the letters to Polycarp, see also 17 nn. 94, 95. On this see N.A.Dahl, 'Der Erstgeborene Satans und der Vater des Teufels (Polyk.7,1 und Joh 8,44)', in ΑΠΟΦΟΡΕΤΑ. *Festschrift für Ernst Haenchen*, BZNW 30, 1964, 70-84.

87. John 4.9. For the attitude towards the Samaritans see Billerbeck 1, 538-60: the view of the rabbis was controversial. R.Eliezer Hyrcanus to some degree identified them with Gentiles; his pupil Akiba and R.Gamaliel II with proselytes. But we must assume that before 70 there were groups which rejected the Samaritans even more radically. The hatred between the two groups was considerable, cf. John 8.48. Josephus, *Antt.* 18.30; 20.118-36 = BJ 2.232-45; cf. 9.288-91; 11.303, 347; 13.74-9, etc. Only against this background does the revolutionary destruction of an old 'image of the enemy' as this can be found in the parable of Jesus in Luke 10.30-37 become clear. The conduct of a Christian has to be orientated on that and not on the obsolete forms of early Christian polemic.

III. I John and the Split in the School

1. For the attestation of all three letters of John but especially the first, see R.E.Brown, *The Epistles of John*, AB 30, 1980, 6-11. The letter is attested by Papias, Polycarp and perhaps also by Justin, *I Apology* 32.7,8, cf. I John 1.7; 2.14; 3.9; *Dial*. 45.4; cf. I John 3.8; *Dial*. 123.9, cf. I John 3.1 (2.3; 3.22; 5.3) and strikingly often in the Letter to Diognetus 10.1-4, cf. I John 4.9,12,19-21; Diognetus 11.4, cf. I John 1.1. For Irenaeus, who is the first to name John as author, see above, 2f.; for Clement of Alexandria see *Stromateis*, 2.66.4 = I John 5.16f.: 'John teaches in his long letter'; 3.32.2 = I John 1.6f.: 'John in his letter'; 3.44.5 = I John 2.4; 3.45.1f. = I John 2.18f.: 'the word of the apostle John'; 4.100.4 = I John 3.18f.: 'John says'. Clement expounds the first and second letters in the *Hypotyposes*; we have a summary in the translation by Cassiodorus, *Adumbrationes Clementis Alexandrini in Epistolas canonicas* on I John 1.1; GCS 17.2 = Clement of Alexandria III, ed. O.Stählin, 1970, 209ff. Tertullian already quotes I John very frequently, above all in *Adv.Prax.* and *De pudicitia*, but also often in *De praescriptione haereticorum* and *adv.Marcionem*. He particularly likes the designation of the heretic as 'Antichrist'. The letter becomes an important arsenal for him in the fight against the heretics.

2. I John 1.4 puts on particular stress by the first person plural pronoun καὶ ταῦτα γράφομεν ἡμεῖς; 2.1,7,8,12,13 (twice) γράφω ὑμῖν; 2.14 (three times),21,26; 5.13: ἔγραψα ὑμῖν.

3. J.H.Moulton, *A Grammar of New Testament Greek*, Vol.IV: N.Turner, *Style*, Edinburgh 1976, 135. Cf. also G.Hoffmann, *Das Johannesevangelium als Alterswerk*, Gütersloh 1933. See already H.Ewald, *Johanneische Schriften*, Göttingen, I, 1861, 436f. That a work written in old age can take on a particular stamp is evident from a comparison between Bultmann's commentary on the Gospel of John or his *Theology of the New Testament* and his commentary on the three letters of John (which appeared in 1941, 1953 and 1967 respectively, the last when Bultmann was eighty-three). See also below, 133.

4. The diminutive τεκνία appears seven times: I John 2.1 (τεκνία μου),12,28; 3.7, 18; 4.4; 5.21 (for the closing verse see n.5 below); παιδία, 2.14,18. Cf. also the address to the disciples of Paul in the Pastorals: I Tim.1.2,18; II Tim.1.2; 2.1; Titus 1.4. This pseudepigraphical work is a 'historicizing adaptation', but in I John the address is genuine and appropriate to the historical situation. For the historical Paul see Philemon 9f., the 'old man' Paul and his 'child' Onesimus. For III John 4 see above, 35 n.45. Alongside this the address ἀδελφοί appears only once (3.13), though in the letter the relationship to the 'brethren' plays a major role (2.9ff.; 3.10-17; 4.20f.; cf. III John 3,5,10). For the juxtaposition with the Johannine Jesus cf. John 20.17; 21.5; 13.33. R.E.Brown, *Epistles* (n.1), 214f., gives a good survey of Old Testament and early Jewish terminology. The picture of the elder from I John continues in Jerome, *Comm. in Ep.ad Galat.* 3.7, PL 26,462, with the address *filioli* as a translation of τεκνία in the Vetus Latina (*filioli mei*, 2.1 etc., cf. VL, *Epistulae Catholicae* 26.1, ed. W.Thiele). The same thing is also true of Clement of Alexandria, *Quis dives*

42.13, where the old John calls out to the young robber captain: 'Why do you, a child (τέκνον), flee from me, your own father, who is an old man?'

5. Nor can one explain this remarkable conclusion by literary-critical artifices. A redactor had no better reasons than the author for making a letter close with this sentence! 'Idols', εἴδωλα, may here, like the term *gillūlīm* in Qumran, simply be a periphrasis for grave sin, in the context of the letter above all apostasy and heresy, which are to be identified with idolatry, see R.Schnackenburg, *Die Johannesbriefe*,HThK XIII.3, ³1965, 292f., following W.Nauck, *Die Tradition und der Charakter des ersten Johannesbriefes*, WUNT 3, 1953, 137; see also R.E.Brown, *Epistles* (n.1), 616ff., 632. It is already said of the false prophets and the lawless in Deut.13.2ff., 13ff. that they lead people astray into apostasy: 'They are lawless men who have gone out from you (LXX: ἐξήλθοσαν... ἐξ ὑμῶν καὶ ἀπέστησαν πάντας... 13.14, cf.11 and also I John 2.19, see below, 51f.). Irenaeus, *Adv.haer*.1.15.6, quotes an iambic poem which recalls the Gnostic deceiver Marcus, εἰδωλοποιὲ Μάρκε καὶ τερατοσκόπε (*Idolorum fabricator, Marce, et portentorum inspector*). It was composed by a θεῖος or θεοφιλὴς πρεσβύτης, possibly his old predecessor as bishop in Lyons, the martyr Pothinus. These parallels not only shed light on the origin of the author but also make clear the Johannine, dualistically-motivated rigorism, cf. also III John 7b and Rev.2.14, 20. It is improbable that I John 5.21 is 'completely incomprehensible in terms of the letter', 'presupposes another situation', namely persecution and the danger of apostasy, and therefore 5.14-21 comes from a later author, as is conjectured by K.Wengst, *Der erste, zweite und dritte Brief des Johannes*, ÖTK 21, 1978, 224ff. The stylistic unity of the text suggests one author. E.Stegemann, 'Kindlein hütet euch vor den Gottesbildern', *ThZ* 41, 1985, 284-90, follows him, but he wants to maintain the literary unity. The *status confessionis* certainly exists for the 'elder', but in the context it is not over against persecution from the state, but over against the heresy which amounts to apostasy and to idolatry.

6. Brown, *Epistles* (n.1), 32, 101f.

7. The relationship between the Gospel and the letters has been argued over since F.C.Baur and is discussed in detail by H.J.Holtzmann, 'Das Problem des ersten Johanneischen Briefes in seinem Verhältnis zum Evangelium', *JPTh* 7, 1881, 690-712; 8, 1882, 128-52, 316-42, 460-85. It was already argued by Scaliger that the letters do not come from the apostle, and the dispute went on in several variants throughout the nineteenth century (462ff.); see e.g. F.Bleek and W.Mangold, *Einleitung in das NT*, ⁴1886; A.Jülicher and E.Fascher, *Einleitung in das NT*, ⁷1931, 224-33, or the introduction by A.E.Brooke, *The Johannine Epistles*, ICC, 1912, I-XXVII, in a critical discussion with Holtzmann. Overbeck defended the identity of authorship with good arguments, see *Das Johannesevangelium*, ed. C.A.Bernoulli, Tübingen 1911, 465-75. Later E.R.Dodds, *BJRL* 21, 1937, 129-56, and *The Johannine Epistles*, MNTC, London 1946, 764-78, argued for different authors, but in my view W.F.Howard, *JTS* 48, 1947, 12-25, advanced good arguments against this (his work is partly identical with id., *The Fourth Gospel in Recent Criticism and Interpretation*, rev.ed. by C.K.Barrett, London 1955, 103-10; 276-96) as did

W.G.Wilson, 'An Examination of the Linguistic Evidence adduced against the Unity of the Authorship of the First Epistle of John and the Fourth Gospel', *JTS* 49, 1949, 147-56. I need not repeat their arguments, with which I largely agree. See also E.C.Hoskyns, *The Fourth Gospel*, London 1947, 48-57; Brown, *Epistles* (n.1), 19-35, differs. For the German discussion see W.G.Kümmel, *Introduction to the New Testament*, Nashville and London ²1975, 442ff.; E.Haenchen, *ThR* 26, 1960, 1-43; H.Thyen, *TRE* 17, 1987, 186-200 (and bibliography). Following Overbeck, Thyen stresses the connection between the letter and the Gospel (191) and sees the opponents (certainly incorrectly) as Jews. G. Strecker, 'Die Anfänge der johanneischen Schule', *NTS* 32, 1986, 31-47, and U.Schnelle, *Antidoketische Christologie im Johannesevangelium*, FRLANT 144, 1987, 65ff., 249ff., also put forward an interesting theory which already had a predecessor in the Tübingen school. With arguments some of which seem to me to be worth noting, they now reverse the sequence which is usually argued for, 'since the Gospel already presupposes the acute controversy of the letter and works over it theologically' (Schnelle, 249). The hypothesis was vigorously discussed in the nineteenth century: see already A.Hilgenfeld, *Historisch-kritische Einleitung in das Neue Testament*, Leipzig 1875, 681f.; *Die johanneischen Briefe*, 471f., cf. 68ff. In reality both the preparation and the subsequent theological overcoming of the conflict can be seen in the process of the composition of the Gospel. It was already a long time in the making, and indeed a good deal of it may already have been fixed (see below, 105f.) when the letters were written, but it was only edited and circulated by pupils some time after the letters – soon after the death of the author, in my view along with the letters. P.-H.Menoud, *L'Évangile de Jean d'après les recherches récentes*, Neuchâtel and Paris ²1947, 71f.; see also Schnackenburg, *Johannesbriefe*, 39.

8. H.J.Vogels, 'Der Einfluss Marcions und Tatians auf Text und Kanon des NT', in *Synoptische Studien, Alfred Wikenhauser dargebracht*, Munich 1953, 278-89; id., *Handbuch der Textkritik des Neuen Testaments*, Bonn ²1955, 140-4; M.Metzger, *The Canon of the New Testament*, Oxford 1987, 97-9.

9. Probably already towards the end of the second century I John was termed the 'Catholic' letter of the apostle in Asia Minor, see Eusebius, HE 5.18.5; cf. also *Muratorian Canon*, 68f.; and above, 162f. n.9. Origen knows the term, and Dionysius of Alexandria in Eusebius, HE 7.25.7,10, calls I John 'the Catholic letter'.

10. The monarchical episcopate came from the East, probably from Jerusalem, see M.Hengel, 'Jakobus der Herrenbruder – der erste "Papst"?', in *Glaube und Eschatologie, Festschrift für W.G.Kümmel zum 80.Geburtstag*, Tübingen 1985, 71-104. It may have made its way into the West via Antioch. The letters of Ignatius show that by then it was not fully established in Asia Minor. The Pastoral Epistles, which are later (around 110 or 120), also still describe it as in process of coming into being; it made its way even later in the Philippi of Polycarp's letter and in Rome. See also above, 15.

11. R.Schnackenburg, *Johannesbriefe* (n.7), 142: 'The author looks towards the parousia (2.28) and sees the emergence of "Antichrists" as a *characteristic*

of this last time' (see above, 41). Here the relationship to the Apocalypse becomes particularly clear. There too the fight against false teachers and 'libertines' in the seven letters is an expression of the imminent end.

12. John 6.70; 17.12; cf. 13.18f. In II Thess.2.3 the 'son of perdition' is the Antichrist. In no Gospel is the betrayal of Judas so clearly presented as a problem as in John. He is to some degree the prototype of the *antichristos*, a deceiver and possessed of the devil: 13.2,27,29,31. The fantastic parody in Papias (fragment 5 in J.Kürzinger, *Papias von Hierapolis und die Evangelien des Neuen Testaments*, Eichstätter Materialien 4, 1983 = fragment 3 in F.X.Funk and K.Bihlmeyer, *Die apostolischen Väter*, SQS 2.R 1, 1924) brings this defamation of the traitor to a climax. With its bizarre and often misunderstood hyperbole it has a whole series of rabbinic parallels (e.g. b.Gitt 56b; Num R. 20.25).

13. 6.65,70; cf. 6.37,44; 10.29; 12.39; 15.16. As in Paul, the Johannine conception of election and predestination is a means of expressing the radical grace of God.

14. Cf. the fine account of the 'adversaries' in Brown, *Epistles* (n.1), 47-68, and the reconstruction of the 'separation' underlying the letters, its consequences and its theological reasons, 69-115; id., *The Community of the Beloved Disciple*, New York, Ramsey and Toronto 1979, 103-9: 'The Intra-Johannine Schism'. 'Both parties knew the proclamation of Christianity available to us through the Fourth Gospel, but they interpreted it differently' (106). But see his cautious qualification, n.209. The completely opposite position is taken by G.Strecker and his pupil U.Schnelle (see above, n.7) who think that the conflict was integrated theologically by the Gospel of John, which came into being later: see below, 68ff. In reality the crisis represents a landmark in the history of the origin of the Gospel, which can be made quite clear from it.

15. His dialectic, in some respects similar to Paul, but expressed even more sharply, is fundamental to an understanding of his thought, see C.K.Barrett, 'The Dialectical Theology of St John', in *New Testament Essays*, London 1972, 49-69; id., 'Paradox and Dualism', in *Essays on John*, London 1982, 98-115, in an argument with E.Käsemann.

16. John 17.20-23; 20.21; cf. 10.16; 11.52; 12.20. The saying of Jesus in 6.37 will also have held for the teacher: 'All that the Father gives me will come to me; and him who comes to me I will not cast out.' The closest parallels to the Johannine school that we can recognize seem to me to be those of Paul in Ephesus (Acts 19.9) and of Justin and the Alexandrian catechetical school. We should also apply to John the elder the statement 'and he was known to all the Jews and Greeks who dwell in Ephesus' (Acts 19.17). One could also compare the school of a Basilides, Marcion (before his separation) or Valentinus. But in the later schools the level of philosophical and rhetorical education was higher, see above 12 and below, 119ff. A modern English analogy may be the Auckland Brotherhood founded by Bishop Joseph Barber Lightfoot, which was completely under the influence of this great charismatic scholar and pastor, see G.R.Eden and F.C.Macdonald, *Lightfoot of Durham*, Cambridge 1933, 21-55, 160-73.

17. Pliny the Younger, *Ep.* 10.96.9: *multi enim... omnis ordinis*: 'many from every social class...'

18. The alleged successor to Simon Magus, see Irenaeus, *Adv.haer.* 1.23.5 (cf. Eusebius, HE 3.26.2): *Resurrectionem enim per id quod est in eum baptisma accipere eius discipulos et ultra non posse mori, sed perseuerare non senescentes et immortales.* See already Justin, I *Apology* 26.4: ὃς καὶ τοὺς αὐτῷ ἑπομένους ὡς μηδὲ ἀποθνήσκοιεν ἔπεισε, cf. 56.1; Irenaeus, *Adv.haer.* 2.31.3; 3.4.3. Cf. John 11.25f.; 5.24 etc.

19. Irenaeus, *Adv.haer.*1.24.1f. = Hippolytus, *Refutationes*, 7.28: τὸν δὲ Σωτῆρα ἀγέννητον ὑπέθετο καὶ ἀσώματον καὶ ἀνείδεον, δοκήσει δὲ ἐπιπεφηνέναι ἄνθρωπον... ἐπὶ σωτηρίᾳ τῶν πειθομένων αὐτῷ, εἶναι δὲ τούτους τοὺς ἔχοντας τὸν σπινθῆρα τῆς ζωῆς ἐν αὐτοῖς.

20. The texts relating to him are collected in A.F.J.Klijn and G.J.Reinink, *Patristic Evidence for Jewish-Christian Sects*, NT.S 36, 1973, 102ff., cf. 3ff. Hippolytus, *Refutationes*, Prologue 7 and 7.33.1, stresses that he received his teaching and his training in Egypt. There is no reason to follow E.Schwartz in explaining the 'Docetist Cerinthus' and 'John the Elder' in Ephesus as fictions of Irenaeus, thus in 'Johannes und Kerinth', ZNW 15, 1914, 210-19 = *Gesammelte Schriften* 5, Berlin and New York 1963, 170-82 (176f.). Probably he really was a historical counterpart of the 'elder'. In the *Epistula Apostolorum*, in which John stands at the head of the disciples, and his Gospel is the most important Christian writing, Cerinthus is explicitly termed a 'false apostle' alongside Simon Magus: ch.1 n.7, see C.Schmidt, *Gespräche Jesu mit seinen Jüngern nach der Auferstehung*, TU 43, 1919 (reprinted 1927), and *New Testament Apocrypha* I, 192, 194. Cf. also n.38.

21. Apart from the brief references in Rev.2.6,15 to the 'works' or the 'teaching' of the Nicolaitans, who, as Balaam once taught, 'eat flesh offered to idols and practise fornication' (2.14; cf. 2.20 and Acts 15.20,29), we have no reliable information about them. Possibly they also made the claim to have known 'the depths of Satan' (2.24). The later patristic tradition (Irenaeus, *Adv.haer.* 1.26.3; Hippolytus, *Refutationes* 7.36.3) derives them from the proselyte Nicolaus of Antioch (Acts 6.5) and connects them with the beginnings of Gnosticism (Irenaeus, *Adv.haer.* 3,11,1; Hippolytus, loc.cit.); this is developed in a fantastic way in Epiphanius, *Panarion*, 25. However, Clement of Alexandria, *Strom.* 2.118.3 and 3.25.5-26.2, defends him against such a connection. For literature see Arndt/Gingrich/Bauer, *Lexicon*, 539, s.v.Νικολαΐτης. See also n.38 below.

22. Acts 20.29f. One is almost tempted to see here, among other things, a polemical reference to the fascination which John and his flourishing school exerted round about 80 CE and which was too 'spiritualistic' and 'anti-Gnostic' for the matter-of-fact Luke, but this is perhaps too bold a thought. We just do not know where Luke-Acts was written: probably in Rome rather than in Asia Minor.

23. I John 4.5, cf. John 3.31; 8.23,47; 15.19. This is a typically Johannine notion, which has a predestinarian basis. I John 4.1 has points of contact with

the warning against false prophets in Matt.24.11 (cf.7.11), in an eschatological context.

24. Brown, *Epistles* (n.1), 'I John offers much less specific reference to the Spirit than does GJohn.' But cf. the detailed exegesis, 345-8, 371-4, 410f., 465f., 578-86 etc., which shows what great importance the Spirit has in the letter. If we take into account the lesser extent of the letter, which amounts to only around a seventh of the Gospel, it does not fall behind the latter in any way – quite the contrary! In the Gospel the Spirit (of God) is mentioned nineteen times, and in addition there are the four Paraclete passages; in the Epistle there are seven instances: 3.24; 4.2,6,13; 5.6 (twice),8. In addition χρῖσμα occurs three times (I John 2.20, 27 [twice]). In the last-mentioned passage Sinaiticus has the interpretative πνεῦμα, see also the Bohairic translation. In addition τὸ σπέρμα occurs in I John 3.9. We find the verbs which are connected with the 'anointing' and the *pneuma* used in an analogous way in the Gospel of John: I John 2.27, χρῖσμα ὃ ἐλάβετε, cf. John 7.39; 14.17; 20.22; ibid., τὸ αὐτοῦ χρῖσμα διδάσκει, cf. John 14.26; I John 3.24 (4.13): ἐκ τοῦ πνεύματος οὗ ἡμῖν ἔδωκεν, cf. John 3.34; 14.16; I John 5.6: τὸ πνεῦμά ἐστιν τὸ μαρτυροῦν, cf. John 15.26; I John 3.9: σπέρμα αὐτοῦ ἐν αὐτῷ μένει (see the same also of χρῖσμα, 2.27), cf. John 14.17: ὅτι παρ' ὑμῖν μένει; 1.32: τὸ πνεῦμα... ἔμεινεν ἐπ' αὐτόν.

25. Rev.12.10; cf. John 12.31; 14.30. See already Luke 10.18. For the rabbinic loanwords see S.Krauss, *Griechische und lateinische Lehnwörter im Talmud, Midrasch und Targum*, II, 1899, 496, *prqlyt*: mAb 4,11; tPeah 4,21, etc. 524 *qtygwr*: mAb 4,11, bRH 26e, etc.

26. John 14.16. 'Preparing a dwelling in my Father's house' (14.2f.), or 'drawing to me' (12.32; cf. 11.52), are also part of the 'heavenly' support (cf.17.24), while as the 'earthly' support sent to the community the Spirit keeps the disciples in the right understanding of the word of Jesus entrusted to them and at the same time attests this before the world through the disciples.

27. Cf. 6.69. For the disputed question whether ἀπὸ τοῦ ἁγίου in I John 2.20 refers to God or Christ see Brown, *Epistles* (n.1), 347f.

28. I John 2.20ff. For the 'knowledge of faith', i.e. the right recognition of Christ, see I John 2.20 and the Johannine connection between faith and knowledge generally. The reading πάντες instead of the accusative object πάντα is the *lectio difficilior*. πάντα may be an assimilation to John 14.26; for πάντες see John 6.45 = Isa.54.13, cf. also Jer.31.34 (MT) and Jude 5 = II Peter 1.12.

29. I John 2.24; cf.1.1; 2.7; 3.11; II John 5f. and John 15.27; also I John 3.8 with John 8.44.

30. I John 2.27f. (see above n.24), cf. John 8.28: καθὼς ἐδίδαξέν με ὁ πατήρ.

31. Cf. II John 9, see above, 42.

32. See my 'Rabbinische Legende und frühpharisäische Geschichte. Schimeon b.Schetach und die achtzig Hexen von Askalon', AHAW.PH 1984, Abh.2, and above 41 n.66.

33. The whole struggle with the Jews in the Gospel is over whether Jesus

is 'Messiah' and therefore at the same time 'Son of God', see 1.20; 3.28; 1.41; 4.29; 7.26,41f.; 9.22; 10.24 and as a conclusion 20.31.

34. For this disputed passage see A.Harnack, 'Zur Textkritik und Christologie der Schriften des Johannes', SPAW.PH 1915, 534-73 (556-61) = *Kleine Schriften* II, 1980, 265-304 (287-92) and now B.D.Ehrman, 'I John 4.3 and the Orthodox Corruption of Scripture', *ZNW* 79, 1988, 221-43. The information in the apparatus in Nestle/Aland[26] is inadequate. By way of a supplement see Arndt/Gingrich/Bauer, *Lexicon*, s.v.λύω, 484. The key to this passage lies in the learned gloss by the minuscule Lawra 184.B.64, see E.von der Goltz, *Eine textkritische Arbeit des zehnten bzw. des sechsten Jahrhunderts*, NF II.4, 1899, 48ff. This marginal note indicates that Irenaeus, *Adv.haer*.3.16.8 (the Latin translation here has the corresponding *soluit*), Origen in Book 8 of his commentary on Romans (on which see Harnack, 288 n.8) and Clement of Alexandria in his work on the passover (no longer extant) have this reading (λύει, 48ff.). In Origen we also find it in the Matthew commentary (*Origenes Werke* 11, ed. E.Klostermann, GCS 38, Leipzig 1933, there in Or.65, p.152.28f.). Possibly the great textual expert was aware of the existence of both readings, see C.Jenkins, *JTS* 10, 1909, 30. In *Hom.Ex.* 3.2 (*Origenes Werke* 6, ed. W.A.Baehrens, GCS 29, Leipzig 1920, p.163, 4f.: *qui negant Dominum meum Iesum Christum in carne venisse*), with the editor I regard the influence of II John 7 as probable (against Ehrman, 229 n.24). A further Greek instance is the church historian Socrates (died 439), HE 7.32, who charges Nestorius with having failed to note this warning contained 'in the old manuscripts' (ἐν τοῖς παλαιοῖς ἀντιγράφοις). The heretics are said to have removed this reading from the 'old manuscripts' and the 'old exegetes' to have referred to this fact. The Latin translation reads *solvit* throughout, thus already Tertullian, *Adv.Marcionem* 5.16.4; *De ieiunio* 1.3; alongside it sometimes appears *negat*, which also emerges in I John 2.22, see W.Thiele (ed.), *Epistulae Catholicae*, VL 26.1, 329-33. In the case of Tertullian it should be noted that we should still expect strong direct influence from the Greek text. In other words, towards the end of the second century the reading λύει is attested in Egypt, Lyons and Carthage; it could also be found in the original for the oldest Latin translation and dominated the further Western tradition. The oldest Greek manuscripts, which then all have μὴ ὁμολογεῖ, are at least 150 years later. This less abrupt reading, naturally suggested by II John 7 (and Polycarp, *Ep. ad.Phil.* 7.1), then established itself in an exclusive way. That means that it too must have been widespread in the East and very old.

35. The somewhat lengthy explanations by Ehrman, 'I John 4.3' (n.34), have not convinced me. There can be no question of an 'orthodox corruption of scripture', since if it were secondary, it would have to have found its way into the text at a very early stage, when I John was not yet 'Holy Scripture'. B.F.Westcott, *The Epistles of St John*, London ²1886, 16ff. (still without knowledge of the Lawra gloss 184 B 64), therefore conjectures 'a very early gloss'. Why should it not have been added in the Johannine circle? That could possibly be an alternative: λύει is certainly not the later invention of a heretic-fighter. However, I regard the other possibility as more probable and would

agree with Ehrman's sentence: 'since none of our Greek MSS... attests any other reading, the reading μὴ ὁμολογεῖ τὸν Ἰησοῦν must have been introduced at the very earliest stages of the transmission of I John.' It may have been made by a copyist to whom the λύει, applied to the person of Jesus, seemed inappropriate. Of itself this is in fact a thoroughly Johannine mode of expression (I John 3.8; John 2.19; 5.18; 7.23; 10.35). The μὴ ὁμολογεῖ sounds better here from a linguistic point of view, as this is a conditional sentence. In that case, as in classical Greek, no conjunction is necessary, see Blass/Debrunner/Funk, *Grammar of New Testament Greek*, Chicago 1961, §428.4, cf. II Peter 2.9; cf. also §380.1a.

36. Distributed throughout the letter: I John 1.3; 2.1; 3.23; 4.2; 5.6,20. Cf. also II John 3,7. 'Christos' alone, without Jesus, appears only in II John 9. That Kyrios does not appear does not indicate any fundamental difference from the Gospel, since only there does the address κύριε appear predominantly in connection with Jesus, and the absolute ὁ κύριος occurs only three times in chs.1-19 referring to Jesus. It then piles up in the resurrection stories from ch.20 on and thus in a special way expresses the direct relationship of the disciples to the Risen Christ. Nor was there any dispute that the Son is the 'Kyrios'. The battle was over the relationship of the man Jesus to the 'Son'.

37. First of all in the case of the disciples who are called (1.41; in another formulation, but with the same meaning also in 1.45,49); 4.25,29: the Samaritan woman; 7.26f.,41f.; 9.22; 10.24; 11.27, cf.45: the faith of the crowd relates to the messiahship of Jesus, similarly 12.34,42. The negative confession of John the Baptist is also an indirect reference to Jesus as the Messiah: 1.15,20; 3.28. The name of Jesus Christ, which expresses the christology of the believing community, appears only twice, but does so at decisive points: in the prologue (1.17) and – anachronistically – in the mouth of the praying Jesus in 17.3. There is a close connection in content between this verse and the penultimate verse of the letter (I John 5.20).

38. Irenaeus, *Adv.haer.*1.26.1; see also the collection of reports in Klijn and Reinink, *Patristic Evidence* (n.20), 3-19; cf. further Brown, *Epistles* (n.1), 65ff., 766-71. For the earliest mention of him with Simon Magus, which thus makes him still a contemporary of the apostles, see n.20 above. As itinerant preachers both are 'enemies of our Lord Jesus Christ'. What is decisive for us is the report in Irenaeus, *Adv.haer.* 1.26.1, who mentions him as the sixth heretic between Carpocrates and the Ebionites and Nicolaitans, but thus does not follow any chronological order. That he was a contemporary of John's follows from 3.3.4 = Eusebius, HE 4.14.6. In *Adv.haer.* 1.26.1 Irenaeus compares the teaching of Cerinthus with that of Carpocrates. According to both of these the world was not made 'by the first god' but (thus Cerinthus) by a 'power' relatively distant from God or (thus Carpocrates) by angels of lesser worth (cf. 1.25.1); according to 3.11.1 by his Gospel John means to refute errors disseminated by Cerinthus and already much earlier by the Nicolaitans (see n.21 above), to the effect that the world was made by a demiurge and not by the 'one God who created all things through his word'. He therefore

exclusively cites the prologue of John, 1.1-5. Whereas Irenaeus 1.26.1 starts from the activity of Cerinthus in Asia, Hippolytus, *Refutatio* 7.33 (cf.10.21), who is partially dependent on him, reports that Cerinthus was trained in Egypt (Aἰγυπτίων παιδείᾳ ἀσκηθείς). In Hippolytus' work against Gaius, the *Dialogue* with the Montanist Proclus, in which he rejected the claim of Gaius that the Fourth Gospel and the Apocalypse are a forgery by Cerinthus, he was probably also handing down the report taken over from Gaius that Cerinthus had been a Judaist, i.e. that he had proclaimed circumcision and fought against Paul, because Paul had not circumcised Titus. Moreover he is said 'in one of his letters' to have described 'the apostle and his disciples as false apostles and lying teachers'. In addition there is the denial of the virgin birth and of 'earthly food and drink', see Dionysius bar Ṣalibi, in his introduction to his commentary on the Apocalypse, Syriac text in CSCO, Scriptores Syri 18, ed. I.Sedlacek, 1909, 3f., Latin translation in CSCO Scr.Syr.20, 1910, 1f. The relevant Syriac text can be found with an English translation in Klijn and Reinink, *Patristic Evidence* (n.20), 272f. (but they give a wrong volume number for CSCO!). However, one can ask whether all these reports come from Hippolytus, who is mentioned only by Bar Ṣalibi, or from the work by Gaius (see below, n.41).

On the other hand this charge fits well with the accusation of chiliastic tendencies which occurs in connection with the work by Gaius in Dionysius of Alexandria and Eusebius (Eusebius, HE 3.28.2-5; 7.25.2f.). Support is found for the connection between Cerinthus and Judaism in the fact that Cerinthus and the Ebionites already follow one another in Irenaeus, and Hippolytus further strengthens this connection in his twofold report, by asserting that the Ebionites had taught 'about Christ like Cerinthus' (*Ref.* 7.34.1), here with the addition 'and Carpocrates' (10.22.1; cf. also 7.35.1: the christology of Theodotus of Byzantium is 'derived from the school of the Gnostics, Cerinthus and Ebion' [!]). This connection with a 'heretical' Jewish Christianity would be further strengthened if in the Apocryphon of James (NHC I.1f.) one could supplement the introduction to the letter: 'James writes to [Cerin]thos.' In Epiphanius it is then developed beyond all reason (*Panarion* 28.1.1-8.2, Greek text with English translation in Klijn and Reinink, 160-9, see also Index, 284). Among other things he introduces a 'double', Merinthus (28.8.1), whose supporters are said to use an abbreviated form of Matthew as a Gospel, like the Ebionites (28.5.1). This is also what is meant in 51.7.3. Epiphanius himself is amazed at the attitude of Cerinthus (as portrayed in his distorted picture), who calls for the observation of the law given by angels and thus devalued, which on his own presuppositions canot really be good (28.1.3; 2.1). The disputed problem of a 'Judaistic' Cerinthus is of little significance for our question. J.E.Fossum, *The Name of God and the Angel of the Lord*, WUNT 36, 1985, 16, 215f., 221f., would like to take it seriously in order to preserve a strictly Jewish-Christian 'Proto-Gnostic' (337 n.217). Klijn and Reinink (n.20), 319, however, are extremely sceptical about this and conjecture that the whole Cerinthus tradition may have grown out of the

Polycarp anecdote. For me that would be to go too far. But his christology has a distinctively antiquated character as over against the later Gnostics.

39. Epiphanius, *Panarion* 28.1.7: οὐ τὸν Ἰησοῦν εἶναι Χριστόν, see also Irenaeus, *Adv.haer.* 3.11.7.

40. One could also say that Cerinthus' Christ was 'only apparently' human, since he did not really unite himself wholly with the man Jesus, the significance of whom for salvation is similarly only apparent, precisely because he is and remains only human. Therefore we may speak of 'docetists' in the case of Cerinthus (and of the 'separatists' in I John), even if nowadays the terminology of docetism is used by individual authors in a rigoristic and narrow way. For this see A.Grillmeier, *Christ in Christian Tradition*, Oxford ²1975, 79: 'The false teachers of the Johannines are not docetists in the strict sense. In other words, it cannot be demonstrated that they already denied the reality of Christ's flesh. Thus there was still no christological docetism in the narrower sense of the word. It was rather a matter of a false docetist doctrine in the wider sense, which is, however, none the less a real dissolving of Christ (as the ground of our salvation).'

See also Schnelle, *Antidoketische Christologie* (n.7), 76ff. Basically we are given the use of the term by the fathers after Ignatius: they always used it in a wider sense which is not completely clear nor fully defined. The 'appearance' can relate to the incarnation, the person of Jesus as man and his passion. Here it should be noted that the christologies of the 'Gnostics' and their preliminary stages are more complex than the anti-Gnostic fathers, above all Irenaeus, suggest. See also n.53 below.

41. K.Wengst, *Häresie und Orthodoxie im Spiegel des ersten Johannesbriefes*, Gütersloh 1976, 15-38: 'Cerinthus probably used the Gospel of John and based himself on its authority' (34). The text cited by Wengst, Irenaeus, *Adv.haer.*, 3.11.1, is not a second report on Cerinthus with additional information to 1.26.1 but a mixed product of 'Gnosis' composed by Irenaeus, which the Gospel of John, the prologue of which is cited immediately afterwards, is said to have refuted. In the Nag Hammadi texts, like the Apocryphon of James (NHC I.2, see Wengst, 35f.) and the Second Tractate of the Great Seth (NHC VII, 51.20-52.3; 56.8-11, see Brown, *Epistles*, [n.1]), we have at best analogies to Cerinthus, which do not allow direct conclusions. Brown, *Epistles*, 65ff., 104ff., 770ff., largely agrees with Wengst: 'the contrary traditions, one opposing Cerinthus to John and the other attributing GJohn to Cerinthus, could make sense if Cerinthus interpreted GJohn in a Gnostic manner opposed by orthodox Johannine followers' (770). But the Fourth Gospel clearly contradicts what is handed down to us by Cerinthus, and from all we know of the criticism of the Gospel by the anti-Montanist Gaius, he does not criticize his 'Gnostic' christology but the historical outline which contradicts the Synoptics. For the criticism of Wengst (and Brown) see also Schnelle, *Antidoketische Christologie* (n.7), 82.

42. This marked protological-cosmological interest applies even more to almost all the Gnostic systems, see e.g. the Index in Foerster (ed.), *Die Gnosis*,

two vols, *Koptische und mandäische Quellen*, Munich and Zurich 1971, 428, demiurge: 449, creator, creation...; 424, beginning. That this interest is completely lacking in the letters and widely lacking in the Gospel, and even in the prologue is answered only briefly, but clearly and simply, shows that here we still may not presuppose any fixed, coherent Gnostic system among the opponents.

43. 17.24c, cf. also 1.18. How unexpected for the exegetes is this clause ὅτι ἠγάπησάς με πρὸ καταβολῆς κόσμου, which was certainly constructed with great thought, is evident from the way in which it is completely passed over both in the translation and the exegesis in Schnackenburg's commentary, see *The Gospel according to St John*, Vol.3, Tunbridge Wells and New York 1982, 194ff; moreover v.24e is missing from the translation – without any reason being given. But see the terse and precise comments by C.K.Barrett, *The Gospel according to St John*, London ²1978, 514: 'The beginning and the end of time are here brought together to find their meaning in the historical mission of Jesus and its results.' The creative power of the Son is also visible in the miracle stories, see below, 92 n. 82; cf. also 5.17; 19.30 and Gen.2.1-3; John 20.22 with Gen.2.7. They therefore have an anti-docetic meaning.

44. *Adv.haer* 3.11.7: *Qui autem Iesum separant a Christo et impassibilem perseuerasse Christum, passum uero Iesum dicunt, id quod secundum Marcum est praeferentes Euangelium... Hi autem qui a Valentino sunt, eo quod est secundum Iohannem plenissime utentes...'* On this see F.Neugebauer, *Die Entstehung des Johannesevangeliums*. AzTh I, 36, 1968, 28ff. See also the Latin translation of the *Hypotyposes* on II John by Clement of Alexandria, *Adumbrationes*, GCS 17², = Clement of Alexandria III, ed. O.Stählin, 1970, 215: *ut nemo dividat Iesum Christum, sed unum credat Iesum Christum uenisse in carne.*

45. I John 5.5,6: τίς δέ ἐστιν ὁ νικῶν τὸν κόσμον εἰ μὴ ὁ πιστεύων ὅτι Ἰησοῦς ἐστιν ὁ υἱὸς τοῦ θεοῦ· οὗτός ἐστιν ὁ ἐλθὼν δι' ὕδατος καὶ αἵματος, Ἰησοῦς Χριστός· οὐκ ἐν τῷ ὕδατι μόνον ἀλλ' ἐν τῷ ὕδατι καὶ ἐν τῷ αἵματι· καὶ τὸ πνεῦμά ἐστι τὸ μαρτυροῦν, ὅτι τὸ πνεῦμά ἐστιν ἡ ἀλήθεια.

46. Cf. already I John 5,4; 2.13f.; 4.4: the victory over the false teachers, also John 16.33: the last word of Jesus to his disciples. Furthermore νικᾶν appears seventeen times in the Apocalypse. The depiction of the death of Jesus in John 19.28-30 is at the same time the depiction of his victory over the 'world' and its 'ruler' (14.30).

47. Cf. John 19.34, which refers to the reality of the death of Jesus, but at the same time has sacramental significance. The attempts to make John an opponent of the sacraments were a fundamental error. On baptism: 3.5; 3.22, 26; 4.2; 13.8ff.; on the eucharist, John 6.51-58; cf. 6.11; 21.12f. For the consummation of the work of salvation in the death of Jesus see 4.34; 5.36; 13.1; ch.17; 19.28-30. Here the relationship to Gen.2.1-3 seems to me to be essential.

48. I John 4.2; II John 7: note the different tenses. The perfect I John 4.2, Ἰησοῦν Χριστὸν ἐν σαρκὶ ἐληλυθότα, expresses the abiding connection brought about by the incarnation between the pre-existent Son of God and a

particular man in the person of Jesus Christ. In II John 7 the unusual present participle Ἰησοῦν Χριστὸν ἐρχόμενον ἐν σαρκὶ produces a grammatical difficulty. It might best be translated future (thus Strecker, *Anfänge* [n.7], who conjectures an anti-docetic focus): 'It concerns the confession that Jesus Christ will come (again) in the flesh.' F.Vouga, 'The Johannine School: A Gnostic Tradition in Primitive Christianity', *Biblica* 69, 1988, 371-85, who challenges anti-docetic polemic, conjectures that II John 7 expresses 'the movement's christology as a sacramental initiation', as a variant to I John 4.2 (376). My question is whether this is not just a slip in language in the short letter. See also below, 187 n.52.

49. Eph 7.2:

εἷς ἰατρός ἐστιν
σάρκικός τε καὶ πνευματικός,
γεννητὸς καὶ ἀγέννητος,
ἐν σαρκὶ γενόμενος θεός,
ἐν θανάτῳ ζωὴ ἀληθινή,
καὶ ἐκ Μαρίας καὶ ἐκ θεοῦ,
πρῶτον παθητὸς καὶ τότε ἀπαθής,
Ἰησοῦς Χριστὸς ὁ κύριος ἡμῶν.

The hymn has been shaped with supreme art, and like I Tim.3.16 has much more of the character of Hellenistic, indeed almost 'Asian', rhetoric than the prologue of John with its more marked 'semitic' sound. The antithetical division demonstrates the markedly anti-docetic character which is also expressed in the paradoxical statements; cf. also 19.3: θεοῦ ἀνθρωπίνως φανερουμένου εἰς καινότητα ἀϊδίου ζωῆς, Trall 9.1: 'who was truly born, ate and drank, was truly persecuted under Pontius Pilate, truly crucified and died...'

Here we come upon antidocetic themes which also dominate the Fourth Gospel, cf. Smyrn 1.1f.; 3.3 and Magn.11 and the charge against the opponents that they regard the humanity of Jesus only as a semblance (τὸ δοκεῖν), Trall.10.1; Smyrn.2.1; 4.2.

50. For the old dispute as to whether the Fourth Gospel did not reverence a 'naive docetism' and whether John 1.14 is really to be understood as being antidocetic see now Schnelle, *Antidoketische Christologie* (n.7), 76ff., 230-49, etc.; he works out the resolute antidocetism of the Gospel. By contrast the provocative-sounding theses of Ernst Käsemann are misleading (*The Testament of Jesus*, London and Philadelphia 1968, last revised and expanded German edition *Jesu Letzter Wille nach Johannes 17*, Tübingen ⁴1980; this contains many passages which are not in the English translation): 'One can hardly fail to recognize the danger of his christology of glory, namely, the danger of docetism. It is present in a still naive, unreflected form and it has not yet been recognized by the Evangelist or his community as a danger' (*Testament*, 26). Here Käsemann refers back, as he himself stresses, to what in my view is the mistaken interpretation of John by F.C.Baur, who reads his

own Hegelian idealism into the Gospel, see id., *Kritische Untersuchungen über die kanonischen Evangelien*, Tübingen 1847, 93-9, on the 'subordinate significance' (94) of 1.14; cf. 231-4, where in the controversy with F.Lücke's commentary on John, John 6.63 is played off against 1.14. 'The historical evaporates into the docetic' (286). However, Baur can only arrive at this docetic-Gnostic interpretation of John because he not only forces the Fourth Gospel into the closest association with 'Alexandrian philosophy and philosophy of religion', but also dates it after the rise of Valentinianism, the 'oldest and most widespread form (of Gnosticism)' (376). For the controversy with Käsemann see also Barrett, 'Paradox' (n.15), 103ff.

51. John 20.20 is quite striking, as is the intensification in 20.27. Jesus' reply in 20.29 has a similar relationship to what has gone before as 6.51-58 or 1.14b and c to 14a. The early crude statements about the 'corporeality' of the Son of God are not done away with by 20.29; 6.63 or 1.14bc but their paradoxical character is put in the right light. See also – with less awareness of the theological problem – Ignatius, Smyrn.3 and Luke 24.37-43.

52. Seeing the Christ on his return at the same time means the transformation of the believers: ... ὅμοιοι αὐτῷ ἐσόμεθα ὅτι (giving the reason) ὀψόμεθα αὐτὸν καθώς ἐστίν; cf. the 'transformation' in John 20.19,20b, 25,28; the relationship to Pauline eschatology, I Thess.4.17; I Cor.15.23; Rom.8.29 is present and paraenetic, cf.Rom.12.2 and II Cor.3.18. The nearest, most closely related Johannine text which speaks of seeing in the future, is John 19.37 = Zech.12.10 (Masoretic text), cf. Rev.1.7 and John 8.28a. All these three texts are words of judgment (cf. also 3.36), whereas I John 3.2 is about the transfigured corporeality of the coming Christ, though this presupposes his suffering.

53. See above, n.49. In general cf. Grillmeier, *Christ in Christian Tradition* (n.40), 582, index s.v. Docetism; W.Foerster (ed.), *Gnosis* (n.42), Index 438 s.v.Jesus and 444 s.v. 'Leiden, leidensfähig'. The Heidelberg dissertation by R.Weigand, *Der Doketismus im Urchristentum und in der theologischen Entwicklung des zweiten Jahrhunderts*, 1961, which is hard to get access to because it has not been printed, analyses all the essential texts, but narrows down excessively the concept of docetism, which was already given by the early church. Cf. further W.Brox, 'Doketismus – eine Problemanzeige', *ZKG* 95, 1984, 301-14. See also above, 60 n.40.

54. Within the framework of these lectures, which hardly go beyond a sketch, I cannot enter into the ethical conflict between the head of the Johannine school and the 'secessionists'. The Johannine ethics seems to me to be more unified in the letters *and* in the Gospel, here above all in the farewell discourses, and more within the tradition of earliest Christianity (and here especially Paul) than is generally assumed. The way to the limitation to the community of the disciples (John 13.34ff.; 15.12f.) is already foreshadowed by Gal.6.10b. By contrast there is no constriction on God's love for the (human) world (3.16), cf. I John 2.2. Events in Corinth had already showed that a heaven-storming enthusiasm can lead to ethical irresponsibility. This danger seems to have repeated itself among the

secessionists in a new way. For the content see K.Wengst, *Bedrängte Gemeinde und verherrlichter Christus. Der historische Ort des Johannesevangeliums als Schlüssel zu seiner Interpretation*, BThSt, Neukirchen ²1983, 38ff., 53ff., 67ff. Schnelle, *Antidoketische Christologie* (n.7), 74, is critical of Wengst's interpretation in terms of an ethical libertinism in which the secessionists considered themselves sinless because they were like God.

55. John 5.30b and 17.25. 5.30b is the end of the present-future saying about judgment from 5.22. The future judgment cannot any more be eliminated from the Gospel by literary-critical means than can the future remarks about salvation, see 3.36; 5.29; 8.21,24,28; 12.47f.; 15.6; 19.37; the closing words of the high-priestly prayer in 17.25, πάτερ δίκαιε, also have a special weight, cf. also nn.52, 56.

56. Perhaps one may here recall the report by Irenaeus that for Cerinthus only the mortal man Jesus is marked out by special 'righteousness' (*Adv.haer.* 1.26.1), that among the Simonians 'righteous' actions only rested on the arbitrary commandments of the creator angels who enslaved human beings by them, and that according to Cerdon, Marcion's teacher, the God proclaimed by the Law and the prophets was only 'righteous', whereas the unknown Father of Jesus Christ was 'good' (1.27.1). For John, by contrast, 'good' and 'righteous' are in practice identical: John 5.29; 7.12; III John 11.

57. I John 2.2; cf. 4.14; also 4.10; 1.7. For the Gospel see below, 71f. For Jesus as the redeemer of the cosmos (despite, indeed precisely because of, I John 5.19b), see John 1.29; 3.16; 4.42; 6.33; 12.47; 16.10; and on this 8.12; 9.6; 12.4. Käsemann, *Jesus Letzter Wille* (n.50), 124f., plays down the fundamental significance of this passage in an unreliable way. The dialectic of the Gospel cannot be brought one-sidedly under a Gnostic denominator in this way.

58. The ἐλέγχειν means not only 'exposing' but is itself already the judgment that creates salvation. It overcomes the sin of unbelief (16.9; cf.7.35) and judges the 'prince of this world'. See also 8.34-36. From here a bridge could be built to the statements at I John 3.6,9. The liberation from sin takes place under the aspect of expiation: John 1.29, etc.; I John 2.1; 3.5; 4.10, or forgiveness: John 20.23; I John 1.9; 2.12, and *birth from God*: John 1.12f.; 3.3-8; I John 2.29; 3.9; 4.7; 5.1,4,18.

59. See also I John 3.5b; 2.1; cf. John 7.45; 8.46: union with the Father (10.30; 5.18, etc.) is the natural presupposition for the sinlessness of Jesus. The theme suddenly takes on renewed significance in the struggle over a right way of life in active love.

60. I John 1.7ff.; 2.1f.,12; cf. 3.19f.; John 8.24f.,34-36; 1.29; 20.23.

61. I John 2.28-3.3, cf.2.18; 4.3,17. Despite the increased number of future statements in comparison with the Gospel, as in the Gospel the author can use formulae which stress the massive presence of salvation, I John 3.14 = John 5.24, albeit with a practical focus. The step from death to life becomes visible in love; cf. also I John 5.11f. and the ἐσμέν of the certainty of salvation, 3.1; 5.19. The starting point in the Gospel is given by the ambivalent promises – which are typical of John – in 14.2f.,18,28; 17.24; 12.32, but also quite clear statements about the future like 5.27-29; 6.39f.,44,54; 12.26,48; 21.22. See also

above, 63f. nn.52, 55, 58 and below 194f. n.11. Evidently the closing remark about the Paraclete in 16.13, καὶ τὰ ἐρχόμενα ἀναγγελεῖ ὑμῖν are to be referred to the last things. From here a bridge can be built to the Apocalypse, which belongs to the Johannine corpus in the wider sense: Rev.2,7,11,17 etc.; 4.2.

62. ἵνα ἐὰν φανερωθῇ, cf. 3.2. Elsewhere the aorist ἐφανερώθη relates to the incarnation and the saving work of Christ: I John 1.2; 3.5,8; 4.9; cf. also John 1.31; 21.14.

63. I John 2.29; 3.9, cf. the formula πᾶς ὁ γεγεννημένος ἐκ τοῦ θεοῦ... 5,4,18, see also 4.7; 5.1, also John 1.13. Evidently the opponents were presenting a 'birth from God' without ethical consequences.

64. It is the foundation and goal of the paraenesis which reaches its climax in the 'definition' of God as love (4.8,16). Only through the revelation of the love of God does responsible action become possible in righteousness and love, I John 4.10,16-21; John 13.34; 15.12f.,16.

65. I John 3.9,24; 4.13; 5.6-8; cf. John 3.3-8; 7.37-39; 14.17, etc. The Johannine views about the 'Spirit' and the terminology used are extremely complex and may not be limited only to the teaching and recalling of the Paraclete. The latter is matched in the letter by the talk of 'anointing', 2.20,27, see above 55f.

66. I John 1.7,9. For the sacramental terminology see 5.5-8; the 'birth from God' also has a sacramental component, which points towards baptism; see also 6.53ff. and 19.34f., below 92.

67. Certainly in the LXX ἁγιάζειν is used more than five times more frequently than ἁγνίζειν, but this too appears nineteen times as a translation of qdš in the *piel, hiphil* and *hithpael*, above all in the books of Chronicles. Both verbs are related and come from the sphere of the Jerusalem cult.

68. John 1.29,36. The twofold testimony of John the Baptist has the character of an 'introit' which points the way. It is matched by the emphatic passover sacrifice typology of the day of Jesus' death: 18.28; 19.14,31,36 = Ex.12.10: (LXX) 46; Num.9.12; Ps.34.21. The decisive factor here is not the 'all the world motive' of the suffering righteous from Ps.34, which is so popular today, but the reference to the passover. Psalm 34.21 was understood as additional evidence for the interpretation of Christ as the passover lamb. It is also important that the whole event takes place at the time of the sacrifice of the passover lambs in the Temple. John, like Paul in I Cor. 5.6-8, presupposes knowledge of the passover feast on the part of the hearer. In Asia Minor the Quartodeciman passover of the Christians was particularly widespread in the night after 14 Nisan (see above, 5). For the relationship to Isa.53 see J.Jeremias, *TDNT* 5, 1967, 700-717; id., *Abba*, Göttingen 1966, 191-216; see also R.Schnackenburg, *The Gospel of John* 1, Tunbridge Wells 1968, 298ff., and the connection with the Apocalypse: 5.6,9,12 etc.

69. John 6.51; 10.11,15; 11.50-52; 15.13; 17.19; 18.14. In addition there are numerous other references to the death of Jesus as a saving event which are more frequent than in the other Gospels: 2.4,21; 3.14; 4.34; 6.70f.; 7.34; 12.7,24.

70. I John 3.16; cf. John 15.13. In contrast to the typically Greek terminology

with ὑπέρ, περί is used in connection with a verb of 'atonement' (most frequently (ἐξ)ιλάσκεσθαι περί) in the LXX translation for *kipper'al*. On this see M.Hengel, *The Atonement*, London and Philadelphia 1981. For ἱλασμὸς περί in the sense of vicarious atonement see I John 2.2 (twice); 4.10. In the sphere of the NT, the Apostolic Fathers and Apologists we find the formula only in I John. The nearest parallel in content is John 1.29.

71. LXX: Ἰδοὺ συνήσει ὁ παῖς μου καὶ ὑψωθήσεται καὶ δοξασθήσεται σφόδρα. In John 12.38, the first 'fulfilment quotation' in the Gospel, Isa.53.1 is cited. For Isa.53.4ff.,11 see I John 3.5. In Isa.53.11 the servant of God is described as δίκαιος, see above nn.55,56. For ὑψωθῆναι see John 3.14; 8.28; 12.32,34; the underlying Aramaic *ithpael* of *zqp*, *'izdaqqeph*, can be translated 'exalted' and 'be crucified', see M.Jastrow, *A Dictionary of the Targumim, the Talmud Babli and Yerushalmi, and the Midrashic Literature* I, 410, and J.Levy, *Wörterbuch über die Talmudim und Midraschim* I, 549. For δοξασθῆναι see John 7.39; 12.16,23; 13.31; cf. 12.28; 17.1,5.

72. Rom.5.5-11; 8.31-39; I Cor.13; II Cor.5.14-21.

73. Cf. e.g. also L.Schottroff, *Der glaubende und die feindliche Welt*, WMANT 37, 1970, 268ff., 278ff. Her objection against R.Bultmann, 280, is interesting: 'An incarnation is not reported for Gnostic redeemer figures'; Käsemann, *Testament of Jesus* (n.50), 9f.; see also 192, nn.91, 94–6. Apart from Käsemann see further U.B.Müller, *Die Geschichte der Christologie in der johanneischen Gemeinde*, SBS 77, 1975; id., 'Die Bedeutung des Kreuzestodes Jesu im Johannesevangelium', *KuD* 21, 1975, 49-71; W.Langenbrandtner, *Weltferner Gott oder Gott der Liebe*, BET 6, 1977, 84ff., 231ff., 370ff.; M.Lattke, *Einheit im Wort*, SANT 41, 1975; G.Richter, *Studien zum Johannesevangelium*, ed.J.Hainz, BU 13, 1977, especially 273ff., 365ff., 401ff. Here these 'Gnosticizing' tendencies are regularly attributed to the original Gospel, which redactors are later said to have falsified.

74. Käsemann, *Testament* (n.50), 44. As a reason he refers to Jesus' scandalous and provocative remark to his mother in John 2.4, as though Mark 3.31-35 (which in contrast to the Johannine passage has a historical background) did not sound even more impossible and offensive to people of antiquity! *Our* more or less 'naive' understanding of 'kenosis' and 'humanity' is certainly not that of earliest Christianity.

75. Käsemann, *Testament* (n.50), 45: 'as earthly as we are'.

76. Ibid.

77. Unless we identify him with the seer of the Apocalypse, in which case the latter must have come into being at a considerable remove in time from the Gospel and we would have to assume a great theological change in the author!

78. Peter: Acts 9.36-43; *Actus Vercellenses* 28 (translated in *New Testament Apocrypha* 2, 310); Titus (translated in *New Testament Apocrypha* 2, 278); John: Eusebius, HE 5.18.4 according to a report by the anti-Montanist Apollonius; Acts of John 36f., 63-86 (translated in *New Testament Apocrypha* 2, 233f., 245-54). The text was edited by E.Junod and J.-D.Kaestli, *L'histoire des Actes Apocryphes du IIIe au IXe Siècles*, CRTP, Neuchâtel 1982, I, 227ff., 253-93, cf. II,

506-13, 541-63. The last narrative, with the resurrection of three dead people, attempts to surpass the Lazarus story (see ch.75 and John 11.41). As for the miracles of the apostolic acts from the second half of the second century, one could suppose that they were meant to fulfil the difficult saying about the (ἔργα) μείζονα τούτων (John 14.12). For the Quadratus fragment see Eusebius, HE 4.3.2; for Papias see fr.16 Kürzinger (*Papias von Hierapolis* [n.12]) = fr.11 Funk/Bihlmeyer (*Apostolische Väter* [n.12]).

79. M.Hengel, *La crucifixion*, Lectio Divina, Paris 1981, 69ff.

80. John 3.16f.; 4.42; 6.33; 8.12; 9.5; 10.36; 12.46f.; cf. 1.5,9,29; I John 2.2; 4.14.

81. John 2.2f.: here perhaps the brothers of Jesus are removed in favour of the disciples; 2.11; 7.3-9; 19.25-27. For John 2.1-11 see M.Hengel, 'The Interpretation of the Wine Miracle at Cana: John 2.1-11', in *The Glory of Christ in the New Testament... Studies... in Memory of G.B.Caird*, ed. L.D.Hurst and N.T.Wright, Oxford 1987, 83-112 (102f., 92 n.33).

82. Mark 3.21,31-35; 6.1-6; 10.29; Luke 2.48ff.; 11.27f.; 14.26.

83. John 1.45f.; 6.42; 7.42,52; 18.5,7.

84. John 4.6-9 (κεκωπιακὼς ἐκ τῆς ὁδοιπορίας). The realism of the narrative, including the geographical description, is amazing. That is of course no proof for its historicity, but it is for a knowledge of the scenery on the part of the person who shaped the story, in my view the evangelist. See below, 111. One can conclude from Mark 15.21 that Jesus was no longer able to carry his cross, but that is not said directly. Here John 19.17 differs – for theological reasons, as in its contrast with the Gethsemane narrative.

85. 6.15: ἀνεχώρησεν; 8.59: ἐκρύβη, cf. 10.39f.; 11.54; 12.36.

86. Origen, *Contra Celsum* 2.34: Celsus makes his Jewish informant quote Dionysius, captured by Pentheus, in Euripides' *Bacchae* (498): 'The God himself will set me free whenever I wish it.' 'But the one who condemned him does not even suffer any such fate as that of Pentheus by going mad or being torn into pieces.' 35: 'Why, if not before, does he not at any rate now show forth something divine, and deliver himself from this shame, and take his revenge on those who insult him and his Father?' (translation H.Chadwick). Cf. 8.41f.: the same question in a comparison between Jesus and Heracles and Dionysus.

87. Mark 1.43: ἐμβριμησάμενος, cf. 1.41: Western text: ὀργισθείς. John 11.33: ἐνεβριμήσατο τῷ πνεύματι καὶ ἐτάραξεν ἑαυτόν. 11.38: Ἰησοῦς οὖν πάλιν ἐμβριμώμενος ἐν ἑαυτῷ. Here one cannot get away with resorting to a 'signs source' which the evangelist is said to have copied unthinkingly: rather, the whole scene has been shaped by the evangelist with great narrative art.

88. John 12.27 as a substitute from the omitted Gethsemane pericope: νῦν ἡ ψυχή μου τετάρακται... This is a clear allusion to Ps.6.4f., cf. Ps.31 (= LXX 30), 40 and 42 (= LXX 41), 6f.; see also Mark 14.34 - and at the same time to the Marcan Gethsemane narrative, the account in which is rejected with the subsequent question, which alludes to Mark's version. For the offer of betrayal see 13.21: ταῦτα εἰπὼν Ἰησοῦς ἐταράχθη τῷ πνεύματι. For the

prohibition in 14.1: μὴ ταρασσέσθω ὑμῶν ἡ καρδία, cf. v.27.

89. On this see R.Feldmeier, *Die Krisis des Gottessohnes*, WUNT 2R.21, 1987.

90. See C. Spicq, *Notes de Lexicographie Néotestamentaire* II, Göttingen 1978, 881f.; Arndt/Gingrich/Bauer, *Lexicon*, 805 s.v. ταράσσω: Alexander the Great at the forecast of his death ἐταράττετο τὴν ψυχήν, Diodore 17.112.4, cf. TestSeb. 8,6; TestDan.4.76. For Philostratus see *Vit.Apoll.* 7.10-8.12: Apollonius is completely unshakeable and fearless before the judgment of Domitian. 7.21: 'that this man would never be shaken' (μὴ ἂν ἐκπλαγέντος), cf. 7.32, οὔτε ἐκπλαγείς...

91. John 19.28-30; see above, 67. One cannot in any way conclude from the report in John that the author thought that Jesus did not suffer on the cross. The διψῶ proves the opposite. There are theological reasons for the differences from the account in Mark and Matthew – in the case of Luke more marked hagiographical features have found their way in. In the case of John all historical detail is subordinate to the one goal of depicting the way of Jesus as the one who brings salvation for believers.

92. Cf. 4.34; 5.36; 17.4.

93. Käsemann, *Jesu Letzter Wille* (n.50), 154 cf. 26, see above, 10.

94. John 19.23f.; the detailed description of the division of the garments of course presupposes knowledge on the part of the ancient reader that Jesus was crucified naked and dishonoured. Probably every reader had witnessed such an event on one occasion. Crucifixion involved the uttermost shame for the condemned man. It is precisely for that reason that its description in the Gospels – even in John – must have been so offensive to ancient readers, see Hengel, *La Crucifixion* (n.79). The best commentary on this is the mockery of the Platonist Celsus in 178 CE and the docetic-Gnostic attempts to take the sting out of this event, see above, 60.

95. Against Käsemann, *Jesu Letzter Wille* (n.50), 11. For the *theologia crucis* in John see Schnelle, *Antidoketische Christologie* (n.7), 191f.. arguing with U.B.Müller; also H.Köhler, *Kreuz und Menschwerdung im Johannesevangelium*, ATANT 72, 1987.

96. R. Bultmann, *The Gospel of John*, Oxford and Philadelphia 1971: 'Hence Jesus has to step forth as the caricature of a king... Look at the pitiful figure! But to the mind of the Evangelist the entire paradox of the claim of Jesus is in this way fashioned into a tremendous picture... The declaration ὁ Λόγος σάρξ ἐγένετο has become visible in its extremest consequence' (659).

97. Karl Barth, *Church Dogmatics* III.2, Edinburgh 1960, 64; cf. 40ff.

98. I John 2.20,27.

99. John 16.8-13.

IV. The Author, His Pupils and the Unity of the Gospel

1. See above, 6f. J.Kügler, *Der Jünger den Jesus liebte*, SBB 16, 1988, 25, says: 'No part of the text has been handed down to us which would have had to stand before John 1.1 nor any which would have had to follow 21.25'; he

forgets the *inscriptio* which is already handed down to us by p[66] and p[75], our earliest witnesses, and the almost more important *subscriptio* with the title. They are a part of the work and may not be simply ignored. The New Testament book titles, which have so far been completely neglected in scholarship, had a great practical significance for the liturgical use of the scriptures, since the content of the reading was indicated through them. The Gospels, the letters and the Apocalypse were either written for public reading in worship or copied for these and sent to other communities. Christian writings were increasingly kept and listed in the community archives with their 'Christian Torah shrine' alongside the Old Testament writings. For the use of the title in worship see the introduction to Melito's passover homily: 'The scripture of the Hebrew Exodus has been read out...', cf. S.G.Hall, *Melito of Sardis, On Pascha and Fragments*, Oxford 1979, cf. also I Clem.47.1; Ignatius, Eph.12.2; II Peter 3.16, which already presupposes a Pauline corpus; Rev.1.3; I Thess.5.27; Col.4.16; Mark 13.14; Justin, *Apology* I, 67.3; Eusebius, HE 4.23.12; here a distinction needs to be made between reading and 'canonization', which came substantially later.

2. John 21.24 (cf.19.35; 1.14; I John 1.1-4). The significance of this reference should not be played down, as tends to be done today. The identification of the author and the publication of the Gospel with a title coincide. It is the last historical action of the school which is visible.

3. M.Hengel, *Studies in the Gospel of Mark*, London and Philadelphia 1985, 64-88, 162-83; Mark 1.1 made a title εὐαγγέλιον κατὰ necessary.

4. For Papias, Mark and Peter see ibid., 47ff., 149ff.; for dating, 13ff., 126ff.

5. Luke indicates that he is closer (in time) to the destruction of Jerusalem than Matthew and John: 13.35; 19.27, 42ff.; 21.24; 23.28ff.

6. M.Hengel, 'Zur matthäischen Bergpredigt und ihrem jüdischen Hintergrund', *ThR* 52, 1987, 327-400: 346f., 349.

7. For the Irenaeus fragment POx 405 see A.Rousseau and L.Doutreleau, *Irénée de Lyon, Contre les Hérésies, Livre III.1*, SC 210, 1974, 126ff., beginning of the third or end of the second century. The Shepherd of Hermas also reached Egypt relatively quickly, see C.H.Roberts, *Manuscript, Society and Belief in Early Christian Egypt*, SchL 1977, 1979, 12f., 61. Tertullian, who returned from Rome to his native city Carthage as a Christian and began his activity as a writer immediately afterwards, had read Irenaeus carefully; he mentions him in *Adv.Val*.5.1 and quotes him in 7.3ff. For his part, Irenaeus cites Justin's lost work against Marcion, *Adv.haer*.4.6.2; 5.26.2.

8. This old disputed question now seems to me to be coming closer to a consensus. For the earlier state of scholarship see W.F.Howard, *The Fourth Gospel in Recent Criticism and Interpretation*, London 1931, 142-57; P.Gardner-Smith, *Saint John and the Synoptic Gospels*, Cambridge 1938, still opposed this; R.Schnackenburg, *The Gospel according to Saint John*, I, Tunbridge Wells 1968, 26-43, is restrained. The insights of B.H.Streeter, *The Four Gospels*, London ⁹1956, 424f., were basically correct; the observations of C.K.Barrett, *The Gospel according to St John*, London ²1978, 42-54, point in the same direction. While rejecting the over-complicated theories about source and redaction – which

cannot be verified – put forward by M.-E.Boismard, F.Neirynck, *Jean et les Synoptiques. Examen critique de l'exégèse de M.-E.Boismard*, BETL 49, 1979, 285f., 390, presupposes the use of all three Synoptic Gospels by John and at the same time stresses 'the originality with which the evangelist edits his work, borrowing various elements from his sources, but combining them and transposing them in his own way' (286). We would need to add the fact that the Synoptic material which he takes over has usually gone through the transforming filter of his own oral teaching. H.Windisch's account of the relationship between the Fourth Evangelist and the Synoptics is still the best: *Johannes und die Synoptiker*, UNT 12, 1926. However, the editors hardly wanted to 'suppress' the Synoptics but rather to correct them and 'surpass' them.

9. Gal.2.7; I Cor.15.1ff.; cf. 15.11 and Acts 15.7 suggest that the term *euangelion* also played a role in the Petrine mission. (Acts 15.7 is the first use of the word in Luke/Acts; the second is 20.24 on the lips of Paul.) This would also explain the emphatic use of the term in Mark (7 times, all in redactional texts), a use which is not substantially different from Paul's reference to the Jesus story, see my *Studies in Mark* (n.3), 54ff., 82f.

10. Peter's *martyrdom* is still hinted at in John 13.36 and attested as having been in Rome in I Clem.6.4; I Peter 5.1,13 (cf. also Rev.11.7; Asc.Isa.4.1). For the tradition of his tomb see the Roman presbyter Gaius in Eusebius, HE 2.25.7; for the crucifixion see Tertullian, *Scorp.* 15.3; *Act.Verc.* chs.35-41 and Porphyry in Macarius Magnes 3.22; a basic account is given by H.Lietzmann, *Petrus und Paulus in Rom*, Berlin and Leipzig ²1927, 226-47; id., 'Petrus römischer Märtyrer', in *Kleine Schriften* I, TU 67, 1958, 100-23: 'Moreover the tradition of the death of Peter as a martyr in Rome was preserved in Asia Minor' (107). The manner of his death, by crucifixion, is indicated in John 21.18 by the ἐκτενεῖς τὰς χεῖρας.

11. See above, 65 and below, 104f. The key witness for a 'present eschatology', John 11.25, shows this dialectic very well; moreover according to the rules of formal logic it is contradictory: ὁ πιστεύων

εἰς ἐμὲ κᾶν ἀποθάνῃ ζήσεται

καὶ πᾶς ὁ ζῶν καὶ πιστεύων εἰς ἐμὲ

οὐ μὴ ἀποθάνῃ εἰς τὸν αἰῶνα.

The second, hyperbolic statement seems to contradict the first. Moreover the ζήσεται can be connected with the conception of the parousia and the resurrection of the dead. What is decisive for John (as already for Paul, but in the latter case still not as strongly and one-sidedly) is the certainty of eternal life which is given now through faith in Christ (20.21). This allows the decorative future statements only 'peripheral' significance; however, it does not simply do away with them, but quite deliberately and provocatively sets them alongside – perhaps also in an anti-docetic setting (thus 5.28, cf. 11.38-44). It is also significant that – again as in Paul (cf. Phil.2.21-23 with I Cor.15 and I Thess.4) – the different conceptions can vary (5.24-29; 12.32,48; 14.2f.,18,28, etc.). Here, for example with the references to the (second) coming of Jesus, he loves ambiguity. J.-W.Taeger, *Johannesapokalypse und johanneischer Kreis*, BZNW 51, 1989, has now turned to the neglected theme of the relationship between the Gospel and the Apocalypse, and seeks to demonstrate 'that the Apocalypse is evidence not of the prelude but of the sequel to the words of Jesus' (204). Apart from the chronological difficulties, the 'archaic' christology and the Hebraizing language of the Apocalypse, which takes up less the LXX than the Massoretic text in the form of paraenesis, indicates the opposite. Strecker and Schnelle (see above, 177 n.7) also arrive at opposite conclusions here. The postulate of an 'evangelist' with a chemically pure 'present' eschatology seems to me to be a typically German phenomenon, as does the 'history' of the Johannine school constructed by literary criticism on this basis (18f.). The 'newly accentuated deutero-Johannine dialectic of the Already and the Not Yet' (204) is in reality that of the head of the school himself; here as a result of the crisis in the school the focal points in this dialectic have shifted somewhat. I am inclined to put the basic material of the Apocalypse more at the beginning of Johannine thought. Possibly it was then published around 70 or (I think less probably) it may have been redacted and edited later by a pupil. Taeger's verdict on the eschatology of the Apocalypse in connection with the Johannine circle remains notably independent of that and shows some progress in research (see above 177 n.7).

12. Cf. also I Cor.15.6, 51; 4.1 There is a clear decline here. With the 'delay of the parousia' the circle of original 'witnesses' 'remaining for the parousia' became smaller and smaller.

13. O.Eggenberger, *RGG*[3] 4, 1408. I know a number of older pastors who recall the unrest caused in the neo-apostolic communities by Bischoff's death.

14. R.Schnackenburg, *The Gospel according to John* 3, Tunbridge Wells 1982, 371: 'For with it… a major problem arose: the parousia which was still expected during the disciple's lifetime, had not happened. If it was a saying of the Lord, it could not be allowed simply to be dropped. So an explanatory saying had to be found and it is just that for which the editors strive.'

15. Kügler, *Jünger* (n.1), 406-11. At this point the argument of the author of this book, which at many points is wise and full of merit, becomes artificial and questionable, where he 'leaves the sphere of textual interpretation and enters the sphere of historical inquiry' (411). His explanation of John 21.22f. is quite unsatisfactory (483f.). The desire to do away with this 'block' in favour of an ahistorical *tabula rasa* is overwhelming: 'Now when we drop the rumour in John 21.22f. we lose the last piece of support for the historical existence of a person corresponding to the beloved disciple who is spoken of. That is no loss to our knowledge, but on the contrary is the factor which opens up the way to a comprehensive evaluation of the anonymity of the figure of the beloved disciple' (484). However, this freedom is dearly bought. It comes about in 21.22-25 as the result of doing violence to the text. How could a work which was attributed to a phantom disciple find recognition in the Johannine circle, and in so doing prompt this circle to false speculations about the death of this disciple? Everyone knew that 21.23,24 was an invention. One can attribute something like that to an obscure author, but not to the figure who puts his stamp on a circle! And how did the redactor arrive at 'The Gospel of John', where this anonymity is broken through? The work could easily have

been given an anonymous title; apart from the Letter to the Hebrews and the Letter to Diognetus there are plenty of them in the apocryphal literature. Would the community have accepted this phantom figure as its 'anonymous teacher' (485)? Moreover the anonymity is so arranged that the name is disclosed (see below, 128ff.). Nor was it ever doubted in the early church. Even the Alogoi claimed that Cerinthus had forged the work in the name of *John!* One cannot make convincing judgments about the historicity of texts which outwardly seek to narrate history, solely on the basis of a purely synchronous linguistic approach, without noting historical analogies. Accordingly the 'evaluation of the anonymity' on the last three pages, 485ff., is disappointingly pale and does not convey anything. See already Harnack's devastating criticism of Overbeck's construction of the beloved disciple in *TLZ* 37, 1912, 8-14, which in many respects is similar: '... the discussion of 21.20-24 is so arbitrary that despite repeated reading of it I have not once grasped the formal stringency of the chain of argument' (12).

16. See the survey in A.Kragerud, *Der Lieblingsjünger im Johannesevangelium*, Oslo 1959, 42-6. For Paul as the beloved disciple see B.W.Bacon, *The Fourth Gospel in Research and Debate*, London and Leipzig 1910, 325f. For Jude the brother of Jesus (cf. John 14.22 and Mark 6.3!) see J.J.Gunther, 'The Relation of the Beloved Disciple to the Twelve', *TZ* 37, 1981, 129-48.

17. John 13.23-26; 19.26f.,34f.; 20.2-10; 21.7. See the careful exegesis in Kügler, *Jünger* (n.1), which takes account of the context but sometimes tends towards over-interpretation and does too little to illuminate the historical background. For the problem of the way in which the redaction works in the material, see below, 99f.

18. Sin[2], C, L, Θ, f[1], f[13], the Byzantine imperial text and the Achmimic and Sub-Achmimic translation have the article. The variants may already have found their way into the manuscripts in the second half of the second century, when people began to be interested in the author of the Gospel. For the identification with the beloved disciple or John see J.Reuss, *Johanneskommentare aus der griechischen Kirche*, TU 89, 1966: Theodore of Heraclea, no.355 (p.158); Ammonius of Alexandria, no.579 (p.339); cf. also J.A.Cramer, *Catenae Graecorum patrum in Novum Testamentum* II, Oxford 1840 (reprinted Hildesheim 1967), 379f.; John Chrysostom, *in Ioann.hom.* 83.2, ad loc., PG 59, 449: τίς ἐστιν ὁ ἄλλος μαθητής; Αὐτὸς ὁ ταῦτα γράψας; Jerome, *Epistles* 127.5, CSEL 56.149f.: *unde et Iesus Iohannem euangelistam amabat plurimum, qui propter generis nobilitatem erat notus pontifici et Iudaeorum insidias non timebat, in tantum, ut Petrum introduceret in atrium et staret solus apostolorum ante crucem...* See also J.S.Semler, *Paraphrasis Evangelii Iohannis*, Halle and Magdeburg 1771, 223ff. ad loc. By contrast, H.Grotius, *Annotationes in NT IV in Joh.*, Groningen 1828, 253 ad loc., conjectured *alium quendam Hierosolytanum, non aeque manifestum fautorem Iesu: quales multi erant in urbe...*, 12.42; possibly he was even the landlord at the Last Supper, Matt. 26.16. Augustine, *Tract. in Ioann.*, 113.2, CC SL 36, 636: *Quisnam iste sit discipulus, non temere affirmandum est, quia tacetur. Solet autem se idem Iohannes ita significare, et addere: quem diligebat Iesus. Fortassis ergo et hic ipse est; quisquis tamen sit, sequentia videamus...*, perhaps an

unknown figure or John himself. Kügler, *Jünger* (n.1), 424-8, gives a survey of the various opinions; however, his interpretation in terms of the beloved disciple being a 'semi-disciple' like Nicodemus and Joseph of Arimathea is hardly right. He does not conceal his discipleship for fear of the Jews (19.38), but joined Peter in following Jesus after his arrest; nor is Nicodemus ever called a 'disciple'. This unknown figure certainly does not have a negative character, even if he cannot be identified completely. But the author is sometimes fond of this twilight, see also 130.

19. The secondary reading πρῶτος, Sin, L, W-supplement, imperial text in v.41 probably indicates that the account was understood to mean that Andrew was 'the first' to find his own brother Simon and that after this the unknown figure (i.e. John) found his brother James, cf. F.Godet, *Kommentar zu dem Evangelium des Johannes*, Hanover and Berlin ⁴1903 (reprinted Giessen and Basel 1987), II, 99; T.Zahn, *Das Evangelium des Johannes*, KNT IV, ⁵,⁶1921 (reprinted Wuppertal 1983), 134, though both want to see πρῶτος as the original reading. For the exegesis in the early church see Cramer, *Catenae* II (n.18), 194, on 1.41; John Chrysostom, *in Ioann.hom.*18.1, PG 59,114; Epiphanius, *Pan.*, 51.14.4-6 (GCS 31,267f.); cf. also Semler, *Paraphrasis* (n.18), 53f., 56 on 1.35,51: his view is that the author concealed his own name and that of his brother out of modesty, a view taken by numerous earlier exegetes. Bacon, *Fourth Gospel* (n.16), 202, conjectures that the sons of Zebedee came after John 1.41f. in the original, but that a redactor then omitted them.

20. Peter: Mark 1.16; 16.7. In John 21.23f. the beloved disciple is mentioned last. It is already striking that the sons of Zebedee appear only in 21.2 and are absent from ch.1 (see below, 128f.), especially as it is in the opening chapter that the evangelist presupposes knowledge of the Synoptic narrative. Its absence is not mere chance, but is deliberate.

21. Kügler, *Jünger* (n.1), 421ff.: 422. There is also a survey of the views of more recent exegetes at this point.

22. See above, n.19. For the whole question see below, 125ff. It has to be remembered that the whole work was not planned and written down all at once like a biographical novel but came into being comparatively slowly and developed from oral teaching in the school (see below, 94f.).

23. *De anima* 50.5. It is significant that according to the information given in *Biblia Patristica* this text is mentioned only in Tertullian and once in Origen, *Comm.in Ioann.* 32.260 (GCS Origen 4, 460.30ff.) among the fathers of the second and third centuries, which indicates that it caused considerable offence. Perplexity continued. The view of M.Lattke, 'Joh 20,30f. als Buchschluss', *ZNW* 78, 1987, 288-92, that despite the reference in Tertullian we are to postulate a version of John without ch.21 is quite unfounded. The tradition of the text gives no suggestion of this. For Menander see above, 54.

24. Cf. above, 50f. Against this see now again Taeger, *Johannesapokalypse* (n.11), 18: 'The Gospel of John and the letters are documents of a relatively independent community (a community association) and allow us to make inferences about different phases of the history of the theology of this Johannine community which can be more or less clearly distinguished.

Closer description of this development depends essentially on literary-critical judgments, on the separation of strata in the Gospel of John and the definition of the relationship between the letters and the Gospel (or its strata).' Quite apart from the fact that the attempt at 'reliable separation of strata' which are said to come from different individuals and groups is extremely problematical (see below, 88ff.), this overlooks two very relevant points: (a) the decisive role of the leading figure, the head of the school, who as a pioneer thinker gave the 'Johannine circle' its stamp and who shaped the language of the school; and (b) the fundamental openness of the school to the communities of Asia Minor. No separatism is visible in the Johannine corpus itself, apart from the secessionists who left no writings. See above, 50; below, 101f.

25. We should not forget that there is no evidence of a thoroughgoing persecution of Christians under Domitian which would justify a remark like Rev.17.6 (cf. 16.6; 18.24; 19.2). The seven kings of Rev.17.9-11 can hardly be extended as far as Domitian; rather they fit Nero as the fifth, and Galba, Otho or Vitellius (both of whom were acclaimed emperor in January 69) as rapidly changing rulers, and finally Nero *redivivus* coming from the East (16.32) as the eighth (one of the seven). In other words, here we have a similar situation to that in Mark 13, where similarly the Antichrist is expected, see my *Studies in Mark* (n.3), 18ff. No wonder that at this time, when a general collapse of the Roman Empire was expected, apocalyptic expectations also extended particularly to the Christians.

26. This is largely conceded again today; see the brief account of scholarship in Taeger, *Johannesapokalypse* (n.11), 7ff.

27. Eusebius, HE 2.23.4; 3.32.1; 4.22.1-3; cf. also 4.5.3. The lists of bishops are historically questionable constructions up to the beginning of the second century.

28. This ongoing influence of oral Johannine tradition is visible in Papias and less clearly in Polycarp, the other 'presbyter' according to Irenaeus, indeed still in Polycrates and Clement of Alexandria. I would reckon that the teacher had some influence on Ignatius also, see above, 14f. and 152 n.85. But all this hardly has anything to do with the school proper.

29. Eusebius, HE 5.24.1-7, see above, 7.

30. E.Hirsch, *Studien zum vierten Evangelium*, BHTh 11, 1936, 155 (my italics).

31. See Philostratus, *Vitae Sophistarum*, and G.W.Bowerstock, *Greek Sophists in the Roman Empire*, Oxford 1969.

32. Polycarp's attack on the arch-heretic, 'I recognize the firstborn of Satan', which Eusebius reports in HE 4.14.7, may well have been read out of his letter to the Philippians (7.1).

33. E.Schwartz, 'Aporien im 4.Evangelium', NGWG.PH 1907, I, 342-7; 1908, II and III, 115-88; IV, 497-560.

34. Ibid., 1908, 148. I must concede that I have often not been convinced by the argument, which is sometimes rather violent, and that for chronological, stylistic and theological reasons I regard the comparison with the historical books of the Old Testament as quite mistaken, see below, 87f.

35. See J.Wellhausen, *Das Evangelium Johannis*, Berlin 1908, reprinted in id., *Evangelienkommentare*, Berlin and New York 1987 (to which the first set of page numbers refers), 601-746 (1-146); cf. also the preliminary study, *Erweiterungen und Änderungen im vierten Evangelium*, Berlin 1907.

36. Ibid., 702 (102) on the author of the basic document (A) (my italics).

37. Ibid., 702-27 (102-27). We owe to the first editor (B) the introduction of the festival journeys, an approximation to the Synoptic tradition, the mention of the disciples, large parts of the speeches and the developed christology. The 'almost docetic-seeming treatment of the death' already to be found in A 'made further progress' in B. In A Jesus is still somewhat less ἀπαθής...' (113).

38. Ibid., 719 (119) (my italics).

39. Wellhausen goes so far as on occasion to attribute the two terms ὑψωθῆναι and δοξασθῆναι to two different source strata, the basic document A and the first editor. Statements like '..that the Messiah dies on the gallows is no longer a riddle' (713 = 113) or against the symbolic interpretation of the wonders: 'These miracles are in truth as clear as a plank of wood; no character and no intimation indicates that they are transcendent' (703 = 103) indicate that he has not understood the enigmatic character of the Gospel and that despite numerous brilliant observations the theological thinking of the Gospel was alien to him.

40. See the impressive description by P.Vielhauer (in discussion with E.Käsemann), *Geschichte der urchristlichen Literatur*, Berlin 1975, 439: 'Naturally the reconciliation of the irreconcilable by the Fourth Evangelist leads to irresolvable *inner tensions*. The hopeless divergence in interpretation of John bears witness to this. The tensions can be reduced to one, that is presented by the juxtaposition of the two statements "The Word became flesh" and "We saw his glory" (1.14).'

41. Schwartz, *Aporien* (n.33), I, 343-68.

42. Ibid., I, 368f.; IV, 558f.

43. Ibid., IV, 557.

44. Ibid., IV, 559f.: 'The editing has gone so deep that a good deal remains uncertain; and I openly concede that I cannot explain clearly... how the scene came to be duplicated. However, I think that I have demonstrated the probability that the attempt to balance the Synoptic account with a context which stands over against it has given rise to these peculiarities, and that I have shown that it is impossible that the basis is a single conception, thought up by an individual author' (358); cf. IV,.559.

45. The *Life of Jesus* by D.F.Strauss with its radical criticism of John appeared in 1835 (the fourth, 1840, edition was translated into English by George Eliot as *The Life of Jesus Critically Examined*, London 1848). C.F.Weisse, *Die Evangelische Geschichte kritisch und philosophisch betrachtet*, two vols., Leipzig 1838, largely follows Strauss's criticism and was the first to argue massively for the priority of Mark. However, in the Fourth Gospel Weisse wanted to rescue a 'Johannine backbone'. Three years later he was followed by Alexander Schweizer, who shortly beforehand had protested against the call of

Strauss to Zurich in his work *Das Evangelium Johannis nach seinem inneren Werthe und seiner Bedeutung für das Leben Jesu kritisch untersucht*, Leipzig 1841, for both see A.Schweitzer, *The Quest of the Historical Jesus*, London [3]1954, 121-36 (133); cf. 72. Similar attempts were made by D.Schenkel (from 1840); H.Ewald; K.H.Weizsäcker; E.Renan, see J.F.Bleek and W.Mangold, *Einleitung in das Neue Testament*, [4]1886, 292-5, and as contemporaries of Wellhausen and Schwartz, H.Delff, *Das vierte Evangelium, ein authentischer Bericht über Jesus von Nazareth, wiederhergestellt...*, Husum 1890, cf. id., ThStKr 65, 1882, 75-104; H.Wendt, *Das Johannesevangelium. Eine Untersuchung seiner Entstehung und seines geschichtlichen Wertes*, Göttingen 1900; id., *Die Schichten im vierten Evangelium*, Göttingen 1911; F.Spitta, *Zur Geschichte und Litteratur des Urchristentums* I, Göttingen 1893; id., *Das Johannes-Evangelium als Quelle der Geschichte Jesu*, Göttingen 1910. For English examples see Howard, *Fourth Gospel* (n.8), 111ff.: they are B.W.Bacon, A.E.Garvie and R.H.Strachan. In addition there are the numerous theories about the secondary transpositions of the text, ibid., 124-41. See also the differing results of these theories of redaction and transposition, 258-64.

46. F.Overbeck, *Das Johannesevangelium*, ed. C.A.Bernoulli, Tübingen 1911, 243.

47. A.Hilgenfeld, *Historisch-kritische Einleitung in das Neue Testament*, Leipzig 1875, 734f., cf. already id., *Die Evangelien*, Leipzig 1854, 325; id., 'Das Johannesevangelium nicht interpoliert', ZWTh 1868, 434f.

48. A.von Harnack, *Geschichte der altchristlichen Litteratur*, II.1, *Die Chronologie bis Irenaeus*, Leipzig 1897, 674ff., on the author of the Gospel. Harnack believed that only 21.24f. had been added to the Gospel later in order to characterize it as a work of the son of Zebedee; however, as it is attested in all the manuscripts, this was certainly 'quite some time before 150' (680). See also his fine sketch 'Zum Johannesevangelium' in *Erforschtes und Erlebtes*, Giessen 1923, 36-43: in his view the work was soon published by friends. Cf. also *History of Dogma* ([4]1909), reissued London 1961, Vol. I, 95-8.

49. W.Wrede, 'Charakter und Tendenz des Johannesevangeliums', in *Vorträge und Studien*, Tübingen 1907, 188: 'When Jesus speaks like John the Baptist (and we can add: like the Evangelist himself), and also like the author of I John, in reality only one person is really speaking: the evangelist, who is at the first time the author of I John. This conclusion has often been drawn, and it is compelling.' Cf. 189 for explanatory glosses.

50. H.J.Holtzmann, *Lehrbuch der historisch-kritischen Einleitung in das Neue Testament*, Freiburg im Breisgau [3]1892, 435f.;, id. and W.Bauer, *Evangelium, Briefe und Offenbarung des Johannes*, HC IV, [3]1908, 23.

51. Windisch, *Johannes* (n.8), 54-8: '...that the Fourth Gospel as a whole is the work of *one* author whose aims can be read out of the composition of the work, the choice of narratives and the content of the discourses' (57f.).

52. M.Dibelius, RGG[2] 3, 255f.

53. W.Bauer, *Das Johannesevangelium*, HNT 6, [3]1933, 249-53: 'It has deepened the impression that we may speak of the unity of the Gospel of John only with considerable restraint. But similarly, at least in my case, the feeling has

grown that if certain results which produce a picture of any degree of completeness are possible at all, they can be arrived at only on the basis of very comprehensive and careful investigations which take into account both the language and the content, and also probably the major letter' (249). The reconstruction of a basic document is to be rejected (249f.). See also the admirable survey of scholarship in *ThR* NF 1, 1929, 136-60: 136-8. His description still holds today: 'Penetrating acuteness and a gift of rich combination have been applied to its solution; but unfortunately just as often lack of restraint and a deficiency in self-criticism play their part, and also a faith in the certainty of the results to be arrived at in this way which is as firm as it is touching.' Unfortunately his impression that 'the *method of source analysis* (my italics) has passed its heyday' has not proved true (138). The 'touching faith' has remained.

54. A.Jülicher and E.Fascher, *Einleitung in das Neue Testament*, Tübingen ⁷1931, 382f. (my italics); cf. Vielhauer (n.40 above).

55. Schwartz, *Aporien* (n.33), II, 147: 'So in the last resort the Tübingen school were not as wrong as all that when they put the Fourth Gospel in the middle of the second century; only then was it given its final form and only after 160 did it exert its influence inside and outside the church...'

56. Wellhausen, *Evangelium* (n.33), 726 (126): 'However, this verse is a late and desperate addition', cf. 627 (27).

57. Bacon, *Fourth Gospel* (n.16), 210-25: 219.

58. Hirsch, *Studien* (n.30), 43, with unsurpassed self-confidence: 'A. I have succeeded in extracting a meaningful and coherent work as the original Gospel. B. I have succeeded in gaining a quite definite and sharp picture of the sense and purpose of the redaction.' In addition there is the 'popular' version, id., *Das vierte Evangelium in seiner ursprünglichen Gestalt verdeutscht und erklärt*, Tübingen 1936. A generation after Harnack, Hirsch was probably the German theologian with the most comprehensive historical and philosophical knowledge. Bultmann wrote an interesting review of Hirsch's two-volume work (*EvTh* 4, 1937, 115-42) in which he stressed that in literary criticism '[I] go... even further than H.' (117). With his demand that 'analysis (can) be done... only on the basis of *style criticism*' (his italics, 121), Bultmann contradicted himself, see below, 202 n.70. The same goes for the next sentence: 'This would show that many passages which H. attributes to the redactor go back to the Evangelist himself and that the text which H. thinks original is in fact the text of the source used by the evangelist.' That this too self-assured literary-critical credulity, free of all self-critical reflection, continues to be widely effective today, without interruption, is demonstrated by R.T.Fortna, *The Fourth Gospel and its Predecessors*, Philadelphia 1989. See the unspeakably naive introduction to his book (above, 136f. n.3).

59. Hirsch, *Studien* (n.30), 135.

60. Ibid., 140. Just as the greater Jewish-Christian church before 70 created its Gospel of Matthew, so at some point a Christian splinter group will have created its own particular Gospel.

61. Hirsch, *Studien* (n.30), 71ff. This explains the exact geographical details.

62. Ibid., 170-9: 175f. For ch.21 see 179-83.

63. Ibid., 177f., 187f. With Wellhausen, 5.43 is understood as a reaction of the redactor to the Bar-Kochba revolt, see above, n.57.

64. Bultmann, *RGG*[3] 3, 1959, 842. p[52] forces Bultmann to a substantially earlier date, before 100. He would probably have regarded reflection on the way in which this forces sources, evangelist and the various redactions so close together as being a waste of time. He never really troubled himself with the real historical 'how' – as in his adventurous transposition hypotheses. Cf. now Kügler, *Jünger* (n.1), 21, on the 'attempt to separate black from white'. As a discussion of Bultmann's theories, D.Moody Smith, *The Composition and Order of the Fourth Gospel. Bultmann's Literary Theory*, New Haven and London 1965, is still indispensable. This important book should be reprinted.

65. Bultmann, *RGG*[3] 3, cf. *Theology of the New Testament* II, London and New York 1955, 10.

66. See above, nn.48-55. Mention should also be made of the restrained, indeed warning attitude of W.Bousset, RGG[1] 3, 608-36: among other things Bousset warns – in an almost prophetic way as far as his pupil Bultmann was concerned – against 'unconsciously or with deliberate intent... excluding from the Gospel in its present form the material which to modern susceptibilities seems less valuable and in this way arriving at a basic document which says more to our taste and is a pure spiritual Gospel' (614).

67. K.Aland, 'Der Text des Johannesevangeliums im 2.Jahrhundert', in *Studien zum Text und zur Ethik des Neuen Testaments. Festschrift zum 80.Geburtstag von Heinrich Greeven*, ed. W.Schrage, BZNW 47, 1986, 1.

68. Ibid., see above, 32.

69. ΕΓΩ ΕΙΜΙ, FRLANT 56, 1939, [2]1965, 87-109. 'The style is essential a unity throughout. So the unity of the Gospel cannot be sought in a "basic document" but only in a compilation at the end of the process of development or in a unitary composition' (108).

70. E.Ruckstuhl, *Die literarische Einheit des Johannesevangeliums*, Freiburg CH 1951; expanded reprint NTOA 5, 1987; in addition see 291-303: the list of characteristics of Johannine style with all the evidence from the Johannine writings. For the special case of οὖν in John see Neirynck, *Jean et les Synoptiques* (n.8), 227-83. Moody Smith, *Composition and Order* (n.64), 57-79, gives an extended evaluation of the criticisms of Schweizer and Ruckstuhl (and its limitations). Cf. also B.Noack, *Zur johanneischen Tradition. Beiträge zur Kritik and der literarkritischen Analyse des vierten Evangeliums*, Copenhagen 1954, and Moody Smith, *Composition*, 73-9. Bultmann had a lengthy discussion with Noack in *TLZ* 80, 1955, 21-6, but he did not consider Ruckstuhl's arguments.

71. I have drawn attention to this in my preface to the new edition of Ruckstuhl's work (XI). As the style of the Fourth Gospel is undoubtedly unique in the New Testament, criticism was made of the conclusion drawn from this by Ruckstuhl (and Schweizer) that there was one normative author behind the Gospel: Kügler, *Jünger* (n.1), 35, even says that 'these statistics have been subject to devastating criticism... under the aspect of this claim'; in reality the arguments produced by the critics are generally unconvincing,

most of all that of E.Hirsch, 'Stilkritik und Literaranalyse im vierten Evangelium', *ZNW* 43, 1950/51, 128-43, for his almost novellistic theory of the origin of the Gospel with authors from completely different times and places does not provide the close cultural connection; moreover he was not yet able to come to grips with Ruckstuhl's work! For this see the critical observations by Moody Smith, *Composition and Order* (n.64), 68 n.42. The same is even more true of the objections by G.Richter, *Studien zum Johannesevangelium*, ed. J.Hainz, BU 13, 1977; in his numerous articles he does not quote Ruckstuhl's work once, but dismisses the problem all too easily with the argument that 'the Johannine style and vocabulary and particular theological conceptions could be the common property of a school or circle' (54, cf.67ff., on John 15.17); however, he inexcusably neglects the problem of style which tells against his speculations. Given the unity of Johannine style the main question is not one of primarily terminological (or even theological) agreements, but above all of more unconscious or unemphatic characteristics like prepositions, conjunctions, pronouns, the use of cases or simple decorations: see the fifty characteristics in Ruckstuhl, 291-330, and A.Dauer, 'Schichten im Johannesevangelium in der (den) johanneischen Gemeinde nach G.Richter', in *Die Kraft der Hoffnung. Festschrift J.Schneider*, ed. A.E.Herold et al., Bamberg 1986, 62-83. Against the similar objection by H.Thyen, that there is not an 'idiolect' but a 'sociolect' in the Fourth Gospel, and that therefore the unitary style is 'completely useless' as an argument against a literary-critical division of the Gospel (*ThR* 42, 1977, 211-70:214f.), see E.Ruckstuhl, 'Zur Antithese Idiolekt-Soziolekt im johanneischen Schrifttum', in id., *Jesus im Horizont der Evangelien*, Stuttgarter Biblische Aufsatzbände 3, 1988, 219-64: 266ff. = SNTU 12, 1987, 141-81.

72. R.T.Fortna, *The Gospel of Signs. A Reconstruction of the Narrative Source underlying the Fourth Gospel*, MSSNT 11, Cambridge 1970, 203ff., attempts a criticism of Schweizer and Ruckstuhl. This is countered by E.Ruckstuhl, 'Sprache und Stil im Johanneischen Schrifttum. Die Frage nach ihrer Einheit und Einheitlichkeit', in *Literarische Einheit* (n.70), 304-31. Fortna's new study, *The Fourth Gospel and its Predecessors*, Philadelphia 1988, is totally unsatisfactory; in it Schweizer and Noack are not mentioned at all and Ruckstuhl only in a note (210 n.509). His own investigation of the style in 208ff. is more than scanty.

73. J.Becker, *Das Evangelium des Johannes*, ÖTK 4.1, 1979, 20-48: 41. On this see above, 50.

74. Ruckstuhl, 'Idiolekt-Soziolekt' (n.71), 234, 238; see below, 95, 101f.

75. J.Becker, *ThR* 47, 1982, 312; Taeger, *Johannesapokalypse* (n.11), 18, follows him with somewhat more restraint (see n.24 above).

76. H.Thyen, 'Johannesbriefe', *TRE* 17, 1987, 186-200; 'Johannesevangelium', *TRE* 17, 1987, 200-25. For the aporias see 203ff.; for the source theories, 205ff.; for the text as a basis, 211ff. 'The interpretation of the Gospel of John must begin... from its transmitted text' (211). There was always a tendency in this direction in his work, cf. already id., 'Johannes 13 und die "kirchliche Redaktion" des vierten Evangeliums', in *Tradition und Glaube. FS K.G.Kuhn*,

ed. G.Jeremias et al., Göttingen 1971, 343-67:356; this is even clearer in 'Entwicklungen innerhalb der johanneischer Theologie und Kirche im Spiegel von Joh.21 und der Lieblingsjüngertexte des Evangeliums', in M.de Jonge (ed.), *L'Evangile de Jean*, BETL 44, 1977, 259-99 (260f., 268ff.).

77. R.Kieffer, *Au delà des recensions! L'évolution de la tradition textuelle dans Jean VI, 52-71*, CB NT Ser.3, Lund 1968; id, 'L'espace et le temps dans l'évangile de Jean', *NTS* 31, 1985, 393-409; id., 'Different levels in Johannine Imagery', in *Aspects of Johannine Literature. Papers presented at a Conference of Scandinavian NT Exegetes at Uppsala June 16-19, 1986*, ed. L.Hartman and B.Olsson, CB NT Ser.18, Lund 1987, 74-87; B.Olsson, *Structure and Meaning in the Fourth Gospel. A Text-Linguistic Analysis of John 2:1-11 and 4:1-42*, CB.NT Ser. 6, 1974; see also M.Hengel, 'The Interpretation of the Wine Miracle at Cana, John 2:1-11', in *The Glory of Christ in the New Testament. FS G.B.Caird*, ed. L.D.Hurst and N.T.Wright, Oxford 1987, 83-112: 90-104.

78. R.A.Culpepper, *The Anatomy of the Fourth Gospel*, Philadelphia 1983, index 265 s.v. signs; also Ruckstuhl, 'Idiolekt-Soziolekt' (n.71), 234-50. The unity of the Gospel here comes out much more strongly than in Culpepper's earlier study, *The Johannine School*, SBL Dissertation Series 26, 1975.

79. G.van Belle, *Les parenthèses dans l'évangile de Jean. Aperçu historique et classification. Texte grec de Jean*, SNTAS 11, Louvain 1985; see also Ruckstuhl, 'Idiolekt-Soziolekt' (n.71), 252-8. C.J.Bjerkelund, *Tauta Egeneto. Die Präzisierungssätze im Johannesevangelium*, WUNT 40, 1987.

80. Kügler, *Jünger* (n.1), 23, 24, 35.

81. Becker, *Evangelium des Johannes* (n.13) I, 35, 112-20, and even more Fortna, *Gospel of Signs* (n.72), who postulates a whole 'Gospel of Signs' from the John the Baptist narrative to the accounts of the passion and resurrection, blow up Bultmann's mere miracle source to a kind of basic Gospel which really comes near to Overbeck's 'scholars' *homunculus*' (see above, 86). For criticism, in addition to Olsson, *Structure and Meaning* (n.77), and Culpepper (n.78), see G.van Belle, *De Semeiabron in het vierde Evangelie*, Studiorum Novi Testamenti Auxilia 10, Leuven 1975; Neirynck, *Jean et les Synoptiques* (n.8), 93-174; Schnelle, *Antidoketische Christologie* (n.7); H.-P.Heekerens, *Die Zeichenquelle der johanneischen Redaktion*, SBS 113, 1984. Cf. also Thyen, *TRE* (n.76), 207: 'Of all the hypotheses about sources the *sēmeia* source has been the most tenacious and is enjoying a growth in popularity', see e.g. now again the quite diligent but methodologically naive work of Hans-Jürgen Kuhn, *Christologie und Wunder. Untersuchungen zu Joh 1, 35-51*, BU 18, 1988.

82. Schnelle, *Antidoketische Christologie* (n.7), 229: 'Because Jesus' death is the presupposition for the effect of the sacraments in bringing salvation, αἷμα and ὕδωρ also point to eucharist and baptism.' John uses αἷμα (apart from 1.13) only in 6.53-56 for the eucharist, cf. also V.H.Stanton, *The Gospels as Historical Documents*, III, *The Fourth Gospel*, Cambridge 1920, 239f., 256, on the link between miracle story and the teaching of Jesus as the bread of life.

83. Richter, 'Zum gemeindebildenden Element in den johanneischen Schriften', in *Studien* (n.71), 381-414: 398, 413. See above, 50f.

84. Becker, *Evangelium des Johannes* (n.13) I, 43-8; see also the diagram (46),

and above, 90 n.73. Becker himself has ultimately to concede: 'The question how the relationship of Johannine Christianity to the rest of Christianity is to be described is much more difficult and explosive. However, it is extremely questionable whether the label "sect" really helps here. It is striking that this relationship is not a direct theme in the Johannine literature... Moreover, at no point does the Johannine consciousness of election demarcate itself from other non-Johannine Christian groups... There may be geographical and even theological reasons (e.g. dualism) for the *de facto* special position of Johannine Christianity within the rest of Christianity, but this did not lead to an antagonism including segregation; rather, Christian unity may have been a presupposition of the Johannine communities' (47f.). These – welcome – insights make the whole construction of the 'concrete history of the Johannine communities' questionable, especially as 'for the most part ... they are shrouded in darkness' (44). The 'special position' is connected only with the unique person of the head of the school, not with a demarcation over against the 'mainstream church', see above, 50. A prehistory of the Johannine community would be primarily the 'history' of the teacher who founded it and the editing of his works. But there is still little evidence of this towards the end of the first century. All we can do is make a few cautious conjectures about his 'prehistory', see below, 134f.

85. Nowadays we already have all too many attempts to reconstruct a 'history of the Johannine community'. They are all doomed to failure, because we know nothing of a real history which even goes back to Palestine, and conjectures about it are idle. If we are said to be no longer in a position even to reconstruct a 'history of Jesus', how are we to be bold enough to reconstruct the history of a 'Johannine community' which is almost completely unknown to us? All we know is the old head of the school; we have some indications of a severe crisis in the community at a late stage, and we see the publication of the head's writings after his death. See e.g. R.E.Brown, *The Community of the Beloved Disciple*, New York, Ramsey and Toronto 1979; Oscar Cullmann, *The Johannine Circle*, London and Philadelphia 1976; R.Schnackenburg, *Das Johannesevangelium. IV.Teil, Ergänzende Auslegungen und Exkurse*, 1984, 90-102; K.Wengst, *Bedrängte Gemeinde und verherrlichter Christus. Der historische Ort des Johannesevangeliums als Schlüssel zu seiner Interpretation*, BThSt, Neukirchen ²1983; G.Strecker, 'Die Anfänge der johanneischer Schule', *NTS* 32, 1986, 31-47; similarly Schnelle, *Antidoketische Christologie* (n.7). See also what I feel to be the somewhat overbold attempt at a reconstruction with special reference to II and III John by B.Olsson, 'The History of the Johannine Movement', in *Aspects of Johannine Literature* (n.77), 27-43. All attempts at determining a historical context depend on 'how one reconstructs the historical situation common to the Johannine writings between about 90 and 100 A.D.'(34). Here our possibilities of reconstruction are *very* limited.

86. Ibid., 28f.: 'It is the result of a long, *complicated process*. There are traditions, oral or written, which are essentially independent of the synoptic material. The long process includes revisions, expansions, corrections, and comments, with many people and several historical situations involved. In

spite of this the linguistic material – and here we can include the Epistles – is remarkably uniform, which indicates that there is also a clear continuation in this long process.' I would add: the 'clear continuation' is governed by the 'elder John' as author. The 'many people' are not many redactors, but the discussion partners in the school (including the apostate pupils), perhaps also scribes or secretaries, and (finally) the editors.

87. See G.Reim, *Studien zum alttestamentlichen Hintergrund des Johannesevangeliums*, MSSNTS 22, 1974; M.Hengel, 'Die Schriftauslegung des 4. Evangeliums auf dem Hintergrund der urchristlichen Exegese', *Jahrbuch für Biblische Theologie* 4, 1989.

88. See W.Bauer, *Das Johannesevangelium*, HNT 6, ³1933, 252: 'But certainly we can note a lack of *literary* capability' (his italics). 'But what is beyond doubt Johannine is... a considerable area in which the author has not been involved according to a creative plan, but inadequacy is allied with indifference.' Over a period of slow growth this deficiency could also be connected with advancing age, which in my view is quite clear in the repetitions and the lack of any division in I John. Authors are human beings with human weaknesses and a human fate.

89. See also above, 50. F.C.Baur, *Kritische Untersuchungen über die kanonischen Evangelien*, Tübingen 1847, 314, etc., already saw the connection with Paul. John knows the Pauline tradition, but at the same time we should not overlook the fact that they were both moulded in the particular cultural and spiritual environment of Jerusalem after 30 CE, see below 120 on Wellhausen and Jülicher.

90. Jordan Mejas, 'Susan Sontag', *Frankfurter Allgemeine Zeitung*, Magazine, 10 March 1989, no.471, 11-22: 14,16,18,20.

91. A.von Harnack, *ThLZ* 37, 1912, 8-14:14. Cf. also the remarks by C.A.Bernoulli and A.von Harnack, 157.

92. Cf. D.Moody Smith, *Composition and Order* (n.64), 239: 'Yet I think it quite possible, indeed probable, that the Fourth Gospel has been left to us in an unfinished state.' As 'unfinished' as Overbeck's Gospel of John? On this see Bernoulli's defence, *Johannesevangelium* (n.46), 157: 'As editor of Overbeck's papers on John I have been guided by no other intent than the concern to embody the special character of my teacher with all its peculiarities in the framework of the book.'

93. Even most of the numerous explanatory parentheses (see above n.79) may come from the author and not from the editors.

94. In this way some years ago, a young German journalist, son of a well-known author, sought to get parts of the literary bequest of the dead writer Uwe Johnson to London.

95. See C.H.Roberts, *Manuscript, Society and Belief in Early Christian Egypt*, SchL 1977, London 1979, and id. and T.C.Skeat, *The Birth of the Codex*,1983, 38ff.; Hengel, *Studies in Mark* (n.3), 78ff. nn.96-101.

96. Rev.1.2f.;22.10,18, cf. Deut.4.2;13.1. In the case of I John the framework could have been removed for the purpose of reading the letter aloud in worship. See above, 47f.

97. This does not mean that it was acknowledged by the majority as such; probably the lofty pretensions of the author at first provoked opposition, in the majority of communities which were orientated towards the Petrine synoptic tradition. The last chapter (21) tries to bridge the gap here, but succeeds only partially.

98. Presumably this was deliberately intended by the author. *All* the disciples, including the beloved disciple, did not at that time understand the discourses and actions of Jesus (12.16; 20.9). It is only renewal through the Spirit (20.22) which gives them the possibility of really understanding Jesus' words and activity.

99. Verse 25 was originally omitted in the writing of Codex Sinaiticus but was then added. According to H.von Soden, NT I, 249, Greek catenae contained the observation that this verse was omitted by 'others': presumably the ironic and hyperbolic conclusion was offensive to some copyists. See Schnackenburg, *Johannesevangelium* IV.3 (n.85), 445 on Sin and 448 on v.25: 'The pretentious sentence gives the impression that an ambitious scribe wanted to add a further witty conclusion.' J.Chapman, *JTS* 31, 1930, 379-87: 386f., differs completely: he sees this as the unmistakable sign of the evangelist, who for him is the apostle himself. I would think that this is a last piece of evidence of the irony so beloved in the Johannine school.

100. For my view that it is highly improbable that the son of Zebedee was the author see above, 21f.; for the ambivalence of the beloved disciple, see below, 130.

V. *John the Elder, his Origin and the Historical Setting of his School*

1. Cf. already the genealogy of the family of Mattathias, son of John, son of Simon and his oldest son, I Macc.2.1f.; 9.36,38; I Macc.8.12; II Macc.4.11; 11.17: (The priest) John, father of that Eupolemos who was Jewish ambassador to Rome and author of a Jewish history; *Antt.* 14.14: a John son of John was among the ambassadors to Claudius in 44 CE.

2. See the Hebrew text of Sirach 50.1 and the early *yehud* coins with the inscription *ywḥnn* in D.Barag, *Qad.* 17, 1984, 59-61.

3. D.Barag and D.Flusser, 'The Ossuary of Yehohanah Granddaughter of the High Priest Theophilus?', *IEJ* 36, 1986, 39-44: 40.

4. John of Gischala comes from an influential Galilean family, *BJ* 2.85; 4.121-7; *Vita* 43,45,71-6, etc.; *BJ* 2.287,292; John the (general) tax farmer in Caesarea and leader of the Jewish community there; cf. also *BJ* 2.568; 2.567; 4.235.

5. The name is not significant either in CPJ or in CIJ. In the list of Rabbis in Billerbeck VI, 84ff., fifteen Johns are cited between 80 and the fourth century. For the New Testament see John the Baptist, the son of Zebedee, the father of Simon Peter (see below n.11), John Mark, who was presumably a Levite (Acts 4.36; Col.4.10, cf. Hippolytus, *Ref.* 7.30.1 [Marcowich, 311], and P.Corssen, *Monarchianische Prologe zu den vier Evangelien*, TU 15.1, 1896, 10.10), the high priest John in Acts 4.19 (see above n.3), the author of the

Gospel and the letters according to the title (that also appears in the New Testament) and the seer of the Apocalypse, who according to Irenaeus and the dominant tradition of the later church is identical with him.

6. A.Schlatter, *Die Sprache und Heimat des vierten Evangelisten*, BFCT 6, 1902; reprinted in K.H.Rengstorf, *Johannes und sein Evangelium*, WdF 82, 1973, 28-199: 'As both the title and the content of the book point to a Palestinian who originally thought in Aramaic, read his Hebrew Bible and predominantly taught in Aramaic during the first half of his activity...' The 'positive connections between Johannine Greek and Palestinian language... unshakably demonstrate... his origins in Palestine' (reprint, 28/29). However, Schlatter collects the parallels almost exclusively from the commentaries Mekilta on Exodus and Sifre Num. and Deut. which were written in the Hebrew of the Tannaites. The work was continued in his commentary on John, *Der Evangelist Johannes. Wie er spricht, denkt und glaubt*, 1930, applying further rabbinic material. Both works are still not obsolete by virtue of their linguistic observations, which are fundamentally without parallel.

7. Klaus Beyer, *Semitische Syntax im Neuen Testament*, Band I, *Satzlehre Teil 1*, Göttingen ²1968, 17f. and 297f., see also N.Turner in J.H.Moulton, *A Grammar of New Testament Greek*, IV, *Style*, Edinburgh 1976, 64-79. See already J.B.Lightfoot, *Biblical Essays*, London 1904, 16f., 125ff.

8. See R.H.Charles, *The Revelation of St John*, ICC, 1920, 1, CXLIII-CLII; F.B.Y.Scott, *The Original Language of the Apocalypse*, Toronto 1928, who (wrongly) presupposes a Hebrew original; Turner, *Grammar* (n.7), 148-59.

9. A.-J.Festugière, OP, *Observations stylistiques sur l'Évangile de S.Jean*, Paris 1974, 7, cf. also the comparison of style with Matthew, Luke and Greek secular literature, 115-23: 'The author... has a style which is all his own' (123). J.Wellhausen, *Das Evangelium Johannis*, Berlin 1908, reprinted in id., *Evangelienkommentare*, 1987, 145, 'No disguised Aramaic', and J.Bonsirven, 'Les aramaïsmes de S.Jean l'Évangéliste?', *Bib* 30, 1949, 405-37, cf. also E.C.Colwell, *The Greek of the Fourth Gospel. A Study of its Aramaisms in the Light of Hellenistic Greek*, 1931 passim, challenged the existence of a *direct* Hebrew original.

10. S.Schulz, *Das Evangelium nach Johannes*, NTD 4, ⁴1983, 10: 'Eastern Aramaic dialect may underlie... the Gospel of John.' This assertion is conjured up out of thin air. For Eastern Aramaic dialects see Beyer, *Semitische Syntax* (n.7), 45-8, 59-62. The literary testimonies to the 'Eastern Aramaic' dialect of Edessa begin with Tatian's Diatessaron around 170 and Bardesanes around 200. A few lines later, in a completely hazy way Schulz defines the 'location of Johannine Christianity in tradition and the history of religion as being an oriental-Gnosticizing Jewish Christianity from the frontiers of Palestine and Syria or from within Syria' (10 bottom). Cf. also R.Bultmann, *Theology of the New Testament* 2, London and New York 1955, 10, and id., 'Johannesevangelium', *RGG*³, 3, 1959, 843f. In conclusion, Schulz conjectures that 'the Fourth Evangelist' is *'a gnosticizing Gentile Christian* who is unknown to us' (12, my italics). E.Hirsch, *Das vierte Evangelium*, Tübingen 1936, energetically challenges any Jewish-Semitic origin: 'Here the distance from the emotion-

laden, picturesque and fragmented (!) nature of Hebrew art..., might be so great that it can hardly be believed that this book was written by a Semite. On the other hand some things recall the solemn nature of classical Greek tragedy' (68). 'A view of the language from the right perspective also makes it improbable that a man of Jewish blood (!) wrote this book' (70). The author is 'a Gentile Christian from northern Syria who is also not totally unfamiliar with Aramaic, and that means... someone who is an Antiochene or is shaped by Antiochene Christianity' (71). The thesis of Gentile Christian origin in essence already goes back to K.G.Bretschneider, *Probabilia de evangelii et epistularum Joannis, apostoli, indole et origine...*, Leipzig 1820, 114, and F.C.Baur, *Kritische Untersuchungen über die kanonischen Evangelien*, Tübingen 1847, 331: 'so we cannot... regard him as a born Jew either'.

11. Messiah, 1.41; 4.25; Cephas, 1.42; *rabbi* (in John 8 times, i.e. more frequently than Mark [3 times] and Matthew [4 times: twice only on the lips of Judas]); in John it is a form of address to Jesus and to John the Baptist (3.26) by the disciples and other conversation partners; *rabbuni* (cf. Mark 10.51), John 20.16: this typically Palestinian intensified form fits particularly well at this climax of the first appearance; Thomas/twin 11.16; 20.24; 21.2. For Simon son of John see 1.42; 21.15-17 only in the form of address by Jesus, cf. Matt.16.17; possibly John is interpreting the *Bariona* there: rightly, in terms of content. Behind the *Iona(s)* of the LXX (outside the book of Jonah) there is usually an underlying *joḥanan*, see Hatch and Redpath, *Concordance to the Greek New Testament*, Supplement, Oxford 1906, reprinted Graz 1954, 93. The Hebrew *yonah* = dove is extremely rare as a personal name, and is late; on this see J.Jeremias, 'Ἰωνᾶς, *TDNT* 3, 1966, 406-8, and the Gospel of the Nazoraeans; see E.Hennecke, W.Schneemelcher and R.McL.Wilson, *New Testament Apocrypha*, 1, London and Philadelphia 1963, 148 no.14. For the name of Judas's father see John 6.71; 13.2,26; for the ἀπὸ Καρυώτου see 6.71 (Sin*, Θ, f¹³, syʰᵐᵍᵍʳ: perhaps it is original here); 12.4 (D); 13.2 (De), 26 (D); 14.22 (D). For the whole question see Lightfoot, *Biblical Essays* (n.7), 18f., 144f.

12. John 9.7, Σιλωάμ ὃ ἑρμηνεύεται ἀπεσταλμένος, cf. 9.11; 19.13, λιθόστρωτον, Ἑβραϊστὶ δὲ Γαββαθά; 19.17, κρανίου τόπον, ὃ λέγεται Ἑβραϊστὶ Γολγοθα.

13. John 5.2, κολυμβήθρα ἡ ἐπιλεγομένη Ἑβραϊστὶ Βηθεσδα, thus *certainly* against Nestle/Aland²⁶, which has the 'more learned' (cf.Eusebius) Βηθζαθά, i.e. the new city, in the text. The committee was split on this question, see B.M.Metzger, *A Textual Commentary on the Greek New Testament*, London and New York 1971, 208, ad loc. See also below, 124 n.91. Presumably πύλη needs to be added to ἐπὶ τῇ προβατικῇ, Neh.3.1,32; 12.39 = Ezra 13.1,32; 22.39. For the appearance of the name in the Copper Scroll of Qumran and the archaeology see J.Jeremias, *Abba*, Göttingen 1966, 361-4.

14. 18.1: The garden πέραν τοῦ χειμάρρου τοῦ Κεδρὼν (cf. II Sam.15.23 LXX). This information supplements very precisely that of Mark 14.26,32.

15. John 8.20 (cf. Mark 12.31); 10.23: the hall of Solomon (cf. Acts 3.11; 5.2); 18.13,24: the distinction between the residences of Annas and Caiaphas and

the knowledge of the affinity between the two men, which is also confirmed by Josephus; 18.19,20: the proximity of Golgotha to the city (wall) but outside it (19.20); 19.42: the tomb near to the place of execution. Cf. also 1.28,44; 2.1,12; 3.23; 4.4-7,20f.; 4.46f.,51; 5.2f.; 6.1,63f.; 10.40; 11.54. All this information is fortuitous, but as a whole it is meaningfully incorporated into the narrative and is largely independent of Mark. It also stands out from the novellistic details of later Gospels by virtue of its relative reliability. We no longer find anything of this kind in the Gospel of Peter.

16. John 2.6,13,20; 4.9; 7.2,22f.,37f.; 8.17; 10.22; 11.39,44; 12.13, cf. I Macc.13.51; 18.28; 19.14,31.

17. Hirsch, *Viertes Evangelium* (n.1), 132f., see above, 87f.

18. For the problem of the 'glosses', explanatory statements and parentheses in the Fourth Gospel, which are quite clearly not secondary expansions but are rather the expression of the evangelist's unitary manner of thought and language, see C.J.Bjerkelund, *Tauta Egeneto. Die Präzisierungssätze im Johannesevangelium*, WUNT 40, 1987. Here Bjerkelund points to the interesting parallels in Josephus and the Second Samaritan Chronicle, edited by McDonald; see also G.van Belle, *Les Parenthèses dans l'évangile de Jean*, StudNovTestAux 11, Louvain 1985.

19. 4.4-9,18,21f., cf. 8.48. John is the first author to mention the Samaritan centre of Sychar (Askar) at the foot of Ebal, which appears later in Samaritan and rabbinic texts, see M.Hengel, *Between Jesus and Paul*, London and Philadelphia 1987, 12, 208 nn.136, 138, and H.M.Schenke, 'Jakobsbrunnen – Josefsgrab – Sychar. Topographische Untersuchungen und Erwägungen in der Perspektive von Joh.4.5,6', *ZDPV* 84, 1968, 159-84.

20. John 6.1-59, see P.Borgen, *Bread from Heaven*, NT Suppl 1981; id., in *Logos was the True Light and Other Essays in the Gospel of John*, Trondheim 1983, 21-46.

21. 6.23f.: inhabitants of Tiberias come to Jesus; 6.1: πέραν τῆς θαλάσσης τῆς Γαλιλαίας τῆς Τιβεριάδος, cf. 21.1. For Tiberias see E.Schürer, G.Vermes and F.Millar, *The History of the Jewish People in the Age of Jesus Christ (175 BC – AD 135)*, Edinburgh 1983-1987, II, 189-192, cf. Index III.2, 1002.

22. John 10.22, see I Macc.4.56: ὁ ἐγκαινισμὸς τοῦ θυσιαστηρίου; 4.59, αἱ ἡμέραι τοῦ ἐγκαινισμοῦ, cf. 4.54,57; 5.1, and II Macc.10.1-9, cf. 1.9. There the motive of the cleansing of the Temple is in the foreground, cf. John 2.14-17. Josephus, *Antt.* 12.325, calls the festival φῶτα. τὰ ἐγκαίνια is a rendering of ḥᵃnukka, see Dan.3.2. See also Schürer, History (n.21) I, 162f.; Billerbeck 2, 539f. For the formation of the word and its form see Blass-Debrunner-Funk, *Grammar*, §124.1; 141.3.

23. John 7.2, 37f.; cf. Billerbeck 2,490ff.

24. John 7.47-49; Billerbeck 2,494ff.

25. John 8.33; cf. Billerbeck 2,523; 1,116f.

26. 8.59; 10.31ff.; 11.8.

27. 11.55f.; 12.12,20.

28. 18.28, cf. 19.14; Billerbeck 2,830f.

29. 19.31-37, cf. Exod.12.46; Num.9.12; see M.Hengel, 'Schriftauslegung

des 4. Evangeliums auf dem Hintergrund der urchristlichen Exegese', *Jahrbuch zur Biblischen Theologie* 4, 1989.

30. R.E.Brown, 'The Qumran Scrolls and the Johannine Gospels and Epistles', *CBQ* 17, 1955, 403-19, 559-74 = id., *New Testament Essays*, 1968, 138-73; G.Baumbach, *Qumran und das Johannesevangelium*, Berlin 1958; J.H.Charlesworth (ed.), *John and Qumran*, London 1972; H.Braun, *Qumran und das Neue Testament* I, 1965, 96-138; II, 1966, 118-44. R.Bergmeier, *Glaube als Gabe nach Johannes*, BWANT 112, 1980, also has a critical discussion of the naive Gnostic theories, including the Mandaean hypotheses.

31. 1 QS 1.5; 5.3; 8.2, cf. Isa.26.10 LXX; Tobit 4.6; 13.6; see Braun, *Qumran* (n.30), II, 112; John 3.21; I John 3.6.

32. CD 19.34; cf. 1QpHab 11.1; 1 QH 8.7,16; see Braun, *Qumran* (n.30), II, 114f.; John 4.10-14; cf. 7.38.

33. 1 QS 3.7; John 8.12.

34. 1 QS 4.4; John 9.3.

35. 1 QS 4.21 (cf. the plural in 3.9; 4.23; 13.10); John 14.17; 15.26; 16.13; I John 4.6; Braun, *Qumran* (n.30), II, 231.

36. 1 QS 1.9; 2.16; 3.13, etc.; 1 QM 1.1, etc.

37. P.J.Kobelski, *Melchizedek and Melchiresa'*, CBQ.MS 1981; M.Hengel, *The Son of God. The Origin of Christology and the History of Jewish Hellenistic Religion*, London and Philadelphia 1976, 43ff.

38. O.Betz, *Der Paraklet. Fürsprecher im häretischen Spätjudentum im Johannesevangelium und in neugefundenen gnostischen Schriften*, AGJU 2, 1963. The book was ahead of its time in Germany. Despite the epoch-making criticism of C.E.Colpe's investigation, *Die religionsgeschichtliche Schule. Darstellung und Kritik ihres Bildes vom gnostischen Erlösungsmythos*, FRLANT 78, 1961, the Gnostic mist which had obscured New Testament research had not yet disappeared.

39. W.Meeks, *The Prophet-King: Moses Traditions and the Johannine Christology*, NT.S 14, 1976; cf. also K.Haacker, *Die Stiftung des Heils*, AzTh 47,1972, 88f.,98f., 108-11, 118-28, etc.

40. J.Macdonald, 'Memar Marqah', in id., *Samaritan Chronicles*, see now Alan D.Crown (ed.), *The Samaritans*, Tübingen 1989; especially J.E.Fossum, 'Sects and Movements', ibid., 293-389.

41. J.Bühner, *Der Gesandte und sein Weg im 4.Evangelium*, WUNT 2R. 2, 1977.

42. G.Schimanowski, *Weisheit und Messias*, WUNT 2 R. 1985.

43. See e.g. the fine account in H.Gese, 'The Prologue to John's Gospel', in id., *Essays on Biblical Theology*, Minneapolis 1981, 167-222. Basically R.Bultmann, 'Der religionsgeschichtliche Hintergrund des Prologs zum Johannesevangelium', ΕΥΧΑΡΙΣΤΗΡΙΟΝ: *FS H.Gunkel*, II, 1924, 123-40, 'Nachrede', in id., *Exegetica*, Tübingen 1967, 110-35, had already seen the significance of Jewish wisdom speculation for the prologue, but under the influence of the hypotheses of R.Reitzenstein associated it with the irrelevant theory of the 'redeemed Redeemer' and misinterpreted the Fourth Gospel as 'evidence of the early penetration of Eastern Gnostic speculation into earliest

Christianity' (26 = 35). For the history of research see now the exhaustive account by M.Theobald, *Die Fleischwerdung des Logos. Studien zum Verhältnis des Johannesprologs zum Corpus des Evangeliums und zu 1. Joh*, NTA 20, 1988, esp.54-161; however, this fails in the history-of-religions question because it hardly adduces any sources and concentrates entirely on literary and tendency criticism, which have gone down a blind alley.

44. On this see J.E.Fossum, *The Name of God and the Angel of the Lord*, WUNT 36, 1985, which has abundant material; it takes particular account of Samaritan traditions and refers to the towering significance of Exod.23.20f.; cf. id., 'The Magharians: A Pre-Christian Jewish Sect and its Significance for the Study of Gnosticism and Christianity', *Enoch* 9, 1987, 303-44.

45. L.W.Hurtado, *One God, One Lord. Early Christian Devotion and Ancient Jewish Monotheism*, Philadelphia and London 1988, gives a brief but precise survey. See also A.Segal, *Two Powers in Heaven*, SJLA 25, Leiden 1978. For Hellenistic civilization see my *Judaism and Hellenism. Studies in Their Encounter in Palestine during the Early Hellenistic Period*, London and Philadelphia 1974; also *The 'Hellenization' of Judaea in the First Century after Christ*, London and Philadelphia 1990.

46. This abundance is already visible in the unique commentary by H.Odeberg, *The Fourth Gospel interpreted in its Relation to Contemporaneous Religious Currents in Palestine and the Hellenistic-Oriental World*, Uppsala 1929 (reprinted Amsterdam 1968), which is most significant for the history of religions; see the table of sources on 7-15. Here the large number of rabbinic parallels is interesting; it is also evident in the works of Schlatter and in Billerbeck 2, 302-853. To a large degree Bultmann's commentary is dependent on Odeberg's collection of sources. See also the first part of C.H.Dodd, *The Interpretation of the Fourth Gospel*, Cambridge 1965, 10-130, and his critical observations on the over-stressing of the very late Mandaean sources.

47. G.Schenke, *Die dreigestaltige Protennoia*, Berliner Arbeitskreis für koptisch-gnostische Schriften, *TLZ* 99, 1974, 731-46; J.M.Robinson, 'Sethians and Johannine Thought: The Trimorphic Protennoia and the Prologue of the Gospel of John', in B.Layton (ed.), *The Rediscovery of Gnosticism*, SHR 41, Leiden 1981, 643-62; *Die dreigestaltige Protennoia*, Nag Hammadi Codex XIII, edited and translated with a commentary by G.Schenke, TU 132, Berlin 1984, 3,22f.,101f.,139ff.,153,161f.; cf. also C.Colpe, 'Heidnische, jüdische und christliche Überlieferung in den Schriften aus Nag Hammadi III', *JAC* 17, 1974, 109-25. But on the other hand see the objection by Y.Janssens, 'Une source gnostique du Prologue', in M.de Jonge (ed.), *L'Évangile de Jean*, BETL 44, 1977, 35-58; ead., 'The Trimorphic Protennoia and the Fourth Gospel', in A.H.B.Logan and A.J.M.Wedderburn (eds.), *The New Testament and Gnosis. Essays in Honour of R.McL.Wilson*, Edinburgh 1983, 229-44; J.Helderman, '"In ihren Zelten..." Bemerkungen zu Codex XIII Nag Hammadi, p.47.14-18 im Hinblick auf Joh 1,14', in T.Baarda, A.F.J.Klijn and W.C.van Unnik, *Miscellanea Neotestamentica* I, Leiden 1978, 181-211; R.McL.Wilson, 'The Trimorphic Protennoia, Gnosis and Gnosticism', in M.Krause (ed.), *Papers read at the Seventh International Conference on Patristic Studies, Oxford September*

8-13, 1975, NHS 8, Leiden 1977, 50-4; E.M.Yamauchi, 'Jewish Gnosticism', in R.van den Broek and M.J.Vermaseren, *Studies in Gnosticism and Hellenistic Religions presented to Gilles Quispel on the Occasion of his 65th Birthday,* EPRO 91, 1981, 467-97:480-4; id., *Pre-Christian Gnosticism: A Survey of Proposed Evidences,* London 1973. The text is a relatively late mixed product of a great variety of influences, including Jewish wisdom speculation, but also the Gospels, above all John, cf. 45.5f. and John 1.3; 47.14f. and John 1.14; 47.30 and John 8.12; 50.14f. and John 14.2. The Valentinian features are obvious.

48. Hengel, *Hellenization* (above n.45), 9ff.

49. See my 'Der vorchristliche Paulus', in M.Hengel and A.M.Schwemer (eds.), *Paulus als Missionar und Theologe und das antike Judentum,* WUNT 1991 (in preparation).

50. On this see H.Thyen, 'Johannesevangelium', *TRE* 17, 1987, 200-25: 211-18; also J.Louis Martyn, *History and Theology in the Fourth Gospel,* Nashville ²1979; id., *The Gospel of John in Christian History,* New York, Ramsey and Toronto 1978; U.C.von Wahlde, 'The Johannine "Jews": A Critical Survey', *NTS* 28, 1982, 33-60; id., 'Literary Structure and Theological Argument in Three discourses with the Jews in the Fourth Gospel', *JBL* 103, 1984, 575-84; W.Trilling, 'Gegner Jesu – Widersacher der Gemeinde – Repräsentanten der Welt. Das Johannesevangelium und die Juden', in H.Goldstein (ed.), *Gottesverächter und Menschenfeinde?,* Düsseldorf 1979, 190-210 = id., *Studien zur Jesus-Überlieferung,* Stuttgarter Biblische Aufsatzbände 1, 1988, 209-32; J.Ashton, 'The Identity and Function of the Ἰουδαῖοι in the Fourth Gospel', *NT* 27, 1985, 40-75.

51. K.Wengst, *Bedrängte Gemeinde und verherrlichter Christus. Der historische Ort des Johannesevangeliums als Schlüssel zu seiner Interpretation,* BThSt, Neukirchen ²1983.

52. For the so-called 'synod of Jamnia' and the *birkat hamminim* see P.Schäfer, 'Die sogenannte Synode von Jabne. Zur Trennung von Juden und Christen im ersten/zweiten Jahrhundert n.Chr', *Judaica* 31, 1975, 54-64 = *Studien zur Geschichte und Theologie des rabbinischen Judentums,* Leiden 1978, 45-64; G.Stemberger, 'Die sogenannte "Synode von Jabne" und das frühe Christentum', *Kairos* 19, 1977, 14-21; R.Kimelman, 'Birkat Ha-Minim and Early Jewish-Christian Controversy', *JTS* NS 33, 1982, 9-61; S.I.Katz, 'Issues in the Separation of Judaism and Christianity after 70 CE: A Reconsideration', *JBL* 103, 1984, 43-76. For the term ἀποσυναγωγός see W.Schrage, συναγωγή, *TDNT* 7, 1971, 798-852: 848-52; *TWNT* 10.2, 1273f., bibliography; see Schürer, *History* (n.21), II, 432f., 462.

53. Hengel, 'Vorchristliche Paulus' (n.49), and *Between Jesus and Paul,* London and Philadelphia 1983, 1-29, 133-56.

54. Josephus, *Antt.* 20.200; see M.Hengel, 'Jakobus der Herrenbruder – der erste "Papst"?', in *Glaube und Eschatologie. Festschrift für W.G.Kümmel zum 80.Geburtstag,* Tübingen 1985, 71-104.

55. Eusebius, HE 3.5.3; on the historicity see M.Hengel, *Studies in the Gospel of Mark,* London and Philadelphia 1985, 130f. n.111.

56. Josephus, *Antt.* 20.203; Acts 25.13-26.32; cf. particularly the assertion of innocence for Paul, 26.32.

57. Already Philip and later Agrippa I and II took no heed whatsoever of the Jews (in contrast to Herod, Antipas and the procurators), and from the beginning had coins minted with the head of the ruler on them. Just as in Judaea the death penalty was inflicted by the procurators, so in this client kingdom it was inflicted by the ruler (and in his absence by his representative). Philip himself had travelled round the land holding courts (*Antt.* 18,106f.). The assent which this unfounded theory of Wengst's has met with in Germany is a sign of the widespread lack of historical knowledge. For criticism see also Thyen, 'Johannesevangelium' (n.50), 215. Βηθανία (variant reading Βηθαβαρα) beyond the Jordan in John 1.28 has nothing to do with the kingdom of Agrippa II north of the Yarmuk and east of Lake Tiberias, or with the city region of Hippos which was part of the Decapolis; there also seems to be no reason for connecting this with Batanaea, as is attempted by R.Riesner, 'Bethany beyond the Jordan (John 1:28). Topography, Theology and History in the Fourth Gospel', *TyB* 38, 1987, 24-63. The threefold πέραν τοῦ Ἰορδάνου as the scene of the activity of John the Baptist and the place in which Jesus takes refuge points to Peraea, which was under the rule of Herod Antipas, and not to the remote north-east, which already belonged to Syria, cf. also Mark 3.8; 10.1; Matt.4.25; 19.1, cf. Josephus, *BJ* 3.44-47. In the geographical description of the area ruled over by Agrippa II in *BJ* 3.56-68, there is mention only of the sources of the Jordan and stress on its 'mixed population' of Jews and Syrians. In contrast to the Synoptics, 'Gentiles' play no part whatsoever, if we leave aside the 'Greeks' in 7.35 and in Jerusalem (12.20), who are probably proselytes, and Pilate. The word ἔθνη does not occur in his writings.

58. For the Jewish Diaspora in Asia Minor see Schürer, *History* (n.21), 3.1, 17-35, and my 'Der alte und der neue "Schürer"', *JSS* 1990 (forthcoming).

59. For Sardes see Schürer, *History* (n.21), 3.1, 202; cf. Index 3.2, 990; M.Reynolds and R.Tannenbaum, *Jews and God-Fearers at Aphrodisias. Greek Inscriptions with Commentary*, Cambridge Philological Society Supplements 12, 1987. On this see Hengel, '"Schürer"' (n.58). Among other things the growing Palestinian rabbinic influence is evident in the inscription. For journeys of rabbis to Asia Minor see n.89 below.

60. Rev.2.9 and 3.9, cf. above, 000. Martyrdom of Polycarp 12.2; 13.1: ὡς ἔθος αὐτοῖς εἰς ταῦτα ὑπουργούντων; 18.1; *Mart.Pionii* 4.8-12; 13.2f., see also Tertullian, *Scorp.* 10.10: *fontes persecutionum, apud quas apostoli flagella perpessi sunt*.

61. Hengel, *Studies in Mark* (n.55), 9f., 123f. nn.56-62.

62. Even the sympathizer Nicodemus, a Pharisee and ἄρχων τῶν Ἰουδαίων and teacher in Israel, does not understand Jesus (3.1,9); cf. 5.38-47; 7.40-51; 9.13ff.,40f., but cf.2.22; 6.45; 7.38; 12.37-41; 19.28; 20.9. For the understanding of scripture in the Fourth Gospel see Hengel, 'Schriftauslegung' (n.29).

63. 7.32,45; 11.47,57; 18.3. Earlier the Pharisees appeared only in connection with John the Baptist in the interpretative gloss on the Jews in 1.19; 4.1 and

ten times as opponents of Jesus between 7.45 and 12.42. In Matthew and Luke they are substantially more strongly to the fore: 29 times in Matthew, 27 in Luke and 18 in John (without 8.3). Mention is made of the Pharisees as religious leaders of the people especially in 9.13ff., cf.9.40f. In addition there are three mentions of the ἄρχοντες (cf.also 3.1); this term appears elsewhere only in Luke, in the trial of Jesus and in Acts 7.

64. The high priests and Pharisees appear together for the last time in 18.3, at the arrest. Between 18.10 and 26 we find only the singular ἀρχιερεύς for Annas and Caiaphas, nine times in all; cf. also 11.49-51, the ἀρχιερεὺς προφητεὺων. The ἀρχιερεὺς ὢν τοῦ ἐνιαυτοῦ ἐκείνου is probably to be understood as meaning 'in that memorable year' (of the death of Jesus), cf. Tacitus, *Dial. de orat.* 17.3 and Schnackenburg, *The Gospel according to St John* II, Tunbridge Wells and New York 1979, 348f., ad loc.; cf. already Lightfoot, *Biblical Essays* (n.7), 29: 'The year of which the evangelist speaks was the year of all years; "the acceptable year of the Lord", as it is elsewhere called; the year in which the great sacrifice, the one atonement, was made, the atonement which annulled once and for ever the annual repetitions. It so happened that it was the duty of Caiaphas, as high priest, to enter the holy of holies, and offer the atonement for *that* year.' Baur, *Kritische Untersuchungen* (n.10), 332f., wrongly wants to use this passage against Lücke as evidence that the author 'was not a Palestinian writer'. For Jewish parallels in revelations to the high priest and to unconscious prophecies see Billerbeck, 3, 546 and J.Jeremias, *Jerusalem in the Time of Jesus*, London and Philadelphia 1969, 149; for his *character indelibilis* even after his deposition see 157f. Otherwise the high priests (with the exception of Caiaphas) sometimes changed very quickly: in the thirty-three years between 37 BCE and 70 CE twenty-eight known high priests held office, and in reality it could be even more! In the trial before Pilate Jews and high priests appear together and side by side, see 18.35: Μήτι ἐγὼ Ἰουδαῖός εἰμι· τὸ ἔθνος τὸ σὸν καὶ οἱ ἀρχιερεῖς παρέδωκάν σε ἐμοί. For Jews see 18.31,36,38; 19.7,12,14; high priest: 18.35; 19.6,15,21. The final choice for the imperial rule and against Jesus in 19.15 which seals Jesus' fate is brim full of Johannine irony.

65. 11.47, cf. Josephus, *Antt.*20.200; *Vita* 368; cf. Schürer, *History* (n.21), 218-23.

66. 4.9; 18.33ff.; 19.19, etc.

67. 4.22; Israel/Israelite, 1.31,49; 12.13; cf. 3.10. See E.Grässer, 'Die antijüdische Polemik im Johannesevangelium', *NTS* 11, 1964/5, 74-90 in id., *Text und Situation*, 1973, 50-69; Hengel, 'Schriftauslegung' (n.29): C.J.A.Hickling, 'The Attitude to Judaism in the Fourth Gospel', in M.de Jonge (ed.), *L'Évangile de Jean*, BETL 44, 1977, 347-54. Out of five instance of 'Jews' in Matthew, four contain the formula 'king of the Jews'; in Mark it is five out of six!

68. John 2.23, the almost stereotyped πολλοὶ ἐπίστευσαν, cf. 7.31; 8.30; 10.42; 12.11,42 – seven times in all! See also the fear of the leaders, 11.48; 7.48.

69. 8.33-47 (44). The counter-accusation, which calumniates Jesus as a

heretical Samaritan possessed of a demon shows the same polemical fury. In the taunt poem against the Valentinian Marcus written by an unknown 'elder' (Irenaeus, *Adv.haer.* 1.15.6), by analogy with this Satan is mentioned as his father, see above, 176 n.5.

70. 15.18-25, cf.3.20: φαῦλα πράσσων here means 'not believing'; 7.7; 17.14; cf. also I John 3.13. In I John the problem of hatred in the community of believers then even comes into the centre; it is a theme which the evangelist did not want to put on to the lips of Jesus – it had already long been acute in the church: see I John 2.9,11; 3.15; 4.20; and for the subject-matter III John 9ff., see above, 36ff., 52f.

71. I John 4.5: αὐτοὶ ἐκ τοῦ κόσμου εἰσίν· διὰ τοῦτο ἐκ τοῦ κόσμου λαλοῦσιν καὶ ὁ κόσμος αὐτῶν ἀκούει.

72. Jesus, John 8.17; 10.34, cf. 7.19; Pilate, 18.31; Jesus to the disciples, 15.25; the Jews, 7.51; 12.34; 19.7. S.Pancaro, *The Law in the Fourth Gospel*, NT.S 42, Leiden 1975.

73. 5.1; 7.2, the feast of tabernacles; 6.4, the feast of passover, cf.2.13; 11.55: τὸ πάσχα τῶν Ἰουδαίων.

74. καὶ οὐδεὶς ἐξ ὑμῶν ποιεῖ τὸν νόμον. τί με ζητεῖτε ἀποκτεῖναι; cf. 7.24f.,50f.; 8.15, 37.

75. 5.39,46f.; cf.1.47; 8.56; 12.41.

76. 2.17; 12.14f.,38; 13.18; 15.25; 17.12; 18.9; 19.24,36. The unbelief of the Jews is also part of this fulfilment.

77. *Das Evangelium Johannis* 121 (= *Evangelienkommentare*, 721): 'John is based on Paul'; similarly A.Jülicher, in *Geschichte der christlichen Religion*, Die Kultur der Gegenwart, Teil I, Abteilung IV.1, Berlin and Leipzig 1909, 96: 'The "theologian" John stands on Paul's shoulders.'

78. 11.48; 4.21. Soon after the destruction of Jerusalem Vespasian founded the colony of Flavia Neapolis near the ancient Shechem, see Josephus, *BJ*, 4.449; Pliny the Elder, *Natural History* 5.14.69, see Hengel, *Between Jesus and Paul* (n.53), 124, 206 n.128. With this pagan settlement the cult on Gerizim probably for the moment came to an end.

79. For the kingship in John see my 'Reich Christi, Reich Gottes und das Weltreich im vierten Evangelium', *Theologische Beiträge* 14, 1983, 53-67.

80. But see 12.20ff. and 4.3-42: the Samaritans are described by the evangelist as 'semi-Gentile' and are a symbol of the later Gentile mission, see Josephus, *Antt.* 9.228-91 (the five gods of the Samaritans) and John 4.18. For John 4 see T.Okure, *The Johannine Approach to Mission. A Contextual Study of John 4.1-42*, WUNT 2R. 31, 1988.

81. Eusebius, HE 6.14.7; see above 000.

82. 4.22: ὅτι ἡ σωτηρία ἐκ τῶν Ἰουδαίων ἐστίν; 4.42: οὗτός ἐστιν ἀληθῶς ὁ σωτὴρ τοῦ κόσμου.

83. Schürer, *History* (n.21), III.1, 68f.,70f.; Crown, *Samaritans* (n.40), 195-217; ibid., 'The Samaritan Diaspora', cf. Index 833 s.v.

84. Sibylline Oracles 4.165ff.; Epictetus, *Diss.* II 9.21, see M.Stern, *Greek and Latin Authors about Jews and Judaism* II, 1974, 542f. no.254; Acts 19.1-7. On

this see H.Lichtenberger, 'Täufergemeinden und frühchristliche Täuferpolemik im letzten Drittel des 1.Jahrhunderts', *ZTK* 84, 1987, 36-57.

85. The province of Asia was also popular as a place of exile, see Bill.4,666: BM 83b: R.Yishmael b.Jose (around 180) is advised by Elijah: 'Your father (R.Jose b.Chalapta) fled to Asia; you flee to Laodicea' (in Asia or Syria). Bill.2, 771: Shab 2.6.19b line 39, R.Jose b.Tanchum; Bill.4, 899: for a variety of rabbis Asia is one of the provinces which will fall to Israel in the messianic age. Cf.also Justin, *Dialogue* 1.3: the Palestinian Jew Trypho and his friends who have emigrated to Ephesus because of the Bar Kochba revolt. When R.Meir (c.150 CE) did not find a copy of the scroll of Esther at one point on a journey to Asia Minor, he wrote it out from memory (tMeg.2.4; bMeg.18b Bar.),

86. 7.35: μὴ εἰς τὴν διασπορὰν τῶν Ἑλλήνων μέλλει πορεύεσθαι καὶ διδάσκειν τοὺς Ἕλληνας; 12.20 on the other hand probably refers to proselytes or godfearers.

87. T.Zahn, *Apostel und Apostelschüler in der Provinz Asien*, FGNK VI, Leipzig 1900, 1-224: 158-75, 220ff.; P.M.Peterson, 'Andrew, Brother of Simon Peter', *NTS* 1, 1958. See above, 17.

88. Wengst assumes that the Gospel comes from Syria, but in the case of I John (and then the other two letters), 'Western Asia Minor, where the whole Johannine tradition is located by church tradition.' 'If these reasons are telling, we must conclude that at least parts of the Johannine circle and with them the Johannine tradition reached Asia Minor', *Der erste, zweite und dritte Brief des Johannes*, ÖTK 21, 1978, 30. When and why did this transplantation from Trachonitis 'to Asia Minor' take place? Here again we can see how untenable Wengst's theory is.

89. I John 3.10-18, cf. 2.29; see above, 64f.

90. The interpretation of John 2.1–10 as a 'luxury miracle' (D.F.Strauss) already caused problems in the early church, see M.Hengel, 'The Interpretation of the Wine Miracle at Cana, John 2:1-11', in *The Glory of Christ in the New Testament. FS G.B.Caird*, ed. L.D.Hurst and N.T.Wright, Oxford 1987, 83-112: 84ff., 104ff. F.C.Baur, *Historisch-Kritische Untersuchungen zum Neuen Testament*, reprinted in *Ferdinand Christian Baur. Ausgewählte Werke in Einzelausgaben* ed. K.Scholder, I, Stuttgart and Bad Cannstatt 1963, 119, takes over this slogan from D.F.Strauss.

91. John 9.1-38; 5.5f.: the duration of the sickness (38 years) has symbolic significance, see Deut.2.14; cf. Num.21.12, and Hengel, 'Schriftauslegung' (n.29).

92. John 4.46-54. I regard the βασιλικός as being more original than the centurion in Q (Matt.8.5-13; Luke 7.1-10). Evidently this was one of Antipas's officials, possibly fom the family of Herod. The Syriac translated 'bd mlk', as does also the Hebrew translation by Delitzsch.

93. Nicodemus: John 3.1ff.; 7.50; 19.39, see above n.62. The term ἄρχων, John 7.26; 12.42; cf. Luke 23.13,15; 24.20; Acts 3.17, will probably denote a member of the Sanhedrin, see Billerbeck 2,412f. In rabbinic legend a Naqdimon b.Gorion was one of the three richest inhabitants of Jerusalem before 70 CE, ibid., 413ff; Jeremias, *Jerusalem* (n.63), 96, 223; cf. also Josephus, *BJ* 2.451.

According to bTaan. 19b Bar. he still had the name Buni, which we also meet in connection with one of the five disciples of Jesus in bSanh.43a. The next bears the name Naqqai, which is a short form of Naqdimon. Here (in a very shadowy way) we perhaps have remnants of a Jewish-Christian Jerusalem Nicodemus tradition.

94. John 11.1-44; 12.1f. The narrator presupposes a relatively well-to-do environment for Lazarus's kin, above all in his description of the tomb and the wide circle of family acquaintances. The relationship with the Gospel of Luke, which does not, however, have the local tradition of Bethany and knows quite a different figure of Lazarus (16.20) who has no relationship to the sisters is striking: Luke 10.38-42, cf. John 12.2; Luke 7.38 cf. John 12.3; Luke 16.19ff. cf. John 11.4. I think that *direct* literary dependence of John on Luke is improbable, even if he knows the Second Gospel. They differ very widely over Jesus' attitude to poverty. Whereas Luke reports both Jesus' 'social preaching' and his good connections with the 'upper class', John does not go into the former. He ignores it. For the problem see J.Kremer, *Lazarus. Die Geschichte einer Auferstehung*, Stuttgart 1985, 82-109. For the hypothesis of Lazarus as the beloved disciple and author on the basis of John 11.3,36, see ibid., 55 n.50.

95. John 19.38; cf. 12.42f.; 7.31; see also 9.22; 20.19.

96. Eusebius, HE 5.24.3, cf. the legendary accounts of James the Just in Hegesippus, a contemporary of Polycrates (Eusebius, HE 2.23.6) and on Epiphanius' *Panarion* (29.4.2-4). Here Epiphanius may be possibly be dependent on Polycrates for the πέταλον. See above, 7, 196f. n.18.

97. See T.Mommsen, *Römische Strafrecht*, 1899, reprinted Darmstadt 1955, 964-80 (969, 980); *deportatio* (Kleinfelder), PW 5,231ff.: 'Originally applied in the case of political criminals, deportation increasingly became a political means of removing people who had become suspicious as a result of their reputation and riches, on the grounds of *crimen maiestatis* as *omnium accusationium complementum* (Tacitus, *Annals* III.38)'; id., 'Exilium', PW 6.2, 1683ff.; 'Relegatio', PW 2 R. 1.1, 564f.; P.Garnsey, *Social Status and Legal Privilege in the Roman Empire*, Oxford 1970, 152; cf. Index s.v. *deportatio, exilium, interdictio aquae et igni, relegatio.*

98. Josephus, *Antt.* 20.194-6: *Jewish War* 6.114. Shortly before the outbreak of the Jewish War the procurator of Judaea, Gessius Florus, had two prominent Jews who were members of the Roman *equites* crucified in Jerusalem: *Jewish War* 2.308. The exiling of John to Patmos is a quite unusual event. If it had been a matter of flight during persecution rather than deportation (see Polycarp), he would hardly have chosen an island and would not have indicated its location.

99. See the unsurpassed introduction by R.H.Charles, *The Revelation of St John*, ICC 18/19, 1920, I, LXV-XCI. See also his comments on the relationship between the Fourth Gospel and the letters and on the authorship (XXIX-L). Charles assumes two different authors, but 'some connection between the authors'. 'The Evangelist was apparently at one time a disciple of the seer, or they were members of the same religious circle in Ephesus' (XXXI).

100. It contains λόγοι τῆς προφητείας, 1.3; 22.7,10,18f., i.e. the author understands himself to be a prophet. The apostles are already presupposed to be traditional authorities: 21.14, cf. 18.20.

101. 1.3: reading aloud in worship; 1.9 ἐγὼ 'Ιωάννης (on this cf. Dan.8.1): the self-testimony of the seer at the beginning and 20.8,10,18f. at the end. The securing of 'holy scripture' against changes has its model in Deut.4.2; 13.1, the threatened curse in Deut.29.19.

102. John 6.7-71; 20.24; μαθητής: 73 times in Matthew, 46 in Mark and 37 in Luke. See above, 74f.

103. John 1.35-51. In addition there is the one unknown figure from 1.37f., see above, 17ff. and below, 79.

104. 11.16; 14.5 and in the scene that is completely tailored to him, 20.24-29; also 21.2. He is the type of the sceptic among the disciples and in this sense an 'antitype' of the beloved disciple and Peter.

105. 14.22, cf. Luke 6.16 and Acts 1.13, 'Ιούδας 'Ιακώβου. In Mark and Matthew this name is absent from the catalogue of the Twelve; it appears only among the brothers of Jesus (Mark 6.33; Matt.13.55). In later legend he is therefore regularly identified with Thaddaeus (Lebbaeus is a variant reading) of Matt.10.3; Mark 3.18. The Old Latin has Judas Zelotes in Matt.10.3. John introduces the name in order to contrast with the traitor Judas, who causes him a serious theological problem, a faithful disciple of the same name. So there is the traitor *and* the faithful Judas. The faithful Judas is the last to be mentioned by name in the farewell discourses.

106. Matt.9.9; 10.3, cf. Mark 2.14; 3.18. Probably the old conjecture that the Logia source circulated under the name of Matthew (see Papias, above 17ff.) and that the unknown author of the first 'pseudepigraphical' Gospel *a fortiori* put this name at the head of the whole new Gospel is correct. Possibly QLuke also knew of this attribution. In that case, from his perspective 'Matthew' would on the one hand belong to the πολλοί and on the other to the αὐτόπται καὶ ὑπηρέται...τοῦ λόγου (Luke 1.1f.). For Luke these terms do not seem to be completely anonymous. We should not simply transfer *our* uncertainty to the early Christian authors. They do not say a good deal that we would dearly like to know as clearly as we would have wished because they take it for granted. Other things that they say clearly and plainly are no longer believed by the pseudo-critics who are so widespread today. Cf. also Justin, *Dial.* 103.8, who in my view presupposes the knowledge of all four Gospel titles; see above, 151 n.79. Its 'apostolic' origin gave (pseudo-)'Matthew' higher authority than Mark and Luke, and from the beginning of the second century made it the most widespread Gospel, see W.-D.Köhler, *Die Rezeption des Matthäusevangeliums in der Zeit vor Irenäus*, WUNT 2 R. 1987.

107. F.Overbeck, *Das Johannesevangelium*, ed. C.A.Bernoulli, Tübingen 1911, 416f.: 'If we assume, for example, that for the author of the Gospel the apostle John was... the given man, because he intended to give to its evangelist the same relationship to Jesus *after* his parting as John the Baptist had to Jesus *before*, the mysterious introduction of the evangelist would be automatically understandable' (417). 'In no case should we forget in an

investigation of the connection between the name and the Fourth Gospel and the Johannine letters that it appears in the *Apocalypse'* (editor's italics, 418), cf. the editor's postscript, 517ff.

108. Mark 1.16-20; Matt.4.18-22. In the list of disciples in Mark 3.16f., the order is significantly changed – in accordance with their importance in the *early* community: Simon Peter, James and John, Andrew. Matthew 10.2 corrects and stresses Simon even more with a πρῶτος: *first* Simon and Andrew; only then do James and John follow. Perhaps John puts Andrew so emphatically at the beginning to counter this πρῶτος. In the Gospel of Mark, which stands in the Petrine tradition (see my *Studies in Mark* [n.55], 50ff.; cf. R.Feldmeier, in ibid., 59ff.), Simon Peter stands as an *inclusio* at the beginning and the end of the Gospel (1.16; 16.7). In John, however, the mysterious anonymous figure stands at the beginning and the beloved disciple at the end. Is this a coincidence?

109. In particular the names of the Maccabaean brothers were extremely popular among Palestinian Jews in the first century CE, i.e. Simon, Judas, Johanan and Eleazar (see also above, 109f.). In addition there were the names of the most important patriarchs like Jacob and Joseph. For the various disciples with the same names see Mark 3.16,18: Simon; 3.17,18: James; Luke 5.16: Judas (see above, n.105), cf.also Acts 1.13 and on the brothers of Jesus Mark 6.3; also the sons of the second Mary (Mark 15.40), which are difficult to identify. The reservoir of common Palestinian names was evidently relatively limited.

110. See e.g. the twenty-one reasons against John the son of Zebedee being author of the Gospel in P.Parker, 'John the Son of Zebedee and the Fourth Gospel', *JBL* 81, 1962, 35-43, though not all of them are equally convincing; however, that does not mean that they can be simply set aside. His conjecture that the author is John Mark ('John and John Mark', *JBL* 79, 1960, 97-110), is not at all conclusive. For other advocates of this hypothesis see J.A.T.Robinson, *The Priority of John*, London 1985, 107 n.308, who rightly rejects it firmly.

111. Gal.1.18; 2.1-21. The eyewitnesses were not just limited to the circle of the Twelve. Cf. also the stress on the agreement in I Cor.15.11; I Cor.9.1ff. and the testimony of Luke 10.1; Acts 1.15, 23.

112. Cf. A.von Harnack, *Chronologie*, I, 679, on the 'presbyter John': 'a Jew with a Hellenistic education and a disciple of the Lord in the wider sense'.

113. Mark 9.9,32; 10.32, 35ff., etc. This emphatic 'misunderstanding' of the disciples in Mark and John is not purely a post-Easter theological construction, but has historical roots. After Easter the disciples arrived at the insight that they had misunderstood Jesus' true nature and purpose in his earthly days. Only in his exalted form is Jesus' real messianic status and divine Sonship made manifest.

114. The best account of the problem is still the investigation by C.H.Dodd, *Historical Tradition in the Fourth Gospel*, Cambridge 1963, which has become a classic. This is criticized and supplemented by A.Carson, 'Historical Tradition in the Fourth Gospel: After Dodd, What?', in *Gospel Perspectives*, ed. R.T. France and D.Wenham, II, Sheffield 1981, 84-145: 129ff. on 'the knotty

question of authorship'. In contrast to Dodd I would put even more stress on the connection with the Synoptic Gospels, Mark and Luke, where the content of these works has completely merged into the school tradition (when it seemed to be favourable). Mark was published at least thirty years before the Fourth Gospel and Luke about twenty years before. So these basic works had long since found their way to Ephesus (see Dodd, *Historical Tradition*, 426). I also think it quite probable that a substantial part of the *tradition* worked over in the Fourth Gospel goes back to the time before the Jewish War of 66–70. The elder brought his wholly personal tradition from his Jerusalem home to Asia Minor. In theological terms he may already have had a relatively independent position. The most difficult problem, which because of our scant knowledge is almost insoluble, is that of demonstrating the historical probability of individual features of the Johannine tradition about Jesus.

115. Mark 11.1, 11f.; 14.3. Mark already presupposes knowledge of the significance of Bethany among his readers.

116. John 18.13ff., 24; cf. Luke 3.2; Acts 4.6: only John knows that Annas is the father-in-law of Caiaphas, the high priest in office. See Josephus, *Antt.* 18.26,34; 20.197f., cf. Billerbeck 2, 153f.,568f. He was high priest between 6 and 15 CE and thus displaced the pro-Herodian high-priestly clan of the Boethusians from office. He succeeded in making his family the most powerful family in Jerusalem betwen 6 and 66 CE. It seems quite plausible that he presided over the preliminary hearing on Jesus.

117. F.D.E.Schleiermacher, *The Life of Jesus* (1864), ET Philadelphia 1975. This is a draft of lectures given in the summer semester of 1832, published long after his death. D.F.Strauss wrote a sharp criticism immediately afterwards: *Der Christus des Glaubens und der Jesus der Geschichte. Eine Kritik des Schleiermacher'schen Lebens Jesu*, Berlin 1865. See the description of both works in A.Schweitzer, *The Quest of the Historical Jesus*, London and New York ³1954, 62-7.

118. R.Bultmann, 'Die Bedeutung der neuerschlossenen mandäischen und manichäischen Quellen für das Verständnis des Johannesevangeliums', *ZNW* 24, 1925, 100-46 (144) = *Exegetica*, 1967, 55-104 (102).

119. O.Cullmann, *The Johannine Circle*, London and Philadelphia 1976; cf. id., 'Von Jesus zum Stephanuskreis und zum Johannesevangelium', in *Jesus und Paulus. Festschrift für Werner Georg Kümmel zum 70.Geburtstag*, ed. E.E.Ellis and E.Grässer, Göttingen 1975, 44-56.

120. *Martyrdom of Polycarp* 9: at the time of his martyrdom he had been a Christian for 86 years, Eusebius, *HE* 5.1.29: Pothinus was more than 90 and died as a confessor in prison: Hegesippus according to Eusebius 3.32.6; Simeon was crucified under Trajan at the truly legendary, Mosaic, age of 120. See also (Ps.-)Lucian, Μακρόβιοι and the fragments of the work by Phlegon of Tralles, περὶ μακροβίων καὶ θαυμασίων, in Jacoby, *FGrHist* 257/257a, both from the second century.

121. Josephus, *Vita* 7-17, cf. Luke 2.41-52 and Billerbeck 2, 144ff., 151, tNidda 5.15 on Luke 2.47. Even legends often have a historical background.

For the 'makrobioi' of the Tübingen school see H.Harris, *The Tübingen School*, Oxford 1975, 54, 77, 113, 126f., 133.

122. M.Hengel, *The Zealots*, Edinburgh 1989.

123. See Lampe, *A Patristic Greek Lexicon*, 628 s.v.: since Origen and Athanasius. In the fourth century Gregory of Nazianzus was also given this surname.

Index of Biblical References

Index of Modern Scholars